Ala Tool

Adventures and Misadventures in Saudi Arabia

By

Jewel Dhuru

© 2003 by Jewel Dhuru. All rights reserved.

No part of this book may be reproduced, stored in a retrieval system, or transmitted by any means, electronic, mechanical, photocopying, recording, or otherwise, without written permission from the author.

ISBN: 1-4033-8143-7 (e-book)
ISBN: 1-4033-8144-5 (Paperback)

Library of Congress Control Number: 2002095789

This book is printed on acid free paper.

Printed in the United States of America
Bloomington, IN

Cover Photo Copyright © 2003 by Virendra Dhuru.

1stBooks - rev. 01/09/03

Acknowledgements

I thank my husband for accommodating me on his life's journey and for intertwining his energies with mine, even if it is a mixed blessing at times. In addition, I thank Gauri, Laura, Sandra and Tom for the sparks of encouragement and Ramesh for his technical support. Heartfelt thanks to Diana, Gisele, Karen and Manisha for their unwavering confidence in my insights and to Jill, Larry, Raymond, my son, my daughter and my son-in-law for providing food for thought. Sincere appreciation to John for his constructive criticism and to Cathy, Neela, Steve and Sunanda for their varied comments and assistance. And my profound gratitude to Jackie and Jim for helping me make sense of it all by listening, making observations and providing detailed feedback.

Dedication

Dedicated to the enlightened empowerment of the oppressed, of all genders, ages, origins and creeds.

Table of Contents

Acknowledgements iii
Dedication v
Foreword by Jim Morningstar, Ph.D. (Psychology) ix
Preface xi

Part I: An Arab Adventure 1
Chapter 1: Is This April Spring? 1
Chapter 2: Balancing On A Blade 13
Chapter 3: Home And Campus 20
Chapter 4: The First Month—Work, Weather And Entertainment ... 30
Chapter 5: The Neighborhood 38
Chapter 6: Winter And The Holidays 52
Chapter 7: From One Extreme To The Other 60
Chapter 8: Hospitality Is In The Eye Of The Beholder 64
Chapter 9: Travel To Asir And The Hejaz 70
Chapter 10: On Being Born Female 84
Chapter 11: Tutoring and Time 99
Chapter 12: Religion And The Qur'an 105
Chapter 13: May Day! 110
Chapter 14: A Parting Of The Ways 114
Chapter 15: Second Wind 121
Chapter 16: Dammam and The Island State of Bahrain 127
Chapter 17: Winding Down 132
Chapter 18: Loosening Arabia's Grip 138
Chapter 19: Home Is In The Heart 144

Part II: The Journey That Changed Everything 152
Chapter 20: A Second Dip Of The Wick 152
Chapter 21: The Grip Creeps Back 156
Chapter 22: One Last Interlude 165
Chapter 23: Back To The Land 171
Chapter 24: *Ramadan* 183
Chapter 25: Reunions And New Unions 194
Chapter 26: Christmas In India 211
Chapter 27: Adjustments, Re-Adjustments and More Adjustments 216
Chapter 28: Soaking Up Local Color 232

Chapter 29: Driving: Hazards And Hilarity 246
Chapter 30: Damascus And Environs 251
Chapter 31: Lull and Storm 271
Chapter 32: Treks: Lush Rivers, Coral Reefs And Dune Buggies .. 274
Chapter 33: Reluctant Students and Welcome Guests 282
Chapter 34: Happy Fiftieth 293
Chapter 35: Hitchhikers, Dunes and Souks 299
Chapter 36: The Elusive Saudi Woman 307
Chapter 37: Taking Stock And Counting Down 313
Chapter 38: The Blink Of A Cosmic Eye 326
Chapter 39: Home At Last 333

REFERENCES 347
ENDNOTES 349
Map of the Region 355
About the Book 357
About the Author 359

Foreword by Jim Morningstar, Ph.D. (Psychology)

We are all fellow travelers on the road of life. At times a particular traveling companion stands out in our memories. It is usually because they have touched us in some way that has made a difference in our lives, given us a richer appreciation for our road or perhaps what we encountered along the way.

The author of this story is, I believe, one of the travelers who will touch you and stand out in your life experience. In part, it is because of the timeliness of her saga. This is a time in our human history when the cultural differences between East and West can no longer be viewed with distant curiosity. Political events at the onset of this millennium are thrusting East and West together with a vehemence that demands understanding and cooperation for our very survival. This is not, however, what stands out or touches me as I read these pages. It is rather the poignancy with which one human being interfaces other humans with widely divergent beliefs on emotional, mental and spiritual levels while trying to establish basic daily amenities in our civilized world.

She prepares us for this journey on many levels. We learn the basics of a woman's life, turned upside down by the adventure of following her husband into a foreign culture in which women are treated with a high number of restrictions. We are likewise prepared to undertake this travel coping with particular physical limitations on her part that require utmost care and creative adaptation. The greater preparation, however, comes not for the outward challenges, but for the inner journey of meeting up with oneself at every turn of the road. Through her keen awareness, she paints for us the stark contrasts between cultures. She goes deeper, though, to highlight the mirrors we find everywhere for our own psyche. These mirrors are often fascinating and not always flattering. We journey with her into our own psyche as we share her reactions to the full range of acceptance and rejection for the way we appear and are to others.

The polarities or contrasts which backdrop this self-revealing trip include the myriad of taken-for-granted everyday routines we rely upon in Western culture that are addressed so differently in the Islamic world. This ranges from men's doing most of the grocery shopping and errands to ritualized greetings. How does our mind cope with such diversity while holding onto a common thread of humanity? The author's unique blend of openhearted observation and personal responses allows us to share her exploration and look into our own mirrors.

The second set of contrasts, which permeate the landscape of this inner travelogue, is the divergent approaches to handling male/female differences en route. Steeped in the Western tradition, the author in her lifetime has seen an expanding role of the feminine in all areas of cultural expression. To be immersed in a uniform tradition in which eye contact or uncovered flesh can be cause for a woman to be censored or even severely punished is a shock to the sense of identity. To live in this milieu for ten months requires a reformulation of the psyche. One may emerge from this total exposure intact, but not unaffected. The conclusions we reach as co-voyagers are magnified by the author, but never dictated.

Another point of dialogue throughout is the dance of two partners, wife and husband, whose distinctly different life roles and instinctual responses are sometimes complimentary, sometimes at odds and sometimes equivocal. Their contrasting styles and responses may well remind us of the voices of our own inner repertoire of characters. How do the ongoing encounters of this journey enrich or limit each party? The author gives us both enough honesty and latitude to reflect on our own reactions to our life partnerships, bringing our lessons home to ourselves.

Finally, the most universal of the energies in dramatic tension portrayed by the author might be stated as the yin and yang of self-discovery. She holds a delicate balance between these polarities, never just taking the feminine point of view, nor pretending to justify the masculine—recognizing the dance of both within her and the spirit that goes beyond either. It is on this level that the journey might touch us the most deeply. We recognize the ever emerging clarity and ambiguity that comes as we reflect on our life lessons, then pack them away—only to find we are given a second chance to travel the road again. What will we take with us this time? With what eyes will we revisit our friends and teachers? Let us join the author with open minds and hearts as she invites us to: *Ala Tool*.

Preface

Some say that travel is most fun either when one is sitting comfortably at home, planning the itinerary or after one's return, when showing friends the photographs. In between comes packing and re-packing, immunizations, flight delays, jet lag, adjusting to weather and the unfamiliar, keeping up with the languages, experimenting with unusual food, making small talk with strangers and parting from new friends. I say that lessons acquired from travel are best applied at home, enriching family life, just as an adventurous attitude acquired from home enriches the travel experience.

In 1998-99, we lived in Riyadh for only ten months and did not expect to return there when we left, so we set out to cope with the environmental stressors. While there, I wrote of our experiences to friends, who encouraged me to share my comments with more than just a few. I contemplated waiting until I got home to begin writing in earnest, but recognized my folly about the sixth month. When conditions reached such a pitch that I needed to release pent-up emotions, I realized not only how therapeutic writing is but that I would not have been able to recall the subtle and varied nuances of feelings or their immediate impact, had I waited. So in April, in the hot, arid, suffocating season of spring, writing more than just journal entries and letters helped to diffuse emotion and to make dispassionate sense of what was happening to me.

Eventually I found the silver lining behind dense clouds and saw the value in being immersed in this enigmatic culture, acquiring the knowledge that leads to understanding and some day to wisdom. The trip was an opportunity to be participant observers in a unique culture, to practice accepting what we cannot change, to make the most of the here and now and to learn how to keep interpersonal barriers low. In case my attempts to be inoffensive and fair are not obvious, I would like to point out that the beliefs and opinions, and alas, even judgments, that flow from my pen say more about me than about the people, places and objects of my attention.

Despite the fact that we all come from the same source and share much, in Saudi Arabia, secrecy plays a significant part of everyone's life, for safety's sake, because of numerous prohibitions. Therefore, except for my husband and I, my characters remain nameless or have assumed names, in keeping with the cloistered atmosphere. But their characters exert influence from the shadows, so I dwell on memorable aspects of their stories and personalities while remaining necessarily vague in describing their origins and appearance. I have been equally indistinct about many aspects of the work my husband and I did there and our family lives.

My spellings of Makkah, Madinah, Jiddah, Mumbai, Turkiye, Qur'an and Muslim, usually seen in English as Mecca, Medina, Jeddah, Bombay, Turkey, Koran and Moslem, respectively, more closely approximate the spellings and pronunciation favored by their native users. And metric measurements are used throughout since they are used by most countries, (but measurements in the British system follow in parenthesis).

I have made every effort to give an accurate, though subjective picture of my stay in the Kingdom, using the evidence of my eyes and ears, processed through head and heart. When I first arrived, I was not to know how fundamentally, personally and indelibly this journey would touch the facets of my life, insinuating itself into my thoughts, altering my career paths, prodding me to look carefully at everything I thought I knew about myself and influencing my lifelong purpose, personality, how I make friends, the language I use, my perception and vision, my choices of what is essential in life and spurring me to reach personal goals I wasn't aware I had.

Ala Tool is commonly translated from Arabic as to go straight ahead or to keep going forward. Stretching the imagination, I conjure up the connotations of keeping focused on living, learning, laughing, growing and going onward or of your final destination not being more important than how you comport yourself on the path.

Part I: An Arab Adventure

Chapter 1: Is This April Spring?

"I know a way out of Hell. Find a boy this high and raise him as your own. Only be sure he's a Muslim and raise him as one" [1]
—Gandhi, in the movie *Gandhi*

"I don't shake hands," the jeweler said dismissively when I extended mine in gratitude for his services, right after he'd just exchanged a warm handshake with my husband, Baba. While I felt like the wind had been knocked out of me, the jeweler kept his body oriented to Baba's to continue their farewell.

Somehow, standing in that jewelry shop in the Kingdom of Saudi Arabia, alongside women who were shrouded in black, with reams of gold baubles around their wrists, my choosing a bracelet as a gift from Baba for my birthday in April took on a different connotation. My confusing experience with that particular jeweler left me with a tangle of questions about what was happening in my life.

By the seventh month of our ten-month stay in the country, I thought we'd been adjusting rather well. Baba had been teaching at a university. We'd gone through the usual culture shock, delighting in some experiences and liking others not-so-much. Overall, we thought we'd developed a balanced attitude to this incomparable culture. I was in for a few surprises.

This specific shop lay in a nest of other such shops, in a souk in the capital city of Riyadh, home to 3,000,000 potential shoppers. The nest featured rows upon rows of windows with glittering strings of gold. The shop door opened from one of many narrow, winding lanes in this grand gold souk, into the central browsing area, while counters and locked glass cases occupied the other three walls, in a U shape. Three male jewelers each wore traditional long white *thobs*, and oval black double ringed *egals* holding white *gootra* headdresses in place. From behind the counters, they served Saudi and non-Saudi customers, since this shop was well known amongst westerners. Like other Western women, I did not cover my hair, but we fell into the pattern created before us of treating other women with a certain inexplicable disregard.

This first time we went there, the senior jeweler seemed cordial and accustomed to non-Saudi customers. After he'd exchanged pleasantries with Baba, with smiling black eyes and twitching moustache, the jokey jeweler asked me if I was a doctor, too.

"No," I said, with a smile, shaking my head of short brown hair, continuing to concentrate on my selection. My strained back ached from too much walking, so I chose not to elaborate on my professions right then.

"Well, you're a doctor's wife," was his response. Technically, Baba is a dental educator, but I left that for him to explain. My mind began to cloud with the implications of the jeweler's pronouncement. I would have liked to tell him that being a wife, or a mother, or connected to whomever, were valued vocations, but they did not define me, that I was someone in my own right, not just an appendage. But I decided to say nothing.

The second time we went there, a week later, we picked out gift cuff links for our new son-in-law, whose background contained, among other faiths, the Bosnian version of Islam. From our son-in-law, we'd learned Bosnian Muslims were generally fun loving, hard working and openhearted to friends and family. Mr. Jokey Jeweler, again, spoke warmly to us both and laughed with us from his position across the counter.

On this third visit, we had a certain level of comfort with him, I thought. Over the next ten minutes, his association with us appeared relaxed. Just before we left, I even asked him if he could tell me the weight of the bracelet I had previously selected. I wanted to calculate the price per gram for this intricate work.

"Now that it's officially yours, I'll have to charge you for weighing it," he teased as he put my bracelet on the scale. After a moment of uncertainty, we all laughed. It felt good to laugh out loud, a rare sensation those days.

As we both thanked him for the service, he shook Baba's hand warmly, for the first time, but to me, whose hand was extended in thanks, it was another matter.

"I don't shake hands," he declared and kept his body angled to Baba's to continue their parting. I felt breathless, but life buzzed along around me anyway. No one else seemed to have noticed

Ala Tool

anything. I regarded the jeweler numbly until the initial jolt wore off, but I had learned it was not fruitful to speak up.

I turned to gaze at the tall, lithe figure of the Asian Indian who had been my husband for the last 26 years and counting. His white hair, trimmed beard and moustache shone under the shop lights. His warm brown eyes still held the jeweler's. Even he hadn't noticed anything askance. He was usually kind. The difficulty was the circumstances weren't kind. He had been forced to choose—in public.

Even though I felt like I had been kicked in the stomach, I strolled out of the shop nonchalantly, but I was keenly aware of the rising warmth in my face. This same female-male dynamic, how the level of empathy in a relationship is affected by other relationships, was played out in different ways all over the world. But there in far-from-cosmopolitan Riyadh, it suddenly became more crucial to really listen to each other and work together, if the relationship was not to change substantially.

As we wound back down the lane to the car, I waited for Baba to say something empathetic. An "Oh, that's too bad" or even a shrug of the shoulders and a "what are ya gonna do?" would have put the issue into a semi-doze, but his response was a complete surprise.

"Oh, that's just his way," he said, when I prompted him. "He meant no disrespect ... different social classes behave differently ... you've got to develop a thick skin."

The same old wrangling over what's more important: following the cultural rules or observing a universal standard of courtesy. My head knew most of what he said was true, but my heart still felt the sting. Not for the first time, the two were sharply split.

As I looked at Baba's tanned oval face, a distance seemed to spring up between us. "How did I get here?" I asked myself—a nice Canadian girl, mother of two adults, English teacher, counselor, artist. My mind, searching for escape, recalled still vital memories of earlier months of our adventure. Tucked away in the time capsule of my consciousness, were the grandfatherly Saudi truck driver with whom we unexpectedly shared Arabic coffee and cookies at a rest stop off the intercity superhighway, the kind stranger who Baba had flagged down to tow our sinking car out of suffocatingly soft sand and the group of Filipina women with whom I enjoyed hushed laughter in my kitchen. The delight still filled me of purchasing frankincense and myrrh in a crowded souk, of watching an orange sunset outline camel silhouettes at the Camel Souk while we sat around a fire in a Bedouin tent, of glimpsing a foot long blue and orange chameleon scurry over 350 year old stone cliff dwellings and of absorbing the distillation of a dusky desert day as a luminous full moon ascended over sand dunes of peach and purple. But these memories were from more natural areas and smaller towns. Now, we were in bustling, downtown Riyadh.

When Baba returned to the jewelry shop alone a few days later to pick up the engraved cuff links, at my insistence, he reluctantly conveyed my feelings to the jeweler. The reason the jeweler gave for his conduct was his religion. I might have accepted this explanation as representative of the male populace at large, but in the previous six months, several professional Saudi gentlemen had already shaken my hand without hesitation. In the back of my mind and heart, the memory rankled for days.

The following week, I got background from a new North American friend, Linda, who had lived in Riyadh for years and had studied Arab culture even longer.

"Historically, males are taught that women are tainted by their biological cycles," she explained. "Deeply ingrained is the belief that she is incomplete anatomically and covets certain anatomy from the male."

"What would you have done in that situation?" I asked her, completing my narrative.

She painted a picture of herself briefly latching on to some part of the jeweler's arm, and exiting quickly, before his protestations reached too high a pitch.

Would this have become such an issue had it happened back home, I wondered. I thought not. In Riyadh, I had fallen into an eroded state, tension was mounting and an easy equilibrium was a state maintained only with difficulty. In time, I was to remember that every culture has to deal with not only the unique powers of the male, but also the ultimate creative power of the female. Some cultures are just more threatened than others by the latter. In time, I came to terms with the episode and accepted what Baba said, that this was Mr. Jokey Jeweler's way of practicing his religious-social beliefs and that he hadn't intended any harm or disrespect. Later, I was to discover others who followed the letter, rather than the spirit of the law.

Henceforth, I was determined to be more vigilant about not setting myself up to be undermined or ignored. For now, the way to my Heaven lay on this path through the Middle East. The jeweler was just a leaf in the forest of my life anyway. The real issue was the empathy between Baba and myself, a realization that was to recur numerous times. This minor drama brought us face to face, yet again, with the issue of expatriate husbands being caught in a double bind. They are charged with the protection of their wives, while trying to fit in with the guys at work, to be part of the impregnable fraternity. They are caught between defending her feelings and accepting Mr. Jokey Jeweler's behavior as routine in that rarified region.

Midwest Spring

Where I now make my home in the Midwestern United States, in April, I usually bloomed along with the landscape. I didn't realize how dismally spring was going to start out that year. Spring was the season of birthdays, budding plants and birds. There's something about the sound of birds twittering in the morning that reminds me we are all sisters and brothers with the rest of nature. But this year, spring came to mean dust storms, disappointments and demise. At the beginning of April, I was not conscious of any particular gloominess, but by mid-month, my fertile imagination had turned my surroundings into a lover of spring's version of purgatory. It weighed on me like the heavy, dusty air that rasped through my lungs on hot mornings when I awoke feeling like a wet noodle. To keep cool, I visualized my tall, thin form standing under a drenching waterfall, my hair glued to my head and neck, or soaking in a tub of ice cubes, or sliding down a snowy hillside or even shivering in a meat locker.

Back home, I would have been touring the fenced in back yard of our 0.13 hectare (1/3 acre) twice daily, filling the bird and squirrel feeders, delighting in the minutest new shoots in my gardens. Shading my brown eyes from the sun, I would spot pairs of baby squirrels wrestling in the grass, glimpse camouflaged rabbits, watch bright red cardinals build nests, listen to ratchety sounding frogs and insects and sometimes sight hawks and even deer in the distance. Our weeping willow would have sprouted yellow catkins and the leaf buds of lilacs and violets would be opening. It was the month of two family birthdays, temporal milestones measuring how far our grown daughter and I had come in the past year. Greening up and growth were the watchwords of the month.

Under Siege in Sandy Riyadh

But, instead of warm breezes heralding the return of avian friends, flora, and a general velveting of the landscape, I got temperatures of 41⁰ C. (106⁰ F.) and dust storms, hazy sky, wind and a searing, scorched scent to the air. The advent of this weather unleashed stories from neighbors about the previous summer. Back then, outer walls and windows had been sandblasted by whipped up wind. Cold air blowing from the AC gave me a raw, red throat. The elements were forces to escape from, not to luxuriate in.

As life was opening up back home, it was closing up in the new neighborhood. The view from our campus flat in this capital city, included fantail and date palms, bougainvillea, mesquite, acacia and lantana; all were beginning to crinkle up after a winter's bloom. An unknown hand had been tending a tomato plant under our sitting room balcony, presumably hoping to bring it to fruition. It sat in a square of thirsty sand surrounded by concrete, where the original tree had been removed. It was full of buds and actually bearing fruit, but was under constant siege from clamorous children in the campus playground who picked and smashed the little green globes as soon as they were detected. It was the only vegetable plant in sight but instead of bringing new life, it symbolized stagnation and destruction.

I discovered most flowers in Riyadh bloomed only during the winter and spring. By April, the sun took an intense interest in the activities of all living things and we were under attack from the heat. My potted marigolds had produced their last blossoms, my gardenia dropped its leaves one by one and was reduced to bare sticks and my night-blooming jasmine, *Malaka lael*, looked awful. I suppose this was fair turnabout for the moderate warmth we'd basked in that winter while Milwaukee had the blizzard of the century, 35 cm. (14") of snow in 48 hours and two months later, 6 cm. (2½ ") of rain in only three hours.

To help shield us from direct rays, the local tailor, a Filipina, brought the long awaited curtains I had ordered. She had a sweet voice but probably due mainly to language problems, the curtains were all wrong. The set covering a window was cut too long, the one for the glass door was too short and the wrong material was used on the wrong windows.

Warm water, usually a source of utter relaxation and comfort, suddenly became cause for irritation. Even the cold water faucet ran tepid. The previous summer, we heard, people who wanted to wash clothes in cold water would have to fill the barrel the night before and allow it to cool. A neighbor's twisted tale suggested to us how to access cool water. We could turn off the hot water heater to access room temperature air conditioned water from the hot faucet, instead of the hot water coming from solar heated outdoor pipes streaming from the cold faucet. Getting into a bathtub for a relaxing soak was unthinkable without taking preliminary cooling measures.

Perhaps in protest, one evening the veins of the water heater in the storage room off the kitchen ruptured and bled all over everything we'd stored there. I sauntered into the kitchen in search of a snack and found myself sloshing through 2 1/2 cm. (an inch) of its life's blood. With a broom, Baba pushed it out onto the second story balcony to evaporate. Actually, we had three separate water heaters, one in each of two bathrooms with stone floors equipped with drains and this one in the storage room with a linoleum floor and shelves full of our belongings.

The leaky one couldn't have been the corroded heater in the main bathroom that looked like it had been on its last legs since Day One. Except for the rusty spotted exterior and intermittent hissing, that one never really gave us any trouble. It had to be the one that looked practically new, on the outside, the one that I had only turned on five separate cold days all winter. It had to be the one with suitcases, newspapers saved for Linda's fledgling recycling project and my latest experiment in clay under it. Fortunately, my art supplies were spared.

With the heat and inconveniences, my perspective was getting so jaundiced I'd already made up my mind I wasn't going to enjoy the dinner we were invited to on the evening of my birthday later that month. I decided in advance I wouldn't know anybody anyway and the conversation would probably be prescribed, not spontaneous or genuine. Dinner wouldn't be served until hours after my biological clock told me it was time to wind down for sleep. But, this party would be non-Saudi, so perhaps we would manage to eat before midnight.

Jewel Dhuru

Because intermittent neck and arm irritation had flared up again, I temporarily had to stop doing my needlework, a picture of Saudi apartments with *roshan*, elaborate wooden latticework windows, so women could peek out but no one could peer in. I hoped to finish it and display my work in an art show before leaving the country. Normally this project provided me with hours of pleasure a day, hours that now jangled my nerves.

I had temporarily lost enthusiasm for practicing Arabic, an almost daily delight the first six months. I loved to utter phrases, unknown two months before, to complete strangers and to get fairly reasonable responses. Perhaps because of the Islamic holiday, Hajj, pilgrimage time, my usual conversation companions had disappeared. As the months went on, along with pleasant discoveries and adventures, small tensions had continued to build into bigger ones.

In February, I had written letters to all my close friends and then started on a list of more distant ones who I thought would like to hear about our encounters, whether or not they replied. From this second list, news came of the passing on of a female friend back home, and then, not two weeks later, a report followed of her husband's demise. On their heels came notices of the expiration of two more friends. We wanted to send cards but this was just when the Post Offices would be closed for 6 days for Hajj. The isolation and delay were frustrating.

My birthday inspired a longing for the carefree days of my childhood in Canada. There, in Riyadh, in 1999, I was surrounded by the negative news of the region:
- Yemeni hostages,
- Anwar arrested in Malaysia,
- East Timor, Indonesia in turmoil,
- India and Pakistan testing and re-testing missiles and in conflict over Kashmir,
- Israel bombing Lebanon and
- the Kosovo crisis.

And still there was Saddam. Since his last threat, a month before, to retaliate against countries having American military bases, Saudi Arabia had been officially in the state of a high level of alert. This meant all our valuables and important papers were to be in one parcel so if I had to flee in a hurry, I did not have to hunt for them.

To cheer myself up, I visualized the pillow I'd cross-stitched in shades of burgundy and peach for my daughter's birthday, a few days before mine. I had adapted the pattern from a Tunisian carpet design book Baba had brought from the university library. Such creative pursuits were quiet excitements giving quality to my days. I'd sent the pillow for her with a Saudi Baba knew who was flying to North America, because I couldn't entrust my precious pillow, two months' work, to the mail. Especially not after hearing that a few letters I had sent to friends and a couple of packages of mail our daughter had sent to us never arrived.

Dealing with Disillusionment

I began feeling disconnected from my regenerative source, from which I drew and replenished energy, the source that kept me in touch with who I was and what I was doing there. For two weeks, I was too distracted to get much benefit from daily practices that kept me in touch with my origins. Sometimes a wave of loneliness for our son or daughter would waft over and temporarily engulf me. Focusing on a deep relaxing breath and thinking how grateful I was to have the kids in my life helped me to stay light until the spell passed.

It was my daily practice to lie down and center on my breathing until I reached a point of blissful stillness. I did not often reach it, but working towards it was well worth the effort. I just concentrated on breathing and things started to happen. Sometimes I started with the mental chant 'Jewel, let go' until gradually, a tingle started and eventually a scintillating sensation poured through me until parts of my body detached and drifted off. Eclipsing all other forms of relaxation, it felt like my physical being had melted and the rest of my molecules had floated very far away, without my ever having to leave the couch.

But that April, this state was getting harder to achieve. At its worst, it was a major effort just to keep focused on ten breaths. As I counted from 1 to 10 breaths, if a thought distracted me, I would start over again at 1. Sometimes I was stalled for many minutes between 1 and 2. It was more like 10 thoughts per breath. Sometimes, jerking back to awareness, I found myself mentally counting 42, 43, 44, but the last number I actually remembered was 1.

Welcome email messages from friends of the heart became mere words on a screen. Favorite books did not hold my attention. Things were looking bleak. I knew life's rhythm was ebb and flow. This was definitely ebb time.

Fortunately, this was not going to be my last month there. Three months still remained to turn the situation around. I was determined not to become a connoisseur of woe. But in the meantime, I had gotten to the pessimistic point that when the notoriously unreliable Saudi TV schedule of programs for the day was given, I actually believed they would really show the announced Michael Palin's Pole to Pole. I knew a series could be rescheduled, substituted or just plain disappear without warning or explanation and delays were nothing to fret about. But when not even a single Pole emerged by two hours after the announced time, anticipation turned to disappointment and had the impact of a broken promise.

Before arriving in Saudi Arabia, my attitude included the belief that even if certain rights and privileges were temporarily suspended, what personal power I did have was internal and could be exercised to the hilt. Perhaps only under Riyadh's stringent conditions could unique methods for mobilizing energies be adequately discovered. But I could feel my confidence in my own abilities and powers of adjustment begin to wane along with my patience with having to procure everything through a male, at his convenience.

Since Baba was the one who was officially employed, resources and information came through him. Sending and receiving snail and email, going shopping, getting airline tickets, being able to sit in a café, having groceries delivered, buying stamps and getting spending money, all awaited his convenience, at least initially.

I contemplated this downward spiral. While stuck in this rabbit hutch of a flat, I needed variety to stave off boredom. Back home, besides work and family, there would have been gardening and getting re-acquainted with the neighbors after the winter's cloister. Balcony sitting wasn't done much in Riyadh and the Saudi neighbors wouldn't have relished our proximity to their children in the playground, just below. Going out was difficult, too, as the heat increased and the city geared up to become tranquilized and semi-nocturnal. Nothing held my interest for more than three minutes before discontentment set in.

Suddenly I was disengaged from and disillusioned with what I heard and saw because it all amounted to the same thing: few choices and the mundane, the routine. Radio and TV programs, which generally had interesting discussion topics, like the arts and interviews with accomplished professionals, now provided a steady diet of religion and war.

This was getting serious. It took me a while to turn things around, to reluctantly remind myself that people who find others' conversation boring are usually listening with their own boring filters on. And Louise Hay would say pain in the neck, shoulder and arm signified resistance, feeling burdened and helpless and trying to fix others. [2] Even though the conditions were unusually restricted and harsh, I was probably projecting who I was on my surroundings. This might be a clue as to how to handle this case of Poor me Syndrome.

Determined not to be miserable any longer than it took me to adjust to yet another of life's transitional phases, I awoke the next morning having reclaimed a small measure of *joie de vivre*. I reread photocopies I had brought with me to keep my spirits up, but that I had put away, smugly thinking I was beyond needing them. My favorites reminded me of the natural aspects of my life, that what I give attention to will grow, along with specialized breathing exercises for maintaining connections with my inner nature and rhythms. I mentally invited order into my life, along with self-confidence and the positive thoughts I had let slip away. I began to try and accept what I couldn't change, temporarily. I spurred myself on to doing self-instruction in Arabic while I awaited the reemergence of my conversation partners. And I reminded myself that my resilient body would adjust itself to the oppressive climate.

Respite, but Foreboding

In the relative cool of the next morning, birds sang as they migrated through the city. I chatted on the phone with our daughter for her birthday. She liked the pillow I'd sent her, and apparently her cat took an interest in it, too. In an attempt to surround myself with new life, I planted onion bulbs and garlic cloves already sprouted in the vegetable bin, along with orange pips and guava seeds and every other kind of fruit seed I could find in my kitchen. Over time, I watched the seedlings with maternal interest as they came up. Then, incredibly, what was left of the gardenia sticks were putting out new leaves.

I had a pleasant birthday, despite myself. Linda came over, made us drinks, Saudi style Virgin Mary's, and gave me a prophetic Hallmark card. It read, 'To have a friend is to invite someone closer and closer to the sacred chamber of the heart. To be a friend is to tread softly there.' The sentiment got me thinking about what I had accomplished in this perhaps not so desolate land, rather than how hard it was to achieve anything. Linda's interest in writing fueled my own attempts, and by supplying practical information about Saudi life, she taught me how to open doors for myself.

I guess I had been treading rather heavily of late. The disparity between Baba's and my views would not disappear overnight, but nourishing my friendship with myself would be a positive step. There was only one thing to do. I put on a gentler pair of shoes and went to the dinner party. The get-together, contrary to my expectations, but not my hopes, did not lack interesting conversation, or camaraderie. I saw more familiar faces than I thought I would. It felt great to laugh out loud for a while. Dinner was not served until 11:00 PM though, but after all, with greater adjustments ahead, it was in my best interests to learn to switch gears quickly.

Chapter 2: Balancing On A Blade

"I like trees because they seem more resigned to the way they have to live than other things do" [3]
—Willa Cather (1873-1947)

Perhaps it would be best to go back to the beginning. Our journey had already begun by the time Baba came home from work one day and asked a question.

"For our sabbatical, how would you like to go to Riyadh, Saudi Arabia for a year?"

For Baba, an Indian raised Hindu but considering himself a world citizen, this would be a professional stint, teaching at a university. He'd been negotiating with several colleges for opportunities to teach, but had not settled on just the right one yet. For me, adventure awaited. Being born and raised in Canada, of mixed European ancestry, and raised Christian, I could experience a different way of life, removing myself completely from my own element, discovering and developing skills I didn't know I had. The trip would temporarily take me away from three professional activities, all part-time. It would be a change from exhibiting paintings in galleries and advertising my readiness to serve prospective counseling clients. And I had recently retired from teaching English as a Second Language to college students. I had just completed the sale of a painting to a local health institute. The view through a window of woods and waterfalls was packed up and sent off just days before we departed. That year, my personal taxes still reflected a profit. What the next year would bring, who knew?

So Baba tended to be the scientific part of our duo and I the psychological part, with overlap on each side, just like the Yin and Yang symbol, in which a white dot appears centrally in the black paisley piece and a black dot appears in the white.

Actually, we had taken a sabbatical fifteen years earlier, when Baba exchanged his professorial and research expertise with professionals of other nations. Back then, for a month, we had gone with our son and daughter to India, Baba's motherland. Then, for three months, while he beavered away in Nigeria, where his accommodations were suitable for himself alone but not for a family, the kids and I stayed with his family in India, I playing tutor at home. After that, he collected us and we flew to Sweden, to tour the Volvo factory and pick up our new car. From there, we drove through Denmark, Germany, Belgium and England, stopping briefly to meet friends and colleagues and arriving within a week in Scotland to begin two months of further sharing and exchanging. It was a trip to remember.

I had hoped this sabbatical would be equally enjoyable. Now the kids had grown and flown so it would be just the two of us. But Saudi Arabia? That would take me out of my element all right! Because of my shy nature, I feel most comfortable and productive when adequate emotional support and a variety of resources are within easy reach. But ideal conditions are not a given. Sometimes I needed a nudge. This would be a shove.

What I anticipated missing most was hugs, laughter and music, those staples of health. In order to do professional activities of my own, I would have to mobilize all my ingenuity, self-support, determination, and perseverance. It would be like entering the home turf of an entity with a strong grip and a sharp sword and trying to live peacefully alongside it. I could learn more about Islam from its cradle and to learn not to judge. I had already heard the Western biases, but this trip was a chance to formulate my own thoughts. I could see the culture first hand, with its own strengths and shortcomings.

Keeping my mind active would be the main challenge, with so many decisions being made for me. But I could teach English in Saudi Arabia, too. And if I did any painting or ceramics, I could sell my pieces later. Being a counselor might be tricky in another culture, so that would have to be approached gingerly. At least my education would help me make personal adjustments, or so I hoped. I didn't think my philosophy books would get through the censors, so I would have to rely on what I carried in my mind and heart.

Delays

To complicate matters, since our first sabbatical, the condition of my health had changed. I was younger and stronger back then. A congenital lower back problem, a back and hip injury in 1979 and the onset of an annoying muscular condition a few years earlier culminated in my developing a lasting case of what the medical field calls CBPS, Chronic Benign Pain Syndrome. Stated simply, I hurt all the time and the sites of previous injuries were the worst spots. Chronic benign meant I was stuck with it over the long haul, but I wouldn't die of it. Sometimes I'd just wish I could. Over the last decade, climbing stairs, lifting more than a pound, walking much and sitting at a 90-degree angle or less or in chairs not shaped to accommodate the human body were particular millstones. Not one to give up autonomy easily, as my right side weakened, I pressed my left leg and hand into service for driving and writing.

Symptomatic relief was valuable, like massage, chiropractic, and learning to make the best of life despite difficulties, or because of them. I really had to just accept this as my body for this lifetime and make friends with it. Practically, it meant I was sedentary and lacked physical endurance. If I awoke of a morning with five sore spots, I felt rickety but could function, but if pain zoned in on only one spot, I felt much more unbalanced. Every day was a new adventure.

From my self-description, I sound practically decrepit. But unless an observer knows about sagging energies, my condition actually doesn't show much. Posture and gait don't usually give me away unless I've been walking too much or sitting in a grossly misshapen chair. My lack of endurance, however, does show. To cope, my constant aim, although my grasp often falls short, is to do everything interesting in moderation, to respect my limitations, to think positive, to avoid overload and to do the best with the present moment.

Baba and I would be like the pioneering family on Little House on the Prairie, in early 1900s Minnesota, when the family was uprooted because Papa wanted to go far away, panning for gold. While he was thinking this was a chance he'd never get again and he wanted to explore to the hilt, Mama wondered if they'd get home before winter. That sounded familiar, although Baba's opportunity was to teach in a state of the art Middle Eastern college, combined with always exciting travel. While the men folk in the TV episode went off to play with the other boys, the women were left to figure out how to keep the family's bodies and spirits intact. For me, contact with our families would be through limited email, super slow snail mail, or costly telephone. In the episode, when greed reared its ugly head, and the proximity, to the husbands, of alcohol and gambling, became hazards for the wives, their solution was to relocate the womenfolk and kids and pay a higher price for safety. What problems would rear up for us,

I wondered, and what price would we pay for this educational endeavor.

Alcohol and gambling were not allowed in the Kingdom, not officially anyway, so said the Islamic books and lists of official restrictions we received in the mail before we ever left home. Papa finally admitted it would be better to maintain family health, develop strength of character and go home. We endeavored to carry support for our inner sanctums with us

We didn't have long to wait before complications arose. We'd completed the medical check-ups for visas and packing was underway for our departure in mid-August, 1999. Then Baba chose, in the end of July to undergo one more not-so-routine test for intermittent chest tightness while brisk walking. When he phoned from the hospital to say one of his arteries was as close to 100% blocked as one can get without using triple digits, and he was scheduled for by-pass surgery that very afternoon, I knew our lives were about to change drastically.

Overload threatened with a capital 'O'. Over the next few days, a million thoughts raced through my mind and fears clogged every cell. Some needed acting upon and some, in the middle of the night, had to be just thrust out so I could get a little sleep. With his already being in the hands of competent professionals and on the mend, and my condition being chronic, my own well-being was more dubious than his. Riyadh would have to be notified, of course.

When Baba got home to convalesce, he phoned them.

"*Mafee mishkole*," no problem, the Dean in Riyadh said. "When you're better, *Inshallah*, you can come."

When I contemplated what could have happened to Baba had the condition not been caught before the last minute crunch was created, from now on was all bonus time.

Baba's recovery zoomed along—a textbook case. Still, I asked him not to rush, to give me time to recuperate as well. I teetered on the brink of exhaustion. His diet, mode of handling stress and attentiveness to interpersonal issues were to change overnight.

A week after Baba's homecoming, while we were wrapped up in matters of the heart anyway, our daughter and her fiancé decided to confide in us what was in theirs. Since we were unexpectedly still going to be in the country a while longer, their wish was to advance their wedding plans, to be married on the anniversary of the date they'd met, August 20, two and a half weeks hence! We wouldn't have to do much, the kids assured us. They would make all the arrangements.

"Oh, why not?" we said. We had all the time in the world for what was really important. On August 20, Baba felt very well and enjoyed, along with the other parents and very few friends, a small private ceremony. We were not to know then, but on the same day as Baba was given new life, somewhere in the city a Siamese-Russian Blue mother cat was giving birth to a nameless gray kitten, who would one day wriggle his way into our lives and hearts.

Bon Voyage

So finally after more convalescence for both of us, on October 6, 1998, Baba and I sat at JFK airport awaiting our flight. We would find out later that 40% of the population, about 6,000,000 warm bodies, was expatriate, expat for short, those, like ourselves, who were originally from elsewhere, and 60% was Saudi, making a total of about 15,000,000. Of the Saudis, approximately 43% are age 14 or younger. We learned non-Saudi women were not required to wear veils, or scarves, or even *abayas*, black robes blanketing a full set of clothes, but most donned the sable colored raiments for their own emotional comfort. *Mutaween*, morality police, also called *mutawas*, would try to enforce strict rules anyway, we heard. They were recognizable by their slightly shorter than floor length *thobs* and bushy beards. And music would not be heard in public.

But we did not know any if that yet, on October 6, when we caught the 13-hour Saudi Arabian Airlines flight. I had met Baba's male, Saudi students so those impressions were already part of my repertoire, but my first personal encounter with a Saudi female occurred in New York.

Awaiting the announcement of our flight, Baba and I occupied two seats at the terminal. We'd already waited four hours, after having taken two previous flights that day. He got up and walked about. I had been aware of three women, cocooned in black, who had walked by earlier but I'd not given them much notice. No sooner had he vacated his resting place then they returned. Other empty spots sat nearby, but one woman began to literally back up towards Baba's seat and sat down askew with half her back to me. Her companions sat on her other side. As she bent to sit, I spoke to her.

Jewel Dhuru

"Mam'n, Mam'n, this is my husband's seat," I said, but she didn't seem to hear me. I was prepared to just let it go, but not 15 seconds had elapsed when, from behind us, an air hostess who witnessed the entire exchange, leaned over to the woman and said, "Mam'n, this seat is taken." Since the woman showed no response, the message was echoed. As it happened, Baba reappeared just then. The lady, along with her companions, had already gotten up. She was muttering, unintelligibly to me, and continued to mutter as she and her companions stalked away. When he took in what had happened, Baba spoke directly to her back.

"It's alright; you can sit there," he offered once, and then again. But she kept on walking and left the area. That was the last we saw of her until we reached King Khaled airport. There, we found a Bangladeshi bearer with a cart and were moving to the baggage section to await our bags, when we became aware of shouting in Arabic going on behind us. We three all looked around and saw a woman, lending her voice to a blistering tirade, aimed at our bearer. All we could decipher was the repeated word *"araby"*… *"araby"*. The bearer might have deduced her meaning, but just shrugged and we continued to wait.

When we two compared notes later, we guessed she had objected to the bearer's helping a non-Arab first. We might have been mistaken, but we'll never really know, so that's where it ended, except for the memory.

While we watched bags circle and stumble over themselves, Baba recognized a pleasant young, single French Canadian gentleman, an engineer, whom he'd met on the flight. Baba introduced us and as this new acquaintance spoke about his brothers and sisters in his familiar French Canadian accent, I immediately felt at home with him. I had been raised in a French Canadian community in Canada. As we bid each other adieu, we asked his name, but not for contact information.

I felt sure the Canadian embassy would have a social at Canadian Thanksgiving at the end of October. But, all three of us had only been in the Kingdom for half an hour. Little did we know parties were not allowed in the country, unless done in secret in a Prince's private palace or at an embassy. Even if allowed, 7000 Canadians were far too many for the embassy to accommodate in such a festive fashion. We were not to know then we would not see him again.

We got through Customs in three minutes, after having to barely open only one bag and I wished I had brought my philosophy books. Paul, a colleague of Baba's was waiting for us behind a security rail. While passing through the airport, we couldn't help admiring the architecture, intricate designs on stretches of walls, around fountains and on metal gratings in window openings. While catching up on news, we three rode to where we would stay until we secured a flat, the campus Guest House, or so we thought.

However, Paul, a gentle man of African origin insisted that arrangement would not be suitable for us. The closest I got to the Guest House was to drive by, but later, Baba went inside and from what I heard about stagnant water and cockroaches, scourges of old buildings in many warm countries, I'm grateful for the initiative.

Chapter 3: Home And Campus

"The heart is a house with a room for every one it loves" [4]
—Governess Miss Madrigal, movie *The Chalk Garden*

The Marriot

We stayed at the Marriot for a week before a flat was selected and furnished. The hotel gym and swimming pool were off limits to women but Baba went as part of his cardiac rehab. We knew that religious etiquette prohibited Saudi men from looking at women other than certain relatives, but I couldn't have known how it would feel until that first week in the hotel. True to predictions, men wearing *thobs* with either a *gootra* or a red and white-checkered *shmal* and *egal*, and usually a cell phone spliced to their ears, did not look in my direction.

When I walked in the hall of the hotel, I moved hurriedly to the side for fear the herd of downward gazing men would mow me down, because they did not appear to have seen me. When I was the sole occupant of an elevator, when the doors opened, before I could exit, two or three such men, sometimes in pairs welded at the shoulder, would begin to enter from the hall as if I wasn't even there. As the car became aflutter with robes and flooded with a strong musk scent, I had to squeeze out the side. It was as if we were on opposite sides of a two-way mirror, I on the sighted side while they faced an impenetrable reflective lens.

The non-Saudi staff, however, was accommodating and friendly. The only other women in the hotel were expat, some saying hello and others keeping to themselves. I felt schizy, not knowing when or with whom to establish eye contact or to utter a greeting.

We slept half days and half nights for the whole week. Before Baba went to work in the morning, he dropped off breakfast for me in our room. That, and snacks from the mini bar, along with the Discovery and movie channels for entertainment, sustained me until dinner. When a Pakistani fellow, Abdulla, came to straighten our room, I covered my hair with a scarf and took a book down to a couch near the main café and tried to look busy for a half hour.

Ala Tool

Asian waiters asked if I needed anything. When I answered, "No, thanks, I'll just sit here for a while, if you don't mind," I got quizzical smiles and then they left me in peace. We were not to know for two months that women were not allowed in that lounge or the central café.

In the evenings, a campus employee drove us around while we scouted out flats. For three days, we looked off-campus and then tried closer to Baba's office. These were the only times I saw the natural light of day, the window in our room being a mere slit.

Taking us on the walking circuit of available campus flats was within the province of Mr. Mustafa, a Saudi in *thob*, *shmal* and *egal*. He joked with Baba as we walked and Baba offered him a cold drink, but he declined, patting his protruding ponch and saying the walking was good exercise for him. My back muscles signaled their dismay at the sight of four stairs at the entrance to each building, even more so when I realized Mr. Mustafa was leading us through some buildings, instead of walking around them, just to get to others with vacancies.

The first empty flat we perused had a pale flamingo carpet and off white walls. The combination of the carpeting and the view were unbeatable and I liked it immediately, but Baba wanted to look at more, so I allowed myself to be dragged through three other buildings on all corners of the campus before we settled on the same first one. We went back to the office and between jokes, completed the paperwork, and then Mr. Mustafa gave us a copy of the Qur'an.

Naturally, overload hit, aggravating chronic muscular complaints. Past experience told me the best treatment was bed rest for a couple of days, along with other symptomatic treatment. The spasms would abate. I relied, more than ever, on the TV, puzzles, reading and whatever I could do to keep my drooping spirits up. The isolation did not help.

The next day, when Abdulla came to straighten the room, I got up off my ice pack to open the door, to give him a cursory explanation and to ask him to just do the bathroom near the door and leave the rest for the next day. He complied but before leaving, he didn't actually enter the room where I was lying down but he leaned against the edge of the wall and started to chat. Being quite cut off from people, I didn't mind a few minutes' chat, at a distance. He told me how much his own back pained him from lifting mattresses, how he missed his family, how little his pay was and that there was nothing to do besides work and sleep. I sympathized, but when he started on how he wished he was married, I got up off my ice pack again, said what I hoped were encouraging words and opened the door for this little boy in a man's body. It was sad and there wasn't much I could do but listen and commiserate, but there were limits. I was new to the place and was just starting to learn just how prevalent his feelings were among expats and how little he had exaggerated.

Baba's fatigue after work lessened day by day and we could keep less curious hours. We went to a secluded restaurant in the hotel, in a so-called Family Section, legitimate entertainment for women accompanied by their men. I'm glad I didn't know better when I previously sat in the main café. It would be much harder to deliberately expose myself to such scrutiny now, not to mention how much more caged I would have felt then.

Hindsight being 20/20, that explained why, when we lunched in the café near a fountain and potted palms, one of two Saudi males at the next table almost sustained whiplash suddenly swerving to stare. I attributed his sharp swing to my having no *abaya* yet, even though I was draped practically from head to toe in loose fitting earth tones. No wonder no other females were around. Baba, in his dark suit and tie must have stood out, too, when every one else was in either long white garments or white uniforms. This was a chance for me to better understand how Baba felt as an Asian in North America all these years.

Campus

The day we moved into our flat, Paul pointed out one of the two spots where skud missiles had landed in Riyadh during the Gulf War. One was beside a school 1.6 km. (a mile) from the campus and the other was out in the desert. Architecturally interesting campus buildings were a hospital, mosque and glass topped atrium, where men lunched and women were only allowed ½ a day a week. Rows of palms and flowers accentuated fountains and sculptures.

Down the street by the campus supermarket, a tailor, barbershop, hairdresser/dressmaker, bread shop, stationery shop, another mosque and fish market all kept each other company. Center stage in a roundabout near the entrance sat a gigantic, open marble Book, *kitab kibeer*, 45 meters (150 feet) high, surrounded by grass and colorful blossoms. Gold lettering in Arabic contrasted with the dark cover but the pages inside were blank, and the whole area was singularly solitary. In another land, it would have been a popular picnic spot.

Friends to whom I had reported we'd found a campus flat gushed about how pleased they were for us and proceeded to list all their favorite aspects of campus living: students lying about on lawns, live bands and bowling alleys. This would be nothing like that. In our Housing area, it was fairly sedate much of the time, except for restless kids playing late on Wednesday and Thursday nights, weekends in the Arab world.

The landscape included squares of salt and drought tolerant trees and rows of flowering plants sprinkled around concrete walkways, sand playgrounds and benches for cool evenings. Plant names read like Who's Who in Horticulture—tamarind, Ficus, mesquite, Jerusalem thorn, eucalyptus, acacia, neem and olive spotted the grounds—all names from antiquity. Middle Eastern palms like Washingtonia fan palms and phoenix dactylifera date palms, adorned the grounds. Some sounded like species of dinosaurs. In season, bloomed yellow trumpet vine, jasmine, aloe, oleander and bougainvillea spectabilis, the latter sounding like a lurking phantom. I looked out to see live exotic plants, formerly just two-dimensional reproductions in a landscaping text.

What a paradise, I thought. Paradise? It was a strange word to associate with scorching sun and shifting sand. Ironically, one theory of the original whereabouts of the Garden of Eden placed it on the island of Bahrain, only a four-hour drive away, just as the Hanging Gardens of Babylon was in present day Iraq, a couple of days drive north. The brilliant flowers and trees of various shades and textures helped to give color to this sandy beige country.

New Flat

Our apartment building was shaped like a cloverleaf with three rectangular petals and a stem, so no common walls connected us with neighbors, only the one attaching our entry to a common hall. This provided maximum privacy, views on three sides and good air circulation. I wasn't to know it at the time, but the combination spoiled me for living in apartments forever after. The buildings appeared to be all the same color, a pale yellow, but at different times of the day, depending on how the sun struck them, the walls waxed from a bleached off white to yellow to peach to beige to ochre to light brown.

Upon entering our modest flat, a left turn from the hall took us into the rectangular sitting room-dining room, with the pale flamingo carpeting. Two sunny windows and a glass balcony door on the far wall lit area. A patterned couch in reds, flamingo and black and a rosewood finish coffee table were situated near the glass door. Four matching armchairs and two side tables bordered the same room while a blond dinette set occupied the dining room. The folding screen between, we usually kept open.

We were to share smiles and belly laughs with people from all over the world in those rooms. Frankincense and exotic ood would smolder in a pot pourri on the side table. We would pour over tour books and maps that covered the coffee table, making plans to visit historic cliff dwellings by cable car and neighboring Bahrain. Near the balcony door, a potted gardenia and a night-blooming jasmine would reside and a little gecko would appear one day clinging to the ceiling. We were to be roused with a jolt at 6:00 A.M. the morning Saddam was bombed, to answer the phone, our daughter calling to see if we were safe. Neighboring expat teens would sing in our dining room, plugging their karaoke microphone into our boom box. On TV, we were to watch, briefly, a British royal wedding, apprehensively, the search for the missing plane of JFK Jr. and his family, and sadly, the funeral of King Hussein of Jordan. But we didn't know any of this at the time as the room stood empty and expectant

From the main entrance, on the immediate right, was the Saudi style bathroom, like a powder room with a shower, but with a toilet level with the ceramic tiled floor. This became a private room for me to line up my little bottles and jars in front of the mirror.

Proceeding down the hall, the kitchen opened on the right with a storage room off the far end of it, containing the infamous leaky water heater and private garbage chute. The kitchen, at first, was stark white. Breaking up the monotony were only a brown table for two and the bright red seats of two chairs by the window, right beside the balcony door. The room looked like a surgical theatre. I'd soon do something about that.

Still, its coziness brought back fond memories of our flat in Dundee, Scotland, on the previous sabbatical. Back then, I buttered

Ala Tool

scones and prepared steak and kidney pie in the kitchen and spread out maps on the table, trying to pin point Loch Ness or Edinburgh Castle.

This time, it was chicken kebabs and still warm Arab bread. In my new kitchen, I was to make Christmas cookies with powdered, non-alcoholic, vanilla extract, and quietly give them away, because yuletide wasn't celebrated openly. A frazzled neighborhood teen, searching for respite from the effects of memorizing eighteen books for exams, was to drink calming chamomile tea with me. While garlic grew in a little pot on the windowsill, visiting kids were to toast marshmallows on shish kabob skewers over the gas cooker. And a young English student was to snack on cookies during her break while she selected her sticker for the day.

Further down the hall came the bedroom on the right where we were to sleep for ten months. The main bathroom occupied the tip of the cloverleaf. We felt quite privileged with our two balconies, off the sitting room and kitchen, the latter providing hooks for double clotheslines. Each room had doors sectioning it off from the others and each, except bathrooms, had its own ceiling AC, which doubled as a heater in winter. The compressor, driving both heat and AC, resembled the first univac computer, so huge it filled an entire room with lights and buttons. Our compressor was a diminutive version, only more rattley and obscured in silt, in a semi-private, separate room right outside our front door.

Colored glass and metal light fixtures, unique in texture and shape, added appeal. The main bathroom had a mini basket washer whose ½ minute tune signaled the end of the cycle. In the main bath, we were to wash off the local color we and our clothes soaked up from the camel/sheep/goat souk and swept out prankish missiles of sand accidentally finding their way through the window into our tub.

Within two weeks, I had transformed our plain white kitchen, where even the window and balcony door were frosted, into the heart of the flat. I had packed pictures from art magazines to personalize the space and create a warm atmosphere. Sketches of herbs, spice charts, paintings of party settings and rustic country roads were stuck onto cupboards and walls and fine art magnets clung to the fridge. The effort was worth it for myself alone, but over the next months, neighbors noticed, too.

"You have such a nice kitchen," they were to say. "We don't have pictures on our cupboards."

Of course, I missed what they took for granted, their kids sitting around the table.

Another item most other kitchens didn't have was a rolling chair. Because of my muscular limitations, I did not stand to cook. So one of Baba's first actions was to roll the computer chair into the kitchen and put a dining room chair by his laptop. The first time I sat and cooked a package of mildly spiced chicken kebabs from the supermarket, the whole flat was filled with the most delectable aroma.

In the campus sports club, doubling as a social club, on distinct women and men's days, we could use the swimming pool, sauna and exercise machines. Baba went regularly, but the pool proved to be too far for me to walk the round trip. And the sauna was upstairs, but no elevator. Inaccessibility to fun activities was a disappointment but dwelling on it wasn't going to get me anywhere.

In the clubhouse, banquet rooms could be reserved for meals with one's relatives only, but men in one room and women in another. Very few expats had many relatives there so a creative definition of the word relative was a must.

Points of View

Other compounds boasted better grounds, more flowers and fountains, outdoor swimming pools, a shuttle service, gift shops and coffee shops with European style decor. The compounds I saw were attractive and for the most part, no *abaya*s. But there was a price to pay. The aura of secrecy clung to the 3-meter (10-foot) high walls around them, bulwark to keep the allure contained. Even the windows of the president of a European corporation's elegant abode, where I was to be a guest for a poetry club meeting, looked out over a lovely garden, then onto walls.

Our campus compound had no walls, but one thing we all shared was guards at the gate. Our flat was in the privileged position of being on the front outskirts of Campus Housing, containing flats for non-Saudis and villas for Saudis. The villas were more spacious but had high barricades around individual courtyards, and such recessed windows as to afford near zero view.

Ala Tool

We were advised, in campus buildings, to avoid first floor flats because of occasional water back-ups, cockroaches and the smelly spray to exterminate the latter. And fourth floors, at the top, were suspect because of the strain the sun baking on the roof put on the AC. So we settled into this second floor flat.

The view from our kitchen balcony was a rear window experience involving fifteen other neighbors. Visible activities nearby were workers digging, cleaning, repairing or accidentally cutting phone or electric cables, trucks full of furniture being relocated, exuberant kids at play, and their mothers chatting on benches before dinner. We admired the designs on the carpets, airing on a balcony clothesline across the way. Starting on our corner was the tree-lined avenue that Baba walked to work each morning. At his destination, near the bus stop by the campus hospital, shrouded female figures silently collected on benches, but they didn't take the bus, because women weren't allowed.

Before the effects of jetlag finally abated, I was sometimes up at 2:00 AM looking out the sitting room glass door at the lit up nighttime skyline. At those times, my Id more awake than my Ego, it was surreal. When morale was low, the full impact of the challenge I had undertaken showed through a fog of fatigue. With a knot in the pit of my stomach I wondered if I was up to it. Was I really there? I loved to learn about other cultures but what was I doing leaving my friends and kids and going there?

Circumstances looked different in the cold light of morning. Our view was no Vermeer, but it was just the right amount of busyness for someone who was used to working from home but who was going to be inside more than usual. I liked it from the start but it grew on me even more.

Our sitting room balcony was situated above the more frequented of the two building entrances, so we were privy to the muffled sounds of everyone's comings and goings. The elevator operating down the hall was audible as well. It occurred to me that in an Agatha Christie mystery, we would be in the strategic position, inadvertently, to witness critical events, like slamming doors and the loading and unloading of small trucks at odd hours.

From the window, three small streets were visible, along with a park of sorts, tennis courts and the white minaret of a mosque whose arches were lit up all night. The three parallel streets also paralleled to the length of our balcony. The closest street was about 23 meters (25 yards) from me as I watered my plants outdoors. On this nameless two-lane road, I could wave to people I knew, mostly Baba's colleagues. Since mail is obtained only through a sponsor, it wasn't necessary to have a home address or for streets to be named. Landmarks like *kitab kibeer,* the big Book or IKEA or the only Sheraton were more useful for finding your way around.

Across the street from us, tendrils of dark pink bougainvillea bordered the tennis court whose fencing was no obstacle to viewing the second farthest street, a four-lane divided street with more traffic. Beyond that, a narrow part of a park was sandwiched between this four-lane thoroughfare and Prince Abdullah Road. I loosely refer to this area of trees as a park, but there were no benches or activities of any kind, because gathering is discouraged, so opportunities for it are not provided. Squinting between the tall stems of palms and acacias in the park, just detectable were the small shops and restaurants on the far side of Prince Abdullah Road, the main street in our area. Alas, most restaurants, even American franchises, some with bright pink furnishings, were for men only. With no Family Sections, they couldn't admit women.

By car, we explored the area behind the main street, latticed with long side streets of walls, behind which lay private residences. Intermittent ornate iron gates in an infinite variety of designs broke up the monotony of the endless parapets, one gate for each residence.

Flanking each gate were individual bushes or trees taller than the walls. Most picturesque were small trees trained to fit flatly against the wall, so as not to invade the narrow thoroughfare. The trunk rose up right against the wall and the branches were pruned to grow and spread flatly against a square of concrete, framed by the street on the bottom and the top edge of the wall, where the leaves contrived to touch flowering bougainvillea cascading over the top. The sides of the frame for the lateral sprawls were the gate on one side and intermittently situated lanterns, which provided patches of light and disappeared down the long streets to their vanishing points.

These blank facades and gateways belied luxurious gardens and walkways that lead to expansive, sumptuous interiors. Just inside each gate, walkways wound through gardens like an enclosed courtyard, leading to the front door, the pattern repeated to a lesser extent in the back. From inside, the view was whatever was within the fortifications. Gazing out through even the most gracefully curved French doors at a stately palm inevitably ended with looking at a wall.

Before the present day police system, these barriers were for privacy and safety. If anyone scaled the wall and stole a peek into your house or grounds, the Qur'an permitted you to have their eyes put out for peeking without permission. Still, I preferred the open feel of our small flat where I could drink in a scene from a distance.

A playground was practically underfoot, just to the right of our balcony, with a seat along the edge shaded by eucalyptus and mesquite trees. The latter, Prosopis juliflora, rolled up their fern-like leaves into tube shapes every night. Three times a week, water tank trucks crawled along the streets while diminutive Asian boys dragged the attached heavy hoses from tree to tree and flooded the squares of soil with the restorative elixir. With rain only falling in the winter, if at all, these trucks were a necessity throughout dry areas.

For ten months, this was our domicile, our base camp, where we unburdened and fortified ourselves mentally, physically, emotionally and spiritually, and where we enjoyed our privacy. We met expat neighbors, and although we saw the Saudi ones through windows or in halls or playgrounds, we seldom made the acquaintance of any. We heard their children playing with balls and bicycles in the halls, though. Expats were from all over the world, all educated and teaching or doing research in various fields like mathematics, engineering, linguistics, chemistry, dentistry, and all areas of medicine, to name a few. Of course, one cannot always feel on the same wavelength as everyone else. Vibrations of all types were to come our way, some smooth, some interrupted and uneasy, and some charged with static.

Chapter 4: The First Month—Work, Weather And Entertainment

"When we grow, it is because we are working at it, and we are working at it because we love ourselves. It is through love that we elevate ourselves" [5]
—M. Scott Peck, *The Road Less Traveled*

Work

The reformulated Arab workweek, with Thursdays and Fridays off, meant Baba would work on Saturdays and Sundays. To adjust, we thought in terms of both systems. Friday, *Jumma* in Arabic, had that Sunday feeling because the streets were quiet in the morning except for the lengthier prayers over loudspeakers, and a Saudi Saturday felt like a North American Monday. That 'Thank Goodness It's Friday' feeling came on Wednesday.

I looked forward to seeing what good news Baba bore in his briefcase each day. For me, as for most females, contact with the outside and access to resources, at least initially, were through the male in my life: invitations, spending money, visas, stamps and our very identity papers and reason for being in the country, all came through him. I would have to wait until February before we could access email from home, and through his account at that. It felt juvenile. It added strain to our relationship to know that not only did solutions for some problems come through him, but the causes as well. Novel strains cropped up, too. A thought ran through my mind: the only thing that can hurt Superman is green kryptonite, a piece of his own home planet. I still had my heart, imagination and voice, though, so I'd have to develop contacts and resources of my own. With the help of neighbors, I did.

I'm not really a tea party kind of person, one who can talk about the latest cake recipe or fashions for an hour. I've become more versatile, but with limited energy and endurance, I'm still a 'Here I am with my skills and limitations and with the intention to help' kind of person. So I didn't immediately fall into step with a particular social set. It would have been great to have congenial company more often but to fill in the long hours with ingenuine talk with people I

Ala Tool

didn't know just to minimize being alone would have led to profound loneliness. But, some of my very best friends were strangers at first.

So I went to 'coffee mornings', the only sanctioned non-Saudi gatherings aside from soccer games. Some were casual, with brunch food, fruit juice, shared laughter and little gossip. And others offered chocolate dainties and coffee, served on china by hostesses who talked incessantly. Initially, I had anticipated the closest people to me would be from Baba's work, but eight and a half months would elapse before I even saw his office.

Basically, for the first three weeks, when Baba went to work with both male and female, Saudi and expat colleagues, I was alone, except for campus electricians, plumbers, carpenters and furniture movers who serviced the water heaters, washer, gas stove and sticky balcony door. It was too quiet. I longed for strangers to drop in, like a troop of Christmas carolers. Then I could offer them hot apple cider. Or maybe a bunch of juvenile scavenger hunters with cheery faces, begging a bit of string, a shoelace, a stamp or a sponge.

But no such luck. I spent my considerable free time reading the books I had brought with me. Anticipating needed mental escapes, a companion from my suitcase was Tolkien's *Lord of the Rings* trilogy. I studied Arabic, from books and cassettes and hoped I would eventually get some field practice. Baba was too busy to learn much Arabic, except for technical work-related words and the all occasion *mafee mishkole*—no problem, that everyone learned the first day. His knowledge of Hindi, though, an East Indian language, was sufficiently close to the Pakistani Urdu, to facilitate conversing with most taxi drivers. We only had one Saudi TV channel and its hours of transmission were limited. So mornings were for listening to cassettes or a walkman radio, cooking whatever Baba brought from the supermarket, painting with the art supplies I had tucked into my luggage and missing my kids, friends and everything familiar I'd left behind.

Many times, thoughts came, as though from a great distance, about Helen Keller, who alternated gaining proficiency with her new world with being plunged back into darkness. I told myself my day at the water pump would come, when all would become clear.

My appointment book, blackened with scribbles the last couple of months before we arrived, suddenly appeared quite blank. There usually was a client or student to prepare for or artwork to submit for juryng or a few phone calls. Joseph Campbell would say I was changing from one kind of achievement to another and ought to observe what beauties lay on the way.

During the last couple of weeks before we left home, such a lot of paperwork needed attention. When piles of mail came, I remembered thinking I'd be glad to get away where no one could send me any more mail. But the very next day, I realized mail from friends would take a long time to come to us, so for a long while there wouldn't be any mail. The absurdity of trying to live in either the past or future and wishing for life to be other than what it was, hit me. Scientists who study the nature of time tell us all the moments of our entire lives are already coexisting here anyway, that they're not somewhere out there. These were good reasons, I thought, for staying grounded in the present moment.

Still, I missed the wonderful feeling of growing I relished when involved in something meaningful. That, and having a female around who knew me well enough to give feedback on how I was coping and changing. When I had acquired experience that made a difference in my life, being was a joy. I often achieved it through reading and applying, but in Riyadh, reading material was limited and so were the days females could enter a library.

Weather

In early November, we were still experimenting with whether to close all the windows and doors and keep the six separate ACs on or to enjoy fresh air in some rooms and cool air in others. It was pleasant enough for open windows, 32 to 38° C. (80 to 90° F.), except for peak heat at mid-day. But that meant wiping tabletops every day or I would literally be able to write my name in the dust, a layer like patina that replenished itself when removed. Baba's secretary back home phoned on business about this time and asked how everything was. When I grumbled about the ubiquitous shower of sand coming in through the window, geography not being her long suit, the sweet lady queried.

"Sand? Are you at the beach?" she asked.

Sure. The beach. Millions of years ago, this was all a sea, but not now. We tried cooling just the sitting-dining room and leaving the rest natural. Perhaps these discordant temperatures led to my contracting the grandmother of all colds. Baba had one, too, but he generally got them more often than I did with more severe symptoms and longer duration. This matriarch lasted three days and involved a sore throat, nasal, sinus and chest congestion, rheumy eyes, more fatigue than even jet lag brought on, a cough and laryngitis. Feeling wretched, it occurred to me that I had both figuratively, and now literally lost my voice! A week after the virus was gone, my voice was still ragged and crackily. Whether because of relative disuse or lack of lubrication from the 15% humidity, I wasn't sure.

The sun drew moisture so greedily from whatever was available, bananas left in a closed plastic bag for an hour, fogged up the bag. Oranges, guavas, papayas—every fruit had to be refrigerated so they wouldn't either over ripen overnight or develop rhinoceros skin and shrivel. I could almost hear grapes left on the table pucker into hybrid grape-raisins. No wonder dried dates and figs were so popular. Fresh, warm breads would mould within two days if left out, but refrigeration removed the yeasty softness, so they had to be eaten up quickly.

Skin required special care. Considering the extent to which bodies were draped, the low incidence of skin cancer was not surprising. But regardless of how well I kept myself under wraps, after a wash, without heavy skin cream, my skin itched and felt like parchment. If neglected further, nails began to crack and chip. When oil was applied, marinating began, but at least the itching stopped. Sipping water often was a must, mainly in the form of desalinated, but not fluoridated, bottled water. The jury of popular expat opinion was still out on whether it was safe to lubricate one's throat with fluoridated tap water or not.

Entertainment

Entertainment was a problem. No movie theatres or Blockbusters. One had to buy from the limited number of pirated videos offered at very few shops. We didn't have a video recorder anyway. There were hardly any libraries. Apparently the concept of lending and then returning things was not understood. Saudis were accustomed to just giving things away. The university library had women days, but I had not begun to go out alone yet. I didn't have an *abaya* yet either. We'd heard they were required, but in time learned the requirement was only a custom of very few countries, not part of Islam as such.

Jewel Dhuru

Technically, the religion only required modest attire and that *something* is covered—some Arabic word. The *something* remained shrouded in mystery. Translations came up with cover your beauty, or cover some anatomical equivalent of your pocket, but that was as clear at it got. It made sense to me that when everyone else has a particular mindset, it was best not to attract undue attention until I knew the lay of the land. We couldn't put a couple of balcony chairs out and people watch, either. The emotional atmosphere was too secretive for that and the meteorological one was too hot. Concerts, plays, bazaars, luncheons and poetry clubs were only whispered through the grapevine and held in seclusion.

I was to attend a poetry group, hosted by the wife of the president of a European corporation. A handful of women met in their sunken living room, all chauffeured in to the gorgeous upscale walled abode, where we read and discussed our amateur attempts at rhyme and were served refreshments by smiley Indian boys in white jackets. After the rare and wonderful occurrence, my back only took two days to uncrook from the couch. By the next month, circumstances had changed and the organizers became elusive.

For in-house entertainment, the university had provided a TV. The first morning alone, I turned it on and waited. Tiring of the blank, blue screen, I left it on and turned my attention elsewhere. Gradually the blue turned to multi-colored bars and then finally, at Noon, the day's transmission began. The only Saudi channel began and ended its day with the national anthem, and a recitation from the Holy Qur'an and its English translation. The early programs were for children, the later ones becoming more adult in nature. Certain words were bleeped out of all programs, altering plot lines. Mother Nature, dating, cross your heart, angel, dance, girlfriend, strapless, royal blood, cherish, church, any reference to alcohol or drinking, pig, pork and anything not understood by the censor—all bleeped. Even juke from jukebox vanished into silence. Once, the last comment in a comedy was just silently mouthed, the whole punch line bleeped. And on to the next show. It was humorous to hear muttered or subtle, but innocent, comments that slipped through anyway. I always wondered how censors worked. Did one group of elders spend their days sitting in a room searching for objectionable phrases in films while others tore or inked out bare legs and arms in *Time* and *Newsweek*?

Ala Tool

The children's interval showed delightful Eastern European cartoons accompanied by only orchestral music. One featured two Czechoslovakian boys, Bolek and Lolek, who went on fantasy adventures. Their stagecoach trip through the American Old West involved hats hybrid hats, crossed between cowboy hats and sombreros and playing a guitar shaped suspiciously like the triangular Russian balalaika.

Episodes of Zoo Cup featured fanciful soccer games, called football almost worldwide, with teams made up of caricature anthropomorphic animals. The Cathedral Cats played the Lab Rats, Slow-but-sure Snails vied with Gastropod Turtles and Dairy Cows challenged Pasteurized Sheep, all with an enthusiastic Snake commentator, named Chuck Adder, wearing a cap and one running shoe, hopping up and down behind a microphone. The Monkeys' star player was Kong and Tyrano was the counterpart of the Lizards'. When the Cobras played the Octopi, the Cobras fouled the opponents by spitting and paralyzing them. The Octopi fouled the Cobras by spitting ink into their eyes. The game ended when a Cobra paralyzed the referee, frozen into a starfish position, his red cards splayed all over the ground, and an Octopus spit ink onto the lens of the camera allegedly filming this animated game. Then, everything went black.

The Saudi channel showed 1940s and 50s B movies, called feature films, Australian or American in origin, many westerns, mostly violent, mainly all-male roles, and showing no friendliness between males and females of similar age. All profanity was removed.

Captivating old British, Canadian and Australian comedies and dramas could crop up or submerge overnight like volcanic islands, like Chinz, The Campbells and Water Rats. Cooking programs, Saudi and Australian travelogues, health instruction, documentaries on Saudi history, water desalination, oil refining, Arabian horse racing and animal conservation abounded. Saudi dramas appeared in the afternoons along with a delightful spoof on Saudi culture itself, *Taj Mataj*, only shown during *Ramadan*. Snatches of Mr. Bean or Northern Exposure were inserted between Saudi programs. Sometimes interruptions were interrupted by a movie. And almost everything could be pre-empted by sports. Movie endings were chopped off in favor of All Sport, usually highlighting soccer. On the other hand, when the *muezzin*'s plaintive voice emanated from the loud speakers of nearby mosques, to remind us of prayer five times a day, called *salah*, feature films and documentaries were rewound a few minutes when they resumed.

Commercials were rare, cumulatively less than an hour a day. One reminisced about King Abdul Aziz, who is credited with integrating all the regions and rival tribes of the Kingdom. The words DON'T WASTE WATER appeared over images of parched, cracked earth followed by 'Water is in trust for us all'. And cameras noting available bargains roved through malls bristling with shoppers.

Programs rarely started on the hour or half hour, but at odd times: 3:11, 5:23 or 7:42. News programs featured what the King and princes were involved in that day and on Press Review, a man in *thob* and *gootra* actually read the news aloud directly from the newspaper. Movies after midnight were more interesting and modern, but not being originally desert dwellers, we didn't keep those hours yet.

And there was religious instruction: Islamic Culture, Understanding Islam and Focus on Islam. It came in many forms, especially during *Ramadan* and Hajj. It was no coincidence that a deep, authoritative male voice translated from the Qur'an.

Arabian horses raced on weekends, but quite differently from the Kentucky Derby, Preakness or Belmont Stakes. No half hour of hype beforehand and no betting. Mostly dark horses shot out of the gate without much preamble. Generally, one horse led by a wide margin from the first lunge and maintained the lead throughout. The announcer did not periodically give a rundown of all the steeds, from first to last. He just kept repeating the names of the first three, Jabbar-Sayeed-Omar, in quick succession. The repetitive nature lulled me into a doze. But once, while I half listened and half read a book, the audience started going wild, jerking me to attention. Six horses were striving, abreast of each other, to be the first to reach the fast approaching finish line. They zipped across and the uproar died down. Once the tangle of legs and noses was deciphered and the winners proclaimed, a camera scanned the animated crowd, indicating royal personages sitting in the front row. I caught myself humming The Sheikh of Araby. Then within seconds of the win, on to the next gate.

Within a month, an African neighbor allowed us to splice into his satellite cable. We got CNN, BBC, TNN, Indian and Arab channels. Still, I missed the educational and cultural programs on the Public Broadcasting Stations back home. But for a while this would do. Once we got a boom box, radio offered mainly Arab stations. The Armed

Forces played music for teens and Riyadh Radio offered a variety all day. A weekly interview featured local people of interest, Arab and non-Arab alike, French programming and plays, and talk shows. Before we figured out how to get English stations, some days, in those first weeks, with the isolation, the friendliest voice I heard, besides Baba's, was the silent one written on the display dial, saying "H-e-l-l-o" when I turned it on and "G-o-o-d-B-y-e" when I turned it off.

Shopping, particularly for women, who acquired merchandise at bartered and bargain prices, was synonymous with entertainment, so browsing was a new option. When we wandered into women's clothing shops, the selection! All manner and shades of leather pants and low cut, sheer, suggestive tops and gowns represented very racy glad rags. Baba and I exchanged questioning glances. Who wore these clothes, we wondered, not for the last time. Not the expats, surely. In department stores, the sections for feminine sleep ware and lingerie took up more floor space than daywear and were just as colorful. We tried to reconcile the cocooned black figures on the streets with these styles, but couldn't, not at this early stage of our stay.

Chapter 5: The Neighborhood

"The first human being who hurled an insult instead of a stone was the founder of civilization"[6]
—attributed to Sigmund Freud (1856-1939)

The evening *salah* had just finished, that 20-minute episode that sometimes soothed like a symphony and sometimes scraped the senses. Vociferous prayers flooded from loud speakers, the first official one commencing at about 6:00 AM, sunrise. A bonus one began at 4:15 AM and the others were at around noon, mid afternoon, sunset and an hour after that. The timings are based on the moon, so vary by a few minutes each day, and change from city to city.

That day, two voices, in mid-cry, had intertwined and built to a crescendo, like the spectacular end to a fireworks display. Those times were truly melodious. At other times, though, the wails and rumblings brought images to mind of a giant with a booming complaint, like Gulliver waking to fetters on the beach. Shopping and eating out had to be done before or after *salah*, because all offices and shops closed then. Baba and I went riding frequently in the evenings, exploring the city or purchasing essentials for our bare kitchen. And I bought needleart materials to occupy my time. For just ten months, it was not cost effective to buy a car because taxis were inexpensive, 15 Saudi Riyals (SR), $4.00 US for a 10-miute ride.

After one excursion, as we passed the playground under our balcony, Baba asked if I wanted to introduce myself to the Saudi women sitting by the side. I had considered it before, but decided to wait until my Arabic was better, or one of them spoke to me first, or I wasn't so shy or any other excuse. But, since he was there, I decided to plunge in. Unable to think of the correct phrase in Arabic, I just said, "Excuse me" to a woman standing nearest, and then continued, "I've just moved in and wanted to say hello."

Only her eyes showed from under a sea of black as she turned to me. She stared for a long moment and then, playing only a supportive role in this little drama, she managed a "no English" before pointing towards another figure in black sitting on a swing. I moved in that direction. As I approached, she asked, "What do you want?" Perhaps she had only a rudimentary working knowledge of English, I thought,

Ala Tool

so I repeated, finding it difficult to smile by then. Our brief conversation was confused and centered on her asking what I was looking for. She seemed to think I sought the building right behind me, although I was only trying to tell her that was where I lived. When she said, "Go there," I thought under the circumstances, it was a good idea and turned my steps towards home. Baba trailed thoughtfully behind.

What a contrast from my experiences eight years earlier in Egypt. There, absolute strangers in a post office in Aswan welcomed me to their country and entire classrooms of kids on a field trip to the museum in Cairo, identifying me as a foreigner, stopped to smile and ask, "What is your country?" and to say, "Welcome to Cairo." I recall thinking these kids had hit the jackpot when it came to having History to study—3000 years of it.

Perhaps the timing was bad with these Saudi neighbors, perhaps my approach lacked warmth, or the language was a problem, or it was the no *abaya* or a blend of them all, but I resolved never to do that again. Giving in to my first impulse to smile and say hello to other fully paid up members of the human race was going to have to be curbed. At the same time, I wanted to keep my heart from shutting down when I had stolid company. A new balance would have to be achieved, for my own sake, if not for others as well.

Batha

Three weeks after our arrival, Baba and I went shopping to an old market, called Batha. He was looking for a telephone, but wasn't sure where the shop was. We learned later that Batha a very conservative area of the city. The market itself had a newer area, where we were, which gave the impression of a meandering labyrinth of stalls and shops, and an older one, with even more winding ways, if possible. A visit to the old section a month later revealed a maze of concrete walls and floors resembling a giant's basement. On makeshift shelves, older local families sold their discards, most of which had antique value. All manner of goods and chattels cluttered this gigantic scrap yard: incense burners, camel bone boxes, carpets, silver toe rings and other jewelry, old fashioned brocade clothing, brass lamps in the Aladdin style and other everyday curiosities of yesteryear, blanketing every inch of shelf and wall space.

But this first visit found us in the new area, looking for a phone so we could call our kids. When my legs got tired, Baba found me a pillar with a wooden bench built around it, one of a string of such pillars along the sidewalk between the main road and the outermost shops. Immediately, I noticed few other females around, only a couple of Filipinas clad in black. By this time, we had not yet bought an *abaya* for me, a phone being a more pressing need. Mostly middle class males, of various origins, perused the merchandise in toy, clothing, kitchenware and stationery shops, and sat in a café. Shopkeepers, appearing to be unoccupied, took an inordinate interest in my inactivity. I thought Baba was going just to the end of the block and returning, within my range of vision. But after I followed him visually for half the distance, I looked away to settle myself onto the bench. When I looked up again, the only human being I knew in that vicinity and one of a handful in the country had vanished into an entrance of the rabbit warren.

Even though not swaddled in black, I was wearing a loose fitting, long, earth-toned skirt, long-sleeved sweater and scarf. Every square inch of my skin was covered except for my hands and face with a bit of hair showing at the forehead. Sitting there in apparently provocative garb, I wasn't to know I had wandered into a more or less no fly zone for women. Inadvertently, I had invited the lingering, unabashed stares of the men walking by.

To keep from getting too unnerved, I tried to dissociate myself from the passing populace, as if I wasn't really there. My breathing became shallow as I varied my gaze from the squealing electric car one toyshop keeper was operating in the walkway, to the signs on the shops across the street, to the distant approaching traffic, but always coming back to the spot where I'd last seen Baba. The traffic, practically at my feet, was copious and constant and above the general din, the occasional honks took on an annoying connotation. Several times I wondered if my Arabic was good enough for me to jump into the nearest taxi and flee back to the university, giving in to a fight or flight response, but by that time, I was probably too frozen to my bench to move anyway. If only I had had a book or drawing paper with me. All I had was a dinky notepad and pen; that would have to suffice.

That was the first time I had seen feral cats, tucked into corners, subsisting on scraps. Dogs are not allowed in the Kingdom, prohibited by the religion, although we did catch occasional glimpses of mangy looking strays on the dunes and saw private pets tucked away in unlikely nooks in the city. The pets probably had a comfortable, if limited existence, but the strays had a forlorn, hunted look. Scavenging cats were a common sight. Fish markets supplied scraps and there was plenty of sand for litter boxes, even the sand in playgrounds.

Sitting there on my bench, hoping mild trauma didn't show on my face, I felt alternately like a dog tied to a post awaiting my master's return and a display in a red light district. Baba returned in a mere fifteen minutes, but it had felt like an age. All my feelings culminated in one short, unvarnished phrase: "You owe me one." Although he was sympathetic, there was no way he could empathize, not so soon during our stay. He had not been able to find the phone shop but had a lead as to its whereabouts, a short way into the snarled labyrinth. So I pulled together the tattered remnants of my composure and fled like a fugitive to an inner bench with less human traffic and fewer shopkeepers, who still stared curiously but less conspicuously.

To restore presence of mind, I began an exercise that fosters calm and confidence. I recalled situations when I felt really content, escaping into the world of special conversations with selected friends and relatives or light-hearted scenes of verdant valleys and bubbling brooks. Fortified by this reverie, I could then deal from a position of strength with my current challenge. And I learned to always carry a book or notepaper with me.[7]

The next day, arriving with Baba and Paul at a fish market in a more liberal neighborhood, I protectively avoided eye contact with the merchants, all male of course. I felt as though my every movement was being watched. Just before leaving, the Indian clerk unexpectedly handed me Baba's change and I caught sight of his face, warmly beaming at me, a quiet fountain of mirth. At me? The forbidden fruit. Taken aback, I hazarded a look at the others, all Indian and Pakistani. I eventually learned that anyone who did any actual work in the country was expat and the schizzy feeling recurred when I tried to remember not to smile around certain people, but that it was all right to be natural around others. As it was, they were watching me, but perhaps because they needed a smile as much as I did. The cats, out in number, were watching too, for scraps. After all, it was a fish market.

I got my *abaya* and scarf before the week was out, and this was the first time I had seen black converted from basic to burden, like a cloak of lead. Eventually, I discovered that it was common knowledge in the desert that birds with black feathers could keep cooler than white ones, but only if the air was moving. Ironically, the *abaya* freed me to go out by myself, without being so conspicuous. I carried the scarf in case we went to another traditional neighborhood, but I rarely covered my hair. On the campus, the atmosphere was freer and when off campus, I was careful about where and with whom I went. When I did don a scarf, it was for my comfort. Being deprived of the sight of the ordinary modest female form, that of more than half the population of this planet, can result in males' forgetting that the form contains a brain, a heart, a sense of humor and decision-making capabilities. To expose more than other females did to males who were in deprivation's grip would be to invite unnecessary discomfort.

I began learning how and how much women could do for themselves. Still, because of the cloistered nature of life, those of us who were out and about were surrounded by men. If I needed anything, a taxi, take-out or groceries delivered, I almost always had to ask for a man's assistance. Where were the days I could publicly be greeted by a pleasant smile, when I could be at ease and take the time I needed for what I was doing? When I interacted with those who accepted the ways of others, I felt a sense of men's being the neighboring, rather than the opposite sex. When in the company of those who didn't, the atmosphere felt adversarial.

Mr. Wrong Number

Once our phone was hooked up, a complex process involving several electricians' coming and going, the innumerable wrong numbers could commence, all starting with *Salam wa laqum*. When I accidentally dialed wrongly, Arabic-speaking females shouted at me, males uttered a curt 'wrong number', an occasional polite response reached my ears or they'd hang up.

In-coming calls fell within a certain range. Besides bad connections, and frequently changed numbers, young expat men without their families, men who had nothing to do besides work and sleep dialed random combinations, hoping to add relevance to their days. I got my share of such calls, but through one in particular, I gained insight into the lives of bachelors. Usually I said I couldn't talk and was going to hang up. I disengaged gently, because I understood the plea behind the calls and after all, they had my number.

But, once when I answered, an Indian Muslim male in his mid 20s was on the line. Perhaps his entreaty was more distinct from the others. Without having to divulge much more about myself than the usual country of origin, configuration of family and religion, a matter of public record anyway, I learned he worked in a jewelry shop, had few friends and his parents back home had arranged a marriage for him in a few months' time. I suggested reading and letter writing to him, but even as I said it, I knew he had little access to books and it's hard to write when you're depressed. By week's end, I almost forgot the incident, except that it was sad.

I was not to find out for months what a difficult life he led. An article in the (2001), shone a spotlight on bachelors. The male journalist published a message from one who described himself as an oppressed Saudi bachelor, past what society considered marriageable age. He complained both young and old bachelors were discriminated against as though they belonged to a lower class or a sub-human group. He claimed the Commission for the Prevention of Vice and Promotion of Virtue, traffic police and security guards targeted them, that they were chased from restaurants, amusement and public parks and malls and from hotels and campgrounds when they traveled domestically. They were accused of harassment, their eyes seeking out other men's wives and daughters. The gentleman continued that it was not fair to generalize because of a few transgressors. He claimed plenty of married men flirted shamelessly except when their wives were looking, adding that sometimes it was the girls who flirted. The result, according to him, was that they found themselves living and working in unpleasant neighborhoods, as if they were foreign. His two suggestions were to take each case individually and to build compounds, apartments, parks, shopping centers and clubs only for bachelors.[8] Although I could see difficulties with the second suggestion, the journalist thought it was a good idea. But, I wasn't to know any of this for months, certainly not when Mr. Wrong Number first called.

He called the next month. In my naivety of the system, I asked what progress he'd made in getting a hobby or a pal, but he had no answers. He asked me about Canada, helped me with Arabic words

Jewel Dhuru

and instructed me on the types and qualities of gold in his sponsor's jewelry shop.

His impending marriage back home, the next month, preyed on his mind.

"What do you think brings more happiness," he asked, "married or single?"

We tossed the topic back and forth without clear answers and I, again, encouraged him to involve himself in something that was worth trading for each day of his life. For the next while, Mr. Wrong Number called monthly. The day came when he spoke agitatedly. His sponsor's domestic help, a South Asian lady, was trying to entice him to the house when the sponsor was away. They had chosen a day the following week for their rendezvous.

"What do you advise me to do?" he asked.

This was one of the strangest situations I'd ever found myself in. Nowadays with counseling being done on the Internet, between unseen strangers, this would have seemed tame, but I felt like Frasier dispensing offhand advice on a radio show, except Mr. Wrong Number didn't know I was a counselor when he'd first called. Hearing the anxiety in his voice, I faced the situation straight on and give him the benefit of my experience. I encouraged him to visualize his life in two years and see where an incident with this domestic would fit into his overall plan. He sounded relieved by the time we rung off. After that, impulsively, he wanted to come and meet me in person. I told him after he was married, we would see.

The next time he called, in answer to my casual query, he said he had gone to see her, but he didn't elaborate. His wedding had been postponed due to complications in the family. He would be going home for vacation time and would straighten it out then. The saga went on.

The time came to face the reams of red tape and register at the campus hospital. Baba enrolled himself while at work, but for me, it would be a separate trip. I still had no *abaya*, since medical concerns were the next priority after getting a phone. So I dressed in similarly modest long, loose attire as the apparently provocative Batha outfit, but and headed for the hospital.

Ala Tool

Faiza

I did, in time, find a kind, Canadian, male physiotherapist off-campus who treated me. Chiropractors were all men, and as a rule, did not treat women. I did find a non-Muslim male, though, who gave me one adjustment at a relatively exorbitant 300 SR ($75.00) and expected me to come back twice more that week. Leaving price aside, the atmosphere in his office was so artificial and patriarchal, the way he interrupted my appointment with alleged phone calls from princes and the way he scolded his female assistants in front of me, that I never went back.

Getting registered at the hospital was a tedious process. Baba came to collect me in a taxi, customarily called a limo when engaged from the limo stand near the campus hospital. After 1½ hours of going to one office and waiting, then another and more waiting, then my going into a ladies-only area and Baba's waiting outside, I secured a plastic ID card with my Father's first name as my middle name and an appointment with a female doctor in two days time.

Two days later, Baba again arrived in a limo, locking up our flat with his key and reminding me of where the limo stand was. This time, he escorted me to the clinic for Family of Faculty and once he was sure I knew my way home, he walked back over to his office.

The waiting room chairs were very low and straight backed, unlike my back, but the Egyptian doctor had a kind voice and called me 'my dear'. I had brought all my reports and test results from home, but not the actual x-rays. It became clear there would be no treatment or referral to physical therapy without the x-rays. So I agreed to have my hip radiated, got lost in the maze of hallways and finally got to x-ray with the help of a non-Saudi Samaritan.

Another waiting room. The women looked straight ahead or down, except for one non-Saudi with a round smiley face. I was not there long enough to converse with her, but the soft expression in her eyes was refreshing. Her having joy to spare gave me hope.

A Filipina nurse came in, clutching a file, and called "Jewel Martin?" In a cubicle as posh as a wooden box with a narrow bench fastened to the wall, I donned a gown, air-conditioned from the back, the design of which is mimicked the world over. It was in this hot, stuffy box that the image came to me of my newly acquired flat key, just where I'd left it—on the kitchen counter.

Jewel Dhuru

Nausea was heaped onto tired, achy and hot and just when I felt like I had come to the last pinch of the vice that I'd put my back into, I was twisted and prodded some more to get the x-ray. Afterwards, a Filipina nurse let me use her phone to call Baba, for his key. But there was no answer. I knew where his building was, generally, in the opposite direction from the limo stand and I was certain there was a flight of stairs. So with tired legs and now a sore hip, I trudged over to get a limo, amid stares and sightlessness, but not enough to immobilize.

I asked the driver to drop me at the Housing Office, from where we procured the first keys. The drive was only a few minutes in duration but long enough for the Pakistani driver to ask my nationality, religion, how long I had been there and if I liked it.

At the Housing Office, I recognized Mr. Mustafa, the same Saudi who'd shown us around campus a few weeks earlier. Anticipating a little sympathy, I felt relieved. I explained the situation and he remembered our building and flat number without my reminding him.

"Nice to see you again," I said, as he rummaged for a spare key.

But this Arab cousin of Dr. Jekyl and Mr. Hyde did an about face and unsympathetically told me to sit down on the couch and wait. Fortunately, I had a book with me this time. After 15 minutes, he silently offered me what he claimed was a spare key, which I assured him my husband would return later. I hiked on home. Now which building was it? Across one building and down two on the campus grid. Thank goodness the elevator was working, but the key was another matter. I tried all angles, depths and directions until my wrists ached, but the lock wouldn't budge. I plodded back to the office—down two buildings and across one. After ten more minutes, Mr. Mustafa announced with his most sullen expression that he had no other key. Back on the phone, I did manage to explain my predicament to Baba's secretary. Forty-five minutes later, Baba appeared and we trailed back to our flat.

After that, I safety pinned my key inside the durable black travel bag I had bought just for the trip. It was 30 x 25 x 15 cm. deep (12"x10"x 6") with a large main compartment and ten zippered pockets. I took it with me everywhere. Besides carrying everything of importance, pens, notebook, a copy of Baba's official papers, a photograph of myself as a child to connect me to my roots and both Saudi and American money, it came in handy as a cushion to tuck behind my back when I sat in a chair shaped like nothing on Earth. The key would be safe there.

The explanation for what I'd interpreted as Mr. Mustafa's Jekyl and Hyde routine? It's true his uncle had offered to help me find a chiropractor if I phoned him at Mr. Mustafa's number. But Mr. Mustafa didn't sound too cooperative when I called then, either. I wasn't to know it then, but even on a campus replete with expats, some construed smiling at a man who was not my father, brother, husband or son, particularly when I wasn't wearing an *abaya*, as tantamount to answering the door to a traveling salesman wearing only the smile.

Not knowing the convoluted medical system, I was yet to learn that the second trip to the doctor, x-rays in hand and new *abaya* encasing my person, merely secured a prescription for the Physical Therapy department, located in the wing farthest from the limo stand. The mazelike hike secured an appointment six weeks hence, with eventual access to therapy and a hydro pool.

On the day of that second appointment, a gentle looking lady played with her infant son in the waiting room. Faiza removed her scarf and exposed a neckline that could not be described as prim. In broken Arabic, I asked her child's age. She answered in Arabic that he was eight months old. They made themselves comfortable on the floor and she and I silently followed his antics, crawling under the table and coveting her keys. After a time, she spoke in fluent French, telling me her Arabic was limited, because they were from Tunisia, in northwest Africa. I was delighted because as a child in Canada, I also learned to speak French, but I was rusty. She elaborated that she also had a three-year old daughter and that her physician-husband was taking a six-month course and then they would return home. The four of them lived about 3.5 km. (2 miles) from the hospital but she came monthly for the children's check-ups.

Only a few minutes ticked by before one of us was called into the office, but that time was delightful. We each had legitimate appointments, but I inadvertently stumbled onto a typical Saudi female past time. Some come weekly to sit in waiting rooms or at bus stops for entertainment and a change of venue. I counted my blessings. What I considered a step down as a form of social interaction, was considered by some in that waiting room as a step up. Faiza and I resolved to exchange phone numbers so we wrote down particulars, but with time constraints and carelessness, I did not check what she wrote.

After the appointments, we re-connected for a brief moment. She offered to catch a limo with me but as I was going to physical therapy, we bid each other adieu and parted ways. When I went home, I planned to ask Baba to get a copy of the campus map so when I invited her over, I could mail it to her to guide her driver. I could show her the Tunisian needlepoint I had started.

A week later, when I finally looked carefully at the paper Faiza gave me, I saw her husband's last name at the top with another name below. Whether her last name or his first, I didn't know, since Muslim women do not change last names when they marry. Next came three phone numbers. The first had a B- in front of it. Could it be for Business? And it had an S in place of the fourth digit. Maybe a 5? Anyway, I never got any answer at that number. Then I recalled she'd said the second number was for her husband's office and was the one she preferred anyway, so I tried it. The last three of the 7 digits were 8s. But the first and last of the three 8s were in Western numerals, usually known as Arabic numerals. The middle 8 was the Arab Arabic number 8, shaped like an upside down V, incidentally East Indian in origin. Why the switching back and forth, I couldn't say. I got an Arabic-only speaking woman at this number and after my second attempt, she lost her patience with me and started shouting and I lost the inclination to try again. The third number, I recalled, was their residence, but it had more than seven digits, so I left a message on the answering machine connected with the first seven. A Saudi woman called back and politely said it was a wrong number. So that was that.

The most practical suggestion from Baba was to call the hospital where we met. I tried it and told my story, asking if they could contact her and give her my number. I expected them to protect her privacy, and wasn't disappointed. They said there was nothing they could do.

Perhaps she just forgot all about the encounter as soon as we parted, or perhaps she did phone when the phone cable was cut, a frequent occurrence those early days. At low moments, I feared the whole endeavor had been doomed from the start and all I was ever meant to have with her was those fleeting moments. Much was fleeting there.

Faiza's husband must have completed his course long before we left the Kingdom and their kids must be half grown by now, but to this day, I remember her gentle face and voice. I also thought of the French Canadian gentleman from the flight when we first arrived and I left our contact information at his embassy for him. But that wasn't to be either.

Neighbor Women

The day after I gave up on Faiza, my doorbell rang. It was a woman, shrouded in black.

"I'm your neighbor. I heard you're new and I've come to say hello," she ventured. She was the answer to a prayer. I subsequently met Anita's husband and a whole brood of congenial, well-behaved children. They were expats, too. In my quest for a key, days earlier, she was just on the other side of her door; I could have phoned Baba from there. But I had not met her yet and was in too delicate a state to cope with the thought of rebuff at the time. Excuses? Maybe. Anyway, things were looking up and since it was early November, the weather had gotten cooler.

A couple of times we came home from evening excursions to find sand on the windowsill and all over the main bathroom. The tub had to be swept out. At first, I thought it was a neighbor's commentary because we had not yet purchased curtains.

The four bathrooms on the tip of our cloverleaf, one on top of another, had windows overlooking the playground. A small, thick opaque glass window, about 30 centimeter (12") square, opened out and a pressure-fit screen opened inwards. Since we were on the second floor and it was winter, we kept the glass open and the screen closed.

One day, in the sitting room, I heard intermittent thuds and lulls coming from the end of the hall, like a virus resting between epidemics. As if I was answering a sharp summons, I went to the bathroom window and peered out. Five little boys, ages 8-10, potential products of misspent youths, stood there, apparently turned into pillars of salt with upturned faces. I pulled on my ebony coverall and went downstairs. Most of the pillars had recovered mobility and scampered off. The one who remained had a whole row of sand clods lined up at the bottom of the slide. He told me with an air of genuine innocence that he and his accomplices were competing to see who could throw the clogs highest on the side of the building. The eldest one could reach the fourth floor window, but as I looked up, ours was the only one open. As he talked, an older boy, about 12, was taking an interest in our conversation. He sidled closer and eavesdropped, eventually forming a trio with my tormenter and I.

Once I saw the look of big brotherly chastisement in the eyes of the elder, I knew steps would be taken in the Saudi fashion to ensure the transgression wasn't repeated, at least not too soon. I couldn't really be angry with them, knowing how hobbled their sources of entertainment were, although I'm glad the benediction of our bath came to an end.

Over the weeks, expat males in our building came to introduce themselves, but wouldn't cross the threshold unless Baba was there, so outside the doorway they wrote their numbers down for him. Baba did call and was glad of their companionship and advice.

I decided to pass the gesture along by visiting the wives, taking small gifts. Baba had spirited away their phone numbers so at mid morning, I just rang doorbells but was prepared to return if they were busy. I was ready for the inevitable offering of more food and drink than I could digest in a day.

The most memorable one, Farhida, was Pakistani, about 40 and good-natured but didn't speak more than a few words of English so she just hovered with food and drink.

"Women should not go out of the building unless it's with their husbands," her husband had stated with conviction, the day he came in to visit us both.

So in fancy Pakistani garb, Farhida took to dropping in on me often, with one of her kids as translator, and with plates of steaming food. She was inquisitive about my belongings, picking up and examining my watch from the kitchen counter and rubbing the clothes I wore between her fingers. I began to regret acting on my impulse to go visiting in the first place.

Another colleague of Baba's, the mention of whose name still brought a smile to everyone's face long after he'd left the country, had a flamboyant personality. Everybody knew him. He was Asian, energetic, intelligent, animated and outspoken. Some described his behavior as bombastic, so I came to think of him as Dr. B.

Dr. B could be warm and funny, with a quip for every occasion, but he tended to dominate conversations with his extended, blustering narratives, in the middle of which he usually jumped to his feet to demonstrate his point, often dragging an unsuspecting accomplice out of a seat to assist in the exhibition. He was amusing, but with a sting. According to Baba, he was a patient and caring teacher. It was he who'd made the comment with which we all agreed, that education and instruction are not synonymous. Even at a university, if one does not learn to think for oneself, that is mere instruction.

He made some good points. In their making, he bounced back and forth between affectionate companion and harsh critic. I liked parts of him, but at times no one could get on my nerves faster. Within a nanosecond of his arrival, a visceral irritation began rising at something he said. I wasted exasperation dealing with him until I finally remembered that in some schools of spiritual thought, all the warm bodies in our lives act as mirrors for us. They help us become more fully functioning, self-confident human beings. So perhaps he was my mirror and it was our common negative traits that I found unnerving. I could see the traits in him, but not in myself. My annoyance wasn't with him at all; it was with myself. Once this dawned on me, he was off the hook. I could even thank him for revealing hidden parts of myself and I was free to take pleasure in his brand of humor.

But how was I like him, I wondered. He had such energy that I didn't. Did my character contain such extremes? Was I kind, but critical? Did I demand such attention? Was getting the answers to these queries part of what I was sent there to do? Things were definitely warming up.

Chapter 6: Winter And The Holidays

"It is not by our money but by our capacity for enjoyment that we are rich or poor. To strive for wealth and have no capacity for enjoyment is to be like the bald man who struggles to collect combs" [9]
—Antony de Mello, *The Song of the Bird*

Slam went the sitting room doors! It was the warmest, breeziest November I had ever experienced. I smiled when I first saw a quilt included with the furnishings, but on winter nights, we buried ourselves under it. After all, deserts are known for extremes in temperature. *Shemal* winds, from the north, whizzed down the east coast, and right through our flat. In October, it had been pleasant, in the 20s C. (70s F.). It only got sticky at midday and windows could be left open day and night, if I didn't mind wiping 1/3 cm. (1/8 inch) of silt off the furniture every day. But on breezy days, leaving the windows open on opposite sides of the flat invited doors to slam. By mid-month, one heavy sweater, indoors and out, all day, was a must, and by November, the windows were kept closed.

It usually rained on and off November through February. The previous year, heavy downpours had carpeted the hills with blossoms. But this year brought few liquid assets. I only remember six separate days of cloudbursts. The sky would haze over, it poured for five minutes and before the rain even stopped, the sun began streaming through dappled clouds again.

In early December, I remember the first day I smelled rain as soon as I woke up. An earthy aroma was making the air thick, ponderous and pregnant. But when I looked out, the ground was dry. Could my senses be deceiving me? It was the unmistakable scent of unquenchable earth being sprinkled with moisture, a treat I had been denied for two months.

"It drizzled early this morning," said Anita, across our kitty corner kitchen balconies, as she shook her rugs. My senses had not abandoned me. She'd witnessed the event, worthy of mention at coffee mornings. The rainy season was beginning.

Winter and early spring were the only seasons with appreciable cloud cover, changing shape rapidly, and a welcome variation from stolid azure. Dawns and dusks were vibrant with pink or yellow marbled skylines. Early one morning, we would have slept through corrugated neon pink and gray clouds if our daughter had not phoned at 6:00 AM, all breathless concern.

"Are you all right?" she opened. She'd wanted to call as soon as she'd heard, in the middle of our night, but our son-in-law persuaded her to wait. During our slumber, we'd been oblivious to the fact that Saddam's people had been bombed. I thought of the innocents, the skud that had dropped the year before near a school, the gas masks Baba's colleagues had been issued, my bag of valuables in the cupboard and the heightened level of alert. We were so near, but I could neither see nor stop the sad events from unfolding.

Thanksgiving

If there was a harvest celebration, in some form, it escaped our notice. So Thanksgiving weekend was spent on the new, usual activities of our reformulated week. Two days before Thanksgiving, the brother of Baba's Saudi student back home invited us to dine at a Japanese restaurant. When I asked about his wife, our host responded she was very religious so she wouldn't join us but he brought a Pakistani male friend instead. The dinner was ample and delicious, complete with a performance of airborne cleaved, tossed, sliced and diced meat and vegetables. But it was our first time out with such a group, so when we were shown into a private room for just the four of us, I was uncertain of whether to remove my *abaya* or not. Fearing being considered an exhibitionist by two males I had just met, my long gown remained unrevealed except for a few inches at the neck, where I had allowed myself the luxury of undoing the top button. When we got home, Baba saw the gown, bought for the trip, for the first time. Before putting on my pajamas, I mentally ran through the preparations I'd made to go out and wondered what that was all about.

We dined out quite a lot. In many restaurants—Turkish, Indian, Lebanese, Chinese, Italian and Pakistani—one could partake of an elegant meal with excellent service for about $10.00 US per person, with food left over.

The next day, Wednesday, Thanksgiving eve, was the day of my first physical therapy appointment and as it happened, the electricity in our flat went out. On our little anthill, some crew or other was always digging a new hole in the ground and at the bottom of the most recent one, was either our electric or telephone cable, just waiting to be cut. So, with no working elevator, I clambered carefully down the stairs with a rumpled shirt and uncurled hair. The appointment was mainly a lengthy assessment, but it only began after I was shooed out of the men's waiting room, in which I had sat by mistake. Thanksgiving Day itself, being Thursday, was weekend. We stayed home and were grateful the phone worked so we could talk to our kids.

Two days later, we supped on Chinese food with Paul. I had celebrated by making cookies, which we quietly gave away, after discovering chocolate chips were hard to come by and vanilla was available only in a powdered, nonalcoholic form. Unusual activities for the occasion, but the unavailability of giblet gravy or pumpkin pie did not prevent our thankfulness for the good in our lives. On Saturday, it was back to work for Baba.

Christmas

Christmas Day was even quieter. By that time we knew gathering for Christian occasions was particularly perilous, inviting arrest. So like other expats, we improvised. I taped cheery pictures on the walls, strung a garland over a door, dangled a large paper snowflake in the main entrance and candles brightened tabletops. One shopping center sold Christmas decorations, but I didn't see the point in buying much. We'd arrived with four large suitcases and had the illusion we'd leave with four. And I wrote letters, which wouldn't arrive until mid-January but which I hoped would be welcome whenever they came.

Shopping centers upgraded our education as well. There were few benches, except for secluded café areas, and for good reason. It not only prevented gathering, but fraternizing between the sexes. The human spirit, however, being ever creative, the Saudi version of cruising was born. In malls, young people kept on the move, trudging back and forth along thoroughfares. Using a sort of black market communication system, bits of paper with cell phone numbers and emails of males were discreetly dropped on the floor at the feet of oncoming females. Exchanges were initiated by males or by suggestive looks from females. The paper bits were either picked up or not, at her discretion. The bases for selecting females were personal but included the quality of shoes and handbags. Then, like the parting of the Red

Sea, couples went to opposite sides of the hall, maintaining eye contact and whispering into cell phones. The outdoor variation of this exercise entailed young men's numbers' being thrust through young women's car windows, cracked open in cooperation, or remaining closed if she so chose. My flaxen-haired acquaintances confirmed often being approached in this way as well.

Downtown, red and yellow tube lights spiraled around the trunks of palms and green lights extended the length of the lowest fronds. They weren't really for Christmas, but they looked festive and I luxuriated in whatever I could. But before a week, they were gone.

"They looked too festive," a British expat confided.

Memories came to me of past holidays, especially of my first Christmas in India, 25 years before. I knew it certainly wasn't going to be a white one unless we visited Kashmir. At least there were no traffic jams, Christmas commercialism or crowded shops, but no carols, either. So, since I loved this holiday season, I safeguarded myself by adopting a mindset of just skipping Yuletide this year and doing something else, of an Indian nature, instead. I was in for a surprise.

Baba's family and friends rallied round with quiet, yet sincere wishes for a 'Happy Christmas'. My sister-in-law followed the chicken curry with plum pudding. Enormous six pointed stars made of bamboo, plastic and tissue paper clung to the sides of apartment buildings, the largest stretching across four windows. One German lady, married to an Indian, the parents of Baba's student, brought over cuttings from an evergreen bush in their back yard. She'd tied the bundle at the base with a red ribbon and hung gold and silver foil origami stars on it. My brother-in-law came up with a tall, slim, ornate brass vase to cradle the cuttings and that was our tree that year. I was engulfed by undiluted goodwill, a fundamental of Christmas and it was heart-warming. Compared to our Saudi Christmas, that time in India was like the moment Dr. Seuss's Grinch's sled, filled to the brim with stolen trimmings, snapped and showered treats down on the unassuming residents of Whoville.

On the brighter side, in Riyadh, after dining with Linda at a Saudi restaurant on Christmas Eve, we were introduced to frankincense and myrrh in the giant's basement at Batha. They were the highlight of the season for me and I was subsequently to learn about the treasured bits of gum resin I held in my hand. Linda had lived there for years. She was a veritable fountain of information about Islamic culture and local history. Her enthusiasm was contagious.

I can never smolder frankincense without thinking of her. What times we had! When she came to my door, her effervescent smile and "Hello" brightened everything. I didn't have to fuss with tea and cakes for her. We both preferred just water while she taught me Arabic. I considered her help invaluable but she dubbed it the blind leading the blind. We started with a list of English phrases I was having trouble with and ended with Arabic conversation, in two different accents. Before long, we lapsed into English. We'd cover every subject imaginable and the walls would ring with laughter. At times we'd phone for a campus limo and go to an embassy library and gift shop or to the Diplomatic Quarter for embassy business to conduct or to a souk in search of Arab fabrics and laces or to The House of Talents for art supplies.

On one such foray in late December, we were at Kuwaiti market, an older sprawling souk. While sitting on a high curb trying to remember what other incidentals we needed before we headed home, a big black Mercedes rounded the corner and stopped in front of us. A Saudi woman, encased from head to toe in black, opened the right side back door and let herself out. At the precise moment her door opened, the driver's door swung wide as well and without hesitation, her Indian driver started toward the rear. By the time he reached her door, she'd gone into a shop, leaving her door wide open. He swung it shut, reversed direction and regained his seat, whereupon he drove into the parking lot to await her. Their movements were so well orchestrated they looked rehearsed. I looked at Linda with an unspoken question on my lips and her comment was "probably a princess."

That Christmas, a package of ten letters and cards came from friends back home. Under the circumstances, a real treat. Our daughter had sent us three such packets, but only one surmounted all the obstacles. Christmas Day, being a Friday, was *Jumma*, so there was no work. Baba was in bed all day with the flu anyway. Several colleagues had it, too. Occasional inclement weather alleviated dryness but added to the chilled atmosphere. Neighbors dropped in for quick visits over the week or phoned to whisper 'Merry Christmas', since religious topics were prohibited over the phone. Like the month before, the scarcity of family and friends did not preclude exchanging goodwill. Besides family, what I missed most was music and greetings in voices not artificially hushed. On the other hand, if there is any season we are able to communicate with our spirits, this must be one.

Ramadan

Just before New Years, the month of *Shaban* ended for the year 1419 *Hejera*, using the Islamic calendar, and the month of *Ramadan* was about to begin—the month of contemplation and meditation. Baba wasn't quite over the flu, so he still needed early nights and I always like to start a day, in this case a year, with a good night's sleep. The celebration of the day was conspicuous by its absence. We dined in an almost empty hotel restaurant with a friend, who explained that the year before, merrymakers in that very room had been arrested for gathering, so we were home early. Being *Jumma*, the usual prayers boomed out over loud speakers.

Throughout the year, Saudi TV news broadcasts opened daily in precisely the same way. "King Fahd Ibn Abdul Aziz, Custodian of the two holy mosques" did such and such. Then, his brother, "His Royal Highness Crown Prince Abdullah Ibn Abdul Aziz, deputy premier and commander of the National Guard" visited so and so. And then, "His Royal Highness Prince Sultan Ibn Abdul Aziz, second deputy premier, minister of Defense and Aviation and Inspector General" did this and that. The word Ibn tells us they are all sons of King Abdul Aziz, but in this case, they all have different mothers. The names and titles fairly rolled off the tongues of the announcers, as if they'd been practicing in their sleep. But now, during that special month, the news was also full of which other Muslim King or Ambassador or President or dignitary "phoned King Fahd Ibn Abdul Aziz to congratulate him on the occasion of the advent of the holy month of *Ramadan*"[10]

Practically the whole country became semi-nocturnal, waltzing to the rhythm of *Ramadan*. Compulsory prayers began early, so eating was done before sunrise. Shops were open from 6:00 AM until noon or 2:00 PM and from after the 7:00 PM prayer until midnight or 3:00 AM. There was no eating, drinking or smoking in public or sexual relations during daylight hours that month, for anyone, at least in theory. Most cafeterias were closed and public water fountains turned off. Non-Muslims on campus went to the hospital cafeteria, ate cold

Jewel Dhuru

lunches in locked offices, or they went home. In case a non-Muslim was tempted to engage in the discourtesy of eating or drinking in front of those who could not, warnings were issued that, anyone, regardless of religion, observed breaking the rules would be lashed or arrested Young children, the aged and those with serious medical conditions were exceptions and did not have to fast, but still had to seek seclusion before sustenance.

Baba's vacation was nigh, so our schedule changed drastically. For the 11-day vacation in January, we escaped to the city of Baba's birth, which had reverted from the British name of Bombay to the original Mumbai. For Eid, at the end of *Ramadan*, our family, Hindus, had days off work. The streets in the predominantly Muslim area of Mumbai were filled with revelers and fireworks. For dinner, Muslim neighbors' kids brought over a platter of delectable lamb biryani, mirroring the Saudi lamb and rice feasts enjoyed in Riyadh in solitude.

In Riyadh, some took personal enrichment more seriously than others. And some just got better at engaging in the clandestine. The range of motivations for behavior was probably as wide as it would be for the practices of other religions, but the character of the range was different. In Saudi Arabia, my sense was that a scant few avoided carrying out their obligations, but most just complied, or cultivated the appearance of it. School children, on vacation, slept until 1:00 PM and stayed up playing outside until 1:00 AM. At month's end, the more incorrigible of the bunch, along with their better-behaved compatriots received gifts for Eid

The *Hejera* calendar is based on the migration of the Prophet Muhammed (peace be upon him)(abbreviated pbuh) from Makkah to Madinah, on July 16, 622 A.D. The calendar shifts forward 11 days each year in its correlation to the Gregorian calendar because the *Hejera* calendar has only 354 days, with the full moon coming at mid-month. So *Ramadan* can and does coincide, eventually, with every season. That year, 1999, it was during the winter, when days were shorter and cooler, so it was relatively easier to do without water. But the time would come when it would coincide with the longest, hottest days of the year, and that must really entail sacrifice. And, after thirty years of shifting 11 days a year, they gain a whole year.

Combined with the intention of self-improvement, sacrifices build character. It was hard to reconcile inconsistencies between what was professed and what was practiced, though. But Linda pointed out that the atmosphere outside after the last *salah*, was very spiritual. So, I went out on my balcony then, while families were breaking their fast, and it was very peaceful. It was like a Sunday morning—quiet. Most people dined in the homes of relatives, at one brother's house one evening and another brother's the next, the men in the front public sitting room and the women in the private ladies' sitting room in the rear.

On TV, more time was spent on religious instruction than usual. A friend suggested at least as many devoutly spiritual people exist there as in the West, and upon reflection, the statement seemed fair.

Jewel Dhuru
Chapter 7: From One Extreme To The Other

"All changes, as well as balance or equilibrium, are produced and given life by the intersection of opposites" [11]
—Georges Ohsawa, *Unique Principle*

After the holidays, our lives in Riyadh settled into the usually unusual again. Between January and March, I began noticing causes and effects, patterns and opposites. This was a land of extremes, but not necessarily clashes. Perhaps the inhospitable terrain and weather that could hot up from downright nippy without warning, and vise versa, set the pace and everything else followed. Conditions required self-protection and taking quick, decisive action. Considerable energy was needed for survival; perhaps there was none left over for frills.

One day, Linda brought over a canary yellow fruit called a Trunge and described it as The Saudi fruit. It was asymmetrical, 20 cm. (8") in diameter, and bore similarities with animals, plants and people. It had rind with a texture like hardened brain tissue, 5 cm. (2") of insulating white pith, a juicy but face convulsing sour core, lots of Vitamin C and many seeds.

The camel scrubby exterior showed the same adaptability, insulation from the elements and a husky voice. It was similar for lizards. Plants were resilient, too. Hardy flowering shrubs coexisted with aphids. Coincidentally, the difference between native Wisconsin clay, with the smallest soil particles on Earth, and Saudi sand, with the largest, was like night and day. So we went from cultivated clay to the land of sand.

I had plants of my own now. Indeed, my own night blooming jasmine's virgin leaves unfurled with aphids already inside. But with little water and even less care, a sort of horticulture by neglect, blossoms appeared anyway. The extremes of weather, stunning to shivering, took their toll on all living things. The harshness of life permeated the environment and was perpetuated with the blossoming.

Arabic vocabulary ranges from accurate in the extreme to a shotgun sort of meaning. *Khali* refers to one's aunt on the mother's side, the masculine version of *khal* for the uncle and completely different words, *ammi* and *amm*, revere the aunt and uncle on the father's side. On the other hand, *itfaddaal* is oblique and is used when a guest arrives. Literally meaning 'kindly accept', it can mean anything from welcome, to come in, to make yourself at home, to here you are, to please take this, to help yourself, to sit down. The all purpose *mafee mishkole* stretches the gamut from no problem, to it's all right, to no worries to *hakuna matata*. And of course, the ubiquitous *Inshallah* covers all and sundry, becoming less personal on the way from I'll do my best, to I hope, to if Allah is willing.

Extremes of behavior occurred in people, too. Much has been written by Graham (1991) about how Saudi Arabia, desperate for skilled labor after the oil boom, pulled illiterates, educated only on the Qur'an and tribal traditions, into the 20th century.[12] After fifty short years, rough edges between tribal ways and sudden affluence still needed smoothing. The image of a volcanic eruption sent flares through my mind. The cataclysm causes upheavals for rocks, beasts and humankind alike. What was previously well integrated was displaced by a powerful thrust and changed form. But polished manners do not evolve with the wave of a pen over a checkbook. Old traditions endure in tandem with outside influences.

Greetings entail approaching closely and bestowing kisses on both cheeks, uttering superlative statements of welcome, even to unfamiliar non-Muslims. But relationship-building courtesies may be absent, minds on both sides staying closed to the others' perspective. It never failed to catch my attention when men embraced other men intimately, even in public, but wives, with whom they shared children, were prohibited from such displays. Maybe because, as John Gray (1992) says, *Men Are From Mars, Women Are From Venus*. In addition, social rules varied with social class. With urbanization, instruction and affluence, the heart becomes more remote.

In Riyadh, we heard and sometimes saw for ourselves that one can procure any illicit substance or service, regardless of prohibitions, along the lines of the North American roaring 20s, but kept to a dull and cushioned roar. On the other hand, since historic Makkah and Madinah afford the country the position of the cradle of Islam, it is thought the most devout believers in moral behavior reside within those borders. Both may well be true.

Secrecy was generally very much the order of every day, but at Baba's office, organizers for the voting for officers of professional societies wouldn't even consider a secret ballot. Along with his choice of officer, a signature and membership number was required.

Conventional wisdom tells us men cover their women because purity is the desired impression. But men's sidelong glances in public places and leering looks down from upper levels of malls, at non-Muslim women, until observed and then transformed in a heartbeat into chaste stares into the distance, told me the highest thoughts were not uppermost in all minds. Why leave eyes uncovered, I wondered. Provocation can easily be transmitted through the eyes, especially if elaborately made up. Maybe the nose or ears would be more neutral.

Even surface wraps were either black or white. But for females, from underneath, flashes of opalescent colors revealed the sharp contrasts, especially at weddings. Either it was flash, or dressing gowns and slippers. I recalled my first quick rounds through clothing shops. Women completely smothered in black eagerly fingered clingy gowns with fishnet inserts or brightly spangled with necklines cut lower than plunging or slacks made from simulated cat skin in neon colors. But the significance was not to dawn on me for some time. Not everyone was the same, though. Uncovered, some Muslim expat faces were quite natural, colored only by inner glows while others used make up which I can only describe as fortissimo.

While on the phone with a female friend one day, coming over the wire from the room next to hers, Saudi men, her husband among them, used raucous voices like bad plumbing when left to themselves. But when she entered their room, they adjusted their volume, order was temporarily restored and gentlemanly phrases like "Yes, beautiful lady" and "I am your servant" rolled off their tongues. From tempestuous to tranquil in a heartbeat.

Raspy sounding words in Arabic were transliterated into romantic expressions and conveyed eloquent, subtle meanings. When I heard genteel promises to get me whatever I wanted, or a shopkeeper's assurance "Madame, we have exactly what you're looking for," or a fellow traveler pledging "my home is your home," I realized the reality was somewhere between that and the opposite extreme. It wasn't uncommon to hear a conversation between two men go, mercurially, from calling each other brothers to vowing retaliation against those taking the other's side.

Like in *Midnight in the Garden of Good and Evil*, where quirks and foibles flourished as if in a greenhouse, in Riyadh, instead of individual eccentricities, the whole culture developed the same ones. Expats weren't immune. A shopping nut or a gossip could go wild. In

Ala Tool

my case, the solitude I needed some of the time could turn into a career. I could become wrapped up in my inner world if I didn't avail myself of the balance Baba's presence offered.

The concept of mercy was confusing. TV programs about Islamic religion and culture reiterated certain phrases. Excerpts out of context, perhaps misinterpreted, but broadcast daily, rattled around in my brain. Along with the adjectives, merciful and gracious applied to Allah, I tried to reconcile the Wrath of the most Gracious, required, compulsory, prohibited, submission, punishment, wrongdoers, unbelievers, transgressors and painful chastisement. The colorful language and lyrical expression left an impression. Sudden, frequent, seemingly inexplicable jumps from pole to pole seemed to be the norm. The attitude prevented acceptance of other ways of doing the same things. Rather, sharp distinctions delineated right from wrong, friend from foe. I would relegate this raw material to that part of my brain still trying to sort out the purpose of Christianity's Fear of the Lord and Hinduism's Shiva the Destroyer.

Balance did not come from measured words or behavior. It teetered between extremes, resulting in an overall enduring balance. This disorderly order was different, yet perhaps not so different, from the unstable stability going on in many other spots on this planet. Balance, for me too, would come from between East and West. I had read that transformation is the process of challenging something in relation to its polar opposite. With this voluntary exile, more seeds of ongoing transformation had been planted.

Jewel Dhuru

Chapter 8: Hospitality Is In The Eye Of The Beholder

"all things share the same breath—the beast, the tree, the man …the air shares its spirit with all the life it supports" [13]
—attributed to Chief Seattle

What names spring to mind when the average North America thinks of Arabs? In my sitting room, I recalled Bill Moyers' interview with intelligent, articulate Arabs. They pointed out most Westerners could not name a famous Arab if asked, other than Ali Baba, Aladdin, Sinbad, Shaherazade or Saladin. The well-read might come up with Kahlil Gibran or Omar Khayam of Rubayat fame. The image that usually accompanies the word is a sword-brandishing, bearded warrior or a dancing harem maiden. Outsiders generally don't hear about the best parts.

Arabs are known for superb hospitality, wanting the visitor to feel at home and granting their every wish. When combined with genuine respect, beginning with self-respect, validating the worth of another individual regardless of religion, country of origin or sex, hospitality goes a long way toward creating meaningful bonds. But, creative cooperation and collaboration have to be experienced in order to be cultivated. And, hospitality is not the same as courtesy and consideration. One can exist without the other. At its worst, what is meant to be hospitality can be prescribed, assembly line behavior, following specific formulae and acted out grudgingly.

The traditional greeting is a variation of kisses on both cheeks. At its best, it involves the full personal attention of the bestower, exuding all the genuine warmth of an affectionate gesture, even between strangers. At its worst, it is mechanical, taking on the feeling of satisfying a duty without involving the heart. Since I could never be sure what the other person intended to do, I sometimes found myself, figuratively and literally, thrown off balance by an embrace, like a high wire walker encountering someone on my wire who was moving in the opposite direction.

Ala Tool

Ramadan **Dinner**

One *Ramadan* evening, in January, we were invited to the home of a Saudi couple, professional people, for dinner, after the last *salah*. Our host picked us up in his car and upon arriving at his home, I was pointed to a coat-rack where I hung up my *abaya*.

The outdoor path from unassuming walls and typically ornate gate had opened into a colorful and elaborately decorated living space. As I lingered in the hall, Baba's wry smile and "see ya' later" prefaced the men's disappearance into the host's private sitting room. From the doorway, my glance followed them in and uncovered a large, luxuriant room, with couches, tables and chairs, in predominantly intense blue and gold. I vacillated in the hall near a dining room, uncertain of what to do next, but long enough to notice the table was set for only three.

In a moment, his wife, Hanan, appeared all smiles and motioned me to her own lavish sitting room, the enclosed section of the dining room, behind a screen. The room was comfortably furnished, in turquoise and shades of peach, with large vases of fresh flowers, their lines reflected in the drapery patterns. Her command of English approximated my own of Arabic, so the subjects stayed superficial. Both coffee tables were laden with the usual break fast foods, prepared by herself and their live-in Filipina help. When *salah* sounded, she and I began on the customary dates and water first, to replenish sugar and water to her fasting body. I partook of a glass-topped table full of hors d'oeuvres with her, while Baba did the same with her husband. Delicacies included sticky coconut balls and small fruit flavored milk shakes. A Saudi host is required to prepare and display much more food than guests could possibly eat. The extra food is distributed to the help and neighborhood workers the next day.

We had a pleasant 20 minutes. Hanan showed me her wedding album and photos of her trip to the West and we commented on the TV news. Then, at a signal understood by servant, hostess and host, dinner was ready. As he called Baba into the dining room, she vanished, not to be seen again that evening. If she made any subliminal gesture of adieu to me before she left, I missed it.

Our host knelt for a quick prayer in a room just off the dining room before he called us both to the table, which, along with the buffet were saturated with a steaming selection. He offered us lamb

Jewel Dhuru

and rice and explained about seasonal desert mushrooms and after all this feasting, three desserts. We conversed about his family history, the inevitable shoptalk and we touched on second, third and fourth marriages, historical and present-day. He said it was rare to see more than two wives these days. After a suitable interval, our companion drove us home. Fortunately, I was able to send a note of thanks to his wife, because I never saw her again.

Masmak Fort

While exploring the city one weekend, we visited Masmak Fort, near the ramparts of the original city gates. Actually, we agreed Baba would take a quick round by himself because I needed a rest. Seeing no benches, I sat on one of a bunch of boulders encircling a fountain. In less than a minute, he was back. He couldn't enter without his wife, the guard had admonished him. This was not a Men's only day. This was a Family day. Single men were kept away from married women and unmarried girls his way. I peeked around Baba towards the fort and standing by the wooden door at the entrance was the stern-faced guard, eyeing us suspiciously. So, I dragged myself around exhibits of armaments and army paraphernalia, including, to my delight, a pinned up chain mail suit, such as I was just reading about in Tolkien.

Before too long, now both tired and lost in the winding channels, our paths crossed that of a short, wiry Saudi gentleman in *thob, shmal* and *egal*. He trailed several small children. He flashed us a big grin, said, "Welcome to Riyadh," asked if we were enjoying the fort and said he hoped we had a nice stay there. Tired as we were, we stopped and talked, answering mostly in the affirmative. It was all over in thirty seconds before he and his satellites moved on, but the memory lingers. His courteous attitude was so different from the usual stoic one and was so welcoming it even boosted our energy. His behavior was in sharp contrast to the guard at the entrance, who followed our departure too, with such serious stares that told us he was not over-endowed as far as joviality was concerned.

The wooden door touted a point of interest. A spear, thrown generations earlier with force and fury by a cohort of King Abdul Aziz, stuck so deeply in the door, it could not be extricated. Eventually, the handle was broken off, leaving the spearhead on display where it was.

Thesis Presentation

In February, I accompanied Baba to a thesis presentation and luncheon, at the women's college, where the presenter and hostess was his student. Baba had attended several, but since I had helped edit this thesis, I was included. Weekly, Baba commuted to the women's college, a few kilometers from the men's, to give the same lecture he'd given the men. He had more personal access to the women than some. Our neighbor, a math professor, claimed when he lectured in class, some women sat behind screens and watched him on closed circuit TV.

The lunch was so sumptuous, I would have filed away the almost incomparable experience for years, had I not noticed all the feasts we attended had been much the same, following the formula, give or take a dish or two. Saudi food, generally, started with roasted lamb or chicken, dripping into a bed of rice, or shish kabobs with cubes of lamb, onions and peppers. Salads included mixed vegetables, avocados and lemon slices, continuing with doughy deep-fried meat or cheese filled squares, rice wrapped in grape leaves, and flat breads with Tahina or Humus, pastes made from ground lentils. A dozen sweets followed: custards, date and fig preparations, trays of baklava and other yummy concoctions.

Before lunch, Baba introduced me to a group of women and a few of them took me under their wings, just before Baba disappeared with the guys. Later, Baba popped his head in the door where he'd left me, to say he was invited to eat in the men's-only lounge—in this women's college. Traditionally, men eat first and when more than half of the allotted lunchtime had elapsed, we women, including the hostess-student herself, served ourselves from what was left over, serving dishes un-replenished.

Over time, various women moved in and out of our group. When I was half done eating, the male professors made gestures to the women to finish eating and resume their seats so the presentation could resume. I felt rushed. There was probably five minutes left to still eat but I had not really understood the system yet. I surrendered my plate, still half full, adding it to a pile of others, and found a seat in the women's half of the room. At this scientific meeting, Baba and I had

Jewel Dhuru

to sit across the aisle from each other, he with an assembled line of colleagues and I with strangers of my own sex.

At times of high anxiety, my brain temporarily cut out, using dissociation as a safety mechanism. At such moments, I used mindless oblivion to cope with the culture. It helped me not get caught up in the drama of their cultural rules, too, some of which perhaps existed nowhere else in the world but there and Afghanistan. It helped me, too, not to get defensive when a Saudi woman who'd been to the West tried to unload the chip on her shoulder on me, telling me which Western social habits she didn't like.

When I drew my mind back to the present, Baba and I exchanged silent glances and smiles across the aisle, at humorous moments during the afternoon segment, just as we had done at poignant moments during the acceptance speeches before lunch. After the presentation, the awards, the lunch and the congratulations, there was the matter of getting home, since Baba was going back to work. I could have taken a taxi but women being out alone or riding with another male without their husbands present was frowned upon. So Baba's male colleague drove his own van and they dropped me off before they went to the men's college. Technically, our threesome wasn't allowed either, but complete immobilization wasn't an option.

The Hospital Waiting Room

The receptionist was away at prayer. Several males sat in the waiting room, awaiting his return. I stood near the desk with others. The receptionist rounded the corner, and before he even reached the desk, I was spellbound, watching all the men rush up to him and clamor for attention. Soliciting bids at an auction for a prize bull couldn't have raised more of a ruckus. Two other women in veils and I edged into the background. When the receptionist finally noticed us in the throng, we were dispatched quickly, presumably, to get us out of sight.

Another experience in February involved my first therapy appointment. A Pakistani male receptionist, to whom I had chatted previously, told me to sit down for a minute. I had met him six weeks before when he made the appointment for me, but I had not stayed long. He asked all the usual questions, establishing identity. No one else being around then, I casually sat down for the info exchange, in the waiting room across from his reception desk. I made my appointment and then started on the walk to the limo stand.

The day of the appointment, I inadvertently deviated from the norm by sitting down in the same set of seats, the only ones I could see, across from Reception. Subliminally, it registered that only men were waiting in that room, but I dismissed it. Within 15 seconds, I was literally chased out by an older man, shouting "*hinek, hinek,*" "over there" and waving his arm in my face, pointing to the women's waiting room, cloistered behind a heavy drape. What staggered me was that neither the receptionist, nor another female patient near the desk said anything to me to attempt to intercept this fiasco. It was a singular and solitary experience.

I was looking forward to the next vacation, out of Riyadh, to smaller towns, filled with history and friendlier by reputation.

Jewel Dhuru

Chapter 9: Travel To Asir And The Hejaz

"Heaven is under our feet as well as over our heads" [14]
—Thoreau

City Tour

Just back from India in January, a map spread out on the coffee table got us started planning our next getaway, to the country's southwestern regions. Hajj vacation would be in March 1999. But before it got too hot for daytime excursions, we put off the half-day bus tour of Riyadh no longer. Meeting in a hotel lobby with other North Americans, we boarded a cramped bus, were reminded of the prohibition against taking photographs and set off.

Only a little was of architectural and historical interest on this tour. The name Riyadh means gardens and the city has a population of 3,000,000. We were acquainted with lancet windows, long vertical slits for defense. Wind towers, rising 6 meters (6 1/2 yards) above roofs, were pre-electricity ACs, which sent the slightest breezes racing down through Gulf buildings, cooling the air before they exited from the other side. The headquarters of a military general extended 12 stories underground. Traditions in a Muslim cemetery dictate that bodies be buried within 24 hours of death, facing Makkah, with no grave markers and no mourning and that at last the segregation of the sexes ceased.

The new Central Museum was constructed on the site of and still contained original mud bricks from the palace of King Abdul Aziz, the man who is credited with integrating the nation's tribes. A book restoration laboratory lay on route. Near Masmak Fort, textured, colored stones embedded in the street, still discernible from the ancient city ramparts and towers, ran obliquely across the thoroughfare and under present day shops. Not far away still stand two 16-meter (50 foot) high, arched, brick, city gates. At the mosque adjoining the fort, water is for purchase from the River Zam Zam, created, so the story goes, when Abraham's wife and child were searching for water and the infant kicked up a spring. Behind the main street, lined up rows of brown, mud brick houses. Their wide, wooden doors opened to rooms with ceilings, walls and sagging floors,

Ala Tool

constructed of reeds, stones and grasses slathered with thick layers of glutinous mud. Electrical connections going out into the desert were traced to Marconi himself. And officers with red berets, the 9th royal brigade, guarded the royal family's abode as we passed.

Since we are amateur history buffs, the tour had zipped through the interesting bits far too quickly for our taste. We subsequently rented a car and on a Friday morning, we reinvestigated the city ramparts, Masmak Fort and the mosque. As luck would have it, at 11:00, on the stroke of the *Jumma salah*, when the *muezzin*'s protracted voice began to lilt over the loudspeaker, we unexpectedly witnessed the Friday phenomenon. Male bodies, cloaked in long, white *thobs* emerged from each building and every direction, marching in lines, in unison, all converging on the central apex of the mosque. We parked the car and watched. They came down stairs and along walkways, crossing streets one behind the other. With pensive faces, there wasn't much chitchat. Each stopped at a low outdoor tap to wash his feet and then entered the mosque for worship. It was eerie as I tried to recall where I had seen this type of behavior before. The unfortunate phrase running through my mind had the word Stepford in it. We drove on.

While on the bus tour, other bits of information had been of monetary interest, the guide's forte: where to repair a Rolex watch, or to find the most modern kitchen utensil, exceptional computer, jewelry, grocery shop or tailor who will copy any foreign design. Numerous shopping centers and bookstores had exotic names: Al Mousa Center, Al Azizia, Euromarche, Al Akaria, Oruba on Aruba Street, Al Shegrey and Al Jarir. Most of us on the tour had seen crowds of women in shops, sometimes with kids and sometimes with males waiting on benches. The guide asserted that for women, shopping could be a career choice.

When we passed royal residences, the guide's enthusiasm reached a climax as we heard about the charitable works of princes, and how queens are pensioned off, since only four wives are allowed—at a time. We heard about the 7000 princes and only Allah knows how many princesses who reside in and around the city. The guide offered two opinions: 1) the only consistency there is inconsistency. You never know what's going to happen next, in Africa called 'shifting sands', and 2) Riyadh is no more Saudi Arabia than Washington, DC is the United States, so get out of the city and see other places, too. So we took another trip.

Hajj Vacation

Whenever we had an opportunity to explore, we grasped it with both hands. Baba had ten days off in mid-March for Hajj, the month of pilgrimage, which commemorated the flight of Muhammed (pbuh) to Madinah. That was the other holy time of year, besides *Ramadan*.

Pilgrimage is one of the five pillars of Islam. The others include testifying Allah is God and Muhammed is his Prophet, praying at the five prescribed times a day, fasting during *Ramadan*, giving a percentage of one's salary as alms, (a 10% tax was fist proposed in 2002) and if one can afford it, to take a pilgrimage to Makkah for Hajj. Only recently were women allowed to participate in the latter. Neighbors who went to Makkah returned exhilarated, thinner and balder, since a little hair is clipped off. On the ritual walk, Anita's husband said the crowd was so firmly packed, if he'd picked his feet up, he would have been carried along anyway.

We rented a Honda Accord, after Baba got the required Saudi drivers' license and spent eight days driving around small mountainous towns in the southwest of the country, near the Yemeni border—the Hejaz district. Busloads of people, from all parts of the country and neighboring Muslim nations, were on the road, their roof racks precariously tied. Some vehicles looked like glue had been poured onto their roofs, a large fan had blown the contents of their basements onto it, and whatever stuck, it was bon voyage. They were heading for Makkah, in the same direction as us. But our path had a compulsory twist to it. Had we not planned to turn off to Taif, we would have reached a bifurcation in the road. That intersection sports a sign, backed up by guards, pointing the way to the non-Muslim road, around Makkah, so we would have been compelled to detour anyway. It would have been like attempting to get near the alleged UFO site of Area 51, near Roswell, New Mexico.

We drove passed the King Faisal Center for breeding hunting falcons, nestled in *Jabal* (Mt.) *Soodah*, cresting at 2900 meters (9500 feet), the highest point in Saudi Arabia. As the road wound along, a sign read Mt. *Soodah* and an arrow pointed the way. A half-mile later, another sign announced Mt. *Sooda*, then around another bend, *Mt.*

Ala Tool

Soudaa. Yet another variation detailed our map. We wondered if the sign makers ever consulted each other. The reality is, recopying the original name in Arabic script would not have presented a problem. But when spelled phonetically using a foreign alphabet, alternate pronunciations due to accents or stressing the wrong syllable, or elongating a vowel, resulted in a variety of spellings, each only approximating the original. On shop signs, the same thing occurred with Resturante, Restrant and Restarent, or Barber, Barbar and Berbar and especially Jewelery, Jewellery and Jewlery.

Besides mangled signpost spellings, baboons with red bottoms inhabited these natural surroundings, including the couple that traversed the hood of our car. Flocks of sheep and goats, in brown, black, white and variegated entertained us, along with occasional colorful lizards or birds. More Arabian camels wander the Australian desert than anywhere else, leaving dromedaries in off white, beiges and browns in the Middle East. Once the only living creatures on a barren ribbon of highway bordered by sand and rock were the two of us, and the gem in the setting was a mother dromedary with her child in tow, striding languidly with a certain majesty.

Mirages gave the road a shimmery wet look, the illusion caused by simmering heat, sand and sameness. The blush of a disintegrating desert dusk, drawn out across the horizon on a full moon night was inspirational and calming. I collected stones of all colors and cluttered my suitcase without regret with bits of black and yellow lava rock and petrified wood.

Childhood remembrances with cousins flashed through my mind of choice chunks of petrified wood, discovered behind our Grandmother's house. At first, they were coveted and hoarded, but long since misplaced and lost. Ancient wood shaded this sandy area once and these new bits of the petrified variety would serve as replacements for childish chunks. Small bags of naturally colored sand: white, tan, maroon and mauve, would be transported home, too.

Unfamiliar plants were superbly adapted to the harsh environment; they were blooming. Eventually, aided by a local horticulture book, I identified Castor Bean, Yellow Trumpet vine and Jerusalem thorn bush. Trained grape vines clung to hill dwellings. A friend of Linda's would show me highly prized gray rocks, shaped like blooming roses, varying from 2-20 cm. (about 1-8") in diameter, called desert roses. Gathered in the rough and sold in rock shops, they'd been struck by lightning and crystallization gave them the appearance of flowers.

In the Hejaz region, Taif exuded charm, with its bridges lined with old-fashioned white globes and flowers. While I read in the car, Baba wandered with his camera. An Egyptian shopkeeper and his Pakistani neighbor, chatted and laughed with him, so different from the big city. As in all the big hotels, an arrow on the ceiling pointed to the Kabah in Makkah so at prayer time, we would know which way to face.

"Can't it be disconnected?" Baba protested, misunderstanding the bellhop's explanation at first. Baba thought the arrow was our own personal loud speaker, positioned directly over our pillows. Most of my life, living West of Makkah, the cradle of Islam was East, but since we came to Riyadh, the arrows always pointed some variation of West.

The day after arriving in Taif, as Baba waited for me in front of our Safari Hotel, across the street from the Grand Mosque, the driver of a fully packed big white car began gesticulating to Baba, then ran over to his window and began what looked to me like a pantomime.

I was just coming to the car as the performance concluded so Baba explained the scenario. Baba thought the fellow, in Saudi garb, wanted to ask about the quality of the hotel and he prepared to say that once he learns to go right back to sleep after the 4:15 AM *salah* booms in from the mosque, it was fine. But no. The fellow had begun a lament about this, his first Hajj, about not having money for benzene, about his large family and more in similar vein. Baba made a contribution and on we went.

At a spacious hotel in Al Baha, in response to Baba's query, the bell captain regretted *mutawas* wouldn't allow women in the pool or sauna, even after Baba, with tongue in cheek, offered to let the *mutawa* come in with us. So Baba didn't use the facilities either. Well padded *mutawas*, we came to know were originally chosen as enforcers because of their brawn, but later there came to be a educational requirement.

The road between Al Baha and Abha, further south, snaked through mountain ranges and spectacular yawning valleys. Tunnels, bridges and small bunches of grazing sheep or camels broke up the monotony of seven hours of winding roads.

Nearing Abha, the Asir region unfolded, with small mortarless stone towers dotting the hillsides. Located strategically on high

Ala Tool

ground, these relics were probably once watchtowers. The City Center in Abha was incandescent with red, blue and yellow tube lights wrapped around tree trunks and along branches during the Hajj evenings. Roundabouts were abundant both there and in Taif. Large sculptures, signifying characteristic aspects of life, adorned the centers. Artwork wrought of concrete and metal, were shaped like incense burners, pomegranate fountains, clocks and stone towers. One large Saudi coffee pot, roughly resembled an hourglass, bigger on the bottom and not too tiny a waist, with a lid, handle and long, slender, curved, toucan beak shaped spout. Tourism, inviting people from different cultures just to visit and explore, wasn't encouraged in the Kingdom, but if it had been, Abha would probably be the first city to be able to handle it. A lovely lake was surrounded by accommodations and attractions to entice tourists, almost of the caliber of Canada's Lake Louise or Switzerland's Lake Geneva.

We wandered between one small town and another. The weather was cooler than the 41^0C. (106^0 F.) days of Riyadh. We had only ten minutes of precipitation the whole week, even though abundant greenery told us it rained more frequently. But in that ten minutes, we picked up a hitchhiker, an elderly local gentleman, a non-English speaker, complete with prayer beads.

When Baba first stopped the car, the gray bearded gentleman approached the front door, but I was occupying the back at that time so I could stretch out whenever I needed to and the front passenger seat was cluttered with all and sundry. So he reluctantly climbed into the back, confining himself to the extreme edge of the seat. When chanting and a clicking of beads became audible, I realized I wasn't wearing my *abaya*, so I hurriedly pulled a sweater over my bare shoulders and then his discomfort lessened. I was able to find out he was going to the next village. He emanated a delightful musk scent. And over his cloak, a traditional leather belt and sheath were strapped to his waist, housing a silver dagger, detailed in design.

A hospital nurse in Riyadh had shown me a photo of her six-month old son, in a *thob* and *gootra* and for accent, the same little dagger wrapped around his chubby middle. Baba admired the dagger before our guest left the car. Although not Baba's intention, we remembered too late that traditional Arab hospitality included their actually giving you anything you admired out loud. But not to worry. Our passenger had not read that book. In a gruff voice, he offered the dagger for sale; Baba smiled but declined. Once we got him home, we took his photo as he shut the door. He appeared to ignore it, but I was sure he was aware of the flash as he moved off for home, from the ghost of a half smile that played on his lips like a pale sun on a winter's evening.

A highlight was visiting an attraction outside of Abha called Al Habala, a deserted traditional farming village, clinging to a cliff face. Our Lonely Planet tour book explained it was settled 350 years ago by the Khatani tribe who escaped the Ottomans and it was inhabited until 1980. The only access now to the village is by cable car, *telefrik*.

It was fascinating. Terraced land stretched down a steep slope, facing sheer precipices. Ropes once dangled from poles attached to the brink, aiding the natives in climbing up to the city. While investigating the outcrop of a dozen low, stone houses, a foot long blue and orange chameleon crossed Baba's path. As he described it, he swung his camera into action, only to experience total inaction. The camera had seized. It's a good thing his memory was working. The setting invited lingering, but with the heat rising, the only chairs being round stools or stone ledges with no backs and much more to see before we put head to pillow, we kept moving.

Security checkpoints punctuated our movements. Sometimes I was lying down on the back seat when Baba announced a checkpoint, saying there was no need for me to get up. I replied that I wanted to get up anyway, because I had to check. Some guards were businesslike as they examined the papers he passed through the window. A few just waved us on from their jeeps while looking the other way. And others were downright kind.

The papers Baba carried were an *Iqama* and a letter from his employer saying he was free to leave Riyadh for this particular jaunt. The *Iqama* was a small brown leather booklet, like a passport, given by the employer to replace both our passports, which the employer held while we were in the country. Since I didn't officially work, I didn't have any papers.

As we approached one particular checkpoint, Baba reached for his *Iqama*, but it wasn't there. We were just outside Najran, near the Yemeni border. As controlled panic hovered at a convenient distance to descend, we wondered what kind of guard we would get this time. At the previous checkpoint, Baba had tired of extracting his *Iqama* from his briefcase each time, so he raised the lid of the compartment

Ala Tool

between the seats and popped it in. But when he reached for it, it appeared to have been transformed into a cassette cover. One guard, reading the signs of our bewilderment correctly, used the all-purpose phrase whenever trouble, large or small, loomed.

"*Mafee mishkole*," he said. "No problem," and motioned for Baba to pull the car over. With sign language, the other guard suggested we look between and under seats and mats. For seven anxious minutes, we searched the car and our memory banks and laughed nervously. This was tantamount to losing a passport. We didn't think we were that careless. We kept returning to the compartment where we were sure he'd put it. Retracing our steps for the fifth time, doing the dance of non-discovery, our nerve centers jangled, Baba again reenacted how he'd opened the compartment lid. As we were examining the resident cassette cover to see if it had grown a false bottom, the compartment lid itself stirred slightly revealing a second upper section, and miraculously, the precious *Iqama*! When we showed the guards what had happened, we all laughed. What could have been a harrowing experience is even now a bittersweet memory, partly because of the concentrated generosity of spirit of those two Saudi gentlemen.

In Najran, still a warm memory, the Okhdood Hotel in our tour book sounded appealing, but we couldn't locate the street. WE asked directions from a police officer in a jeep at the side of the road. From the moment our car slowed near him, he graced us with a grin, so uncommon in the big city. He insisted on driving to the hotel and bade us follow, showering us with more warm smiles, then and the next day as well, when we passed him again at the roadside.

Actually, Okhdood was the subject of local lore. Najran has Jewish, Christian and now Islamic, history. Rodinson (1971) explains *okhdood* means ditch and tells about how, for religious reasons, bodies were burned in a particular ditch. Conventional wisdom has it that the locals still know where to get the best fertilizer for their plants. [15]

In these smaller towns, the attitude to my attire and conversing with females was more liberal than in Riyadh, but especially in Najran where some people were downright friendly. My no scarf and only the top button of my *abaya* being done up brought only one gasp. Refreshing—yes, but the majority of people on the streets, by far, were still men. The scant few women were exiting mosques or

Jewel Dhuru

sitting fully veiled in cars, awaiting drivers. A unique aspect was that veiled women, revealing only eyes, had stalls in the Old Souk, alongside men. I bought bags of freshly ground cumin, coriander and frankincense from one, and learned to identify henna from another.

I was first introduced to frankincense while perusing the antique section of Batha, with Baba and Linda on Christmas Eve. Because the shopkeeper didn't have coins for Linda's change, he gave her two paper packets instead, one containing bits of frankincense, and the other, nuggets of myrrh. Without hesitation, she handed them to me. Frankincense is chunks of crystalline gum resin, in off-whites, pale yellows and greens, from the genus Boswellia, to put into an incense burner to smolder on a piece of charcoal. Driving pests from the house leads a long list of uses. The gnarled, low-growing, thick-trunked trees grow only in Yemen, Oman and Somalia. Myrrh is a reddish brown resin, dissolved in water and drunk for medicinal purposes. At the time of the first Christmas, gold was the least valuable of the gifts the three kings brought for the babe swaddled in the manger.

Later, I got a whiff of smoldering ood, slivers of wood from trees that only need morning dew to sustain them. The fragrance was indescribable. Perfumeries selling ood and frankincense also carried Arabic gum for chewing and liquid perfume cocktails, made from combinations of jasmine, sandalwood, musk and other scents. With an eyedropper, a merchant could custom-make a concoction that would cling to the clothing for several lifetimes.

One morning, while I rested, Baba drove out to Okhdood Dam, following a winding road, in and out mountain tunnels. He returned exhilarated and full of stories about guards who gave him Saudi coffee in demitasses, and told jokes. He looked like he'd had a night out with the boys. He'd sat with half a dozen guards, on a Persian carpet with blocks of cushions, drinking both tea and coffee and eating dates. This sporty bunch clowned and didn't even mind his photographing either them or the dam. One officer playfully pinched Baba's sunglasses and another took him to an adjoining museum of local artifacts, swords and incense burners.

We both went back the next day on our way out of town. The drive through the hills was beautiful, one of the tunnels being 1 ½ km. (about 3 miles) long. Some of the same guys were there and they offered me the same coffee, brewed with cardamom, their backs remaining half turned. Naturally the chemistry had changed with the addition of a female.

A warm memory was a truck driver at a lay-by outside Najran. When we pulled up some distance from his dusty freight truck, no other human or beast was in sight besides us three. Baba called to me that the driver, in *thob* and cutwork cap, had beckoned to him, so I pondered how to amuse myself for a while. But when Baba called back that we were both invited for coffee, I shoved my arms into the sleeves of my *abaya*, as a formality, and trudged over.

As we approached, Hesham sat on the edge of a lowered platform hinged to the side of his truck, with a piece of blue threadbare carpeting on it for padding. My *abaya* flapped in the wind, covering only my arms with black. He gestured for me to perch on the carpeting, which I did. From his lack of scrutiny, I got the distinct impression Hesham wouldn't have cared if I were in street clothes. He poured diminutive cups of Saudi coffee from his thermos and I had brought a cellophane packet of cookies from the car—an impromptu, no-frills desert picnic. Our companion with a well-trimmed white beard asked where each of us was from, but didn't even mention children. The soft look in his grandfatherly eyes smacked of unflappability, the calm born of experience and knowledge.

Our brief associations with both Hesham and the hitchhiker were memorable. And I got some Arabic practice. Despite raspy and choking sounding versions of the letter Q, and letters that are to be pronounced as if you have two pairs of socks in your mouth, for the most part, it's a beautiful language. I conveyed to Hesham the idea that the people we met in Najran were kind.

"*Ana Najrani*," "I'm from Najran," he exclaimed, grinning broadly and patting his chest.

The only jarring note to the encounter, occurred when, in mid sentence, Hesham loosed the empty cellophane packet to the wind, to join a string of such litter, skewered by the camel fencing paralleling the highway. His ancestors were probably rugged Bedouins and turned their garbage into Arab tumbleweeds, rather than carry it around. But my fondest recollection was the warm look in his eyes when he greeted fellow human beings without reservation, regardless of sex or origin.

On the drive home, we noticed the system truck drivers worked out to let tailgaters know when it was safe to pass. When a car approached from the rear, if a truck signaled a left turn with clearly no place or preparation to turn left, it was not safe to pass. The right signal was the all clear. Despite this courtesy, Saudi driving was scary. Their thinking seemed to be 'if I'm not destined to die on this road, I'll be able to squeak between these cars, approaching this hill, on this curve, crossing the double solid line, in the dark, with only one headlight—and the guy behind me will make it, too, *Inshallah*! Baba grumbled that driving needed 200% attention. Drivers wanted to save on time and gas as they came barreling down in the wrong lane. He believed they imagined themselves taking the straightest possible curve in their grand prix daydreams. We didn't see many accidents, but heard of stunning ones, involving teens in the wee hours of the morning, heart breaking for families on all continents.

In Riyadh, we remembered being inconvenienced by dozens of young males, ages 12 or 13, who drove cars or pick-ups, seemingly without any instruction. The backs of their trucks often cradled a dromedary, sitting passively, head raised regally. For stability, two bungee-looking cords were stretched across the bed, one on either side of the hump. Women were not allowed to drive, except Bedouin women who answer only to their families. This is one country where, in cities, you don't have to wonder if there's a he or a she behind the wheel of the car that just pulled a spectacular stunt at your expense. Apparently, the Qur'an does not oppose women's driving. The prohibition stems from the Saudi requirement of veils and the fear that, in case of a flat tire or mechanical difficulty, a woman would have to expose her face to ask for help.

Seven days had passed quickly. As we steered towards home, we bordered the Empty Quarter, *Ar Rub al Khali,* the treacherously almost uninhabitable southeast corner, near Oman. Just before our arrival, a couple of adventurous, hardy young men from Calgary, Canada retraced the steps of a British explorer who'd trekked across the barren badlands decades before with camels and Bedouin guides. The youngsters had camels and guides, too, supplemented by Jeeps, notebook computers and a satellite modem. Most Bedouins had left the land to oil pipelines.

We got lost in sprawling Riyadh on the way home. Arriving during daylight in the smaller towns and going around in circles served the practical purpose of soaking up local color and unique architecture. Once familiar enough with the surroundings, we could find a hotel and tourist attractions. The antiquity of the towns gave their winding streets and landmarks charisma.

But arriving after dark on the freeways of gigantic Riyadh, lined by predominantly white and beige buildings, only produced the result of delaying our homecoming until 2:00 AM. We stopped to ask for directions and strangers gave all sorts f advice. One hospitable Afghani told us he knew where we wanted to go and bid us follow him. With initial relief that finally turned to despair, we followed his twists and turns for 45 minutes. When he stopped, a clock was chiming midnight. Although he said we were near the university, we found ourselves in front of his house, where he invited us in, for a cup of tea! Not being permitted to drive, I had become complacent about compass directions. At length, Baba recognized the pointy-topped Faisalia Center, Riyadh's only tall building, and thus being oriented, it was only another ½ hour to home.

Understandably, the next evening we were asleep by 9:00 PM. That didn't stop the doorbell from sounding at 10:00, though. Baba slept right through it and I wish I had, too, but our doorbell was a buzzer that riveted into my skin. I threw a long dress on over my nightgown and weaved down the hall on automatic pilot. In a semi daze, I found myself opening the door. It was Farhida and her daughter, come to visit. They were all smiles, a plate of steaming food in hand. Raking my fingers through my hair, I mumbled that we were sleeping, hoping they would offer to return the next day. To my surprise, they edged past me towards the sitting room and sat down anyway. It was their vacation time, too, and they were bored. Finally after a little chitchat, my eyes closed half the time, and more unashamed explanation that I really had been sound asleep, they got up to leave, but not without Farhida's fingering and oohing and ahhing over the lacy bit of my night gown that was showing at my neck, from under my dress.

The Camel Souk and *Diraaya*

Two vacation days remained. With one, we went to the local livestock market, the Camel Souk. The 40 hectares (100 plus acres) of pens at the side of the highway had such a selection, especially goats whose colors and ear shapes seemed infinitely varied. A group of small boys ran up to us, offering a baby camel. *"Le, shukran"*- no thanks, we said and tried not to imagine a roasted camel in our flat. I thoroughly enjoyed every shape, sound and lungful of our visit. Baba used up two more rolls of film. And the flies in the car as we drove away were thrown in free.

The cooler mountain area out west became just a memory. In our absence spring had taken a firm grip. Vacation ended with touring the ruins of the mud brick houses, palaces and palms of *Diraaya*, and there went more rolls of film. The original Saud family settlement, with a population of 4000, where Saudi Arabia actually started, was being spruced up for its 100th anniversary. Present day *Diraaya*, otherwise written on maps and signs as *Diriyia, Dirayea, Daraeya, Darriyah* and *DeRiyah*, is an outcrop of the old one with shops, mosques, residences, vehicles and townspeople. On roads and grass verges between the old and new, herds of multicolored, shaggy coated goats and sheep grazed on the green and brown bits while their herders ambled alongside. *Diraaya* is considered the First State and when the Turks burned the original town down, a Second State, *Dira*, was started downtown near the old city ramparts, where we happened upon the ritual event of the Friday morning *salah*. *Diraaya* was just a ten-minute drive from us, but it had taken us six months to get there. Perhaps the close at hand is more easily taken for granted than the distant and exotic, no matter where one lives.

A Golf Course

Baba started back to work and I fell into my usual routine at home. On a Thursday morning, Baba got up early and joined Paul and other colleagues for golf, as an unofficial photographer. When he got home, he described a modern, though sandy range for taking practice shots, a gravelly course with scrubby, thorny plants here and there and a 'green' of brown hard packed sand. His general view was flat beige terrain under a sizzling blue sky, not the undulating green occasionally shrouded in mist we customarily associated with golf.

A 60 by 120 cm. (2 by 4-foot) piece of green Astroturf, the only bit of green in sight acted as the tee. The thought of green was incongruent with these surroundings. During winter in the desert, plants were greener, many blooming, but this was spring and it was already 35^0 C. (98^0 F.) at 7:30 AM. At each player's turn, a 10 by 30 cm. (4 by 12") piece of Astroturf went down, preventing their swinging out of a perpetual sand trap. On the first golf course in St. Andrew's, Scotland, the birthplace of golf, Scots prided themselves on their use of natural terrain, resisting weed control and using animal burrows as the original holes. Something along those lines was going on there in the desert, too.

As required after each hole, they swept the brown 'green' with a wide push broom, which they replaced in its own rack at the brink of the green. Sand traps were raked, too, to remove footprints. At each hole, a water tank with a spout stood to refresh the clientele. Black insects and small lizards scurried while the game droned on.

Other, lush green courses were maintained at considerable expense for CEOs and princes and some were co-ed, not requiring *abayas*. We saw videotape of one owned by a prince. The several thousand members of the royal family each collected considerable monthly salaries, consuming a chunk of the national budget and most did not lack free time, either. This prince chose to expend his resources by walking through his course, greeting players and bringing tea to the workers. Balancing extremes. Baba came home clutching his precious camera, exhilarated, though a little dehydrated and with a deeper tan to show for a Thursday, morning well spent.

Chapter 10: On Being Born Female

"Nature has given women so much power that the law has very wisely given them little" [16]
—Samuel Johnson

During those early months, while Baba frequented golf courses, shopping centers and the gym, from my home base, I mulled over my situation and that of other women I encountered.

Veils

In a restaurant lobby one evening, as we passed three veiled women, a Western expression came to mind: 'If one wants to see how a man is doing, one only has to look at the face of his wife'. If ever there was a saying that couldn't be simply applied cross-culturally, this must be one. But it gave me pause.

One morning, our faces brazenly unobstructed, blue-eyed, blond Linda and I made consecutive appointments with a physician. When we checked in, we were surprised when the Filipina receptionist asked if we were sisters. My companion's response was "of the heart."

I saw the doctor first and when I returned, she went in. True, we were approximately the same age, height and weight, had similar haircuts and both wore *abayas,* but no scarves. But to the practiced eye, the differences made a longer list than the similarities. What we didn't expect was that when she went in, the doctor and her nurse thought I was back again!

I started to wonder what we actually see in a face. The TV sheikh's claim was veils are worn in public to preserve purity. Just after I met Mr. Jokey Jeweler, Linda had elaborated on the male belief that females covet a certain aspect of the male anatomy.

"There is a myth in the Arab world," she said, "that the woman is 'incomplete' 'a hole in her center'. It's in literature back to the middle ages. *One Thousand and One Nights* is full of this imagery and the idea that left to themselves, women basically become sex addicts. In ten years of living in Riyadh, I've never heard a Saudi woman espouse the philosophy," she concluded. [17]

Ala Tool

I, too, had heard the popular belief that females were incapable of controlling erotic impulses, so if not covered, they will dishonor their families. Some women argued that women were thought to be tempting, rather than inferior, but their education was still frowned upon. The implication seemed to be that if her face was exposed, impure thoughts would take over and impulses would run rampant. The emotional development in that region of both males and females being what it is, there seems to be little appreciation of how the physical form also embodies thoughts, deep feelings and a spirit. Could it be they understand themselves well, that in Saudi Arabia, running rampant is exactly what would happen?

It's up to the husband whether or not his wife wears a veil in public, its presence preventing her from being gazed upon by any male she could potentially marry. If an extended family inhabits one house, other males occupy separate levels. Of course, this business of covering the eyes works both ways. Can anyone tell where she's looking?

It seemed easier for Saudis to distinguish one from another when facial features were not the primary cues. To my untrained eye, women walking in darkness resembled a sea of black, occasionally exercising disembodied voices or levitating a pair of eyeglasses over the sea. They recognized each other, nonetheless, by picking up on all the small nuances and lesser elements of style, presumably below my threshold. Scarves could cover the forehead in a straight line from temple to temple or be hitched up in the middle in an inverted V. Some veils had short cords running vertically over noses, separating the eyes. Some had trailing ties and others had velcros.

Abayas, with endless permutations, could be plain or elegant, with embroidery, lace or braid on the edges. Some women wore gloves as well. The design of shoes and handbags was of particular relevance. Baba collected refrigerator magnets with humorous depictions of Saudi life. One such magnet illustrated children approaching one ebony clad figure after another, calling "Mama? Mama?" I had no doubt they easily identified who's who, using more cues than those in my meager repertoire. I was not alone. Indeed Paul revealed how female students would ask, "Dr. So and so, why don't you ever say hello to me in the hall? Don't you recognize me?" Actually, defeating the purpose of deflecting attention, all the preening and adjusting of slippery errant folds every few minutes drew attention to hair and face

Jewel Dhuru

more than not covering would have done. One becomes accustomed to the commonplace. It's still mystique that attracts.

Variations showed in men's *shmals* and *gootras*, too. For each, a square of material was folded on the diagonal. It could flow longer down the back or shorter. Under it, on the head, goes the small white, cutwork Arab cap and over it goes the double ringed, black *egal*. From the juggling I observed in public, I have no doubt considerable time was spent in mirrors fashioning just the right look Pointed ends of *shmals* were often left down on the shoulders or, in winter, crossed in front of the neck and flipped back like scarves. In summer, when worn pointed straight down, I had seen men flap them like wings, perhaps for cooling. Some tossed only one side back and brought it round to artistically adorn the opposite shoulder. On top, sides could be carefully curled back, resembling, to my untrained eye, the brim of a cowboy hat. Careful folds of a *gootra* could produce a big bow on top of the head. More careless flicks and swirls overhead, particularly in the hot summer, resulted in rabbit ears or a bird's nest effect.

White *gootras* sport a V-shaped crease at the center front, extending outward with prescribed waves bordering forehead and face. From the number of times I had seen hands go up to check that undulations were in place, they seemed a principal part of the appearance. Not using an *egal* is considered progressive, not separating oneself from God. But then, without the ringed fastener, *gootras* became less manageable and even more susceptible to slips and slides.

At restaurants, eating in veils posed no problem. In Riyadh, some restaurants didn't allow women at all. Men's Sections were open and airy. Family Sections accommodated whole families, but were divided into booths with curtains or moveable screens, obscuring the decor.

One evening, we and another expat couple occupied a booth in the Family Section. We doffed *abayas* and left our curtain open, so we could shun that boxed-in feeling while watching the floorshow. Saudi champagne gave the illusion of a glass of bubbly. To white soda and apple or grape juice were added apple, orange, strawberry and banana slices and mint leaves. We sampled all the gastronomic delights, Arab bread, tahina, mousaka and chicken and vegetable preparations. As the evening progressed, the booths filled up. When a Saudi family moved in opposite us, their curtain closed. Inside, veils came off.

Watching the waiter take their order and serve them was amusing. He knocked on the wobbly partition between booths to alert them to his presence before the husband opened the curtain. Food was juggled in through the slit in the curtain while the waiter averted his eyes. As we left two hours later, at 10:30 PM, by then bursting with families with clamorous kids, I wove my way down a winding aisle between rows of closed curtains. I gripped the curtain rails on either side as I sidled along because I felt like I was in the sleeping car of a train and kept expecting the whole room to lurch.

A Communication expression also thrust itself onto my conscious mind—'An individual cannot not communicate'. The eyes are thought to be the most expressive part of the face and most communication is sent through them, followed by other facial features. However, so the theory goes, even with facial stimuli concealed, if one deliberately tries not to leak information about oneself, freezing in position and becoming non-responsive, one is still sending a glaring message for all to see, of wanting to be left alone. This might even backfire and attract unwanted attention. Taking measures to obscure what is in one's heart or mind could communicate something quite different from what was intended. For some, the very prohibition of thoughts and actions facilitates resignation, creating a self-perpetuating suffocation, like babies who are neglected from birth, who abandon their spirits and shrivel. For others, the prohibition invites curiosity and surreptitious experimentation in the very behaviors that are condemned.

Feelings, on the other hand, can't be controlled so easily. They may be only suppressed. I may not have been able to read veiled faces, but other cues like the inclination of the bodies, the energy or lack of it in the steps and audible gasps when seeing something disagreeable, spoke volumes. This was Riyadh, of course. Spirits in smaller cities were lighter.

Power

Yet another phrase came to mind, this one attributed to Ginger Rogers, about a female dancer having to do everything the male does, except going backwards and with high-heels.

Every individual in every culture has challenges to face. There may be more strains of one kind on females and of another on males, the aged or children. But societies, their characteristics and rules, are shaped by all their participants. Some develop more like the Irish Riverdancers, where males and females have equitable or complementary backwards and forwards time and both wear the same clickity heels. Perhaps in some societies, not all the voices involved are as loud as in the Greek play Lysistrata, where the women threatened to withhold carnal pleasures from their husbands unless the men stopped warring with each other. But a change in the behavior of one creates reverberations through all, just as a tug on a single silken strand of a spider web shapes the whole system. Acquiescence, compliance and obedience are degrees of accord making statements and inviting responses, perpetuating the system. In Riyadh, even men, alleged protectors of their women folk, are restricted from doing some of what they want and women, in their turn, have ways of articulating dislikes. Wherever a union exists, remote controls do as well. Whether exercised or not and how or how much, is up to us.

The power of the female can be so overwhelming to some, they feel threatened by it. Paula Gunn Allen, a native North American, summed it up this way.

"Women who are at the peak of their fecundity are believed to posses power that throws male power totally out of kilter. They emit such force that, in their presence, any male-owned or -dominated ritual or sacred object cannot do its usual task."[18]

A counseling service, accessed through an embassy, told about the emotional atmosphere that brings out characteristic marital problems with power, especially for mixed couples, Arabs and non-Arabs. To be clear, Arabs are often defined as those who speak Arabic, but there are exceptions. The people of twenty-two Middle Eastern countries, around the Mediterranean and in northern Africa, speak Arabic. Iranians are not Arab. They are Persian and speak Farsee. Turks speak Turkish and are not Arab, either. Pakistanis speak Urdu and Afghanis speak Pashtoon. Some Egyptians are Arab and some have pharonic ancestry.

We met a lot of mixed couples: Saudi and non-Saudi, Arab and non-Arab, Bedouin-Mexican unions and all manner of expat non-Muslim blends. My two male Saudi counseling clients, both middle-aged, had cumulatively fathered seven children. One was divorced from an American and one was unhappily married to a Saudi. From them, I learned about how patterns of marital control or non-appreciation were passed down from families of origin to families of procreation, from parents to children to grandchildren. It happens in every culture, in every marriage. We are handed down the legacy our heritage and our environment have to offer, for better or worse, unless fate or self-awareness and personal choice, intervene. Ways of being mothers, wives and friends are handed down from mother to daughter to granddaughter. To the extent that we are unaware of the dynamics of the pattern, and do not objectively determine which actions are healthful for us, we are doomed to repeat it. As always, the first step towards fashioning a new pattern is to take a hard look, without shame or blame, at what we do to create and continue our present situation.

For mixed unions, upon arrival in Saudi Arabia, a bond of friendship between husband and wife has to be shared by the bond is formed there among men only and another among women only. These two types of bonds could compete. More enlightened would be to invite compatibility and the complementary—no small feat.

On days I felt particularly forlorn, it was tedious to listen to what fun Baba had at work, lecturing on a favorite subject with bright students or exchanging jokes with pals at lunch. I was glad he was enjoying himself and I usually managed an abysmal smile at the height of his jocularity. I knew he was trying to cheer me up but it made the contrast between our situations more apparent. To the extent that I could wrench myself from self-pity and he could develop an empathy for the disparity, we were then able to salvage the rest of the day. Eventually, as I toughened up and he softened, we were able to start getting the new dynamics to work for us.

Blended couples can be content and productive and indeed enrich the planet, just as other kinds of couples contribute in their unique ways. But in blends, maintaining the identity of each member, while working together takes perhaps more ingenuity and cooperation. If one of the pair tries to dominate, the union and any good that can come from it, are jeopardized.

One day, Baba brought a notice that was taped to his office door. He recognized it as a copy of the announcement from the office bulletin board. The flyer said "The committee on sports activity organized a one day 'SPORTSFEST' ... Everybody is invited to come and join in ... Anticipating your presence with your children on this day." It sounded like fun, so Baba said he would find out more about it. When he came home the next day, he said his male colleagues looked at him in surprise at the suggestion that I thought the likes of me would be able to come, one even saying, "There will no *abayas* there."

Momentary shock on my part gave way to a strong emotion or two, and when the tempest passed, to gratitude that my repertoire included experience with places on this globe where the term every body meant human beings of all descriptions. Along with small crises, opportunities for humor and self-empowerment arrived. I was reminded of the 1968 comedy, "The Private Navy of Sgt. O'Farrell." Bob Hope suggested something was going on between an unattractively made up Phyllis Diller and a commanding officer. The officer protested, "That's ridiculous. I'm engaged, to a woman!" as if Phyllis Diller had been pronounced some third form of life!

Not long after that, Baba came home saying a general appeal had been announced for medical caregivers to volunteer in Kosovo for two weeks and he was considering volunteering. After all, 2,000,000 people are accommodated annually for Hajj, in Makkah. Within a couple of weeks the world would witness the donation by gulf countries of five star tents. The next news flash was that a superior had taken Baba aside and told him it was understood that the request was intended for Saudis only.

My impression, supported daily, was that the men's world and the women's world are very separate there, lived in compartments, more so than in most places. The women's world seemed to be primarily other female relatives and children and the men seemed more involved with other men. Husbands made dinner plans with male friends at the last minute, called their wives and announced, "We're going out," meaning the men. Men learned young how to placate females and after they've taken their wives and kids shopping on Wednesday and Thursday evenings, they were free to vacation separately with men friends. Women, on the other hand, might have been asked by their husbands to wear veils but not gloves but some women will wear gloves anyway as part of a 'see what you made me do' philosophy. Coffee mornings, for women only, began at 10:00 AM with sweets, caffeine and gossip. Bazaars were frequent, held in seclusion, and involved the selling of all manner of interesting ethnic crafts, some even bizarre.

Ala Tool

I contemplated the parallels between the Irish family in *Angela's Ashes* and Saudis, the former with economic challenges and the latter, with primarily social. The Irish father kept the money he earned from occasional employment for himself and used only the charity allotted him for family upkeep. When his wife asked him to use a portion of his earnings for the family, in effect to cross boundaries, he argued "its different for a man; you have to keep the dignity. Wear your collar and tie, keep up the appearance, and never ask for anything."[18]

Men and women seemed to have clearly defined roles, responsibilities and jurisdictions, like white and black, not a lot of gray areas involving both. Men did not seem to be encouraged to share information or major decisions with womenfolk and I suspected the reverse was true, too. The woman of the house occupies an exalted position when it comes to the domestic and influencing her sons' behavior. Generally, in the realm of Islam, Egyptian women are the most powerful, but they still need husbands' signatures to be able to travel. When relationships evolve such that the male remains immature in the home while the female is put on a pedestal, then in order to maintain balance, outside the home the situations have to be reversed.

Men got the blame for wives' indiscretions. Baba's male expat colleague had to sign a paper at the police station acknowledging his wrongdoing when his wife was climbing a curb and pulled her skirt above her ankle. My limited experience told me Saudi men who wanted to ease the path for their wives felt just as stuck as their wives. These social features can be contagious to non-Saudis if we aren't aware of what's happening. Some days, consequential email messages for me coming through Baba's account were considered inconsequential by him and so delayed. On days when I felt more rapport with other recently acquainted females than I did with my husband of 26 years, I became aware of how the system was sneaking up on us.

Good fortune smiled on me when I met a Saudi male who worked on campus, with whom I had infrequent, though valuable opportunities to talk. He radiated energy, from his insatiable spark and inquisitive eyes to the spring in his step, a thin but wiry half man and half rubber band. He wore the usual *thob*, *shmal* and *egal* and all men had moustaches. It was one trait that theoretically distinguished them from boys.

It was he and his Indian helpers who delivered the bed frame and bookcase when we moved in and he brought us a Qur'an. I thanked him but we already had one. Another day, the helpers inserted curtain rings on our rods while their overseer watched. My Arabic, only slightly better than his English, we shared information piecemeal, non-verbal cues on both sides being indispensable. As we became better acquainted, and my vocabulary expanded, our conversation became less superficial. On one particularly difficult day, our paths crossed.

After some preamble, my reply to his query about whether I liked it there or not was *"nuss,"* half. I grumbled about enforced seclusion and unfriendly neighbors, generally giving my power away left and right. His two-word comment was like a tonic. Accompanying it, he touched his index finger to his temple and at the moment he uttered the words *"Saudia bent,"* he dropped his arm and hand suddenly without severing the finger-to-head connection. His finger, with oil under the nail and a faint scent of benzene clinging to it, demonstrated the shape of his expression, which still rings in my ears. This uneducated man had succinctly spoken volumes. Not for the first time, I noticed his weather-beaten, leathery feet, shod with worn sandals.

"Kayf t'araf?" I asked him. 'How do you know?' so much about what I interpreted as twisted thinking. What I deciphered of his answer told me he'd traveled here and there, all Muslim countries, and from what he saw, even he thought the Saudi experience was—different.

Given the state of flux of relationships, whatever expat female friendships I made would have to be tested by time and other trials. Honoring the company of ones own sex provides strength from sharing experiences, airing feelings in safety and getting feedback, without competition or jealousy, putting female politics aside and just being at home. And when life deals one of us a blow, it's comforting to retreat for a moment to the refuge of female friendship.

Acquaintances numbered more than friends, of course. When I luxuriated in the warm hospital hydro-pool, 7 x 3 x 1 1/3 meters deep (22 x 9 x 4 ft.), at times, up to four Saudi women paddled with me. We all wore suits covering elbows and knees, as required. I smiled to myself about the Western one-piece I'd packed that never left the closet while I was in the country. The simple one piece Saudi suit I obtained was devoid of extraneous design and was lime green, the color of the national flag. But the one or two-piece outfits worn by others were colorful and embroidered. As each additional woman entered, saying *Salam Wa Laqum*, I added my voice to the murmured response, *Wa Laqum Salam*. It felt good to be part of the group, even though I didn't know the members. A gentle Pakistani female therapist, who supervised the pool, sat and chatted with each of us as we exercised. During *Ramadan*, though, she mumbled aloud from the Qur'an, head bowed so low, from hunger and devotion, I thought she'd tumble in.

Over time, I distinguished between the reticent, even glacial ones, who avoided eye contact, and others whose nonverbal behavior demonstrated their ease with themselves and others. Giving in to the temptation to ignore another first before she ignored me was easily done but meant falling into the trap of self-fulfilling prophecy and did not produce the desired result of camaraderie among equals. It would take strength to not only sustain myself but to be compassionate with others as well. Superficial as it was, when a *Kayf halik?*—How are you? came my way, I answered with *quayesa, shukran*—fine, thank you. I resisted falling into the pattern of answering *Il Hamdoolileh*—thank God.

Those who attempted to converse used prescribed questions, following the script, about nationality, family and children. More than one expat couple that was childless by choice admitted to fabricating children living abroad just to avoid the horrified looks when they insisted neither of them was "the problem".

Marriages, where male and female powers will theoretically be balanced, are arranged. Women come into unions having inherited private fortunes. Banks have distinct entrances, marked LADIES, around the sides or backs. Saudi couples have a different type of relationship to begin with than couples that are friends beforehand. The sense of duty was different in each case as well. Duty was not restricted to marriage. Since giving alms is a pillar of Islam, no street people adorn those desert streets.

Actually, it's quite the opposite. A woman might get dressed up even with no place to go, just to keep her spirits up. If spirits drooped anyway, a widespread problem treated with multiple medications, some actually went out with nightgowns on under *abayas*. Unless you went visiting and removed the shroud, who would know? Why not be naked under wrappings? At least, the skin is a God given layer. I sometimes found it hard to muster up the energy to put on something pretty just to smother it in shadow, until I made up my mind to dress for my self.

The closest approximation to street people is women who sit, with or without children alongside, on steps outside restaurants to gather alms. They might be widowed or divorced. Although the society has safety nets and all women are cared for in some fashion, like a widow being taken under the wing of her husband's brother, some women do slip through the cracks and collect alms. I was oblivious to the practice until we were leaving a restaurant and Baba turned back to give money to the black bundle on the step. That's when he elaborated.

One place for women to go was Saudi weddings. Men's and women's festivities occurred in different rooms, though, sometimes even on different days. The fashions that had caught my eye months before had taken human form. They were all there. Slacks in animal skin patterns with revealing cutouts, furry textures and wild colors, low cut, sheer gowns with adornments to direct the beholder's eye. Guests wore elaborate, incandescent, gilded gowns and female entertainers belly danced, sometimes on tabletops, with considerable tossing of long hair. Loud trills, using voices and tongues, expressed their joy. As it was explained to me, Saudi women have only small windows of opportunity to experiment with identity and comparative self-expression, so when a window opens, overstatement is understandable.

When a man occasioned to enter the room, after his knock, a flurry of veils and *abayas* thrust the room back into shadow. Maybe he was the lucky one. The dazzle of resplendent, sequined and beaded gowns was enough to blind you. As always, dinner was served last, just before everyone went home, sometimes at 2:00 AM.

History's Impact

Family obligation is extremely important in the Arab world. The Prophet and Kings are role models for how to construct and conduct family. Much has already been written by Wilson and Graham (1994) about political threats from outside the country translating into rivalry between royal brothers and cousins, in turn disturbing national stability, and also about relationships among the religious establishment, military and technocrats.[20]

Since the leadership of Abraham's two sons, Itzhak and Ismail, diverged into two major religions, Judaism and Islam, respectively, the potential has existed for exceptional cooperation and collaboration or alternatively, exceptional rivalry. In this region, political power is generally in the hands of one family. The behavior of brothers is an example for all. Brothers can be disinherited or worse, over power and control and sisters and daughters are for perpetuating the male bloodline. It was sad when Jordan's King Hussein passed on during our stay. His more or less peaceful attitude was much needed in the region. Power puts strains on relationships. It could also lead to incomparable allegiances and healthful integration, when relatives truly admire each other and are of an accommodating mind.

It has been said, that in days past, one young son in each family was sent to live with Bedouins. The convention was that once the Bedouin mother nursed the baby five times, she became his mother. We met a gentleman with a jovial disposition who had been the chosen link in his family and we heard stories of his childhood, including a scorpion sting or two.

On a religious question and answer program, a viewer's letter asked what happens if you find out you've married your brother. My mind reeled. How could one not know? Now I know the desert was full of connections to urban families. It was thought to be a political move because when election time rolled around, one's vote was decided by family affiliation.

History tells us King Abdul Aziz Ibn Al Rachman Al Saud, Ibn meaning he was the son of Al Rachman and the grandson of Al Saud, had between 44 and 60 sons. Apparently he had at least as many daughters, but they aren't mentioned initially, because as I was told frequently, they don't count. Perhaps not so well documented is the national belief, also stated often, that there is no adultery in Saudi Arabia. Combine this with the knowledge that the official limit is four wives per male and that all he has to do to divorce one of them is to say, thrice, in front of the proper witnesses 'I divorce you', then it's not difficult to understand the system—four at a time. However, the culture is not alone in this practice of multiple couplings. The Egyptian Pharaoh, Rameses, had many wives and hundreds of children. In Europe, in feudal societies, Ireland for example, the first night of any bride's married life was spent with the Lord of the Manor, resulting in his progeny dotting the fields.

A book we picked up on our travels enlightened us. In Bahrain, *Gender Equity in Islam* (1995) explained polygyny as a man's having up to four wives at once, as long as he can treat them all justly in every way. According to the author, "no text in the Qur'an or Sunnah, the two revelatory sources of Islam specifies either monogamy or polygyny as the norm."[21] ... and "Islam did not outlaw polygyny, as did many other people and other religious communities; rather it regulated and restricted it."[22] It also states "the Koran urges husband's to be kind and considerate to their wives."[23] The reasoning behind polygyny goes back to earlier days. An all-female talk program on Riyadh Radio claimed that since these are typically war-like nations, at least 2,000,000 men have died in recent decades. To my mind, this made women even more of a numerical majority in a country where their lives mirrored minority. The logic behind polygyny was that it's better for a woman to have a husband and father around for the children some of the time rather than not at all. Men made the rounds, residing in each house for the same length of time and got very polished at placating. The wives often did not get along but kept their peace for public appearances.

Polyandry, a woman's marriage to multiple husbands, on the other hand, is not allowed. "It's practice raises thorny problems related to the lineal identity of children and the law of inheritance, both important issues in Islamic law."[24] Divorce for females involves tedious, drawn-out, not to mention, male-governed, court proceedings.

Women keep their last names when they marry but the children bear their father's surname. Female first names showed variety—Anoot, Noor, Nada, Rana, Adeela, Shok, Hanadi, Johara, Dahlia, Roqaya and Najd, although everyone knew the meaning of her name and its connection to history. Men's names, however, were repetitive. It seemed to me that a quarter of the male population was called Muhammed. A quarter was Abdul Aziz and another quarter was Abdul Rachman, after an ancestor of Abdul Aziz.

We had the honor of being invited for dinner to the home of a Saudi family with six children and the subject of names came up. Upon arriving, once we passed the outer walls, gate and garden, the enormous foyer opened into a living room with a striking but restful color scheme of peaches and golds, comfortable couches, glass topped tables and interesting paintings. Dinner was the usual sumptuous feast, although the Indonesian kitchen help who served hors d'oeuvres had a harried, anxious look in her eyes.

"No Saudis work in this house," the father said apologetically, after she'd juggled heavy platters of lamb and rice and went back into the kitchen.

In this well educated and traveled family, the mother was working on a Ph.D. They lamented that their own neighbors considered them too progressive. One of their teen daughters was traditional in her beliefs, covering her hair and remaining speechless all evening while the other was quite the opposite. She wore modern clothes and was talkative and lucid.

When Miss Modern proclaimed her happiness at keeping her own name, my thought was that the only name that is really mine is my first name. I didn't see much fundamental difference between their system and the Western one. We can keep one man's last name, our father's, or take another's, our husband's, or combine the two or add our mother's or grandparents' in the Spanish style. My maiden name will always be part of my personal history and experience, regardless of new events. All the stages and ages of my evolution are still right here, within me.

The father objected to his daughters taking any other man's name. My strong impression was that to Arabs, surname and identity were considered one and the same thing, whereas to me, surname is an indication of bloodline, not a substitute for a separate personality.

When it got late, we headed for the door and the father's car. The mother asked me to keep in touch. Believing her request to be genuine, I asked if she preferred snail or email. She said she didn't have email, preferring the anonymity of chat rooms and that despite her best intentions, she never got around to responding to snail mail. The same two daughters had gathered at the door to see us off but as soon as we headed down the path, I heard them scamper off. When I got to the gate, I turned back to give the mother one last wave, since I didn't anticipate hearing from her soon, but she was gone, too, like water from a bath, and the door was closed. I did phone to say goodbye before I left the Kingdom. I left a message with Miss Modern for her mother to call me but Mom's busy week must have been extended indefinitely.

Jewel Dhuru

Thinking back, the most memorable part of our conversation occurred when the mother said that when a woman gives birth, she is forgiven all past transgressions. With each subsequent birth, the sins from the interval since the last child are absolved. I asked what the male counterpart to such forgiveness was. I got simultaneous but different answers from mother and daughter. The mother answered "nothing" and then elaborated that this was a perk of being born female while Miss Modern answered "Jihad" (self defensive military action)!

Chapter 11: Tutoring and Time

"I know that the more I open myself to the wonders of nature … the more willing I am to let life happen and to cultivate the inner resources of my imagination. The more I allow myself to simply *be*, instead of always *doing*, the more I see a wondrous growing all around me" [25]

—Eda LeShan, Counselor and author of *How Do Your Children Grow?*

"I would like you to tutor my children," Dr. Shebib said, from his end of the phone line.

I remembered Dr. Shebib well. He was the colleague of Baba's I had met when I went to the college one day with blond Linda. As soon as she'd left me in search of a particular office, he began asking questions about her.

"Who is she? … Where is she from? Who is she married to? …." He fired one question after the other, but my answers didn't come as quickly.

Two weeks later, he was calling about a tutor. He could send his driver to pick me up twice a week, he said. After ascertaining that his house was accessed only by a flight of stairs, I explained my physical predicament and said I would gladly have the girls come to me instead.

Even though he taught on campus, Dr. Shebib sounded reluctant to agree, saying his driver only took his teen daughters to select sites. Safety seemed to be the issue. I didn't see the problem. They could go from home, veiled, into his driver's hands and then into mine, reversing the process on the way home. Who didn't he trust, I wondered. The campus? The driver? Me?

At length, he extolled the charms of his neighborhood, some distance from the campus and continued to try and convince me to come. Reaching an impasse, we engaged in face-saving on both sides, agreeing to "perhaps another time." So there it remained, all the women involved still in their homes and he on the lookout for another tutor.

When Baba came home one day, soon after that, with stories of how Saudi spies were planted in organizations to report on compatriots who deviated from the straight and narrow, Dr. Shebib and his rapid-fire questions uncomfortably sprang to mind. Eventually, he went on to become head of a department and I made the acquaintance of 6-year old, Egyptian Rana.

We learn from our students. While this young lady, born in the desert, scraped green crayon off the North American winter scene she'd colored for homework, I tried to think how best to explain about our seasons. Saudi, American and British schools taught in the Kingdom but she attended an International school. Her day went from 7:00 AM to Noon. By the heat of the day, playful, longhaired, dark-eyed Rana was home. About 5:00 PM or so, kids headed for their tutors'. Either her mother or brother would walk her over for 1 1/4 hours, twice a week. We'd catch up on her news and then she'd settle down to work on the low coffee table, on whatever needed most attention that week. At break time, a snack waited in the kitchen.

As I helped her with lessons, I learned students generally crammed for exams at the last minute and memorization was required. I had misgivings as I helped a 6-year old try to memorize the definition of a Capital city—where state leaders work. In a workbook exercise, on words that rhyme with Sam, she didn't recognize a picture of ham, because pork is prohibited in Muslim countries. I explained the four seasons, even though there aren't that many in the Arab world. Rana had to learn to respond 'sad' to a question about how we feel about rain and 'happy' to no rain, in a desert where rain is an event to celebrate. She stared at me in disbelief as we scraped green crayon off the winter picture and I showed her a Christmas card with snow and mostly bare trees. Explaining autumn colored leaves, I would save for another day.

I learned another lesson from this little lady about the female's power to shape behavior. One way women express disapproval is by clicking their tongues, producing a sound of annoyance. I recalled an incident at Al Habala, the cliff dwellings, the month before. Photography had to be done reservedly. It was prohibited to capture much of Saudi life, like public buildings, mosques and especially women.

I had taken the cable car back up to the parking lot before Baba. He needed just a few more photos. I was the sole occupant of a car approaching the top when four young non-Saudi males pointed their camera in my direction. This wasn't unusual in this setting. The sheer

Ala Tool

drop and agricultural terraces made the area exceptionally photogenic, and it would have been difficult to steer clear of every cable car. I didn't think anything much of the boys at the time. Since I was scarfless, I assumed they knew I was not Saudi. But before my car stopped, I could see them jostling each other, presumably as a reminder to get my permission first. They gesticulated, to which I responded with thumbs-up. It was all over in less than a minute.

But as I vacated the cable car, I discerned a senior Saudi woman and her family sitting in a row, waiting for their ride. As I passed them, I heard her *tsk tsk* and jerked my head to her in surprise before I walked on. I guessed her paralinguistic comment referred to my attire and the photograph. I chose not to reply. I found disregarding both approval and disapproval more prudent than arguing. But I didn't forget.

The way in to the *telefrik* had been a gentle downward slope which I had managed with only a little difficulty, but as I turned the corner to reach the parking lot, I faced a flight of stairs, and Baba was nowhere in sight. I laboriously mounted them, the thought crossing my mind that if I were to fall and injure myself, the same lady's family would probably be among those who would come to my aid. Extra blessings went to those who helped others in need.

A month after the trip, Rana came for her lesson. She was a sweet child, with a stubborn streak that surfaced now and again, sometimes too playful, but bright and generally well mannered. Still, 1¼ hour for a six year old, after a full day of school was not ideal.

The time came when my mild frustration showed with the circumstances of that day's lessons. The spelling words were difficult, time was short and she was especially resistant to study that day. In her mind, it was playtime. Teetering on the edge of exasperation, a dreaded single *tsk* inadvertently escaped my lips. The effect was electrifying.

The little lady interpreted it as chastisement. The poor dear jerked her gaze to my face and I saw fear in her eyes before she lowered them in dejection and disgrace. It was the first such exchange between us and I regretted it immediately, especially since it was unintentional. The remorse on her face for the alleged transgression couldn't have been greater than my regret for inadvertently scolding this sweet, bright child. I talked about it right then and we cleared away the emotional rubble. Locating her worst fear, I assured her even if she misspelled every word, I would still like her. Rana's forgiveness was openhearted and complete and that day we allowed each other to shape the other's behavior, I hoped towards gentleness and self-confidence. The incident was laid to rest.

But the lessons of that day came back a few days later. Looking up from the sitting room couch one afternoon, I discovered a small 10 cm. (4") long gecko, on the ceiling. Reading up about geckos, I learned of their uniqueness among lizards; they alone utter a sound other than hissing. This desert inhabitant makes a clicking sound with its tongue!

Time

And the lessons kept coming, in all forms, often when least expected. Time, for example, is used differently in various cultures. I experienced this first hand in a practical sense. Every *Inshallah*, every half-hearted promise, every utterance with the best intentions to be helpful, but which was never really under the speaker's control in the first place, taught a lesson.

It used to feel accomplishment when I thought in a linear fashion, following a straight line. I made a plan, took the necessary steps to achieve my goal, organized for the best possible outcome, left energy to cope with last minute changes and spontaneous bright ideas and saw the plan reach fruition. Then I could relax, without that niggling feeling of something being uncompleted. I realize every westerner doesn't use time this linear way, but it is, generally, the norm. But working with Rana required every ounce of innovation and imagination I could muster to keep her involved and learning.

A more Eastern, circular view treated life as a process, juggling events and relationships and adapting to changes while staying in the here and now. Revamping my attitude had the added benefit of unlocking horns with Baba's casual attitude to time.

After my slice of life in the Middle East, where this style of diplomatic circumlocution flourishes, I could derive more joy from the power and haven of living from moment to moment, because in Riyadh, speedy results were not always forthcoming. This was not a straight-line sort of culture in other ways, either. In banks, postal centers or anywhere service is needed, standing quietly in line was not

Ala Tool

the way things got done. The expression 'the squeaky wheel gets the grease' was tailor made for this part of the world.

With a circular, life-is-a-process attitude, actions, events and living generally took on a more circuitous route, at the end of which, if there was an end, outcomes were unpredictable. If anywhere in the world lends itself, indeed attracts the serendipitous, the Arab world must be it. Not to relax through it all could sustain tension for a very long time.

It took some time to get the hang of not trying to control everything, to let the process evolve, in this flighty lifestyle. At times it was a choice between learning to listen to life, to see the beautiful in what was happening and to accept the natural flow or to try and enforce what I thought should happen, making myself miserable along the way. It was humbling.

Inshallah was tailor made for the culture, too. An exact translation might be written in stone somewhere. In practice, though, individual differences were applied. At its worst, it absolves accountability and excuses having no initiative. At its best, it means doing one's utmost to formulate and initiate personal plans, but being willing to surrender to a will greater than one's own and accept the immediate and long-term master plan. When I requested a campus limo by phone, they confirmed by saying *"Naam (*Yes) *Inshallah."* In other words, if God is willing, we'll be there. Actually, 98% of the time, they were there when I needed them. But there was always a doubt, or an out.

Theoretically, it can be used conversely, to get out of obligations—God was not willing. The goal, instead of completing a task, was to keep one's dignity while reaching for results, going through the maze of burocracy, gathering opinions from family and friends, placating each one and dealing with the plethora of small emergencies that come up in life. And with an extended family, one that extends all the way to the near neighborhood and ancestors, a lot of things come up. There were priorities of course, but the sand was always shifting.

The original plan might fall through at the last minute or be cancelled, usually without hard feelings, or it could just undergo countless transmutations—to include another individual, to accommodate forgetfulness, compromise, collaboration or being put in jail. In the disconnected, elliptical course, one learns who one can count on and trust under what conditions and who one cannot and one develops liaisons and alliances that can last a lifetime and into the next generation. And therein lay the quality of life, to enjoy the process in the present moment, the only moment for action in any case, and to accept what came.

Privacy and personal space, topics related to time, are luxuries of the West. In the East, private thoughts show and are scrutinized publicly. The influence of family and neighbors is conscripted to keep one on the straight and narrow. There, privacy is in the mind. No wonder meditation originated in the East.

Interestingly, the Arabic words for soon and near are one and the same—*qereb*. Young and small are *sarir* and old and big are *kabir*. The first word of each pair is related to time—soon, young and old, and the second relates to space—near, small and big, respectively. Could it be that this connected use of the abstract, elastic concepts of time and space showed a profound understanding, way back at the dawn of the language, of space being the third dimension and time being the fourth, of the speed of light, of gravity and of the real nature of time, even before Einstein's theory of relativity? Why not?

We were not to know it yet then, but the continuous orbiting of the International Space Station was to be a twinkle in the eye of my life-is-a-happening husband. The search for it in the heavens was to take up quite a bit of Baba's time and afford him needed abstraction as well.

Ala Tool

Chapter 12: Religion And The Qur'an

"Parents are duty-bound to **support and show kindness and justice to their daughters.** Prophet Muhammed (P) said, Whosoever has a daughter and does not bury her alive, does not insult her and does not favor his son over her, Allah will enter him into Paradise" [26]
—J. Badawi, *Gender Equality in Islam*

Language transmits culture. We can tell a lot about a culture by listening to the literal meaning of the words used and uncovering their connotations.

At social occasions during the long, warm winter, I heard traditional greetings and responses, and the distinctive vocabulary of the religion. A whole string of expressions are used when friends come through the door. The most common exchange is *Kayf halik?*—literally What's your situation? and the response *Il Hamdoolileh*—Thank God. A similar string is threaded into the beginning of TV news, rattled off at super speed, without the replies, so in the first ten seconds of broadcast, we've been really and truly greeted and blessed but haven't heard any news yet.

The Arabic for holiday is *Eid,* the word for both holy days. More culture is transmitted at presentations and meal times, where it's customary to begin with *Bismilleh Al Rachman al Rahim*, a blessing invoking peace and mercy upon all and reminding them of their heritage. The month of *Ramadan* is called just that, *Ramadan*. Before it comes the months of *Rajab*, then *Shaban*, and then comes *Ramadan*. It's not just a few holy days. It's a real month, like March or June, with a whole square to itself on a calendar.

Electric and phone bills and notes with the date scribbled on top recoded the 1st or the 5th or the 20th of *Ramadan*, with all the overtones of fasting, spiritual obligation, sacrifice, nocturnal office hours and breaking fast with relatives, surrounding that label, everyday of that month. And the month with the Hajj in it is *Dulhijj*, with images of pilgrimage, the long march around the black stone Kabah and throwing stones at the devil.

I hope, I'll try or I'll do my best are translated as *Inshallah*. *Mashala* has the nuances of 'touchwood' but with religious connections, invoking protection from the curse for gloating.

Likewise, the roots of many disciplines can be traced to religious beliefs. Books about the culture occupied a spot on our coffee table. I read and learned from the TV and then went out and saw the religion in practice.

About 600 AD, Islam evolved from the roots of Sufism, which valued all religions. Phillip Hitti (1970) wrote about Sheikh Muhyi al-Din ibn Arabi (1165-1240) from Spain, a Kurd who has been called the greatest monist and pantheist Sufi, and the greatest speculative genius of Islamic Sufism. In his influential writings, one charmingly called *The Bezels of Wise Precepts*, he waxed lyrically about his heart being capable of every form, finding the path to God in a synagogue, a pagan temple, a church altar and mosque, wherever love is.[27] From his book *Tarjuman al-Ashwaq*, a paraphrase states the "true mystic has but one guide, inner light, and will find God in all religions."[28]

Much of what was valued then still influences even Western systems now. The mystical expression of Sufism underlies and is infused into numbers, geometry, music, poetry, architecture and other disciplines.[29] The very floor plans of buildings are influenced by geometric forms[30] and "the form of the traditional city is based on its movement systems," the most important example architecturally being the order of the bazaar.[31]

The Sufi-Arabi style affected the courts and selection of rulers until the end of the 18th century. Then came Western intervention in the forms of France, Britain and the United States. By post-WWI, when Arab leaders were re-instituted into their own countries, it was under foreign tutelage. The attitudes of the Whabbis could not have been more opposed to Ibn Arabi's, and from them comes today's leadership. McLean (1989) writes about three goddesses, Allot, Minot and Al Uzza, revered in the matriarchal, pre-Islamic society to the point of having their likenesses chiseled onto venerable stones. The only remnants now of their features are all but scratched out, scarred relics of another time and like the roots of Islam, relegated to history.

Qur'an

The Qur'an did not sit on our coffee table. From TV and radio instruction, it seemed clear that the subject was so vast, I would never be able to grasp very much. Since I did not plan to make it my life's work, the best I could hope for, beyond the basics, was to get impressions.

Still, I had learned about Islam, at least the Saudi version of it. Being one of this planet's six major religions, I'm grateful for that. Still, no belief alters the fact that all human beings come from the same source.

Regardless of not being a scholar of the holy book, I couldn't help but hear and see. I gathered background to start. The Qur'an was written in Classical Arabic. It is said that through translations, one can acquire understanding, but not the taste of the message. The two revelatory sources of Islam are 1) the Qur'an itself, passed on verbatim through the Prophet Muhammed (pbuh) around the 7th Century AD containing, among other parts, codes of conduct and stories from prophets and 2) the Sunnah, a form of revelation to Muhammad (pbuh), but not verbatim. The Qur'an was sent down so those who embrace Islam can gain wisdom. Re-reading it penetrates to the heart and is in itself a prayer. Prisoners, depending on their offenses, can get their sentences reduced if they memorize it, but even law-abiders are instructed to do so anyway.

The Arab News cluttered our coffee table, too. In the series, Guidance from the Prophet, the author wrote, "The Qur'an is revealed in substance and form, i.e. meaning and word. Every word is used by God Himself as He revealed it to His messenger, the Prophet Muhammed (peace be upon him) who conveyed it to us in God's own words." [32] It is believed that to add anything to the original is to suggest Allah was incomplete. In another column, "the Qur'an achieves full expression of the intended meaning in a most economic style" [33] and "the Qur'an always invests the minimal possible wording to generate the broadest possible meaning." [34] Our Bahraini book, *Gender Equity in Islam* (1995), added that "Disregard or ignorance of Sunnah may lead to serious errors of interpretation" and "Errors are multiplied when an erroneous literal meaning is translated from the original Arabic text." [35] Scholars still hotly debate strategic passages, perhaps no more or less than discussion over other key religious books. It doesn't make it any easier on lay people to understand the tricky bits, though.

Quotes on a variety of topics caught my eye. Concerning manners, Salahi wrote: "The more civilized a community is, the more refined sense of duty its members have. That sense translates itself in practice into good manners. ... Since Islam, by definition, promotes every good, it encourages the adoption of all these virtues, and promises reward for them." The virtues were "... all universal virtues such as forbearance, forgiveness, truthfulness, sincerity, generosity, bravery, humbleness, self-respect, fidelity, etc. ..." [36]

This sounded good, in theory. Other religions espouse the same beliefs. Hoff (1992) tells us Confucianism's "most vital principles are Righteousness, Propriety, Benevolence, Loyalty, Good Faith, Duty and Justice" but also "Confucianism is stern, regimented, patriarchal." [37] Duty with heart always felt best to me, ideally leading to an elegant though effective touch, caring relationships and deep contentment. Duty out of obligation, however, when one's heart is not in it, bore other fruit. How suppressed strong feelings are ultimately discharged while the required appearance of good manners is being maintained, is a personal endeavor.

Perhaps the conflict between the two ways of doing one's duty accounts for the behavior of the Saudi medical student, in his 20s, in expensive clothes and a high-powered car, who streaked through the parking lot where Baba's 'Everybody is invited' college picnic was being held. He was oblivious to the fact that Baba had to jump out of his way just in time not to lose his life, or a leg. Only after his passenger pals convinced him he really was at fault did his prolonged stout denial change to effusive apologies.

Conversely, at their best, these high ideals produced behavior that was gentle but strong, polite, capable of picking up and responding appropriately to the subtlest looks and gestures and considerate of self and others.

About the character of the Prophet, Salahi (1999) wrote "His love and compassion to others surprised the Arabs a great deal. They were hard people who did not even show their children any love. The Prophet, on the other hand, kissed his grandchildren in public and some of the Arabs were taken aback by this action of his." When questioned about it, "The Prophet said to them 'How can I help it if God has taken mercy away from you'." [38] We met Saudis who were affectionate with children, even in public. Men with children frequented grocery stores more than women. But as in every nation, there is a range of personalities. Sometimes, human behavior falls short of its high standards and sometimes it exceeds it.

Concerning females, *Gender Equity in Islam* (1995) sums it up well, saying "There exists a gap between the normative behavior regarding women outlined in the Qur'an and the prevalent reality among Muslims ... Their diverse cultural practices reflect both ends of the continuum—the liberal West and the ultra-restrictive regions of the Muslim world. ... Some Muslims emulate non-Islamic cultures and ... in some Muslim cultures undue and excessive restrictions for women, if not their total seclusion, is believed to be the ideal." [39]

On the TV program, 'Rights of Women', not a single woman was even on the panel. I searched in vain for a program about the Rights of Men. That day, the topic was Dowry. The Dowry in Saudi Arabia must be given from husband to wife, they said. He must give it before the marriage is consummated. The amount is not relevant. If the only thing he has to give is verses he has memorized from the Qur'an, that will suffice, but he must give something. The gentlemen on the panel ended the lesson by emphasizing this was a gift, not an obligation.

I must have missed something.

More caught my eye, either prompting a narrowing of the eyes, raising of the eyebrows, or feeling like a poke in the eye. Finally, I decided learning more only added to my confusion and could lead to fruitless argument and counterargument. Where would it all end? Would learning more open my heart wider? Perhaps. In stages.

What it ultimately comes down to, I decided, is what sort of thought governs peoples' behavior, how they treat themselves, their families, including pets, and their neighbors. That is the stuff that gives value to our present moments, our days and our lives.

Chapter 13: May Day!

"When you get into a tight place and it seems that you can't go on, hold on, for that's just the place and the time that the tide will turn" [40]
—Harriet Beecher Stowe

Remember April Spring, which brought dust storms and distress instead of birds and blooming? Well, April Spring had urged me to dig deeper within myself for value, whether anyone else shakes my hand or practices Arabic with me or has the same sleeping and eating schedule as me or not.

May had new lessons in store. Conversations with Muslims in Saudi Arabia followed a predictable pattern. The question from men that caused a warm sensation to rise to my throat was their asking why I don't have another baby, as if they were applying for the job of donor!

Exceptions to the pattern occurred as some respected one's privacy more than others. The order of the questions or how directly a subject was broached varied with the questioner's educational level. But regardless of whether the speaker was Pakistani, Eritryean, Moroccan, Egyptian, Afghani, Bangladeshi, Sudanese, Algerian, Ethiopian or other variety of Muslim, conversations began the same way.

"What is your nationality?" they began, meaning citizenship. Then, "Are you Muslim?" ... "Christian?" ... "How long have you been here?" and "Do you like it?" It was as if a faucet was turned on and got stuck in the ON position until the flood of questions was drained dry.

When I asked questioners in return how they liked it, I got grimaces or the vacillation of the open hand, palm down, that doesn't signify over joy. Taxi drivers and servicemen sang the 'nothing to do but work and sleep' blues. I was asked if I had babies, how many, and whatever the number, they suggested why not one more. The gender of my children came next and then whether my daughter was married or not. Those I would see again did their duties as good Muslims and brought books entitled *Repentance, The Way to Happiness* and *The True Religion*.

Ala Tool

Since the second month of our ten-month stay, I had been having difficulties with taxi drivers, which worsened with my familiarity with the system. When I went to physical therapy during the day, I phoned for a campus limo. When we both went out in the evenings, we got taxis from on and off campus.

In retrospect, I neglected to notice how drivers' demeanors changed when Baba was with me. Those who had previously conversed with me now talked only to him and didn't even look in my direction. On the other hand, a few Indian drivers who chatted animatedly with Baba while the two of them waited for me grew suddenly cold towards him when I joined them. Baba's guess was they were dismayed that I wasn't Hindu.

In further retrospect, going back to Abdulla in the hotel, I had noticed the extreme responses of non-Saudi men to common courtesy. By courtesy, I mean using occasional eye contact and smiles and answering questions without being curt. Expat males without families in the country subsisted on scraps of softness wherever they could find them, and warmed to anyone who was moderately kind, perhaps carrying on imaginary intrigues, but we didn't know this at the time. My heart opened to them, but I was newer at surviving the severe than they were and I hadn't created the system, either. I was just trying to make sense of it.

One non-Saudi, but Muslim taxi driver, from the early months, stood out. Baba had sat in the front when we went out one evening. The two fell into immediate conversation and remained so for the whole 20-minute trip, seemingly forgetting I was there.

"This guy has given me a lot of information," Baba voiced when we alighted. We dropped the subject until we got back home and then he picked up the thread again.

"He kept asking me if I was sure *Babi* (wife in Urdu) didn't understand the language," he continued. "He was saying you can get any kind of illicit substance you want in Riyadh," listing the liquid, crystalline, powdered and human varieties. After the shock abated, I began the climb out of the trap of thinking these things happened on the far side of the city, not on our campus.

Then I remembered Mr. Saudia Bent and how excited his reaction when he spied a bottle of wine in a photo of a still life I'd painted. He had gone into a long unintelligible harangue, pointing at the bottle, moving his hands with palms up in and out of his *thob* pockets. It took me a minute to figure out I was looking at someone with black market connections. Memories continued to come back from the fall months. Now it was well into spring.

I got suspicious when one driver, balding and middle-aged, turned up at the door for the second time in as many weeks, on the pretext that he got a message saying I had requested a limo. I was reluctant to let him in a second time to check with his office by phone, and had Linda not been visiting me at the time, I wouldn't have.

In a moment of lucidity, I finally figured it out one evening when we were out shopping and the driver and I were waiting for Baba, who had run into a shop for five minutes. As it happened, it was May 1. We'd had this driver before, and although I didn't remember him at first, he remembered me. He was from an African country and reminded me I had told him my nationality and all the usual bits. He sent money home to his wife and five young children, who were living in a country where jobs were scarce. He had a sister in Canada. He handed me his pager number, common used at those times when getting through to a limo was difficult, like at *salah* when offices closed. I had an envelope full of such numbers.

Although a red flag threatened to go up in the back of my mind, I took the slip of paper. I suppose this is how men met second, third and fourth wives. No wonder they wanted their own wives covered. And no wonder women were aloof from each other. But I was taken aback when this Muslim male pointed out he was alone there and assumed when Baba went to work, I was, too, so he asked for my phone number and the times I would be on my own. May Day!

The warm patch in my throat gripped my vocal cords. The situation was sad. He sounded sad. The saddest part of all was that some of my normally human tendencies would have to be severely curbed so as not to inadvertently lead on people who were already confused.

The month had started inauspiciously, but as May progressed, I finally finished the stitchery of landmark status apartment facades with intricate wooden windows, in Jiddah, near Makkah. The windows allowed women to peer out while concealing their features from the stray glances of in-lookers. But Linda, who knew how to get it into an art show was notified of a death in her family in North America, so within six days, she was gone and would not be back before I left. She had helped me find students and taken us to out of the way restaurants and souks.

Until that time, when Baba and I considered extending our stay another year, with the summer in the United States, I thought of her and decided that with a few arrangements back home, it might be doable. But when she left, much was to change. Suddenly I was not so keen on lingering. As it happened, Baba's American job wouldn't release him for another year anyway, so that laid the matter to rest, or so I thought.

The month ended with international news claiming our attention. Between gleeful shrieks filtering in through the walls from local kids who'd finished final exams, we followed the Ocalon trial in Turkiye, pronounced Tour-quay'-yeah. Turks do not find it complimentary when the heart of the former Ottoman Empire is treated synonymously with a bird, or a nerd. And, in stark contradiction, the space shuttle Discovery was loading the new space station, housing celestial ambassadors, but Belgrade was still being bombed.

Chapter 14: A Parting Of The Ways

"You gain strength, courage and confidence by every experience in which you really stop to look fear in the face. You must do the thing you think you cannot do".[41]
—Eleanor Roosevelt

As the hammering heat kept up a slow simmer, June brought its own set of challenges. Almost everyone we knew was leaving for the summer, not to return until mid-August. Even familiar taxi drivers who knew the limits were going away on vacation. But we were on an alternate schedule. Since Baba's heart surgery had delayed our arrival by two months, we had to stay two months longer. There would be a lot of *mac salamas*, good-byes with blessings.

Before leaving the Kingdom for good and all, Dr. B developed complications. For travel, faculty was expected to participate in the expat sport of signature gathering, obtaining up to fifteen for final departure. Clearance was needed from three libraries, the Housing Office, an equipment store, electric, gas, water and telephone services and more, in order to re-secure passports and retrieve the damage deposit for the flat. The origin of this system was Egyptian. In Egypt, it provided needed *baksheesh*, tips, for breadwinners at each step of the way. In Riyadh, perhaps having to go to separate agencies for each service, provided checks and balances, or maybe it just removed accountability. We didn't expect it to change any time soon.

Dr. B. gave up his phone a week before leaving so his final bill could be tabulated. While zigzagging the campus to secure permissions and with the inevitable complexities of selling his possessions, furnishings and car, having no phone-fax were major inconveniences. He was heading for a meltdown. He asked for our help and my being at home became a boon for him. Once again, I was grateful the crime rate was so low that we had the luxury of leaving our front door unlocked without giving up safety. He could just buzz and enter to use the phone or pick up notes, without inconveniencing me. It was hectic, though, making calls, relaying messages and getting faxes to the right people, but it was good preparation for our own eventual departure. Of course, agreeing to be a captive audience whenever he popped through the door put me in the position of hearing the dynamic details of his process blow by blow, but we got through it.

The atmosphere was charged with emotion as we bid one colleague-friend after another farewell. On the 9th of June, five people left and two more were to go the next day. Anita's family was leaving in four days. The place felt even more arid than before. The phone was quiet, not even wrong numbers. We took to finishing each other's crossword puzzles again and our supplies dwindled to meager minimums. Playgrounds and parking lots were less than half occupied. The morning after the five left, I looked at my watch and mentioned to Baba that so-and-so must be home by now. Without looking up, he uttered, "They all are." I understood.

Our hearts and minds were slowly slipping back to the basics with which we'd come. The silence became deafening. Alas, even my favorite Maamoul date pastries, pie like and sweet, inexplicably disappeared from supermarket shelves. Other brands remained, but the crusts weren't the same. They were familiar now, providing false solace at times. I had planned to take a box home, but they were gone. We were going to have to depend more on our own resources for support and entertainment. That, too, was becoming more familiar, even comfortable.

A counseling service gave pointers to out-going expats, especially those leaving for good. The same service had advised the in-coming to prepare for the fact that events might befall loved ones back home that expats can do nothing about, for example, concerning health or jobs. A delayed letter or call of commiseration might have to suffice, and then we must care for our own emotional well-being, because we don't have the old support system as near at hand as usual.

We tasted this first hand when a close female friend of mine back home was having a biopsy. We would have liked to exchange hundreds of words, but a few lines on a screen and a couple of phone messages had to do. We waited for the results. Then came the surgery, and then the chemotherapy. The card I wrote with shaking hands wouldn't be touched by hers until three weeks after it left mine. Eventually, she recovered, and we all became a little more patient.

But the time I wished most ardently I could dematerialize and reappear sitting next to my daughter occurred one day when I was reading in the sitting room. The phone rang and I heard her quavering voice sputter over the line.

"M-Mom, sh-she's suing me!" she moaned.

As she explained about unethical behavior on the part of the other party, I wanted to put my arms around her and my cheek against her face. The combination of our coaching with her innate good sense and competence got her into touch with local authorities that could help. The wholly unjust lawsuit was speedily dispatched—in a month or two. And we all became a little wiser. It was at such times that Baba and I pulled together with ease, all other annoyances seeming petty.

Out-going expats were reminded everyone has changed back home, just as we have. To expect to pick up just where we left off would be counterproductive. Some, from the old neighborhood, will not be interested in our escapades, we were informed. After their "welcome back," their conversations will circle around their own local activities and politics. Also, leaving behind new friends in Saudi Arabia, with whom we shared unique feelings and experiences, who it's possible we might never see again, needs special adjustments. Still, we resisted getting steeped in loss. How many of us could have predicted the chain of events that led us to those enriching liaisons in the first place?

In the thick of decisions and emotions, I recalled advice from centenarians who shared their secrets for longevity. The consensus was that along with moderation in all things and a stress resistant approach to life, they had an incredibly healthy attitude toward what is commonly thought of as loss. They didn't think of changing circumstances, or growing up or moving away or even death, as loss. It was just change and that is the nature of life. Using their energy for more positive pursuits proved more healthful.

Solo Shopping Trip

Even fortified with positive thoughts, the strain of being in transition yet again was taking its toll, so one Monday morning, I felt sluggish when I awoke. I went from room to room searching for something interesting to do. The same old books and CDs. There finally were fledgling Internet connections in the country, but the faculty was notified of consequences for anyone who attempted to access the Internet from home. So, not an option.

I could go to the exhibit of architectural models of mosques at the university. Baba had admired it so much he went back twice more,

Ala Tool

with his camera, encouraging me to go on the ladies-only day at the end of the week. But I didn't want to look at mosques. From Baba's photos, the patterns and designs were beautiful, some showing Sufi influences, but I didn't want to be bombarded with religious symbolism. Perhaps unfairly, I associated mosque shapes with the limitations that bound me. And I was reminded of them every *salah,* whenever a lament loomed from the minaret loudspeakers just down the street.

It wasn't that I minded hearing *salah* five times a day. It was a spiritual and emotional speed breaker reminding me to get in touch with my own purposes and goals. What irked was the fact that everything in town came to a standstill for that time, that sincerity was expected on demand, as though that was the only way to devoutness. For that kind of sacrifice, one would think life would improve in quality with every shop closing. But did it? Couldn't prayer be carried through daily life, even into work? Even though this system claimed to be a model for all Islamic countries, other Muslim nations followed their own consciences.

So looking at mini-mosques was out. I tried to work on my Spice Souk painting, but I had only brown, yellow and white paint with me. I had lent the rest of my colors to a neighbor child who'd had a wisdom tooth extracted and needed the distraction. I really wasn't in the mood for painting anyway. Feelings of disquiet reached a critical mass.

From past experience I'd learned that if I once let apathy get a grip on me, the whole day could pass in that mood. So to jumpstart my battery, I decided to go shopping, by myself, for the first time, in the Kingdom. Now, this wasn't going to be a frivolous foray just for accumulating unnecessary trappings. The Jiddah landmark stitchery needed framing and I wanted some ood to take home, too. I had heard of perfumeries at a mall ten minutes drive away and I knew where the framer was. It would take courage to go alone, though. Since Linda, my main souk buddy had left, I would have to depend on myself. Before I lost my nerve, I phoned for a limo.

The ride was uneventful—a driver with no tangle of questions on the tip of his tongue for a change. At the mall, scarfless females walked purposefully. I kept mine off, too. Two circular sets of benches had only men on them, rigid with decorum, waiting for their

Jewel Dhuru

wives. All those eyes were daunting. I gritted my teeth, prepared to run the gauntlet and went about my business.

A personable young Indian fellow in the framing shop took my order. When I finished there, I wanted to sit for a few minutes before I continued my reconnaissance for the ood. I found the only unoccupied gap in a circle of benches, sat down, pulled out paper and pen and scribbled down how I felt about this spree, as it was unfolding. When I glanced up from time to time, to look off into space and think, quizzical looks came from the males in the seats, but I was determined not to take more notice than necessary, of either approval or disapproval. This feigned indifference would be dysfunctional under normal circumstances, I thought, but after all, normal would not be the adjective I would choose to describe the circumstances of that day.

Actually, I had found a world of difference between the feelings and energy movement that sprung up in me when people walked towards me with smiley faces, as opposed to those who looked away, shepherding kids away from me or clicking their tongues. One is uplifting and one could be draining. The undertaking of maintaining composure and good humor and smiling when I wanted to anyway, was formidable. It entailed remaining centered, not getting caught up in another's personal drama and suspending defensiveness. It took conscious effort and practice to remain in charge of my own lifts and drains, but it could be done.

Mustering self-support, I intercepted scarfless women to ask the whereabouts of a perfumery. This alone took nerve, because of the aloofness among Western women. A group of three actually did help, because an ood and incense shop lay not far away.

In the perfumery, ood came in three grades. On display in the same brown battered suitcases used to transport it, it looked like bits of chopped up tree trunk. I bought a handful of the Excellent grade of Indonesian ood, for 200 SR ($50.00US) per ounce. From past experience, I knew Medium and Low grades smelled little better than charred wood. Special shops sold varieties of Cambodian ood at 3000 SR per ounce, but I didn't go there. It would have been like setting $100.00 bills alight for kindling.

Just before leaving the mall, I stopped at the entrance and looked back to see if I was forgetting anything. When two-dozen male eyes

Ala Tool

stared at me from the benches, I went out the door, pulled my scarf over my head and fled toward a taxi.

Three days later, on Thursday evening, Baba and I went back to pick up the framed stitchery. I was pleased with the work, more or less. It had lost its third dimension, as if ironed flat and the hook was on the bottom. But it would be easier to moisten and fluff up the stitches and to reposition the hook myself than to try to explain and leave it with the framer any longer.

As usual, whole families were enjoying weekend outings in the mall. I sat for a bit, gasping, because even at 9:00 PM, it was still 38^0 C. (100^0 F.). The effects were savage. Baba felt it too, but over his clothes, he wasn't wearing a full-length cloak of lead radiating heat. Before I wilted, Baba got me a cold drink. I didn't know it then, but my malaise was partly because my Hemoglobin level was dropping for medical reasons. Two months hence, it would plummet to half its normal level, but with treatment, the situation would be corrected.

All I knew then was I felt as limp as a boned fish. While I sipped my cold drink, I chatted with a Lebanese woman on the same bench and she admired my artwork. She called her husband out of the jewelry shop across the aisle, where he worked.

"Bless your hands," they both said with appreciation. I, in turn, blessed their hearts.

During my time in the Kingdom, I had completed four pieces of handiwork: two Tunisian, one Bedouin and this one of Jiddah. This was the only one I had considered selling. Somehow, I felt it belonged there, not in North America. But after this chat with these two kind people, how could I sell the piece that was the impetus for such a genuine blessing?

After my solo-shopping trip, I closed the frosted kitchen window and used the enclosure to experiment with frankincense and the ood I bought. The shopkeeper at the market provided charcoal, called Modern Coke, in the shape of wide, flat pencils, chopped flat at the ends. They were 8 x 2 ½ x 1 ½ cm. thick (3"x 1" x ½"), painted silver on the outside, presumably to keep everything they touched from getting black and sooty.

Previously, when I had burned incense, I turned off the AC in the sitting room and lit up my terra cotta pot pourri. The scent was lovely while it lasted, but the air soon became stifling, and when the AC

Jewel Dhuru

went back on, like a whisper, the scent dissipated as soon as it was produced.

But now, I could break off a fragment of charcoal pencil and turn off only the kitchen AC. It was usually warmer there anyway. Nestling the pot pourri in the sink, I lit the charcoal and breathed in the vapors, each in their turn, from Indonesian ood and four different types of frankincense. My nostrils quivering with expectation, sometimes I spritzed jasmine perfume on a piece of ood, just like they did in the shops. The intermingling of the fragrances was such a powerful assault on my senses, that first time I did it, I found it difficult to get up and do anything else. The olfactory elixir was almost intoxicating.

I sat for half an hour, watched, blew on the embers and allowed the miraculous molecules to drift about me. I couldn't have done it in the sitting room. I observed leisurely as black resin exuded from the ducts in the brown wood, formed a shiny coating and started to smolder. I watched the frankincense, one milky white, one translucent amber yellow, a third the palest sea-foam green and the last variegated in color, begin to bubble, darken and release their aroma. For some time, I became one with the aromas, with all that is natural and timeless.

I looked forward to indulging myself back home—often. The fly in the ointment was certain family members, including Baba, had allergies and were sensitive to strong smells. If I were to luxuriate in this rapture with any regularity, I would have to choose my moments.

The next morning, fragrance still lingering on the air, nothing was quite like entering the kitchen and having my senses re-delighted by whiffs of one exotic scent after another. The feelings of the day before re-kindled in my inner sanctum, the sense of wholeness and stillness while uniting my spirit with that of natural materials, all catalyzed by fire: the frankincense seeped from trees, the ood of the trees themselves, and the coal from Mother Earth.

Chapter 15: Second Wind

"When the forgetful man gets up in the morning, he reflects on what he is going to do, whereas the intelligent man sees what God is doing with him" [42]
—Ibn (Ata) Illah, 13th C. Egyptian Sufi

As June set and July dawned, Israel and Lebanon were expressly not at peace. Ocalon was found guilty and sentenced to death, India and Pakistan competed for Kashmir, conflict involving even women soldiers re-emerged between Eritrea and Ethiopia and the Irish Good Friday Peace Agreement was approaching a deadline. Before July's end, student protests in Iran would take a turn for the worse and Taiwan and China would clash over the One-China policy.

In Riyadh, as the mass exodus of assorted acquaintances and friends was underway, a few malingerers were staying until the end of the month, so there would be time to get to know them. Paul's wife, a lady whose companionship I'd previously enjoyed, lived in an African country. Elizabeth was coming to Riyadh for three weeks, and then the pair would leave together.

The day she visited, after hanging up her *abaya* and making ourselves comfortable, we talked about the affects of being splintered off from cherished relatives. Nevertheless, our mood was upbeat as Elizabeth expounded on how, in her culture, the female achieved a position of eminence, equal to but different from the male. With muffled smiles, we discussed the differences between females and males. As I walked her out, we parted on cheerful terms, having reconfirmed *who* we were on this Earth, but not even a minute passed before she was tapping at the door again. We might have known *who* we were, but both of us had forgotten *where* we were. Elizabeth's *abaya* still hung on the hook.

Other activities nudged the month along. My Spice Souk painting was still unfinished and I experimented with air-drying clay. Two graduate students asked me to edit their theses. I welcomed the distraction and was glad to help, but didn't enjoy haggling over the price of my services, especially since graduate students received salaries for being in such a program. Small wonder many did not complete the requirements in three years, some taking double the time.

In addition, the guava and orange seeds I had planted in April were just peeking through the soil surface. I had rooted a stalk of purple Wandering Jew, Baba had brought home and it was doing all right, but cuttings of bougainvillea didn't take. Our daughter phoned to say she missed my cooking and asked for a couple of recipes to hold her until I got back. By the grace of others, I had borrowed books for the last months, *The Name of the Rose*, *Foucault's Pendulum* and *Modern Arabian Short Stories* and I had access to Joseph Campbell's *The Power of Myth* cassettes. I still had my Tolkien trilogy, one of my lifelines, and couldn't help noticing how some challenges in the journey of the characters paralleled my own.

The heat anesthetized the earth. Outside air on my face felt like I'd gotten too close to a bonfire. Whenever we went out, we closed our eyes from the sting of the first waves, both coming up from the ground and descending from on high. I kept watching for airborne ashes.

Heaven and Hell

Anita and her family had expected to leave the week before for the summer, but were delayed by the non-arrival of official papers. Meanwhile, they embarked on the ambitious and backbreaking project of changing their carpeting. During the installation and its aftermath, they sent over to us, whichever children weren't helping shuffle furniture, potted plants or the tower of already packed suitcases inside their front door. This was a pleasant bonus, if a bit hectic. We left the door unlocked and the kids came in relays. First, we sang using their Karaoke microphone plugged into our boom box and then we played every game they had: Scrabble, Uno, Chess, Parchese, Rummy, Mogus and whatever else they could drag out from under their beds. This interval reminded me of a tete-a-tete with another expat teen. Among her varied topics, she began a garbled narrative about what she was taught in a Saudi school about Heaven and Hell.

On Judgment Day, she had learned, women and men together, would stand in line, but the fear would be so palpable, they wouldn't even notice they were naked. Hell meant having a sun shining very near your head while sand is rubbed into your skin. The heat from the sun burns your skin off, but you grow a second layer, complete with nerve endings, so you can still feel the heat and sand. Seven to eleven guards watch a quarter of the Earth's population, and Hell is forever. But, there is a brand on your face, in case you happened to go to Heaven later.

She continued her tale with mushrooming enthusiasm and with an expose on Heaven, which has seven levels, depending on how much of the Qur'an you have studied. The highest level, attained by studying the most, provides the ultimate shopping experience for ladies while men gain pleasure from white concubines made from clouds. Birds with wings the size of the sky fly around. Good food is everywhere, like rivers of honey and non-intoxicating wine.

The next day, a TV Sheikh spoke of The Day of Judgment. I grabbed pen and paper and scribbled it down. The grave was the first destination of the hereafter, he explained. Souls are alive but bodies vanish ... rewards and punishments are meted out ... hypocrites are tortured twice and then returned to someplace, he referred to in Arabic to be punished twice more ... drowning in flood and then burning in hell fire. Whatever their reward or punishment, what came after that would be better than a garden or worse than hell fire. My senses reeled for days.

Going-away Luncheon

I finally saw Baba's office when the crown on my tooth came loose and we chose a campus dentist to re-cement it. Afterwards, I met a few more of his colleagues. By then, we had only a few weeks left, so personal touches in his office had already been dismantled.

The week after, Baba's female Saudi graduate students gave him a going away luncheon and I was invited. In a rectangular meeting room, Baba's Dean motioned Elizabeth, Paul, Baba and I to seats near the head of a 6-meter (20-foot) long table, but our four hostesses sat at the far, unoccupied end. The event started with short speeches expressing appreciation and gratitude on both sides. The Dean expressed his thoughts, sat down and sighed deeply. Then Baba got up and shared from his heart, which was caught in his throat. Comments came to my mind that I would have liked to add, but the Dean's call for lunch came immediately after Baba sat down.

Jewel Dhuru

I was expecting the usual 'ladies first, after the men' routine at lunch and I wasn't disappointed. Baba said "See you later," as he left and went down the hall with the Dean. Actually, as a line of men filed behind my chair, one gentleman invited Elizabeth and I to come with them opening a space for us in the queue. I considered it for a moment; then looked down to the far end of the table. Seeing the shrouded bunch waiting in the corner, I knew I couldn't just go and leave my hostesses. They were the only part of my reason for being there that had not already linked up with the lunch line. I thanked him but said I'd wait. He shrugged and went on.

What had not dawned on me yet was that once the women got their food, they would have to go to their own private lunchroom down the hall. I had forgotten about their veils. So after sitting with Baba for a while, I took my plate to their room. Elizabeth followed. Baba, too, came in later, after knocking on their door and waiting for the flutter of veils to subside. Leaving aside the twists and turns of getting to that generally comfortable point in the proceedings, once I got there, I could feel the professional fellowship in the air, a kinship Baba must have enjoyed daily. I almost forgot the difficult influences engulfing us—almost. Some conditions ought not to be gotten used to, lest we forget they exist.

The next morning, despite the heat, we were planning an excursion. We wanted to see as much of the region as possible while there. We considered Istanbul, Damascus, Amman, Nairobi, Muscat and the island of Bahrain. For the last time, the coffee table was mounded with tourist information and maps.

I had begun emptying out kitchen cupboards and drawers to minimize the work after our foray. Only a couple of weeks would remain by then. Just as everything was clean, Anita's travel plans got straightened out. So before we said our fond so-longs and they left for two months, the kids brought over all their perishables, followed by boxes of non-perishables and our kitchen was full again. Fearing the bread would mold and recognizing much we'd never use up, I left it in boxes and went to the sitting room balcony to find someone who looked hungry.

I was in luck. Sweeping the stairs tight underfoot was a black bearded figure in an orange jumpsuit, with a *shmal* wrapped like a beehive atop his head. I called down to him and he motioned that he'd come up. He was Kuwaiti. As my tongue tripped over troublesome

Ala Tool

letters, he scooped up a box and toddled off, asking the usual questions on the way out. He routinely got care packages when people left. Within two minutes he was back, his hands empty, volunteering to dust our car for us. His face drooped when I said thanks but we had no car. A few days later, Baba rented one for our trip. We'd decided on Bahrain.

Gecko

Before we set off, though, we had a little excitement when I was home alone, walked into the sitting room and discovered a small 10-cm. (4") long gecko, on the ceiling. When in India, I had heard of their coming in through necessarily open windows and scurrying from one picture frame to the next, but I never actually saw one in the house. I knew this one probably wouldn't bother me if I didn't bother it. Still, I would have minded less if it had been green. But it was an embryonic pink, with green only at the eyes and internal organs. It appeared doughy and translucent. My binoculars told me its alert eyes followed my movements.

I wondered how it had gotten in and how many times it had leered overhead without my knowing it, scrutinizing our crossword or my cross-stitch. I kept an eye on my little friend as it traversed the ceiling. I struggled with the irrational thought that its sticky feet would come unglued and it would drop on me. It retreated into a corner.

When Baba returned, he urged it out of the corner with a mop while I opened the balcony door, but it didn't move towards the hot balcony door. It scuttled directly to the AC and entered the space between it and the wall and that was the last we saw of it. Although I told myself this occurrence must be common in the desert, that room didn't feel quite the same for days.

Like the sound of sanction coming from the woman at Al Habala, this is the only lizard that makes a clicking sound with its tongue. Where it ultimately went, I don't know. If I was a small creature staying in Riyadh through the summer, though, I might have lived behind an AC, too. And if this was a newborn, as Baba suspected, I could just imagine the parents.

I couldn't blame the gecko for staying inside. It was summer and going out was like walking into an oven. From 2:00 to 10:00 AM, the temperature dropped to 27^0 C. (80^0 F.) but during the day, it reached

53^0 C. (130^0 F.) and the air was suffocating. Winter floral displays were reduced to hardy souls with scorched tips and the earth had a moribund complexion.

In July, caretakers of shriveled gardens and those who dusted cars, swept and dug holes to reach our phone or electric cables, worked mostly in the dark, before 6:00 AM and again after 10:00 PM. This reminded me of the short winter days of my Canadian youth. I recalled the words a co-worker, leaving work at 4:00 PM, the sky rapidly sheathing us in shadow. With a sanguine air, my companion had said, "It's dark when we go to work and dark when we come home; it's like being in jail and they let you out for the night."

Chapter 16: Dammam and The Island State of Bahrain

"A direct and superficial examination of things does not always enable us to conclude that reality is identical with perception" [43]
—Lecomte de Nouy, *Human Destiny*

In mid-July, we embarked on another adventure, this time leaving by car at 9:00 AM for Dammam, a few hours northwest of Riyadh, on the Arabian Sea. Black tents, sheep and camel pens and pick-ups nestled in the sand off the highway, signifying that Bedouins camped there.

When a towering sand dune intersected the highway, 12 meters (45') high, we knew we'd reached the wide band of dozing Dahna Dunes. Baba wanted photos, so he pulled our Toyota Camry onto the shoulder, already criss-crossed with tracks and headed down the 14-meter (15 yard) stretch of sloping, sandy shoulder between the highway and a length of camel fencing. When the ground started to give progressively more resistance, we realized maybe those previous tracks were made by 4-wheel drive vehicles, unlike ours. Only after that did Baba the Intrepid recall a colleague's warning not to slow down in sand. Too late. We'd gone headfirst into 20 cm. (8") of soft sand. When Baba reversed, the car repeatedly stalled. With a sigh, he said, "We're in trouble."

I looked at the clock. 10:14 AM, in mid-July, the hottest month. It was already 38^0 C. (100^0 F.) and we sat in the only shade in sight—stranded. Still, we had enough gas to keep the AC running for a few hours. We had cold drinks and abundant traffic just behind us, so no need for panic. We walked around the car to discover the front wheels imbedded in 15 cm. (6"). Baba thought our best bet was to watch the highway and wave down a small truck. He told me to stay in the shade while he watched. He let cars and trucks carrying equipment go by, but within a few minutes a jeep, driven by a Saudi, edged over the horizon, so Baba started waving.

The driver pulled over and the two men talked. When the driver dragged a 2½-cm. (inch) diameter turquoise rope out of his jeep, I got out to join them.

Jewel Dhuru

"This guy wants you to speak Arabic to him," Baba appealed, gesturing towards Ali. I didn't understand every word of the first question but his meaning was unmistakable. Being a sophisticated desert traveler, Ali wanted to know something along the lines of 'why did you go down there?' He'd asked Baba the same question already and Baba's answer had been equally universally understandable, a shrug of the shoulders.

While Ali maneuvered his rope, he asked questions. In those few minutes, he learned where we were from, where we lived, that Baba taught at the university and that we weren't Muslim. While he worked, we sat in one of the Earth's most expansive sandboxes, a realization that added levity to our semi-serious situation.

Afterwards, I offered Ali a cold drink. He thanked me but showed us a cooler as full as ours on his passenger seat. Shaking both our hands warmly, we waved as he drove away. Baba explained later, that as he was waiting for the right vehicle to come by, he had visions of a group of men standing around our car, nodding, stroking their chins and discussing how to best approach the project. But I guess getting stuck was a common enough occurrence that the procedure wasn't too complicated. Ali's compassion and know how didn't hurt either.

I looked at the clock again—10:24 AM. The whole ordeal had just lasted a few minutes. Ten minutes before, we'd been humming along coolly and comfortably and now we were hot and sweaty, from both heat and anxiety. Before we left, Baba took his photographs.

A few hours later, alluring Dammam beckoned. It was smaller than Riyadh, with narrower four lane main streets and tree-lined boulevards and it was startlingly more humid. The temperature was the same 43^0 C. (110^0 F.) as Riyadh, but 90% humidity. The windows of the air-conditioned car fogged up from the outside and when wiped, moisture combined with the ever-present silt turned to streaks of murk. And when we stepped out of the car, our eyeglasses became so clouded with condensation, we stopped in mid-sidewalk, laughing while we wiped them. Drinking water didn't help us stay cool there. The air was full of water already. Only cool air alleviated lethargy and labored breathing.

From a bench by the Corniche, the ocean road, in adjacent Al Khubar, after dark, when the heat abated but the wind didn't, the oceanfront came alive. Bunches of people lay on expanses of grass, picnicking, carrying snacks from concession stands and resting

Ala Tool

between rides with kids at the amusement parks. Several women wore *abayas* and veils but some did not and the sense of urgency and roughness I felt or imagined elsewhere had vanished. It was like a different world, but the still abundant blackness of garb reminded us of where we were. We sat enjoying the green hue of the water and photographing long-beaked terns winging back and forth, inspecting the flotsam and jetsam.

While in the vicinity, Bahrain, across the 20-km. (12 1/2-mile) King Fahd Causeway beckoned. Clearing Customs took half an hour on a man made island halfway across. Once there, the atmosphere was still more relaxed. But it was not until we set eyes on diminutive alcohol bottles in the hotel mini-bar that we knew we really were in a different country.

Bahrain

Baba and I searched for historical places to explore and we weren't disappointed. In the capital city, Manama, Bahrain Fort displayed seven layers of occupation beginning in 2800 B.C. with the Sumerian culture, their civilization called Dilmum. Next a Portuguese fortress had been constructed, then Kassite and Assyrian buildings dating from 1500 to 500 B.C., an alleged Hellenistic settlement of which there are no remains, but archeologists seem to know it existed anyway, an 11th century Islamic Fort and more mid 16th century Portuguese ruins. The best part was, near the miniscule guardhouse, a friendly, though mangy looking guard dog lay down belly up, jiggling as if he was having a seizure and hoping to be petted.

In and around Manama and connected Muharraq Island, pre-electricity ACs, wind towers for cooling, still rose above decrepit buildings. A museum video depicted the history of pearl diving and locally built dhous on the beach were the fragile wooden boats that are to the African coast what junks are to the Chinese. Burial mounds, some excavated, prevalent before Islam, were all over. On the outskirts, craftsmen demonstrated clay pot making and cloth weaving.

Jazra House, built in 1907, of mainly ground up coral and gypsum with palm trunks in the walls for added strength, was the birthplace of the current emir, Shaikh Isa Bin Salaman Al Khalifa. After a quick look, I had returned to the car while Baba climbed up to the terrace and photographed. After a few minutes, he returned chatting with a

Jewel Dhuru

Muslim guard. I braced myself for the usual stiffness. Instead, upon seeing me, the guard plucked a handful of ripe dates from a palm and gave them to Baba for me, along with a handful of herbs pinched from the garden. Baba readily passed along the yellow dates, full and succulent. The most refreshing part of the exchange was that none of the three of us saw anything improper in his actions.

Baba walked through Al-Fatih Mosque, the largest island building. Then, we headed out of Manama, to the island's southern part. There flourishes an enormous lone tree, marooned in only sand for miles around. One theory was that of four rivers named in the Bible, only three can still be found today. The fourth went underground and feeds that very tree. A party of a dozen picnickers on a blanket could spaciously lunched in the shade under the branches of only one side of the tree. This story about Bahrain being part of the Garden of Eden was fascinating.

The main differences between these two countries were no *abayas* for non-Muslims and women actually drove, driving being more disciplined overall. Shops didn't close during *salah*. Probably just my imagination, but even the air smelled freer. People weren't overly friendly, but at least no one stared. But in both Saudi Arabia and Bahrain, the price of gas had doubled since our March trip; now it was 90 halalas/liter (about $0.25 US/gallon) One SR equaled 100 halalas.

As we crossed the causeway back to Dammam, sudden spattering on our windows drew our attention to the wind. In the distance, a whirlwind of sand was whipped up and circulated while another burst of the grainy stuff was being blown from one side of the road to the other. Irregular, shifting lines materialized on the road in front of us like the beginnings of a snowdrift.

A few miles from Dammam, particularly intriguing peach colored dunes, as smooth as ice cream cones, bore investigation. Trudging through them and listening to the wind sigh softly, I felt as though I could tell the shape of the winds by the impressions, streams and ripples they left on the dunes. Baba sat atop a 1½-meter (4-foot) ridge and kicked his heels into the top edge. Fine grains flowed down in rivulets, like liquid glass making small pools in a valley at my feet.

The short jaunt to that 600 sq. km. (about 235 sq. mile) island dispelled half the murky atmosphere from the land next door. In Bahrain, I was broken of the habit of thinking I needed to cover my person with a black cloak whenever I went out my door. With only twelve days left in Riyadh before I headed for home, I was determined not to lose my half restored sense of freedom. It meant walking a narrow ridge, being true to myself while getting along with the ways of the founding fathers, without falling into unhealthy habits of one extreme or another.

Chapter 17: Winding Down

"We have left the rest behind one after another ... almost like a dream that has slowly faded" [44]
—Frodo in The *Return of the King*

Back in Riyadh, in July 1999, the picture was changing. Before our short excursion, tens of other campus residents had been asking Baba if we had anything to sell before we left the Kingdom. He'd responded in the negative. What could they have wanted, we wondered. Our clothes? Our souvenirs? Through miscommunication, we had the misapprehension, for nine out of ten months that our furnishings and appliances were provided by the university and were to be left behind when we parted. But the light bulb finally came on.

"No, no," friends declared emphatically, one after the other. "Your furniture was bought using the housing allowance the university gives you. It's yours to sell."

They did us a great service. I cast my mind back to the early months. We'd learned a lot from neighbors. The kindnesses we'd been blessed with from absolute strangers in the first weeks were heart warming. They came primarily from expats, because they knew the hazards of starting out on this bit of Earth.

Collectively we were like small crafts, having temporary clearance to moor in foreign waters, huddling together for strength and companionship, all in the same global boat, taking pleasure in the diversity in our characters and the ever-changing view. By the tenth month, we were grateful to many more. Our harbor bore sudden influxes and times of dwindling populations. Through it all, we entertained each other and created shared histories.

So at this eleventh hour, ten days before we left for Bahrain, Baba posted ads to sell everything. Then the phone started to ring. While I was packing for both our getaway and my eventual homecoming, I showed scores of people through every room, which was in a perennial state of disarray. We managed to sell half of it, before leaving for the five days. I could have sold the TV, phone/fax machine and washer many times over. Less imperative items, apparently, like the fridge, stove and even the bed, would take longer.

Ala Tool

It was so good to get away from the phone for a while. But when we got back, the situation became compounded. Shopping and frenzied bartering had almost been elevated to the status of a religion. The ad deliberately gave only our phone number because we wanted people to call before coming. But when our phone went unanswered for days, prospective customers had only to give the Housing Office our number to procure our address. People started turning up at the door, bartering skills polished to a sheen.

Those days were a blur. I often ordered tantalizing boneless chicken wrapped in Arab bread called chicken *schwarma*, sesame *tahina* and *tabouli*, a salad, to be delivered from the campus restaurant, because there was no time to cook. Finally, almost everything was sold and the day of my departure was chosen, three weeks hence, a week before Baba. Baba would lecture and visit family, both in India, for a few weeks first.

I wouldn't be there to share his winding down and closing up activities but I had to look forward. I knew he would finish cleaning and distributing odds and ends to other expats.

Uneducated laborers, primarily Bangladeshi, doing taxing jobs for meager salaries, 300 SR, ($75.00 US) a month, would get their share of the spoils. The disparity between their salaries and that of professionals was astounding. They were welcome to our incidentals: a can opener, extra knives, curtains and leftover food. They endured crowded dorms, inadequate meals and daily bussing to and from job sites, just to earn money to send to their families. Seeing them on the road, huddled in small open-backed trucks, I cringed whenever a truck hit a bump.

I considered why uneducated expats volunteered for such work. I knew they sent their salaries home to pay for their wives and children's upkeep. In fact, because their homelands lacked jobs, laborers paid more than they could afford to their local employment agents just so they could work in the Kingdom. The system seemed to work until periodic fluctuations in Saudi economics caused employers to withhold salaries. That, coupled with passports, and sometimes *Iqamas*, also being withheld by the employer, made a sad combination. Still, the spirit with which some accepted their alleged lot in life, shining through sad smiles, was inspirational.

Ironically, they generously donated their energy and time. Some taxi drivers, bread makers and shoe repairers wouldn't accept payment

Jewel Dhuru

from Baba and offered him cold drinks instead, in appreciation of his courtesy. We envisioned the fortresses of the Incas being built on the strong backs of assimilated peoples. One thing was certain. We were in the Kingdom by invitation only.

This chapter of our lives was closing. Just as life had started nine months before—no phone, email, friendly neighbors, or radio, and only one TV station—so it was becoming again. The only movies were temporarily pre-empted by the death of Morocco's King Hassan. When a Muslim monarch died, all Islamic countries mourned for three days. In Riyadh, even soccer was pre-empted. Instead, only excerpts from the Qur'an and their translations all day—for three days.

One by one, the variety of our activities narrowed. Our printer died so no more letters and no more editing leisurely on hard copies. Then a principal computer program became corrupted so even typing ceased. No email from home either, only through Baba's office again.

Pictures came down off the wall and kitchen cupboards, were given away or repacked. We kept just enough household supplies for Baba's last week. Just as we'd acquired things through purchase or gift, everything would find a new home. The homey look we'd created was dispersing, but the feel didn't. This had been our home for ten months and I'd never forget it.

The last week, Tolkien's *The Return of the King* became a constant companion. I took the trilogy traveling as a refuge from reality. I reveled in the facets of the journey. Bought second hand, I intended to reread and bestow them on someone there and I finally found a candidate for the handing-down ritual. Paul had agreed to take them. Having finished the borrowed books, I was soaking up 40 pages of Tolkien a day in order to finish on time.

Some days I did little besides pack, sell furniture, make meals and read. Sometimes I forgot to look out the window or at the plants, perhaps detaching from these features of my life, too. The view would be history soon anyway and the plants, given away. The gardenia that had lost every leaf grew a whole new set.

The last time 'Mr. Wrong Number' called, two weeks before he left for his wedding, we got our signals crossed. We had a visitor when the phone rang, but I wanted to say good-bye and wish him well anyway. He seemed to feel he was intruding so he rung off quickly. Suddenly—click—he was gone. That was the last time we spoke.

Ala Tool

Shoppers who came to our whole-flat rummage sale were rather memorable. Ninety-five percent of the scavengers were male, from a variety of backgrounds: Jordan, Syria, Sudan, South Africa, Afghanistan, Bangladesh and Egypt. But two women left their marks.

One Saudi, who didn't speak English, accompanied two Filipinas who did. When I opened the door, she was veiled and hesitated in the hall until I announced to Baba, who was typing in the dining room, that she was coming in to look at the gas stove. Baba promised to stay where he was, but his voice floated into the kitchen as he continued to comment. At first, the woman rested her veil on top of her head as she scrutinized the stove, the cooker, as they called it. She split her attention between examining it and monitoring Baba's movements. His voice changed pitch as he alternately paced and hovered uncomfortably in the dining room doorway, engaging in long-distance barter. Her eyes looked harried, like a small, frightened bird's.

She reminded me of the haunted, guilty look on the face of the female lead in the movie *The Quiet Man*, when this Irish girl and her beau escaped their chaperone, took an illicit walk together and the heavens seemed to cut loose their wrath with gales, lightning and thunder. My potential buyer was so skittish about Baba's possibly entering the kitchen at any moment, she eventually gave up and lowered her veil for the remainder of the proceedings.

The second female was Sudanese and had a cheerful demeanor. Accompanied by two children, she announced proudly she was expecting her sixth. She was energetic, fluttering from room to room, asking the price of everything in sight. I wondered how and where she lived that she was so enamored with our humble digs. When she inquired about our plants and wall-to-wall pale flamingo carpeting, I had to ask. She said they lived in an older building on the same campus. Then her rather gruff husband arrived and ultimately, they didn't buy anything.

One Saudi male came with a Filipino friend, his spokesperson and negotiator. The Saudi averted his gaze from my face, but my peripheral vision told me he sometimes turned to me with a jerk when I answered the Filipino's questions about the fridge and singsong washer.

The most unforgettable, battery-charging shopping visit, though, was with four Filipinas. Friends of Anita's, they had come,

Jewel Dhuru

supposedly, to purchase kitchenware, pots and pans, mugs and cutlery. But they dispensed with the subject within two minutes.

"We'll take everything," they said. Then we proceeded to have a lovely chat about backgrounds and families, steeping in the sounds of collective laughter.

"Oh, you talk just like the British lady who used to live in the next building," they twittered and continued with "it's too bad we didn't meet sooner."

High praise indeed. We'd just learned that week that the sweet British female friend had passed on in England three weeks earlier. She was already seriously ill when I first met her in Riyadh but her gentle voice never lost its calm. Back in December, she had given me fruitcake, a candle and a small raffia star that I still keep. Her spirit, example and goodwill endure.

Frequent, rapid changes affected my mood. Sometimes I felt heartsick with sadness and disappointment. And sometimes, poignant elation came from facing fear and accomplishing what I never thought I could or that accompanies incremental increases in courage.

Through the last weeks, I remained submerged in *The Return of the King*. As my own tension mounted, my companions were the peoples of fictional lands, struggling to overcome life's obstacles and to maintain inner tranquility. The ethereal, illusionary aspects of what we call real life were brought into focus. The book followed travelers on a journey. Whatever challenges I faced then, the subliminally spiritual sections spotlighted them, too. At times, my anxiety was exacerbated and sometimes, welcome respite was the result.

As the last days crawled along, I raced towards the end of the book. The characters faced final challenges and were homeward bound and I also prepared to make the far-from-seamless transition from my new life to the current shape of my old one. The characters went home changed, the landlord of the inn commenting that they "looked like folk as can deal with troubles out of hand." [45] The members of the group had supported and protected each other. As they approached forks in the roads, just as in our lives, one more went his separate way.

Coincidentally, the year Tolkien's travelers returned to Middle Earth was 1420. Incredibly, I left the Middle East on August 1, 1999, otherwise known as the 17th of the month of Rabi II in the year **1420, *Hejera*.** The number fairly jumped off the page at me and I mentally filed it away for future reference. Frodo's ending admonition to Sam was good for me, too:

"You cannot always be torn in two. You will have to be one and whole, for many years." [46]

Chapter 18: Loosening Arabia's Grip

"We must love them both—those whose opinions we share, those whose opinions we don't share. They've both labored in the search for truth and have helped us in finding it" [47]
—Thomas Aquinas

On August 1, as my flight grappled with gravity's grip, I contemplated what I was leaving behind. No more *abaya* and only 18 hours before I could jump into my car and drive, but also no more poetic verse in Arabic or Camel Souk. I felt a healthy tugging at my heart, pulling in two directions at once, signaling that I had not wasted ten months of my life. I had derived joy while enduring discomfort and learning difficult lessons.

I was on my way home. North American concerns that had temporarily faded into the distance while I lived under an enchanted spell, would become all too real again soon, as I awoke. But they would be mixed with sweetness.

My last week in Saudi Arabia, I contemplated what I would miss and what I would gladly relegate to the past. It was poignant when Baba went to the Supermarket for the last time, brought the last guavas and shish kabobs. And perhaps the last take-out chicken shawarmas and fresh pomegranate-mulberry juices from Mama Noura tasted best. Something akin to nostalgia caught in my throat as the last gas cylinder and 20-liter bottle of water were delivered.

However, I don't miss those sand grains that wriggled so deeply into light sockets, that when the bulb burned out, often both socket and bulb had to be replaced. Much as I liked my little kitchen, I won't miss the claustrophobic feeling of walking into a box when the opaque window had to be closed for religious or meteorological reasons. Still, my ood and frankincense experience more than compensated. I do not miss the lack of variety in music, having to hush impulsive laughter in public, the absence of friendly and affectionate dogs and being necessarily restricted by the budget, phone access to my closest friends.

I did miss, however, the office chair I rolled around the kitchen in, from my low gas stove to my low refrigerator. Everything was low: chairs, tables, the cupboards, and the bed—in Bedouin fashion. If I had been compelled to cook standing up, a chronic crouch would have resulted. Even though I love my comparatively lush Midwestern back yard and more spacious house, this Middle East chapter in my life had its own merits. I missed the flat's compactness. We miss the 99% mildew-free bathroom and the dry cleaners that laundered and pressed a shirt or pair of pants for 2 SR (less than $0.50 US).

We miss the ethnic restaurants and intercultural neighborhood, having access to varied educational and cultural expertise at our fingertips. Perhaps, only a country is at this stage of professional development could provide such an environment, however transient. I miss the contact with a variety of languages at once, associations with people who are not embarrassed to attempt a foreign name and people to whom one can use an untranslatable descriptive word without having to explain it. And our shot, strong flat cleaner, Munawer, who hoovered, dusted and washed the whole flat once in fortnight for the equivalent of $13.00 (50 SR) was a treasure. He was Bangladeshi and had a wife and son there. He was so thorough, we had to shoo him out. After we thought the bathroom and kitchen looked spotless, he was still washing the walls.

The way we conversed with him was unique. Munawer spoke Bangla, Urdu, Hindi, some Arabic and strategic words of English. Baba spoke *Marathi*, his mother tongue and Hindi. When I talked to Munawer, we used Arabic with the odd English word thrown in. When all three talked together, we switched back and forth, Baba and I checking meanings in English. We usually got more from the non-verbal than from the words, and few misunderstandings occurred. There's something about not having a verbal language in common that keeps barriers down. As we look to the non-verbal for intent and feeling, our humanity can become accentuated.

The sounds of neighbors moving around in the halls and under the balcony were comforting. I miss the activity outside the sitting room balcony, our Midwest home being on a pleasant, but less frequented street. I miss being able to wander in an open-air souk, spanning several blocks. We miss the low crime rate. Crime is so severely punished there, I felt safe setting my black bag down on a counter in a shop, wandering for a few minutes and coming back to pick it up later. It hadn't moved. Before returning the rented car after our Hajj trip, we aired it out in the parking lot for a ½-hour, doors wide open, while we were up in the flat and no one had touched it. The little crime that exists is not talked about openly. Officially, executions are announced on the News for serious crimes, like murder, drug smuggling and repeated child molestation, to name three, crimes that "threaten the civility and safety of the country."

Besides the bread shop, Baba misses laughter with other expats at lunch in the cafeteria. It was a bonding and stress-relieving time of day. Their mirth was voluntarily muted by looks from the natives, but even so, at times Saudis actively asked the group to be quiet. We were not to know then that many who had the technological capacity to keep in touch were not to do so. Still, we served as mirrors for each other, providing the feedback that refines, the information about self that develops depth and integrity and makes an examined life worth living.

We were taking treasures home with us. Aside from my prison pallor from rarely being out in the sun, from Abha a brass Aladdin's lamp, actually pronounced Ala ad-din', was stowed away. A silver dagger and leather belt, a silver necklace with indigenous semi-precious stones, little camel bone boxes, weavings copying the designs and material of Bedouin tents, batiks from Bali and handmade clay pots with coral shells stuck on the outside, from Bahrain, were to fill our cases. Frankincense, ood, and a Saudi incense burner followed. An inlaid wood chess set lay beside fabrics and laces. Linda gave me a transparent blue gown with a train and so much gold embroidery on it that it actually felt leaden. Worn on festive occasions over an *abaya,* it was the female counterpart to the ceremonial sword, given to males as parting gifts.

I had completed three paintings, Symbols of Saudi Arabia, Arab Impressions and Spice Souk. And I had completed four stitcheries: two of Tunisian design, one Bedouin and the building facades in Jiddah. A fifth, in rich earth tones, a wide, rustic wooden door of traditional design, with iron hinges and latch, set in a stone wall, was unfinished. This project was intended to get me through hours of awkward inactivity during the last weeks and at airports. From air-drying clay, Tunisian design tiles were carefully wrapped.

We reminisced about good and not-so-good times. We had not visited a Saudi farm. Qassim, north of Dammam, was called the breadbasket of the desert and might have been fun. We had not been on a desert camping trip, on which guided groups searched for fossils and diamonds and admired rock formations by day and the sickle moon by night, then slept on camp beds with metal legs to discourage snakes and scorpions. We had not seen the archeological site at remote Madain Saleh. And purportedly friendlier Jiddah, the alleged burial place of Eve, would have to remain unexplored. It had been, at different times, frustrating and fascinating, infuriating and heart-warming. Little did I know what twists life had in store.

Groundhog Day

Groundhog Day? I looked out the window at palms and playgrounds. It wasn't even February. Why was that phrase repeatedly ticker taping through my mind?

By the time we were ready to leave, we'd spent 300 days and Arabian nights in the Kingdom of Saudi Arabia. At times, I would ask myself how many times I had to endure the askance glances, feelings of distrust, distance and disunity. And the answer was, just like in the movie *Groundhog Day*—until I got it right. Until I stopped judging, pre-conceiving and started to actually enjoy the process of being in this land and with these people that God made.

Travel is an education. So what did I learn from this journey?

- I learned that I fashion my own destiny to a great extent, that I must either be a self-starter or fall prey to isolation and depression. I had mellowed, becoming more at peace with my own thoughts and accommodating of the beliefs of others. While surrounded by historically warlike nations, I found a peaceful attitude is one I had to work at preserving. I delight more now in genuine courtesy, from the heart, and gentleness in relationships, especially between husbands and wives and in women's caring for each other. Hardships borne in the Arab desert must not have been for nothing.
- I felt especially grateful I had been born Canadian and spent my formative years there. The unifying event for early Canadians was the construction of the railroad, not a war or coup. Sadly, the railway just made it easier to nudge the original inhabitants onto reservations. Ironically, as I worked on this chapter in 1999, a controversy had sprung up, over, of all things, the replacement of the Peace Bridge, which connects Canada and the United States.

That singular topic was monopolizing radio broadcasts on both sides of the border. And so life goes. At times I burst into laughter at the absurdity of it all—so many forces tugging in their own directions, but all contributing to the same unstable stability.

- Regardless of what goes on around me, no one can disgrace, insult or belittle me unless I buy into the mistaken belief that they have the power to do so in the first place. Concerning personhood, I am a human being first and as such, share a bond with all other humans. After that, I derive joy from connections to groups—familial, national and numerous others, in my own subjective order—after the first human allegiance.
- I became more intimately acquainted with the subtleties of
  - fear—dis-ease and the feeling of impending hurt;
  - anger—resentment, frustration and disappointment;
  - sadness—loneliness and loss, and
  - happiness—gratitude, a feeling of privilege and contentment.

Over the duration, I had felt all of these, and more.

- I answered for my behavior, thoughts, words and choices to a higher power than anyone on this planet, so became less affected by the fear permeating the atmosphere and less attached to people and places. Beginning relationships with an attitude of detachment freed me to put more of my real self into exchanges and to express genuine feeling without embarrassment or burdening the relationship with my fear of painful parting. I could let others get close enough to touch my heart without the fear of withdrawal. And despite what I miss when I allow myself to dwell on it, I welcome living in the here and now. I enjoy the down-to-earth style of Colonel Sherman Potter on M.A.S.H. when he says, "If you ain't where you are, you're no place."
- Perhaps the lessons of that sojourn were meant to be applied to what really mattered most to me in life—family and home.

- When natural human impulses are prohibited and no reasonable alternative outlet is provided, subterfuge increases.
- And, when a serene nature is provoked or demeaned, it takes thought, self-control, self-confidence and self-support, uniting head and heart, to choose assertiveness over aggression.

The difficulty in leaving Saudi Arabia, from which I had mixed memories, was not that I would never be able to go back. The difficulty is some experiences change everything. In tandem with hardships I tried to leave behind, kind strangers whose names I never knew touched my soul. I shared looks with them that originated from somewhere beyond the hurt, looks that had such depth, they connected me to all humankind. To use words to describe the feeling would be like trying to make music by tapping a rusty spoon on a cracked teapot. My confused heart proved more elastic than I thought possible. But with the increased elasticity came more questions and gaps in understanding. Mixed feelings continued but at an advanced level. If I felt disengaged and disoriented ten months earlier, the rubber band had not yet reached full capacity. Perhaps to cherish and apply what I learned and to draw on the support of memories will have to suffice. Perhaps that is for the best.

I needn't have fretted. Just as the groundhog eventually wakes to spring and new growth, with or without six more weeks of slumber, future springs and chapters were in store for me, too.

Chapter 19: Home Is In The Heart

"We are led to believe a lie when we look with, not through, the eye that is born in the night to perish in the night while the spirit sleeps in beams of light" [48]
—William Blake

Baba secured umpteen clearance signatures for his departure with few flare-ups. Nothing, however, that the customary walking out of one office and right into one of a higher power couldn't rectify. When in Rome …

Tell Them What They Want To Hear

The last week of July 1999, I was touched by more intended hospitality. The first was a courtesy from the airlines. In keeping with airline policy, I could check in my bags and pick up a boarding pass the day before the flight with the idea of just sailing right into my seat the next day. As long as Baba didn't mind doing it the day before, it saved me the hassle. But then an airlines employee told me on the phone I could check my luggage through to Wisconsin and go through Customs there, even though I had a connection in New York. This seemed unlikely.

Calling back to verify this with someone else, I gave my confirmation number:

"D-Delta, J-Jiddah, S-Saudi, T-Tea, FF-double Fox."

"Yes, Madame, No problem, *Mafee mishkole*, check through to Milwaukee."

I asked Baba to inquire again when he took my bags to the airport. If it was true, it was comforting to think I could tackle Customs just on one side of a wall where my family waited for me on the other. I never knew, with Customs, if I would glide through without opening a bag or have every cranny and corner inspected.

At the airport, they guaranteed Baba anew and as their assurance, gave him appropriately demarcated baggage tags stapled to my ticket jacket. Whether they just didn't know the rules and really believed what they said, or another case of the old 'tell them what they want to hear' syndrome, I may never know, but at JFK, it was emphatically

Ala Tool

expressed that before we entered the airport at large, we were going to clear Customs, baggage tags or not, and so I did.

The other variation of hospitality occurred while on the 11-hour flight home. I sat in a window seat and a slim Saudi man with a goatee, wearing Western clothes, sat on the aisle, with an empty seat between us. He played video games and I read. We began to talk. The dialogue, in spurts, did not follow the typical pattern. He was in International Business and had been to 20 plus countries. He was educated and seemed somewhat open-minded. We shared the number, gender and ages of our children. We conversed guardedly about what we each liked and even disliked about each other's cultures. When asked to name one thing I disliked, I took the plunge.

"Being surrounded by fear," was my candid response.

"No religion" was his.

Gaining some respect for this gentleman before we disembarked, I told him if he ever came to my city, he was welcome to phone and I passed him a card with our names and address on it. He bore with me as I pronounced the names.

"My home is your home" he reciprocated. I thanked him but noticed he had not yet offered even his name. Just before disembarking, in response to a garbled loudspeaker announcement about Customs, we brought out tickets and boarding passes to see how far our bags were checked. As we compared notes, I caught a glimpse of his name on the ticket, just as he would have been able to verify mine. We wished each other well, but neither of us offered our hands. He got up to leave and that was the last I ever saw of him.

Home?

Most New Yorkers were in summer clothes. I was in long slacks and sleeves and with a black scarf wrapped around my neck. Nothing in the Qur'an required an *abaya*, which I had doffed at the airport and slung over Baba's shoulder. Since covering the hair is mentioned, over Saudi air space, keeping a scarf handy was prudent. It was handy, too, because it was overcast and 21^0 C. (70^0 F.) in New York. To me, the air felt cool. Having just arrived from months in the desert, I used my scarf as a shawl to keep the chill away while I sat under blowing ACs in the terminal for 2 1/2 hours. My family picked me up and I finally replaced the virtual hugs, on which I had subsisted, with the actual, down to earth, warm-bodied variety.

We exchanged stories all the way home and continued the narratives right into our blue and beige living room, a sight for tired eyes. Suitcases were opened, items distributed and displayed and then everybody went home. Eventually, just our son remained with me and the dust began to settle.

The morning after my arrival, my back yard had the most wonderfully earthy scent, the aroma of moist, green things growing. Like frankincense and ood, it was intoxicating. I sat in my dew laden patio chaise and absorbed the pristine water. I drank in the piercing whistles of bright red cardinals and the clicking claws of baby squirrels chasing each other around the weeping willow trunk. Nothing was quite like reclining in my chaise to give the feeling that all is right with the world. Indeed, it was like being in a Wodehouse novel where absent-minded Lord Emsworth blundered through life, but somehow everything turned out all right anyway.

The joy and relief of being back was mixed with a nagging feeling of bereavement, like something significant was missing. It wasn't Baba because we'd been separated before. I had just spoken to him the last evening and he would be home soon. No, it was that sad feeling of loss. I was here; I was not there. I could not interact anymore with what had for ten months become familiar. No matter how I justified and rationalized, an empty spot bubbled in my heart. Travel brought personal enrichment, but the nature of life is to change, and I could never recover those exact times, or precise relationships or feelings. I had to commit myself to going on, forward, *a la tool*, wherever that led me.

Trying to recapture what was eventually gave way to holding with open hands. When I reentered the house after charging up my battery in the yard, I faced the mountains and molehills that needed attention. To avert overload, I flitted from living room to dining room to family room to kitchen, from desk to computer to table to phone to suitcases, going around and around dealing with the most pressing affairs first. I had already distributed the perishable Arab bread Baba sent for the kids, so I caught up on their urgent news, got out letters that needed mailing, got myself a snack, made a few phone calls, and thought about getting some sleep. I postponed burning incense because of family allergies but to keep stable, I still did my breathwork.

A poignant companion those first days was a talking wristwatch given by a colleague of Baba's. The Hers half of His-and-Hers watches announced the time every hour from its spot on the coffee table. The colleague had laughed at the idea of our being reminded of his friendship every hour. The timepiece took me right back to the Riyadh sitting room whenever the little voice told me the time. After a week, Baba had packed up, left the flat and gone to India and my split body experience began to lessen. That feeling of having one foot on each continent and my head in the clouds was less frequent. I could still cast my mind back to the way the flat used to look but by now all the furniture had been sold and moved out. Whatever feelings of home I'd had there, they were not in the flat anymore. They were within me.

Dwelling on the past was curtailed when the getting re-acquainted inspection of the house and yard began. I had traded my ceiling gecko for wasps nesting in a chipped cinder block on the outside basement wall. So much demanded my attention, my habit before the trip, of gazing out the kitchen window and relaxing into the view of a bird feeder and birdbath was all but extinguished. It would have to re-evolve. I felt disoriented, putting the stuff of suitcases away. Small packages of office supplies, which I had anticipated using, but didn't even open, were redirected to a desk drawer. Oddly, I felt like I had just packed them up the week before. I asked myself if I'd ever really been anywhere at all.

By the time I had been home for two weeks, some things had fallen nicely into place, but others had not. Home? Where was that anyway? Home had increasingly become within me. I was sleeping nights again and even the waves of sudden mid-afternoon fatigue had passed. Immediate business had been dealt with and the suitcases were once more empty and cocooned in plastic in the basement.

A large armload of papers, however, still needed sorting out and putting away. They sat on my oak desk in one corner of the earth-toned family room as if they were glued to the spot. What was disturbing was that although other jobs were speedily dispatched, I resisted tackling this one. The very sight of those pages seemed overwhelming. When I actually sat down to look at them, I didn't know where to begin. I perused already overstuffed shelves, but knew lack of space wasn't the barrier. The difficulty stemmed from the nature of the papers themselves.

- An envelope of Arab articles about delicate cultural and political subjects,
   - like the official statement that there were no foreign troops on Saudi soil,
   - like what happened to the Saudi women who planned to drive and were caught,
   - like the article about American women in a harem.

They were fascinating to expats but now that I was back, what was I to do with them?

- A children's newspaper with *Ramadan* and Hajj activities might interest educators.
- Miniaturized copies of documents were valuable on the trip, but had served their purpose. Still, I was reluctant to discard them. If we traveled again in a year or two, updating them would be easier than starting all over. In the interim, where to keep them?
- I cherished the cards and letters we'd received, but couldn't keep them all. Rana and Anita's kids liked the stamps and snowy picture cards, but special missives did return with me.
- My Arabic notes lay unopened since my return. Proficiency would lessen with disuse, but I had not seen an Arabic speaker for two weeks and really didn't have time to contact one right then. Still, if I didn't keep the notes in plain view, their importance would fade. So they sat.
- Pictures adorning Riyadh's kitchen didn't fit in the Midwest kitchen but keeping or giving them away would require thought as to where, to whom and why. Meanwhile, they also sat.

From time to time, I laboriously chipped away at the pile. I was slowly settling in, but I knew things would never be the same. I was not the same; I had changed, expanded my awareness. My choices were altered. I continued to postpone the final dispersal.

And another issue niggled at me. Before purchasing my black travel bag, I rarely wore black, but I selected this bag to go with the black *abaya* I knew I was going to buy in Riyadh. It had become a symbol of mobility where immobility was the norm. It was like a survival pack. I put the now empty bag in my bedroom closet, but after not even a whole day, out it came again. Putting it away put a premature period to a journey that was far from over. The adjustments of returning to this home were just beginning and I needed to keep the bag nearby, to bridge the gap between the two continents and cultures. More and more, I was carrying within me the ability to feel at home anywhere. That short era had passed, but not without lasting impact. Eventually, the bag rested in the depths of our front closet.

I had become quite unaccustomed to the excessive violence and sex on TV and did not miss commercials, either. But I hit the jackpot when it came to PBS. They were fund-raising, featuring the best programs: theatre, music, horticulture, wildlife and intelligent comedies. I reveled in it, vicariously revisiting dearly missed settings, artists, compositions and characters.

I sought out the only Arabic program, one meager hour a week. As conversations zipped along at the speed of natives, I recognized merely words. But what manner of Arab culture was this? Men, women and children gathered in the same room for activities. Arab Fest on a lake highlighted varied and free behavior associated with the beautiful Arabic language, but somehow it now surprised me. Interviews occurred between Egyptian male human beings and female ones. And even a fashion show with smiling, fully clothed, tastefully and colorfully clad young women. What a treat!

Baba's Arrival

A month after my arrival, Baba returned with stories, questions, luggage and fatigue. When he returned from India, his Saudi issued ticket compelled him to stop in Riyadh for 8 hours. He'd planned to visit pals, but with a visa no longer, the officials wouldn't let him out of the airport. The three 2/3 x 2/3 x 1 meter (about 24"x24"x36") cargo boxes of belongings, souvenirs, photographs, textbooks and notes he'd shipped home had arrived before him. The kids and I had started on the top layers and after doing as much as we could, we pushed the lot into a corner by the back door and the cartons sat.

But, Baba was back. He and I were temporarily out of sync, again. I was long over my jet lag and he was just starting his. Ebb and flow. Still trying to restore my version of order, he brought more bags to unpack, more photographs to see and gifts from people I had not met. Officially, he was due back at work immediately, so with things still in disarray, off he went. Re-establishing relationships with the kids and neighbors would wait.

Reconstituted fatigue and frenzy eventually gave way to controlled chaos. The scattered feeling lessened, but then the old burden of coping with cooler weather was added. Re-acquainting ourselves with the activities and developments of adult children and our still relatively new son-in-law wasn't easy, but it was invigorating to evolve new patterns in the household to accommodate all. Responsibilities would have to be restructured. Deliberations and collaboration began on how to re-organize our effects and time and where and how to store and make use of these 1000 photographs.

Gradually, humor that is a luxury when one is bombarded with decision and information overload crept back into conversations. Quiet, subtle comments that flew over our heads when we were overworked or distracted began to re-engage. Then, optional activities restarted, the kind that aren't pressing but that improve the quality of life. Baba perused digital camera catalogs and began work on a private project in the basement. I baked goodies for the family again and signed up for a monthly spiritual psychology class, with daily inner homework to do.

Things were shaping and clearing up. Then, one day, in September, in the den upstairs, Baba dug up a forgotten packet of papers: Saudi electric and phone bills, take-out menus in Arabic and English, a list of acquaintances' phone numbers and other palaver. As I rustled the pages, an enchanted satchel opened and a spicy mustiness wafted on the air. I indulged myself with deep breaths. Scent, being a powerful memory-evoking substance, mental souvenirs encapsulated me, like a 360^0 theater in a dome.

Sand and scorch came flooding back along with spices and chicken kebabs on the cooker, along with the glow of our little flat, the shapes of light fixtures, the sounds of talks and peals of laughter on the phone, the taste of *schwarma, humus* and Arab bread and the itchiness of the dry air. I wasn't to know it then but these weren't to remain merely memories of times gone by.

Such reminiscences could also be triggered by the sight of someone standing on a street corner cloaked in black. When a lone male voice drifted in through the window with other city sounds, my mind clouded with scenes of minarets and lines of men in white going to pray. Likewise I expected all the shops to shut when a squeaky refrigerator door let out an elongated whine that started softly and built to a crescendo.

After three months at home, we were, again, smearing oil on skins, this time as a shield against chilly weather. Some semblance of a routine had been restored but there had been changes, too. For Christmas, our daughter and son-in-law were off on an excursion of their own, so Christmas would be simple this year and I was back to missing their physical presence again.

The shifting sands of Arabia helped me adjust to the advent of our gray Persian-Siamese-Russian Blue Grand-kitten, the one who'd been born on the day of Baba's heart surgery, who'd been added to the menage in our absence. Perhaps it's easier to accept his intermittent affection and aloofness, after my experience with balancing extremes. On one occasion, my new, little furry friend purred when I reached out to pet him. And when he jumped up on the bed beside me, looked me in the eye, stretched and pressed his little paws against my shoulder and curled up against me for a nap, that, too, gave a feeling of home.

PART II: The Journey That Changed Everything

Chapter 20: A Second Dip Of The Wick

"I don't know the key to success but the key to failure is trying to please everybody" [49]
—Bill Cosby

Did I say we'd never be allowed to go back? Was Saudization not in full swing, expats being sent home and Saudis progressively taking over the running of their own institutions? There had been 6,000,000 expats—40%. The Kingdom had misgivings about being overly dependent on professional and domestic help, office workers and manual laborers, all privy to Saudi secrets, so they sought more independence. But in the professions, autonomy was still a ways away. And until 2001, no taxi drivers, manual laborers, civic cleaners, clerks, hotel receptionists, shopkeepers, security guards, gas station attendants or street sweepers were Saudi.

Baba had been told his help would still be useful at the university, but nothing formal, until 1:06 AM on a working day in May. Seven months after our return to North America, in the middle of a quiet night, a fax came beeping and creaking and squealing through and Baba was officially re-invited. I was invited to come along.

The next week, for me, was a blur of headaches. Baba was excited about his work and the prospect of seeing his pals again—if we decided to go. While he rejoiced, I seemed determined to look at the situation through bleak-colored glasses.

Once the throbbing in my head subsided, I was able to deliberate on whether I wanted to take on the strains all over again or not. I began weighing my options. For a while, I functioned in a fog of indecision. Baba had enjoyed the year so much he had already begun comparing the benefits of taking a leave of absence and traveling the next year, or just retiring altogether. I could ask him not to go, but then what would we do with that year? He would have to make arrangements for someone to cover his current professional responsibilities at the American university if he went. They could just be re-rearranged if we decided not to go. If he really had his heart set on going, I could stay in North America. It would be pretty quiet, but I could resume my professional activities. Or I could move in with my married daughter for a year.

I considered it for some time. Over the last few months since I had gotten back, I had not really been getting too much counseling, artwork, or English tutoring done anyway, except for volunteer work. I had supervised home repairs, helped our daughter and son-in-law move in with us in preparation for their eventual move to New York, talked about the trip and wrote.

So, if we went, there would not be as many ties now to stretch, without severing them altogether, as the first time around—if we decided to go. Those who were truly friends had adapted undauntedly to the distance, time change and price of postage. With some, closeness was not much affected by long absences. We picked up right where we'd left off and applied our energies to maintaining the deeper bonds between us. Using the abundant spare time abroad to write not only helped me process it all. It had been satisfying.

Gaps punctuated the chapters, though, questions left unanswered. I had another chance to get answers—if we decided to go. Had I reached the goals I carried there at first—to truly understand the culture and not judge? Groundhog Day—had I gotten it right yet? Had I become less complacent, more pro-active and in command of my moods as I had intended? Had I learned to appreciate Baba's way of caring for me without being passive about getting what I wanted out of life? That, more than anything else told me I had more work to do. Maybe going back would be beneficial. Perhaps the sooner I stopped resisting my lessons, the sooner I'd breeze onward.

Based on these portents, I had decided I would go along, back to the wilds of Saudi Arabia, to complete the survival course I had started. A week after the fax, while Baba sat reading on the couch, I elected to announce my decision.

"All right, I'll go," I informed him. "But this time I'll come just before your first vacation and stay only the six months."

He looked stunned. I don't think it had occurred to him that I might actually prefer to stay home on my own. After a thoughtful few minutes, he responded.

"We'll buy a car this time, so I can take you out every day if you want," he vowed.

That might work, I thought. Not to depend on the convenience and driving style of taxi drivers, stumped by *salah* and full of quarrelsome queries, would be better. Linda, who had opened so many doors for me, had moved on to another Arab country, though.

It was a good thing I had kept the miniaturized documents. The Arabic notes would go back into the suitcase. And that black bag, never far away, my companion, my symbol of mobility, right in the back of the closet. It was probably still warm, not even cooled off yet and probably knew all by itself in which pocket everything went. I had almost left my *abaya* behind when I left the country. Our bags were so full; I didn't see much point in taking up precious space with something I'd never use again. But Baba said he'd pack it and it had arrived with the cargo. It would have been a shame to invest in a second one, when I didn't have much use for the first. I could borrow back the black Saudi scarf I gave to my daughter as soon as I'd arrived home. Maybe we hadn't had our last chicken *schwarma* or Mama Noura juice after all.

That same week, Baba helped his Saudi students prepare posters for a professional conference. Our daughter and son-in-law went to a crowded convention center to see exhibits and meet students. They came home saying one female student had offered her hand to our daughter. But I felt like we'd come full circle when our son-in-law extended his and met with the same response I had received from the jokey jeweler, "I don't shake hands."

Over the next weeks, I vacillated between spells excitement and dismal remembrances. I could reconnect with acquaintances, if they were still there. The little voice in the wristwatch was getting weaker; the battery was going. It would be great to see the fellow who gave it to us again. And we could explore more neighboring countries. We might get to Jiddah after all.

Now, I was forearmed with a fresh attitude and fortified with a head full of supportive memories, layers of protection. I was more detached now, too. This time, I didn't have to fall prey, in that machine gun sort of existence, to reacting to everything with jolting, exhausting emotional highs and lows. I didn't have to feel caged, getting caught up in the cultural drama of others. This time I would take with me more music, philosophy literature, animal pictures and 3-D puzzles and I already had two new art projects in mind.

When I mentioned our evolving plans to selected friends, to avoid filling my days with the sound of the name of *that place*, I adopted just that euphemism—*that place*. New lessons were about to begin and I prepared myself for incremental and frequent changes.

As awareness of my predicament dawned, the image flickered in my head of a candle. Beginning at the inner core, the depth increases so the resulting candle can brighten its little corner of the universe, and ultimately disperse energy for the use of others. Like fresh wicking, on its way to becoming a candle, accumulates new layers of substance when dipped into a vessel of molten, clinging wax, I was about to be re-immersed into the simmering, homogenous, enigmatic, rarified substance of Saudi Arabia—*that place*. The metamorphosis would not only be thermal, but emotional, accumulating layers of knowledge and experience. I had hoped I could not only sustain my wavering light but perhaps it would even brighten over another 12 months.

Chapter 21: The Grip Creeps Back

"Nothing in life is to be feared. It is only to be understood" [50]
—Marie Curie

Two months before Baba left for Riyadh, I woke up one morning in the grip of something cold and clammy. Negative emotions swirled around my head. My heart felt heavy and dark. It was fear—the fear of being alone and having so much to take care of. Except for me, the house would be empty when he left—no kids, no pets. Our son was in the city, but on his own. I was suffused with a strange sadness, too, over what I perceived as the creation of our parallel lives.

By the time I got there, Baba would have long since chosen campus, compound, or DQ for our abode. My input would necessarily be from a distance. He would have selected the furnishings, arranged the kitchen and be cooking for himself. He talked about getting for a two-bedroom flat, which usually included a second, ladies' sitting room. That way, he explained, I would have room for my hobbies without compromising what I call the museum quality of his sitting room. We would see. He would have a routine by the time I arrived: the gym, eating out and shopping with his buddies. He might even go on a desert picnic or diamond-hunting outing. Whenever I joined the scene, I would walk into a man's world—in more ways than one.

Although I wasn't to understand it in these terms for some time, deep inside I was disquieted by my perception of his comfortably falling into step with the male way of life there. He seemed to be in his element, walking purposefully with his head down, as if on a mission, undistracted by peripherals, with the single-mindedness that got what one wanted but was not especially good for listening between the lines. And it had become easy for me to fit into the female system of occupying myself with activities that excluded males and of keeping disgruntlements bottled up until discharged unpredictably. Or perhaps these were just differences between males and females everywhere.

Baba was to leave for Riyadh in early August 2000. I wondered what I would do with the next weekend. I imagined the long day Sunday stretching out before me. Still, it was my choice not to go along in August. Nobody was twisting my arm.

I meditated on the loving intention behind sadness. In some schools of thought, it is to lead me to what I think I've lost. I was determined not to get stuck in loss, even if stained by it. I concentrated on the enduring parts of my relationship with Baba, timeless, resilient aspects that bore stretching 10,000 miles. Since the loving intention behind fear, in those same schools, is to keep me from making the same mistakes over again, I prepared to do things differently this time.

The biggest part of my fear now stemmed from physical limitations. In some ways, I had weakened. The biggest blow was that I had mounted very few stairs in *that place*, so now back in Milwaukee, soothing warmth water beckoned at the top of the stairs but many days, it was just too great a climb. My bedroom, clothes closet and warm water were only within reach every third day. This was supposed to be home, but it wasn't always comfortable to live there.

This comprised the biggest part of my fear of being alone for three months—93 days—14 weekends. Before this point, I had arranged my surroundings ergonomically so I could work efficiently, but I usually needed some help. I tormented myself with self-doubt.

- How would I pack my two 32 kilo (70 lb.) suitcases?
- How would I get the front door open, when it stuck fiercely in high humidity?
- How would I do my laundry, way down in the basement, where I hadn't treaded for years?
- Who would help me figure out the cryptic machinations of my new laptop?
- Who would fold up and leave interesting articles from the Sunday paper on my chair?

Actually, two months earlier, we'd stumbled onto a chronic Pain Clinic. Combining medications with warm water exercise and dealing directly with the emotional and psychological effects of chronic pain, was helping. My endurance was increasing, by inches. I was delighted. Still, in my darker moods, I wondered how I would cope. Still, no one could do it for me.

The internal dialogue kept running. Temporary thorns in my side weren't insurmountable, I told myself. My son and special friends had volunteered to pitch in. A skycap awaited me at airports so I didn't exhaust myself along marathon gangways. My faithful black bag, slung over my shoulder, magically made 1 kilogram (2.2 lb.) of bare essentials, that I couldn't entrust to checked baggage, feel like just ½ a kilo.

Coming right down to it, the main challenge I faced was the same one awaiting me in Riyadh—entertainment and making the most of each day. Finding meaningful activities that nourished my mind and contented my spirit. On both continents, I didn't want to just use up the days; I wanted to live. Quality of the day was the goal. There was more freedom now than there would be later. The alternative was to go in August, but I still couldn't run away from myself.

As I reflected, gorgeous dark pink peonies bloomed in the front yard. I had missed them the previous year and would miss their short three-week bloom again next year. But here I was this year, not enjoying them to the fullest either, being preoccupied with shadows. Hugs, humor and humming, for health—now, I reminded myself.

Even with the house emptier for 3 ½ months, ways to keeps spirits up were plentiful.

- I could smolder incense whenever I felt the urge, not aggravating anyone's allergies.
- A kit for raising Triops, like brine shrimp, with a 3-month lifespan, awaited me.
- A friend and I would make appointments for soothing massages.
- I would hand make a gift for my Grandniece in Mumbai and get TV art instruction.

But what was that? Our son would move into the house with me? Oh joy! Of course, he would be busy much of the time, but at least my son, who was a great conversationalist, would be around some of the time. My son, who would sneeze from the incense, but on the other hand, my son, who would enjoy the Triops, too. This time with him would be a precious interval. It would also influence the parallel nature of Baba's and my geographical separation, having a third person involved in the care of the house who was equally invaluable to each of us.

Then, a new rite of passage was suddenly inserted into the proceedings, adding a whole new dimension. Baba decided to

officially retire. Loads of preparations had to be hopscotched through already, without the retirement:
- getting papers notarized for new passport applications,
- procuring a written record of our not having any police records,
- getting x-ray and blood work results for the visa application,
- calling in ticket numbers to two different airlines and rattling around in their voice mail jails,
- telling families and close friends about our plans,
- taking umpteen phone calls in anticipation of the sale of our car, in between nuisance phone calls from radio stations offering me a free trip to Atlantic City, Disneyland or Las Vegas,
- making changes to insurance coverages,
- two trips to the attorney's office to update all manner of documents,
- buying and setting up two new laptops and a new portable printer to replace antiquated ones,
- getting the authorization to return the new printer that didn't work,
- tuning up all the systems in the house: AC, furnace, audio, fax and answering machines,
- getting voice mail because the answering machine couldn't be tuned up,
- answering the doorbell to strangers who wanted to sell us frozen steaks, who wanted to put in a security alarm system, or who wanted to spruce up our asphalt driveway,
- updating miniaturized copies of documents,
- secreting a package into Baba's suitcase for the birthday he would have before I got there,
- barely doing the minimum to maintain what was growing in the yard,
- notifying pertinent agencies as to who was authorized to take care of business in our absence,
- all while maintaining my strength by doing warm water exercise twice a week and coping with the accompanying ache and fatigue,

- not to mention Baba's official and social university retirement formalities,
- taking phone calls from students who were looking for their soon-to-be-retired mentor and who volunteered to help him shift his office,
- and all that while trying to keep some semblance of normalcy in our usual routine, like getting an occasional half decent meal on the table.

If all this was not enough, to ease Baba's guilt pangs for agreeing to leave me on my own, he suddenly decided he needed to get someone in to re-grout the bathtub, that the garage needed cleaning and that two large pieces of furniture we'd been asked to dispose of ten months earlier, needed to be advertised for sale, right now. And so phone calls came for that, too.

Through it all, daily, I saved energy and good humor to listen to the dynamic goings-on in the lives of my three kids, including our son-in-law.

"You'll never guess what he's done now!" opened a phone call one evening from our daughter, who'd moved to New York. Keeping me spellbound, she described the escapades of our grand-cat who did a high wire act outside the railings of their 8th-storey balcony, on the 5-cm. (2") ledge, a walk in the park for him, but harrowing for his caretaker-parents.

Once Baba left, there would still be plenty to do.
- coaching our son in the care of the car, house, yard and bills,
- getting my new laptop configured for the Internet and updating the viruscan,
- buying dietary supplements and art supplies for the trip because prices abroad were double,
- generally expecting the unexpected while still trying to get into a warm pool twice a week,

and a multitude of trivial incidentals that took up time but didn't show much, unless left undone.

As one day after another was filled with a barrage of arrangements whizzing around my head, details, documents, decisions, phone calls, and well wishers who insisted we must go for dinner before we left, I reflected that I had never aspired to be an Air Traffic Controller.

Deciding which clothes to pack wouldn't take long. I was determined not to take the same colors again. This time it would be violets, teals, yellows, greens and burgundys, not the beiges, oranges and browns I took last time for easier coordination. I began to understand the opalescent dazzle peeking out from under folds of black there. Sameness was to be avoided. When I envisioned going out again in the same gown I'd worn to the Japanese restaurant when I only opened the collar of my apparition attire 5 cm. (2"), I saw myself sinking into a deep rut.

Thank goodness I was still immune to Hepatitis B and Typhoid Fever. And no matter what North American doctors said, I was not going to take anti-malaria tablets again. When I asked the Saudi doctor to refill my prescription, she suppressed a smile as she patiently shook her head.

"Madame, there is no malaria in Saudi Arabia."

When I thought about it, why would there be. Malaria was transmitted by mosquitoes, in places where water lay thick on the ground and people grew rice. There wouldn't be much malaria in the desert, except maybe during rainy season. True, along with noisy bedroom ACs, most of us did complain about that single irritating mosquito that dozed in a corner all day, awakening just to torment us at night. Still, Hepatitis was a worse threat.

The house began to take on a chaotic look but we'd have to tolerate it for a while. A swirl of packaging, tissue paper, plastic bags, boxes and piles of manila envelopes circulated. The closer we got to Baba's departure date, the higher the rate packages came through the door. Transition again. To keep my sanity, I worked on a 3-D jigsaw puzzle, to force my scattered mind to focus on one thing—only 1000 little pieces at once.

Six weeks before Baba was about to depart, leaving me with everything he hadn't finished, I awoke one morning with my mind in chaos. I'd had a dream in which my son, aided by an unruly mechanical dishwasher, had reduced to rubble the set of Royal Crown Derby china my father gave me when I got married. In my deranged state, I attempted repairs, gluing a turkey wing, also retrieved from the dishwasher, onto the broken edge of a platter, but finally accepted that this set of china had been passed down through the generations for the last time.

Jewel Dhuru

I used the Gestalt method of dream analysis to see what I was trying to tell myself. Identifying the main elements as myself, my son, the platter, the dishwasher, the turkey wing and the glue, I deciphered messages from each of them, presumably all symbolic of deeper parts of myself. I ended up with some understanding of my own advice, to be careful with cherished possessions, to choose caretakers carefully and providing supervision, but the elusive message from the turkey wing not to mix the organic with the inorganic would take due deliberation.

Also as I woke, a melody echoed in my brain. The Mills Brothers crooned "I never would have bet, that my shy Violet, would ever be a w-i-l-d, w—i—l—d Rose." Baba eyed me with amused concern when I told him about it and I made a mental note to keep my sugar intake low that morning. I was anxious about keeping affairs manageable and told Baba so.

"Only six weeks?" he repeated, raising his bushy white eyebrows.

Oh, yes, he would get started on something right away, he assured me. True to his brand of efficiency, he sat down at the computer. While I read to him from my scribbled list of jobs for him to do before he left, he contented himself by creating a neatly typed copy of the list, which he fastened with a magnet to the refrigerator.

His official retirement triggered the rite of passage of wading through every scrap of paper he'd accumulated in the last 27 years, both in the office he was vacating and at home. His secretary half joked that as his office emptied out, her shelves got fuller. I knew the feeling. Suspicious piles kept coming through the door and were spirited upstairs, each with a nostalgic story of a past student or author he'd met. My desk also brimmed. With him preoccupied, I handled more paperwork. My Pending file completely obscured the desk surface. When the car was sold, the contents of the glove compartment ended up there, too. Piles of mail spilled over on to my chair making it more difficult to sit down and work at a time when much needed doing.

Baba took everything in stride, but in the weeks before he left, I woke up, my head stuffed with specific people and long past episodes from adolescence and college days that I had not reflected on in years, rehashing lessons learned. Selected scenes from my lifetime slowly streamed through my brain, in absorbable passages, perhaps in support of this yearlong endeavor.

Ala Tool

During those days, few pleasures were as keenly felt as the warm, tempered sun, caressing my face as I stepped onto our patio and became one with my lounging chaise, glistening with dew. I drank in the yellow of the coreopsis and red of the sedum, memorizing the sounds of birds' wings fluttering, crickets chirping and dragonflies whizzing and contemplating my dreams. Becoming saturated with back yard moisture would sustain me during the dry days ahead. One late-July morning, just before I went out, a loud crack came from the back yard. As if there wasn't enough to do, a 25-cm. (10") diameter willow limb suddenly plummeted earthward, taking smaller branches with it, narrowly missing the neighbor's fence and the whole bunch sat there in the middle of the back yard. Before the chain saw could be oiled up and the tree's discards cleaned up, the rabbits would have a feast on the leaves.

Those last weeks, Baba and I had great talks, short on duration but long on depth. With each chat came the satisfying sense of strength, connectedness and quiet contentment that accompanies the wish to see each other happy and the continued commitment to check with each other about everything important.

June and July had been relegated to memories and notes in my journal. In June, the President of Syria, Hafez El Assad, passed on and his son, Bashar, was being groomed for the position. I visualized the three days of mourning. This would have an impact on regional politics, especially since two other young Muslim rulers had recently also assumed power in nearby Morocco and Jordan. The price of gas had reached $2.23 US per gallon in the Midwest before the Saudis began pumping more barrels of oil.

Somehow, the list from the refrigerator did get done, although the first item on my list was the one Baba did last. Then, he decided the oak kitchen table needed re-varnishing.

Finally, in early August, he was off, but not before announcing on the morning of the alleged departure day that he still had much to do and would leave a day later. It looked like my neglected pool exercise would have to be pushed back again. And my calculations to carefully apportion quantities of the foods only Baba ate so they ran out the minute he left, went awry too. It was time to make self-care a priority. A friend drove Baba to the airport and I went to the pool. He stopped for a day in New York to visit our kids and then was off over the ocean.

Jewel Dhuru

The next morning I surveyed the fallout. It billowed with every phone call from him over the next 48 hours, requesting something else he'd forgotten and needed sending on. Unbelievably, the list began with his laptop, which was still buried under papers on his desk!

Chapter 22: One Last Interlude

"If you don't know where yer at, you can't see where yer going"

—Will Rogers

August

Three and a half months would pass before I saw Baba again. I was determined not to spend all my waking hours preparing for my return to the wilds of *that place*. My attempts to leave it out of conversations or to glide over it quickly and get on with more essential aspects of living met with varying levels of success. During this last interlude, highlights were an unexpected whirlwind visit from our son-in-law and talks over the Triops tank with our son.

In Riyadh, Baba renewed acquaintances. Generally, employees, usually men, arrived in August and left in June. Wives came and went, a minimum six months in residence entitling them to the sponsor's round-trip ticket. One colleague, whose wife away, too, had brought Baba a thermos of tea one morning and another cooked extra dinner to share. With pals, he supped at a Sudanese restaurant, shopped at an old souk and began sparsely furnishing our new abode. Between us, emails buzzed back and forth and our phone bill mounted. For the first time, I was able to hear what my decision to come later was doing to him. He was alone and he missed me.

At home, three springs earlier, a grape vine had materialized at the front corner of our garage and I had argued to keep it. It had prolifically covered the entire side of the garage, rounded the corner clinging to the downspout and provided me with even more pleasure on my patio. Ducks flew so low overhead I could distinguish them as Mallards. I reveled in the sounds of cicadas, buzzing like overloaded wires, as I watched the rays of the early morning sun stretch over our house and spotlight tree tops on the other side of the street, tingeing them with gold.

Jewel Dhuru

September

Baba's busy work schedule changed without warning. When his first check came, he registered at the gym, opening new avenues for entertainment, and he shopped. He had only a short wave radio. He would acquire a boom box and TV closer to my arrival date. He described stray cats lining up endearingly at doors and pigeons perching on the windowsills of friends, wheedling table scraps and seeds. He window shopped at a car souk, like a flea market, owners milled around their wheels, some standing on the hoods with megaphones, touting the attributes of their vehicles to everyone who could hear little else within a two-block radius.

Apparently, Dr. B had applied to return to the Kingdom the next year. What did this mean? More intense work on my character, with him as the instrument of improvement? Actually, the December before, he'd sent a card and note. Since Baba was swamped with other matters, I responded with a card. A month later, Dr. B. called and I answered the phone. Before talking to Baba, he took a moment to chastise me for the way I'd misspelled his name. I started to apologize but didn't seem to be accomplishing anything. I passed the phone over to Baba and tried to put the episode out of my mind. The chance he would be back was slim, but who knew. The day I heard he would return was the day I would know I was also consigned to another year.

Meanwhile, anxiety filled me when my new laptop, dubbed 'the listener', filled the whole house with a scorched smell and Technical Support recalled it for repair. A 50th wedding anniversary party given for our neighbors was heart warming. I celebrated with neighbors who had lived across, beside and kitty-corner from us for more than twenty years. Some referred to our plans as an adventure but others lowered their eyes and shook their heads. They didn't understand what we were doing. Sometimes I didn't know myself.

Trying not to let barriers spring up, I steeped myself in Huston Smith's The Wisdom of Faith video. I particularly wanted to see the parts about the Buddhist belief that whatever happens, there's no conflict or obstruction to a peaceful mind. And the part about meditation and silence providing more understanding of the mind than years of Psychology courses. I fortified myself, too, with Buscaglia videos—*The Art of Being Fully Human* and *Living Fully-In Love*.

Having reflected on no conflict-no obstruction, I restored a topped off level of self-support, felt calm and refreshed and reached for the phone to get the day's business sorted out.

In place of a dial tone, only a hollow echo occupied the line. A rainstorm the previous night had left electric power undisturbed, but none of us neighbors were to have phone, email or fax for three days. I had all the silence and time for meditation I could use, and then some.

My efforts at collecting signatures in a card for Baba's birthday in October resulted in three cards packed with good wishes. But I became reluctant to entrust them to snail mail that was taking 17 days to arrive. I would hand carry them in November and his 65th birthday would just have to be a month later. That gave me time to collect more autographs. Subsequent to the storm repairs, both of our emails remained undeliverable for three more days because of a computer glitch in *that place,* so we just had more to share when we finally could connect.

October

I said so long for both of us to the next-door neighbors and met the new owners. In an email, Baba reported he needed just a handful of the hundreds of Saudi photos he'd stashed in a closet, so I agreed to slowly wade through the lot to find the select few. Were these clips of the past or the future, I wondered as I slogged through them.

One day, coming through the mouthpiece, I finally heard some of the words I'd awaited for months. As the minutes clicked by, he decided that instead of relegating my hobby material to the smaller sitting room with one paltry pane, it would be better, during the long days in my rabbit hutch, if I had access to the more spacious living area with a glass balcony door and more windows. He would compromise on museum quality. His new idea was he would set up the second sitting room for himself and his pals. I knew it was not going to be just as simple as that. The final plan would require collaboration and negotiation, but this was a big step.

My heart went out to him. He was in a difficult position, but so was I. My contention was that any common living space acquires its ambience from the personalities of all who reside there. We each had to assess what of value we brought to the mix. I wondered how many families, where the breadwinner was away working, would prefer having that person around more often, despite fewer funds. We discussed how cultural strains, both here and there, affected us individually and our relationship and ironed out more wrinkles.

My exercise routines, both in and out of the water, underwent refinements, in preparation for the times to come that pool access would be limited, at best, or the times I was too fatigued from the rigors of travel to exercise at all. Strengthening kept on at a snail's pace. Any attempt to quicken it resulted in relapse. I had a long road to go but was so glad to be on the road.

My visa and ticket arrived from the Saudi embassy. Even though they agreed to provide round trip tickets from home for us both, they informed me that Saudi Arabian Airlines could not provide a direct flight for me to New York. I would have to cope with a connection. A further surprise was that they wouldn't allow me the same stopover with my kids that Baba got two months earlier. After much futile hassle, I made my own arrangements for New York.

I didn't dwell on it, being distracted by the news of the latest Middle Eastern eruptions, re-enactments of previous traumas—Palestine, Israel, Yemen, Iraq. Still, I was not too concerned for my safety. Baba's messages lacked alarm as well. My stint there told me, as global distances go, my route lay relatively far from the trouble, barring hijackings. What bothered me was the unnecessary suffering of the innocent and the endless repetition of variations of the same approaches that always yielded the same results.

This interval of exclusive access to my son was coming to a close, too. We might never have such proximity again. There was only today. I had enjoyed this hiatus of indulging our common interests. My spirit was nourished by the cooperative give and take that develops between friends. That we were mother and son was an added bonus.

One weekday, at precisely 6:10 AM, before sunup, in response to my request a few days earlier, he woke me saying only, "The sky is clear." Without another word, I followed him out onto our balmy, breezy patio and he pointed out the three stars of Orion's belt, beaming down on us stargazers from the dark sky. As he coached me, I located Orion's arms and legs. I found the reddish star, midway between the belt and the right arm that was Betelgeuse. Then, I looked up at my firstborn while he drank in the heavens, his hair tussled by the breeze, his face serene and I thought to myself 'What a great way to start a morning'.

Over the weeks, I packed two large cases and phoned several friends to say so long. That and keeping entropy from taking over took up the last two weeks of this yearlong plan. While leaves danced like Astaire and Rogers across our patio, Mother Nature worked on a crinkled patchwork quilt on our lawn, her leaf shaped remnants in vibrant russets, bronzes, umber, burgundy, and periwinkle. Inhaling their musty scent, my head swam, conjuring up images of bonfires and kids crunching through piles of leaves. With the weather taking a turn for the brisk, I sat on the patio, in a jacket, watching a mourning cloak butterfly flutter by and stray cats meander through the yard. Squirrels, doing calisthenics with their tails scampered within feet of me without so much as a backward glance. Amid cheeps, chirps, chatters and twitters, the tinkling of neighbors' wind chimes reached my ears as well as the honks of Vs of Canada Geese, overhead, soaring southward.

November

On November 1, at 6:00 AM, four days before leaving, I awoke from a dream. I was on a city bus in my hometown in the province of Manitoba, approaching my bus stop, but inexplicably, my possessions were strewn all over several seats. I began haphazardly, overstuffing two tote bags that I recognized from high school days. The only familiar items were a sweater and a watch Baba had given me but the bags were so full of the non-descript that these two were half falling out of the top and at risk of being lost. As I deciphered the dream, the primary meaning was that I was too burdened with emotional baggage from the past to appreciate the gifts Baba wanted me to have in the present. My waking up before reaching the bus stop told me to be careful not to dump everything from the past, to take time to integrate.

Another interesting phenomenon involved my little burgundy, leather bound, address book. Before then, I'd changed books several times over my lifespan, either because they'd filled up or as a rite of passage. Since my teens, I still kept four old books, moving appropriate names forward when I graduated, got married and moved to the United States and when my kids started collecting school friends. Different friends sprung from different chapters over my lifespan and were recorded in different books. Some ties stretched through all four. But with this current one, blank space remained only between U and Z. Still, I wasn't at all inclined to replace it. Instead, I started adding more people I wanted to keep in touch with, filling up U through Z with appendicized addresses. An elastic band kept hoarded cards, address labels and notes from jumping out, thickening the book considerably. It would be hand carried safely in my black travel bag, not relegated to checked baggage and would be one of the last items I'd packed.

The day I left home, November 5, 2000, I took the patio chaise cushions in for the last time that century.

Chapter 23: Back To The Land

"I saw that stony indifference to others that was the most fatal disease of the concentration camp. I felt it spread to myself: how could one survive if one kept on feeling! ... It was better to narrow the mind to one's own need, not to see, not to think" [52]
—Corrie ten Boom, *The Hiding Place*

On November 19, 2000, I prepared to re-plant my feet on the sandy substance of Saudi Arabia, *that place*. I'd had a battery-charging visit with the kids and my grand-cat in New York. From their home base on the Hudson River, we set off to explore the controversial haunted house in Amityville and The Cloisters of the Metropolitan Museum of Art, and then I was off again.

The Flight

In bustling JFK, before I left the physical manifestations of loved ones behind, I offered up early Thanksgiving gratitude for the degree of safety, freedom and abundance I enjoyed. It was about to change. I normally did feel physically safe in Riyadh, though in New York, an item in the newspaper gave details of a British engineer in Riyadh, victim to a car bomb. Still, the emotional and mental milieu was more menacing.

The 11-hour flight started at 9:00 PM. In my four-seats across middle section, a late flight was perfect timing for a night's sleep, I thought, if I stretched out over my own seat and the two adjoining ones, which airline personnel had assured me were vacant. Instead, the airlines felt 11 hours was just long enough for another dinner and a breakfast, with a nap sandwiched in between. As it happened, I dozed reclined in my single seat, my right armrest taken over by a guy from Jiddah who was all apologies but claimed his and his friend's real seats had been commandeered by strangers and the left seat being a rotating spot for guys whose friends sat nearby or who were just giving their wives and children more space. Before he sat down, I had already noticed the guy on the right, in his bright orange shirt, but when he stopped in the aisle near me, I didn't trust my vision. A Saudi male face was smiling at me, in public. Actually he was quite pleasant when awake, plugging in my earphones and bringing me an unsolicited piece of fruit when he got one for himself.

When I boarded, I felt defensive, sensing stares. But when I was able to pry my heart back open, I looked with different eyes at one fellow on my left. He sat squeezed into only the far ¾ of his seat, reading his Qur'an and keeping clear of my armrest. He avoided looking in my direction and as I surreptitiously studied him, I got a glimpse of someone who maybe didn't think of me as forward and shameless, tainted and incomplete. Instead I saw a man who might possibly have been preserving whatever purity he shared with his wife by preventing evil thoughts from entering his mind on the scent, voice or look of another woman. Suddenly I didn't mind so much not being able to stretch out to sleep, at least not on a spiritual level.

Riyadh

In Riyadh, on the 20th of November, it was cold all day, 13 to 17^0 C. (50 to 60^0 F.). Kids waiting for their school buses at 6:00 A.M. wore fleecy-hooded parkas. And it had rained, again. It would stop long enough for puddles to sink into partially satiated sand and then start again. Real winter weather, not like what we'd had two years before. The heating was the same, each room having separate AC/heaters. Maybe there would be flowers on the dunes this year.

Back to the Land Through the Looking Glass

The land where Thursday and Friday are week-end, where winter is colorful flowers and summer is like living in a frying pan, where every rule for civilized driving is taken as a personal challenge, where you surrender your passport to your sponsor and need written permission to leave the city, where both females and males flip and flap head scarves and hitch up raiments when negotiating stairs or getting into cars, where you can watch a baker knead and bake the Arab bread you carry home still warm, and where everyday safety from theft of material possessions and physical assault is probably unparalleled.

Ala Tool

Back to the Land Where Time is Used in a Casual, Circular Fashion

Where the gym hours change at *Ramadan* but few know what the new hours are, where the door bell always rings when there is only five more minutes to the end of the movie, where neighbors drop in at 9:30 at night, where a serviceman tells you "Call me anytime and I'll come," but when you call, he's not there but his 4-year old wants to chat, and where you never know what "in 10 minutes" or "see you at 2:00 o'clock" or "on Tuesday" really means. Back to the unpredictably predictable: strangers handing me books about Islam, the sporadic working of the phone/fax/email/electricity and random in-coming phone calls from lonely strangers.

Baba, too, being a lovable last minute lad, probably waited until the last week to get things ready for me. But winter weather and overwork had contrived otherwise. He hadn't felt well all that week and I arrived just in time to urge him to get a persistent, hacking cough and fatigue checked out immediately. By Thanksgiving, he was taking an antibiotic.

As a result, until five days after my arrival, I occupied considerable free time as best I could because there was no TV, no CD/cassette player, which had been unplugged in semi-readiness for the TV, no power strips for laptop, vibrator or curling brush and no help to unpack my two suitcases. And Baba being a shower person, he didn't know the rubber plug for the tub was torn, so not even a comfortable bath. The newspaper on the table sat without a half-done crossword to finish. There wasn't even much conversation because he slept a lot, when he wasn't coughing. And with our circadian rhythms out of sync again, when he wasn't asleep, I was.

It the next weeks, I would hear, through the voices of others, just how Baba had prepared for my arrival: replacing furniture that just didn't work in a certain room, replacing the kitchen floor and two missing water heaters, finding the right rolling chair for the kitchen, having curtains made and taking care of the endless list anyone who has ever moved understands.

Still, a key of my own would have been nice. To our main door, he'd only been given one. Despite Baba's many jaunts to hardware stores and key copiers, it was to be three weeks before my own key to the rabbit hutch could be pinned into my black travel bag.

Just when I thought I couldn't cope without a TV or a decent bath or a female friend or a Christmas cassette inadvertently left in New York, I found I was only beginning to plumb the depths of creative coping. At least I hadn't caught Baba's cold and relied on garlic as a preventive measure. Awakening at 3:00 AM, I prowled, checking out his bachelor flat. I discovered his battery powered short wave radio and listened to Canadian news on NPR.

This campus flat was much the same as the one two years earlier, a leaf on a cloverleaf, on the second floor, except this was a two-bedroom with the extra ladies' sitting room, so walking distances were greater and the floor plan faced the opposite way. The same Saudi style bathroom lay on the left near the entry.

The kitchen balcony, on the left, was quite different, though. The frosted half glass, half metal balcony door, beside a frosted window, was no Rear Window experience. The clothesline looked out over a bougainvillea bush in an isolated alcove near our noisy condenser room.

Baba had decorated the sitting room on the right and the bedroom farther down the hall on the right, both in teal, blues and burgundy, with teal carpeting throughout and a delicate green pattern of linoleum in the kitchen. The walls were all white, as before. All the furnishings were 20 cm. (8") lower than my usual, again. In the sitting room, near the balcony, a blond coffee table with magazine rack underneath stretched in front of a sky blue couch, so I could see out the glass door from the couch. Three matching armchairs circled the perimeter of the room. A TV table and flat screen TV opposed the couch. On the side table and floor by the balcony stood six small plants and a meter tall (3') croton, with bright variegated green, red and yellow leaves.

I looked in the fridge, but without much appetite, not even for the Mammoul date pastries I had favored. The cooker, dustbin and outlets on the wall were all low, too. I ate a *guava*, actually pronounced *guawa*.

To keep my sanity, I immersed myself in the 3-D clock puzzle I dragged out of my suitcase. After three days work, when I activated the hands, they would jerk rhythmically forward, inevitably, towards the day in May when I would go home. It became a special companion, counting down the days. Back to becoming hyper-flexible, ready for anything.

Ala Tool

At 4:50 A.M., the *Fajr salah*, before sunrise, began. I went out onto the kitchen balcony, the *muezzin*'s reverie quavering over to me through the mist and 17^0 C. (60^0 F.) rain. Then, mosques being as plentiful there as pubs in Ireland and pharmacies in the United States, refrains emanated from the minaret on the other side of the flat, so I listened in stereo. Then the third closest one began its epiphany and I had surround sound. I always wondered why they didn't all recite the same words at the same time. I knew the precise moment of sunrise affects *salahs* across the country, but these virtuosos were only three blocks apart. Perhaps they had chosen different verses. Then, like a vampire, when the sun came up, I went back to sleep

Back to Richness For the Senses

Where pungent, personal scent is valued to help identify another's mood and the breath is monitored from a close proximity to tell if the truth is being spoken. The heavenly feast of kabobs sizzling on the gas cooker would soon pour out of my kitchen into the hall, intermingling with the frankincense and ood coming out of the sitting room. Back to the sight, even if true only half the time, of the stereotypic generously rounded physique, for men and women, with sloping shoulders, a downward gazing aspect and slumberous, shuffling locomotion in floppy slippers on leathered feet. The other half the time, femininity fluttered in bright, beaded splendor under blankets of black, and white lines of trim troubadours metastasized with swords and scabbards, dancing and chanting in reedy tenors and bass notes to Arab flutes, violins, stringed ouds and drums. Back to patterned, textured carpets and shapely pots and minarets. Back to the sonorous strains of *salah*, secrecy and whispers, accents, lots of languages and quotes from the Qur'an.

The most insistent sounds thrusting themselves on my consciousness were the intriguing special effects escaping from our bedroom ceiling AC/heater. Air bubbles were trapped in the system so the HIFI gurgling inside was unvarying. Before I got used to it, I awoke from jet-lagged sleep wondering if I was floating in a giant vat of fluid or if a plane was landing on the roof. *Salah* amplified the metallic mumble and even when it was not prayer time, I could swear I heard men's voices subliminally sneaking out of that box.

Jewel Dhuru

The AC/heaters were really blowers attached to the condenser, in the room down the hall. All the heaters warmed their respective rooms within minutes of pressing the ON button on the wall, but the building insulation being non-existent, as soon as OFF was pressed, heat dissipated and chill seeped back in. In order to hear the TV, a CD or conversation, the noisiest blower, in the sitting room, had to be turned off. This meant wearing two or three sweaters indoors and walking around with a fleecy indigo and black plaid blanket wrapped around myself most of the time. Neighbors in the Midwest, buried under a record snowfall of 125 cm. (50") that December, didn't have much sympathy for us, but cold is cold.

Back to the Land Full of Memories

If I'd had average physical vitality, I could have hiked over to the gym on a ladies day and swum, used the sauna and chatted with whoever would talk to me. The Filipina women who bought out my first kitchen might still work there. Things went pear shaped, though, because the pool, although closer, was still too far for me to walk, exercise and then carry heavy wet clothes home again and the elevator to the sauna was still not working from the previous year. While I was thinking about how to build up to this feat in stages, *Ramadan* dawned. The women's hours changed, the new hours were passed on only by word of mouth, and I didn't know any of the mouths that knew the word. I was not to find out until January that when the very late night women's hours for *Ramadan* came to an end, the pool would close for repairs for several months. Meanwhile in the new men's-only pool and sports center a mile down a campus road, business was booming.

What else to do? Other women walked the campus perimeter or called limos and went shopping. I had my choice of garden brunches and luncheons, concerts, crafters and quilters' guilds, natural history meetings, dance and musical instrument lessons and more, all done in seclusion. As it was, though, even visiting Anita in our old building, a 10-minute walk away, would now mean a limo ride for me.

The campus building in which the twice weekly Arabic class was held, was closer now, but that didn't get around the stairs or the sitting in chairs designed not to fit. It wasn't that there was nothing to do; only the choices for me were even more limited than average,

Ala Tool

everything took me longer and the conditions for all women were restricted, at best. If an activity had appeal, it was probably clandestine and therefore, chancy.

Baba had rented a Mitsubishi Lancer. The price of gas had gone up to 6 SR/liter ($0.40 U.S./gallon). In the evenings, between sleeping and coughing, we went to get a bathtub plug, power strips, chicken *schwarma* and Mama Noura juice.

As reminiscences became reality, I felt like Bob Cratchet directed by the Spirits. "Why, it's the old neighbors with their kids! ... And *kitab kibeer*, the marble Book in the roundabout! ... Look at how big the Kingdom Center is. It had just broken ground when we left last time. ... And the Faisalia Center will have a revolving restaurant on top?"

If I could have seen the future on the first trip, I would have known half of what I looked forward to the second time wouldn't be there anymore. The bookstore with a semi-private nook for office furniture, where I would sit for a while, then make excursions to the arts and crafts section, was all different. The few remaining chairs were front and center, conspicuous and far away from anything of interest.

The eyeglass repair shop near the campus, with friendly service and seats for waiting, was now half its former size, another shop having budded next door. No room for seats and only a surly salesperson, which tried to tell me the only frames that fit my glass, garish blue speckled ones, suited my face. The first time I had prepared for a potentially close encounter with a *mutawa* was there. With bushy beard and ample waistline, he had shuffled in on leathered feet, examining frames at the counter while I sat waiting for mine. I was scarfless and my *abaya* was open except for the top snap. Being in a feisty mood that day, I decided if he rousted me about my appearance, I would quickly dispatch him by pointing him toward the nearest mirror. Lucky for both of us, from the counter, he went directly into the back room and didn't reemerge for the duration of my stay.

The captivating Hindi comedy, *Zaban Sambalke*, about a Hindi as a Second Language class, with plenty of non-verbal cues, wasn't on any of our channels. Back to the days when the friendliest face when Baba worked was inanimate, the smiley paper clip on my laptop screen. Even though raised in Canada where, generally, one preserves

Jewel Dhuru

a dignified distance from strangers until introduced, I was half habituated to the casual, friendliness of Americans. But in this environment where we mustered support wherever we could, where many expats were North Americans, it never failed to surprise me how other expat females averted their gaze when I spontaneously smiled at them. It was like we all harbored a dark secret. I guess we did—several.

Back to Extremes

The elegant and the harsh. Amid textured trees, flamboyant flowers and ornate gates, news reached us, through warning letters from embassies, of a second car bomb in Riyadh, although the local news said nothing. Even the articles in the New York Times and Arab News about the first incident were noticeably different, the former giving more detail. A high level of security awareness was urged.

Something new was the police parading the aisles at red lights, imposing fines of 300SR, about $75.00 US, for not wearing seat belts, in conjunction with Saudi TV ads saying "Buckle Up." Like a fad, the new watchwords were everywhere. Peeking out of the fridge, "Drive Safely" was stamped on eggs in their crate. The reality was I couldn't say how many times, in just the first week, Baba screeched to a stop as a Saudi driver cut us off. I stopped counting and started laughing after the fifth time a driver made a U-turn to the left from the extreme right lane on one side of the boulevard, on a red light, while three other lanes of us were stopped! I started ignoring honks and just put my trust in Baba's driving and whatever hand guided our movements, believing we were not destined to die in *that place*, creamed in our car.

Sometimes my heart felt full and light at the prospect of seeing acquaintances in the same boat again and of soaking up whatever I was acquiring from this travel. At other times, sadness sank heavily behind my breastbone, a strange primordial wound leaving no physical scars, only lackluster residue around my aura and showing through my eyes. The first week, catching sight of myself in a mirror, I didn't recognize the strained face and disquieted eyes as my own.

I felt out of step with my natural rhythms. Every so often, I wondered if this whole Saudi experience would ultimately shorten my life. Even two days of oppression could threaten my sense of whom I was—a child of the universe, from the same source as everyone else, put on this planet for a purpose. Negative thinking was not the way out of Hell, I thought. Focusing energies, getting back in step with the uni-vers-al flow, discharging tension and reengaging in the continuous cycle of receiving and giving, was the way to correct this disharmonious dis-ease.

Back to Feeling Schizzy

But with a belief in myself that wouldn't let me quit. So even before making a dent in the unpacking, to keep loss of identity, apathy and resentment from getting a grip, I homed in on the P.G. Wodehouse book in my suitcase, to keep my spirit light. I ferreted out inspirational articles I'd brought to keep in touch with the outside world and began putting up Christmas garlands and discrete transparencies on the windows, all the while pushing past the 'what's the use' feeling that constricted my breathing. This was as far away from daily hugs and laughter as I could get.

Five days after my arrival, the CD/cassette player/radio got hooked up and connections to two TV dishes resulted in replacing silence with 27 channels. BBC and CNN accompanied some with names I had never heard before: Nile TV International, Future Television, TV5, mbc (with English movies, some having such language, they made up for all that was bleeped from the Saudi channel), Indian channels, Lebanese BC (so this is where all the commercials got to), Al Jazeera and all the Arab satellite stations. Arab Sat gave access to cooking, crafts and cosmetics instruction, music and dance programs, kids' and game shows, nature programs, urban soaps and rural dramas that had me wishing I understood Arabic better.

Eighty percent of the programs where women appeared displayed faces with overstated make up and outfits a couple of sizes too small. This wasn't too different from the Indian music programs where dancers looked like they might have left the dressing room in a slight hurry. The other 20% looked professional and pleasing to the eye.

Most Arab Sat channels had that same, casual regard for the clock and continuity, bleeping punch lines and chopping off endings. Except for the 5-minute 5 o'clock Saudi News Brief, which broke abruptly into whatever was showing at precisely 5:01 or 5:02 PM.

Jewel Dhuru

Once again, wrong timing became the right time for whatever was actually going on. Baba missed the variety of foreign films back home—Italian, Iranian, Japanese. Ironically, as these channels offered new avenues for entertainment, the balcony door became stuck shut by the thick cables from the dish on the roof wedging tightly under it, making the balcony more cosmetic than ever.

Saudi channels were much the same, except for the new Program Parade. I watched for it at precisely, approximately 1:10 P.M. or so, to see if a feature film would be shown that day, the only movies I knew of at first. It was still the home of the one-day series. During the wee hours, one morning, the shock starting to abate, a 40-year old Candid Camera sported a massive sign on its stage saying SMILE. I tried but was surprised at how rusty my smiling muscles had become.

Back to Seclusion Tempered with Resourcefulness

During the daytime, I took in our view. Like in the first flat, it was no Eakins, but the sitting room balcony overlooked a strategic bend in the main road between a checkpoint and the Supermarket strip of shops. There was always something going on: teens careening cars around the curve, trimming of the bougainvilleas, people walking to and from the shops and families laboring under bursting weekend picnic baskets.

Over the roofs of the villas across the street, towered the tops of the only two high-rises, some 6 km. (3.7 miles) away, the Faisalia Center and the Kingdom Center. Once a small contingent of Sudanese women came along the sidewalk—no *abayas*, only loosely wrapped garments in mauves, pinks and blues. Their step was jaunty, their faces bright and I was sure I heard singing as they passed. A lovely respite from the usual nondescript neutrals. In a twinkling, they faded away around the corner and I touched my eyes to see if I was dreaming.

As Baba recovered and resumed work, I found a half filled crossword puzzle again and he was able to take pleasure in the birthday cards I had hand carried. In bed, he leaned against his pillow, taking in each name, smiling, nodding, coughing and healing. He told me stories about how and why *mutawas* had approached his friends and about incredible stunts performed on roadways by out of control drivers.

Ala Tool

A week after my arrival, the New York branch of our offspring were in Milwaukee, so all three kids phoned us. Using the family room speakerphone, just feet away from my patio, we had a great five-way chat. There was a price to pay for such frivolity, though—dreariness and brooding weighing me down the rest of the evening and following me into slumber.

It looked like it was going to take longer than the week it took when I went back home, to get my days and nights straightened out. I had not slept 8 hours at a stretch yet, and usually just managed 2 to 4-hour increments around the clock. That wouldn't have been unusual in and of itself, but since boredom can cause fatigue and depression can cause excessive sleep, it was hard to distinguish what was causing what.

I continued my daily practice of starting the day getting in touch with air, water, fire and earth. Deep, slow breaths focusing on my intentions, warm baths, a sunny window or beeswax candles and caring for Baba's plants were part of the fixings, if I could keep my thoughts positive and if I could tell when the start of the day was.

Once perspective prevailed, I recognized benefits to this split-sleeping schedule. Wide-awake during the heart of the night, I painted or cooked up a pot of something that would improve with age. At that hour, I wouldn't be interrupted by the doorbell or phone. Likewise, I valued the midday coma, not only because it broke up the monotony of the solitary day, but also because I could stay up later at night to see what went on in this culture of night owls.

At first, my purpose became skewed. Instead of expressing my uniqueness in a new setting, I protected myself from invalidation. Eventually I hoped to prevent the constraints of my physical form from driving the fact out of my head that I am a spiritual being, only having harrowing human experiences at the moment.

The day after calling the kids, *Shaban* ended for the year 1421 *Hejera*, and *Ramadan* began—the month of contemplation and meditation. TV news would again be full of which Ambassador or President or dignitary or other Muslim King "sent a cable to King Fahd Ibn Abdul Aziz to congratulate him on the occasion of the advent of the holy month of *Ramadan*." [53]

It had warmed up to between 19 and 21^0 C. (65 and 70^0 F.). It had not rained for two days and the sky was its usual silky blue. My moods had stabilized, more or less and I was ready for the earlier,

Jewel Dhuru

longer and louder prayers, the atmosphere of sacrifice and nocturnal work and shop schedules. Now that I had fought my way back in, I had reached a shelter, insulated from the full impact. Back to the eye of the storm.

Chapter 24: *Ramadan*

"The nail that sticks up gets hammered down" [54]
—Japanese proverb

The first day of *Ramadan*, a Monday, we unexpectedly found ourselves driving up to a barricaded gate with a guard holding a 32 x 25 cm. (14"x10") mirror on a meter long (3') pole. After circling the car with it, he tapped on the hood, which Baba opened. He looked in and then repeated the drill with the trunk. He was looking for bombs. Then he came to the window.

"What's the purpose of your visit, Sir?"

This was the usual protocol when entering this few acres of Earth, under the jurisdiction of a Western embassy, surrounded by striated rock formations and palms.

"To go to the Gift Shop and Library," Baba answered.

The guard waved us through.

It all started when Baba came home for lunch that day. The cafeteria was closed, as it would be all month, because of *Ramadan*. He could have walked over to the nearby hospital cafeteria, but he came home instead. With him, he brought the embassy shop hours. This was the day of the week they were open latest and his duties finished earlier all that month. So about 4:15 that afternoon, we breezed through hilly country, our gaze riveted to tendrils of dark pink bougainvillea spilling over expanses of parapets protecting even more expansive mansions. Walls again. I delighted in their absence on the campus, unobstructing our view of the people from a variety of origins.

The ritual of the mirror completed, we wandered into the gift shop and met a warm-hearted woman who told us camping stories about at the Wahba Crater near Jiddah. Baba was equally comfortable there and at his office, but for me, to be in that cheery, colorful environment for just that hour with it's no *abayas*, higher chairs, free and easy conversation, smiles and laughter and even a Christmas shop was such a shot in the arm, I went out feeling quite refreshed. But not without picking up a couple of necessities. Surplus paperbacks in the library were 5 SR each, about $1.40 US and, of all things, I found a beautiful, but inexpensive cane. I had been thinking of getting one,

Jewel Dhuru

just for emergencies. The cane was bamboo shaped and colored, with black rings at 10 cm. (4") intervals, Chinese pictures up the stem and a shapely black handle. Baba's special find was a magnet of a buxom Saudi lady, cloistered in black except for her eyes, with the caption, "Eyes by Yves St. Laurent—Body by chocolate chip".

As the guard waved us through barricade, it was 5:30 P.M. The *Maghreb salah*, at sunset, was just reaching its ending strains. It sounded like a crooner's voice on a victrola that was winding down and being wound back up again while the needle was still on the record. Better voices would appear later that month. We debated whether or not to do errands.

"There'll be a lot of traffic," Baba moaned.

We resolved to risk it, but after a couple of minutes, noticed the roads and sidewalks were practically deserted.

"There's not too much traffic yet," I ventured.

Not even any bicycles, which only came out during this cooler weather. It was eerie—so quiet and still. Here and there were only a couple of *thobs* and black mustaches, standing on street corners with the ubiquitous cell phones attached to their ears and a few Indian workers moving about. *Salah* was finished, wasn't it? Of course— we'd been saying it all day, but it still had not registered. The first day of *Ramadan*. Everybody would be home breaking their fast with extended families, going from one brother's to another on successive days.

Yes, it was quiet on the street, but inside, what feasts and frivolity there must have been. Children lived in anticipation of gifts for Eid at the end of the month. Special *Ramadan* recipes were shown on TV, high in calories, to keep energy levels up. An Egyptian woman told me that typically, women gained weight when fasting, while the men, who pray more physically, upping and downing on their prayer rugs, lose some. The idea of gathering each evening in this way seemed festive, as well as supportive. Leaving aside the matter of whether or not personal choice is available, traditions with which we are raised can give comfort. This was a form of happy living, I thought. The thought struck me that even aware of alternatives, who was to say most people wouldn't choose to continue what they usually do and be happy about it?

If this was break fast time, the shops and bank wouldn't be open until after 9:00 PM either. So we went home to catch *Taj Mataj* on

Ala Tool

TV, a *Ramadan*-only spoof on Saudi culture. We didn't understand 95% of the verbal but the comic non-verbal spoke louder anyway, criticizing the driving, bureaucracy, veils and *salah*. I thought I understood why the program was only shown that month. The idea behind fasting was for experiencing lack of privilege first hand. A program for laughing at oneself seemed in keeping with this tone of self-improvement.

That was the first of 30 hushed days and nights. Most shops were open only from 10:00 A.M. to about 2:00 P.M. and again from 9:00 P.M. until 3:00 A.M. Sleep for fasters was secured in split shifts. Some of Baba's Saudi colleagues were absent from work for a large chunk of the month. Swarms hit the streets, restaurants and shops again after 9:00 P.M. Muslim expats told stories of how, in their countries, daytimes of deprivation were followed by nights of amusements—tents with music and dancing. They related how the best voices were saved for *Ramadan*, raising the tenor of *salah*. Not so in Riyadh. Except for pliable plastic tubes of yellow, green, blue, red and variegated lights spiraled around tree trunks, lamp poles and outlining buildings, and signs proclaiming *Ramadan Mubarak*, to be followed by *Eid Mubarak* at Eid, everything was low key. Mercifully, even the groups of teen Saudi boys, usually cavalierly sitting on expat cars in the parking lots, were lessened. It never failed to get our attention when a *muezzin*, during a protracted prayer, vented fervent feelings, and to complete the cacophony, began crying. We opened the window and listened.

A number of interesting occurrences peppered the month. One *Ramadan* day, we had just stopped at the roadside when squealing tires pierced our eardrums. A slightly creased van pulled up ahead and the offender took the rear position. The driver in the foreground circled his vehicle examining it minutely before meeting the other driver halfway, right in front of Baba's window. Preparing for either fireworks or the opposite extreme, we sat and listened. After a handshake and *salams*, a quiet talk ensued. Within minutes, both were on their way. Some say there are few, if any, swear words in Arabic. Some say Arabs learned the English ones readily enough.

The daily admonition during *Ramadan* to avoid fighting might have had something to do with this sedate settlement.

"If someone tries to argue with you," the TV advisement in a deep male voice went, "tell him twice: I am fasting." Is it possible to be non-violent, but warlike? Coping with the harshest realities of life with equanimity but ready to bear arms for beliefs in a cause?

It wasn't until the streets were quiet that I took more detailed notice of the architecture at a leisurely pace. It was safer for Baba to take pictures, too, because of fewer watchful eyes enforcing prohibitions against photography. One large sandy colored, ministry building still had the historical, long, vertical, extremely narrow lancet windows, perhaps originally designed as protection from projectiles. From the outside, it looked beautiful, but closed in. From the inside, I could only imagine how the windows affected the outlook.

A few office buildings sported a curious shape. The sides were all glass, except for vertical rows of concrete partitions sticking out 2/3 meter (2') between each row of windows, and the windows themselves were angled in such a way that the view was slanted, oblique. The same slant was repeated with elongated side panels on apartment balconies. The design might have been to shield against sun and sandstorm, but also effectively cut off any peripheral view. Your view was only what was right in front of you.

Other ministries were narrow at the base and gradually built up to wide expectations at the top. This meant all the views, starting from the top down were leaning in only one direction. The facades of several apartment buildings were gable steps, staggered, coming forward in stages as I panned from right to left, like a giant horizontal set of stairs, preventing any view of a neighbor. Indeed, the windows of our own bedrooms and second sitting room were recessed two feet. In the bedroom, what I lacked in view, was made up for in surface area for strewing cookie crumbs and rice for pigeons and sparrows. It's fortunate most of our solutions, just like the causes of most problems, are right under our noses, anyway.

The first ever shipload of legitimate foreign tourists, from Great Britain, were given clearance to arrive on the shores of Jiddah during *Ramadan*, just after Thanksgiving, 2000, reported the Arab News. [55] The Kingdom claims hundreds of thousands of tourists each year, advertising hotels, restaurants and amusements. Counted in that number are generally only Muslims from other countries on pilgrimage, expats working in the Kingdom or Saudis themselves visiting other Saudi cites and sites. As I see it, unless I seek contact with cultures having different attitudes, rules and values from my own, I'm just rattling around in my own jar of marbles. No matter how colorful or interestingly patterned the marbles, they're still in a jar. The said shipload came to experience a new culture and shop, but since only allowed in on a *Jumma* morning during *Ramadan*, normal traffic was nonexistent and all the shops were closed.

Now and then, I would go along for the ride when Baba did errands. As we drove along shopping thoroughfares, cavernous interiors of shop after shop, brightly lit but with no customers, surprised us at first. The heights of the ceilings, three times what was necessary to exhibit racks of clothes, carpets or furnishings, were baffling.

At intersections, late at night, young, tired looking girls and boys walked between stopped cars, selling boxes of tissues. Generally, the kids just plunked the four-pack in through the window onto Baba's lap and took his 6 SR ($1.50 US), without a smile or a *shukran*. But once, a young boy, 7 or 8 years of age, came by my window and tap-tapped on the door. I waved the palm of my hand at him saying no thanks through the closed glass. He didn't even look at me but with an air of not taking no for an answer, he tap-tapped again and when I looked over, he pointed down at fringe my *abaya*, sticking out of the bottom of the door, and then with tissue boxes in tow, he moved on down the row.

When we got to Baba's shops, he went and I would get out a book and alternate between reading and soaking up local color. I observed, probably while I was being observed. Short, sinewy Bangladeshi car washers roamed the parking lots. We often had the car washed and swept out this way. A constant layer of silt was falling. It didn't take splashing through puddles to muddy a car there. It cost 10 SR, about $2.70 U.S. for a hand wash and dry, though from a common bucket. Hoses were not to be used for washing cars. This was the desert.

For months, Baba labored under the delusion that these guys brought two fresh buckets of water, one exclusively to wash and one to rinse our car alone. I hesitated to tell him the same bucket was hauled about for a dozen cars. Baba was surprised his meticulous eye had not picked up on this procedure of using used water. The trick was in the wiping. After applying the soapy bucket water to the roof, hood and trunk with gauzy cloth number 1, causing soap bubbles to streak down and intermingle with the brown, silty, sludge, the best washers wiped every square inch they could reach with gauzy cloth

Jewel Dhuru

number 2. Then again with numbers 3 through 5 or 6, the cloths getting progressively cleaner and drier as the numbers increased. I got out while they brushed the floor and wiped windows and dashboard on my side. One windshield wiper raised when finished kept the driver from taking off without paying. That was a way to keep bombers away, too. I could have just given the washers the 10 SRs, but I knew Baba wanted to inspect their work, so I left it to him.

I left a great deal to him and started down the road to complacence again, but only about what was out of my control, like not worrying about

- how to pay the American Express, phone and electric bills,
- how to get a re-entry visa from the bank to be exchanged for the passport held by Baba's sponsor, which in turn, secured a visa at an embassy,
- what our Plan B was when the flight we wanted was all booked up,
- how to get to places we frequented,
- who would buy our car and
- and which cargo company we would used to ship our stuff home.

Eventually, I even became lackadaisical about answering the phone. It seldom rang anyway and was usually for Baba. I didn't even pay attention to who was coming out of which flat in our building. It felt odd but it was temporary and gave me more time to tend to my own emotional bruises and find new strengths to develop.

While at shopping centers, I recalled friends back home who asked me if women were required to walk a few steps behind their husbands. The dance I saw unfolding involved men who got out of cars, snatched up a young child and headed for the mall where his pals were. Women and children pulled up the rear at a more leisurely pace. When they came back to the car, the man with the key was often last because he was burdened with all her purchases and the same small child, so she waited at the locked car door for him.

Twice, during the throng beginning after 9:00 P.M., while at my observation post, half exhausted women from pounding shopping aisles leaned heavily on our car, not realizing I was there. Once, I was sure an earthquake had hit the car in the shape of a short Saudi girl, only eyes visible, who flopped and draped herself cavalierly, arms up-

Ala Tool

stretched, face down, over the roof near Baba's window. I was surprised by the tremor and black curtain moving passed the pane and sighted a sprawled body sliding slowly downwards. When her eyes became visible, I smiled and could tell by the wrinkling at the corners of her eyes that she was smiling, too. She leaned for another half minute and then waved at me when the key arrived for her neighboring car.

The second time, I was reading in a considerably reclined seat when the car suddenly started to rock. An exhausted, buxom lady, was leaning her back against my window, and in her quest to find the most restful position, had collapsed the side mirror. I debated what to do, and decided to jump into the fray by straightening up my seat. It worked. Her young son poked her in the ribs and jerked his thumb towards me. Ready for anything, I watched for her face. It was uncovered, round and very cheerful, in an exhausted way. A black scarf blanketed her hair. She straightened up immediately, smiling and holding up the palms of both hands in a gesture of contrition. With a broad smile, I tactlessly pointed at the mirror, which she straightened and then continued to vibrate her palms. I nodded profusely. Quiet convulsions of laughter escaped both our throats. I regret not thinking to lower the glass sooner, to talk with words instead of gestures, to ask her if she wanted to rest in our back seat for a minute, or just to have a laugh with her without the impervious layer between us. I couldn't help thinking this insulating oneself from the culture business was a double-edged sword. She moved away with hands still in the air and still smiling broadly. As her son passed my window, he was also grinning, the mirth in his eyes passed down from mother to son. I was glad to have shared that fleeting moment with them, and then they were gone.

The next day, a third car bombing occurred in Riyadh. On the hood of the targeted car, near the windshield, an unknown hand had put a juice box with a blast in it.

A week into the month, we went back to the well-guarded embassy shops and library for more second hand books and gifts for relatives. After the guards cleared us, we bumped over four concrete speed-breakers in quick succession and realized the guard had not closed our trunk. When we got out of the car, it must have been a flight of fancy, but even the air seemed different there—fresher. After gathering books, bookmarks and bags woven in Bedouin tent patterns,

Jewel Dhuru

cards and a Thai sarong, we went out to the car, where the trunk was still open.

Yes, feeling so well guarded, we'd forgotten to close it before we went in. Still, the warnings were everywhere. As Baba checked the trunk and put in our purchases, I crossed the parking area to throw away wrappers from candy we'd been given inside. From there, it struck me that I could see under the car. I didn't expect to see anything, but bent to look anyway, so imagine my surprise when I heard my own voice speaking to Baba.

"Oh, there's something under the car!" I exclaimed.

It was light colored and the size of a child's shoe box—right under the epicenter of the back seat. We both peered a little closer, not believing that what we'd been hearing on the news could come this close to home. I walked up to it. It started to move. It was a little white cat!

One particularly magical moment left a lasting impression. We headed for home at 5:00 on a Thursday *Ramadan* afternoon. We'd gone to the gold souk at Kuwaiti Market to get the detached post of an earring I had bought there two years earlier, re-soldered to its main frame. Once we located the right goldsmith, it hardly took a minute and we were off again.

The shops were just closing as the *muezzin*'s moan vibrated softly in the distance. The sun was setting. The sky was changing rapidly and the air was a balmy 29^0 C. (75^0 F.). The few clouds were darkening to blue-gray in their denser centers and the more transparent edges were turning into pink frills, their brightness intensifying by the second. Rays emanating from the setting sun spread upwards in shafts and were superimposed over wispy, straggly snippets of emergent clouds.

The sky reached a medium shade of gray just as we were rounding the corner of a hushed street and to complete this astral scene, two rows of trees parted, across an open area, exposing a mosque. Discerning in daylight what its actual color was would wait for another day. At that moment, the combination of its own floodlighting and reflections from the swiftly shifting sky created the impression of the palest sea foam green dome and a light gray edifice having no clear upper edges, melting into the sky, while the blasts of lighting under a row of small arches all around the base gave the illusion of a liftoff. The effect was disorienting. Baba pulled the car over and we

Ala Tool

just sat and took it in, like watching a time-lapse film. It was moments like this, when no body was around, we decided, that this city might not be half bad.

A few days later, in the middle of *Ramadan*, in early December 2000, we were on our way to the Diplomatic Quarter. We planned on going to India for *Ramadan* vacation, which that year, included Christmas and New Year's. Normally, once the sponsor issues the *Iqama*, they keep the passport, but today Baba had traded his *Iqama* in because we had official business with the passports. Three years earlier, our five-year Indian visas had been stamped into passports that expired two years hence; so two jaunts were required to the Indian Embassy to have new visas stamped into new valid passports.

It was 3:00 P.M. as we approached the DQ. A bald hill with five trees and a stone tower on top, just on the outskirts, had attracted Baba's attention. As we advanced, I saw an access road to the top and wondered if the site had historical significance.

We breezed through the entrance roundabout, scrutinized by guards with rifles. The *Assr salah* had started, mid-afternoon, but DQ business didn't observe *Ramadan* hours. The embassy closed at 3:30 P.M. In the area, besides embassies, private flats with sports facilities neighbored an Italian restaurant, shops and a long wadi, like a sunken, dry riverbed with lots of palms, and a walkway winding like a path through a chambered nautilus. I waited in the car while Baba went in, the bald hill practically over my head. A conflagration of color passed by in the form of six women wearing Punjabi dresses, adding to the semi-casual setting. The car clock said 3:26 P.M. when Baba got back.

"So where would you like to go now?" he inquired.

There was a back seat full of jobs to do: letters to take to the post office, negatives to have printed, and an electric bill to pay at the bank. But nothing was open now, until 9:00 PM.

On the other hand, I had brought a small vial of the ashes of our cherished dog that had passed on a couple of years earlier. Before this, his ashes had been set free in his own back garden in the Midwest, in Central Park New York and in the lush front garden in Mumbai. I wanted to set his spirit to roam in the wadi too, on a green grassy circle under a shady palm.

So we headed for the wadi and afterwards, we'd see about the five-tree hill. We circled several big, beautiful roundabouts on the

Jewel Dhuru

way, 50 feet (16 meters) in diameter, with central sculptures or fountains, and one Baba particularly fancied, with colorful flowers and a small grove of date palms. He pulled over to the curb.

"I'm just going to get a picture," he declared.

Out came his new toy, a digital camera that whirred, beeped, flashed, and had lots of buttons, which loaded pictures onto a removable flashcard that could be printed from a computer, like a file. When he drifted off, no one was on the street except two Saudi guards in military green that had just rounded the corner with a lackadaisical gait, a block ahead of us, coming towards us. I reclined my seat and closed my eyes. Before 20 seconds had elapsed, I opened my eyes to the sound of urgent steps passing the car and a shadow moving over me. The guards had reached us in double time, one perusing the interior of our car and one approaching Baba. As soon as I heard the quick step, an alarm went off in my mind. Of course! Embassies and cameras were mutually exclusive. The colorful garb, the wadi, the flowers, the perhaps historic hill; we'd forgotten we were in the Diplomatic Quarter.

After the shadow passed, I took out a small mirror and tried to see Baba without turning around. Sure enough. He was standing right behind, handing his passport to someone beyond my view. Instinct told me to sit tight. Before long, my door opened and Baba spoke.

"A little trouble. Can you come and translate?" he asked.

I stood up and said "*Marhaba*"- hello, to a gentle faced mustached guard and among the three of us, we sorted out our citizenship, our intention, that we had an *Iqama* but not right there at that moment, that Baba only took one picture which he displayed on his 5 sq. cm. (2" sq.) flashcard screen and that this kind of camera didn't have any film. Oh dear! No film to confiscate! The other guard was already on his radio contacting the Saudi Captain. The gentle faced guard was all apologies but he had to follow the rules. The paperwork began.

The Captain arrived in a jeep within minutes, chewing a Mishwak stick, a bit of tree branch used traditionally to clean the teeth. Also not much English, but enough to say "follow me" and to motion for us to turn our vehicle around. Just before we drove away, the gentle faced guard lowered his face to my open window and said what I understood as the equivalent of "If you just give him the film, you won't need to do anything else. Understand?"

"*Naam*," I said. "Yes." I understood him, but …

    We followed the Captain, who had to slow down once so as not to lose us on a turn. A second time, he actually stopped on a roundabout as we temporarily vanished from his view.

    "Could you drive a little faster?" I pressed.

    Baba's curt "No" told me he had his own agenda. Arriving at the guard kiosk at the edge of the courtyard of the police station, the Captain drove in and we parked on the street. Baba asked me to come and help with the language. I rolled up the glass and opened the door. I had never felt in such demand. But as I straightened up, the Captain had come back, and fanning the air toward me with the palm of his hand, said, "wait, wait."

    I sat back down and lowered the glass again. Through the side mirror, I watched Baba pass the kiosk and disappear. He was only gone five minutes, but during that time, he was the only one of the pair of us who knew that women weren't allowed in the police station, that the Police Chief spoke English and had heard of filmless cameras. He was the one who, before being sent on his way, was getting a squeeze of the shoulder from the Chief, along with being told "sorry," that they had to follow procedure. By three minutes, he was the one who already knew he wouldn't even have to delete the infamous photo that started all the trouble. But for me, those drawn out five minutes were filled with the unknown so the tightness at my neck had begun at four. When Baba got back, we headed for the exit. The ashes and the bald hill would wait for another day.

Jewel Dhuru

Chapter 25: Reunions And New Unions

"Friends are nations in themselves" [56]
—Emily Dickensen

Old Neighbors and New

"Well, Yewel, are you settled now?" asked Baba's European pal. He always pronounced the J in my name like a Y. "I don't know why I ask if you're settled. People don't really settle here. They just do the best they can for this time," he continued.

This interval of my life was a semi-retreat, immersed in philosophy and music, alone with my thoughts much of the time, a semi-contemplative life with ample portions of doubt. Smoothing out the creases in my friendship with Baba was a constant occupation, too, trying to harness the toll the trip was taking for some useful purpose. Opportunities to add to my stores of patience abounded. But the retreat, as a matter of course, was punctuated with various events.

That particular day, five of us had gathered in our sitting room. We were going together to a Portuguese restaurant. Over the next months, with or without company, we began the rounds of ethnic restaurants. With gastronomic juices on overdrive, we partook of *masala dosa* at a South Indian restaurant, Shish Taouk (skewered chicken, peppers and tomatoes) at a Turkish one, grilled hamour at a Fish and Chips, roasted chicken with rice and salad at an Afghani one, and from Arab snack shops, *foul* (ground fava beans), spinach pies or *schwarma*, relish trays with *humus* (chick peas and sesame paste) and *baba ganoush* (eggplant and garlic), each served with fresh Arab bread still too steamy too handle. The only thing missing was a glass of wine.

I met many people that first month. That evening, the only other woman and I agreed to trade paperbacks when we'd finished them. I had met her before. She was pleasant, but labored under the same pressures I did, and carved out her own niche of privacy.

"So how are things in the U.S.?" another visitor asked me a week later.

This query came just while conversations were buzzing about the 2000 Presidential election in the United States and how the Supreme courts would decide the fates of the ballots and non-ballots that were being counted, not counted and re-counted.

That same week, I had phoned Anita, the previous next-door neighbor. She would call in a day or two, before coming to visit, with her children, she said. But then *Ramadan* started so that changed the complexion of everything. Three weeks passed before she and two kids dropped in unexpectedly one morning while I was still in my pre-bath apparel and before I had cleared the sitting room of the remnants of Baba's late night newspapers and snacking. Circular timing, life as a process, I reminded myself. I was still glad to see them, and tried to thrust out of my mind the idea that my state of unreadiness would be a topic at their next coffee morning.

In the Supermarket parking lot, we ran into Tanya, the non-Saudi lady, married to a Saudi, Baba's new next-door neighbors and now mine, too. I met him and their 3-year old the day I had arrived. He let Baba splice into his satellite dish. On Tanya, all that was visible was the sweetness behind her heavily made up eyes and the delicate frame of the hand she extended. She looked young, in her late 20s, and was full of apologies for not having invited me over yet.

"It's *Ramadan*," she explained. "It's busy ... every night we have to go somewhere and tonight we're having company ... and with the fasting ... when it's all over, I'll call you," she concluded.

I understood. With four kids, it would have been busy enough, without the added strains of that month.

"If I can help with the kids, let me know," I offered.

She thanked me, the twisting to and fro of her upper body giving the impression of someone who doesn't know which way to turn.

A week later, my garments brushed briefly against her daughter's, for less than the time it takes to open and close an elevator door. The norm was that Saudis silently passed non-Saudis in the hall, Saudi eyes lowered. If we arrived at the elevator simultaneously, they let me enter alone and waited for its return. But on one rare occasion, a Saudi female asked where I lived. On another, as I waited alone in the hall for Baba, a lone Saudi male entered our building on a windy winter day, eyes downcast, and surprised me by muttering "it's cold" as he passed.

But one day, I was standing outside the elevator shaft in the empty hallway, waiting to ride down, when the doors slid open. When I had first arrived in the country, I'd heard about the configurations, nationalities and religions of the families that Baba knew in our building, just as the neighbors must have heard about me. So when the door opened revealing three Saudi girls, all shorter than my 150 cm. (5'8"), one completely covered and two with only their eyes showing and then one swished quickly passed me with a tired look in her eyes, heading for Tanya's flat, I thought this must be her adolescent daughter. My eyes alternately followed her and tried to take in the whole scene at the same time, so she faded into her flat and her door slammed shut before I could say anything. Marshalling my wits and seeing the elevator still open, I stepped towards it. But before my shoe crossed the threshold, an arm from within the conveyance, draped in black shot across my face and pushed a button for ascension to a higher floor. The door closed and within 15 seconds of the commencement, there I was standing in the empty hallway again!

As I mentally replayed the episode, I could hear a quick-paced Sergio Mendez number in the background, coming to life when the elevator doors opened, picking up steam, racing along towards the crescendo and stopping abruptly, timed to coincide with the closing of the doors.

Profiles and Perspectives

Alone in my sitting room one day, I wondered if I felt isolation and displacement more acutely that others. More than once, I had been described as too sensitive. But sensitivity is an asset and does not equal vulnerability. I thought of the other wives and how they coped.

One was from India, like her husband. The pair had spent the last fifteen years working and moving households from one exotic country to another, staying only three years in each. Twice a year, they visited their grown kids, in school in India. In Riyadh, she grumbled, too, but was committed to riding out the sacrifices for her kids.

Another was American, married to a Saudi, and she'd studied Arab culture and loved the best parts of it even before she met him. She cautioned me about letting tedium and apathy get to me and went around town with a smile on her face, one that she brought out from deep within to keep that caged feeling away.

A third originated in a Spanish speaking culture while her husband was African. At one time, she had presided over a large

Ala Tool

household and three servants in the land of his birth until the economy took a turn for the inconvenient and then they and the children moved to Riyadh. An enthusiast of coffee mornings, bazaars and the campus sports club, she suffered at exam time, dragging the kids out of bed before dawn to memorize textbooks for that day's tests.

Another lived and held a professional position in the African country of her and her husband's births. He made the move years earlier for his career. She came to Riyadh three times a year to visit him and used the solitude to catch up on lost sleep and hobbies. Their grown kids were all over the globe.

One Asian was married to a man from a South African country. She was accustomed, since childhood, to frequent moves. Well educated, she didn't work because of her kids' dependence on her for transportation and because of numerous community responsibilities.

Another, an Asian Muslim, had a college degree but had never worked in her field. She was content to stay home, to take care of the kids and house. She studied Arabic so she could study the Qur'an, went swimming and hosted coffee mornings.

Yet another, part of a social, good natured Asian Muslim family, seemed content after more than a decade there. He golfed and she shopped and cooked. She loved the domestic arts, indulged her esthetic sense and helped the kids with their studies. They actively participated in their party circuit and excelled at keeping spirits up.

A female colleague of Baba's was from a North African country. Her husband remained there because of his job, but her child and parents accompanied her. They traveled back and forth at vacations. For professional families, this was the norm.

It was common to see women walking around the campus, a 3-mile jaunt. But one, a North African, went round and round for two hours every day. Her husband insisted after you get used to the place, it grows on you. If I could have walked that much, I would have gone into IKEA or the adjoining department store, just outside the campus, for a change of scenery.

When she passed the window, the memory of a polar bear at the zoo came to me, its plunging into the water, climbing out, a few steps this way, a few that, lumbering over to the other end of the pool and plunging in again. I wondered if there was a male counterpart to this phenomenon, this dance. Maybe it was going out in groups for the same dinner to the same restaurant time after time or maybe shopping for watches, clothes and gadgets.

My former clients in the United States were individuals who had become semi-aware of their depth of discontent with the status quo, yet unable to change, and didn't know how to expand their repertoire of constructive outlets for sadness, anger and fear and for the joy that bubbled beneath. It was ironic that where I now lived for seven months, a similar state was what passed for an acceptable life for half the population, female and male.

Some expats had long-term goals: to save for their kids' educations or to retire on a ranch and others operated more for the short term, taking each year as it came. Some found living conditions better in Riyadh than in their own countries. Most of the marriages were long term.

Most of us found our sensibilities ruffled at one time or other. Imaginative coping was required. We all learned how to gloss over the unpleasant, to tolerate what seemed intolerable, to turn a blind eye to the unlivable and get on with living. There was wisdom in this temporarily narrowed vision, shying away from dwelling on our larger lives.

I felt a bond with the wives, just from Baba's stories, even if we had not actually met. When a wife arrived, that couple hosted the bachelors of the moment for dinners or outings. She added variety with her voice and opinions. The guys reported our comings and goings, so we women were indirectly part of each other's Saudi experience.

What rankled was the lack of autonomy, that precious commodity with which many are born, but may not deeply value unless we see how others live. To have the run of the town, to enjoy my patio and to drive when I wanted, were privileges I would take for granted no longer.

I must have gotten closer to reaching my goal of detachment because I thought of myself as being launched on my path along with other boats and ships, houseboats, speedboats, yachts and an aircraft carrier, all navigating murky waters, passing each other during the long night, the darkness lit and buoyed by our auras, sometimes serving as lifeboats for each other, our wakes intertwining, each having a splash of life to show and share and then heading back out to sea. Perhaps I was getting too detached. At times, I didn't relish

Ala Tool

hearing a male voice. When Baba asked me for my opinions or preferences, I resisted the temptation to answer, "I don't care," although my tone must have belied my feelings. I knew the time would come when my spark would return, when I would be roused again, animated, galvanized, electrified to full power, but in those early months, I was still working on keeping my candle flame from becoming dim or being snuffed out altogether.

Baba and I Have a Talk

That Sunday, a week since my arrival was a regular workday, in *Ramadan*. Baba finished at 3:00 P.M. I had been looking forward to getting out of the flat in the evening. The only person I had talked to all day, besides Baba, materialized with the buzz of the doorbell right in the middle of my ceramic painting. Half the bells in the buildings had tinny sounding chimes and our half had stabbing buzzers that always gave me a jolt.

Centenarians, also, had recommended moderation in all things, not getting stuck in loss, and when retired, have a daily schedule. This was as unreasonable a facsimile of retirement as I had ever experienced, so heeding the advice, weekday mornings were either for writing or artwork. I needed something worth getting up for.

Baba had bought a plain white, ceramic, soap dispenser and toothbrush holder, and he'd asked me to spruce them up. So we got blue and yellow paint and I started. I lined the kitchen table with newspaper and right in the middle of watching green form where the colors merged, the doorbell buzzed.

"Now who could that be?" I grumbled.

To my surprise, it was a limo driver claiming I had reserved him for that exact hour. Not this again. Reconnaissance? I dispatched him quickly and finishing the project, left it to dry.

"What am I going to do now?" was the question I spent the rest of the morning and afternoon asking myself and answering.

That evening, I didn't have anywhere special to go. We planned to find out about getting the ORBIT channel and to try copying the key again. But then the phone rang. Baba's buddy, Joseph, was going to Batha and asked him to come. ... Would I mind? ... Oh all right. I knew when I arrived I would have to share his attention with his friends; we'd go out tomorrow night. I had given up waiting for that

Jewel Dhuru

key a long time ago. If I really had to go somewhere, I'd just go and leave the door unlocked. The crime rate was low enough that I didn't have to keep myself captive over it.

Baba came home just to change clothes and have a quick chat and then he was off again. I milled about the sitting room, wondering what to do with the dregs of the evening. I had already listened to music half the day. I could have done laundry or soaked a pot of beans, Baba's favorite food since his surgery. There were always socks to darn or cleaning to do, but I didn't feel like doing anything domestic. I didn't feel, either, like watching an Arab channel or playing catch-up with a fast-moving French movie, subtitled by even faster-dissolving French phrases.

At times, there was nothing so soothing as the spell of sounds in a language I recognized. Oh, what luck! The Saudi station was showing an old episode of an English program—Third Rock from the Sun. Okay, I'd try it. And then something called The Walt Street Journal, trailed by Star Track, actually Star Trek—The Next Generation, both with words bleeped and parts chopped. Programs not normally on my agenda, but under the circumstances, welcome diversions. It was ironic that two otherworldly programs provided escapes from this other world.

After TV, I read and began to bring another puzzle to life. I had never really been a puzzle or crossword person, until what I called this Saudi stuff, started. But with days stretching ahead, it appeased my mind and kept some part of my brain active. In an odd way, when the pieces of puzzles fell into place, I felt that the pieces of my life did, too. I finally shelved my book and fell asleep about midnight.

In the morning, I awoke to see Baba already in a gray suit.

"I got home at 1:45 A.M," he was saying. They'd gone here and there and to a third pal's house and "look at the time—gotta go."

"Whoa! Wait a minute!" I exclaimed. He must have sensed I wasn't thrilled so he led me to the sitting room where he gave me a Beach Boys CD he'd bought at Batha. He'd intended to leave on the couch for me to find that morning. Placating? I don't know.

Then he sat down and we had a quick, though imperative talk—the first of many over the next weeks. We talked about adjustments we would each make and what we wanted to accomplish. Then suddenly, there it was.

"I'd like to accept a contact for one more year, if it's offered," he confided.

His statement loomed heavily in the air between us for a minute. I had heard rumblings of this over the last four months, but here it finally was, out loud, in his own voice. We knew the college liked his work and he shared mutual admiration with most of his colleagues. At his age, now 65, contracts were considered by committees on a yearly basis, so if we resolved to go this route, we would have to wait and see. But airline reservations and arrangements for the care of our house would have to be made in advance, so it wasn't too early to incubate plans.

For some time, I'd been mourning the changes in our daily proximity and how touchy cultural subjects had become. Like many momentous times, there was no fanfare and the room was quiet while Baba shared his thoughts. While he was newly retired, but still fit, he wanted to work at his chosen profession where he was held in esteem and reasonably recompensed.

"OK, I can cope with that," I replied, "but I don't want to spend another seven months here next year. At home, I'd like a hot tub and maybe an all climate patio to put it in." I'd wanted to tell him what I'd been thinking for months. The hot tub would do my muscles good. Maybe he had heard my rumblings through the kids. But finally, there it was, in my own voice. The seeds were planted.

Still, when he left for work, my marriage long habit of hugging him at the door evaporated almost overnight. Alone again, I searched for alternatives to the current impasse without behaving like a repellent. It was at such times I wondered if the clock had been turned back 50 years, if my life was really any different than that of my parents, where he was the breadwinner and her domain was domestic. Not for the first time, I examined my own intergenerational patterns, my similarities to my Dad and the fact that my husband and Mother had the same birthday.

I sought inspiration from a book I'd brought with me. It dealt with good medicine and the spirituality of nature, but with a zoological turn to it. It often soothed when I was troubled. I may be destined for a third year, with or without the return of Dr. B. Animal Medicine didn't have definite answers, only inspiration from the characters. All decisions would still be mine.

Two suggestions came to me. The one for the Yang, my right, male side, the outgoing energy, action part of me came from Horse, symbolizing power. It emphasized the power of entering Darkness and finding Light. That sounded familiar. The abuse of power would not lead to wisdom, true power is the wisdom in remembering my total journey, and compassion, teaching, and sharing my gifts and abilities are the gateways to power, it said. The suggestion for my Yin, my left, female side, the intuitive taking-things-in-stride part of me came from Buffalo, symbolizing prayer and abundance. It reminded me that smoke is a visual prayer, to recognize the sacredness of every walk of life, to honor another's pathway even if it brings me sadness, to be grateful for what I receive and that time brings serenity in the midst of chaos.[57] I meditated on this for a while. Then, I got up, went into the kitchen, lit up chunks of frankincense and ood, put spices, onion and garlic into a pot of soaking beans and I lay down to immerse myself in the Beach Boys.

Students with Bedouin Backgrounds

On a Wednesday evening, a week later, events were to start popping. A couple of Baba's students were to come over and translate the Saudi spoof, *Taj Mataj*. The primary student, Faisal, had helped Baba get our furniture and look at cars. And he was going to bring a friend. We made preparations. Two hours before they were due, Faisal phoned and begged off with a sore throat, perhaps tonsillitis. The other had said he was "90% sure" he would come. We waited in limbo. But on the stroke of 6:00 P.M., the buzzer riveted through us, and the 90% sure fellow and yet a third student appeared at the door, with a bowl of red and white carnations.

They sat for a while, explained the program, munched on snacks and glanced at photos. These days, they explained, a Bedouin means simply, a livestock farmer. One fellow's grandfather had been a nomad until their family moved to the city. The other, Mr. 90% Sure, lived as a Bedouin until the age of five, and he did most of the explaining.

He recalled those years as the happiest of his life, telling stories around tents, eating roasted lamb, drinking camel milk, and having lots of companions, since he was a product of his Father's fourth marriage. He was unmarried but planned on two wives himself.

Ala Tool

"A woman is like a diamond—you know diamond?" he asked caressing a giant stone in the air with his hands, one that would make the Hope Diamond blush. Giggling, he continued.

"If you see her too much, she loses her ... how can I tell you?"

He never did say but assented heartily to my suggestion of the word "value?" even though my gut feeling later told me he really would have preferred the word 'appeal' and then he turned to the TV with a dismissive air of finality. He was very matter of fact about it.

I heard myself say, "Does she?" perhaps inaudibly, because the air was full of the sound of the second guy agreeing with the first. What surprised me was I didn't feel compelled to argue with him. To try to change his mind would have been doing the same thing I disliked when people shoved unsolicited Islamic books at me. I could exchange ideas with people who were still refining their purpose, but not with this level of certitude.

The two guys stayed about an hour. Then two minutes before the last, *Isha salah*, while Baba and I were still eating, they suddenly jumped up, announced they had to go for prayer, thanked us politely and left.

I struggled with suspending judgment. I recalled the words of Leo Buscaglia who counseled that the models of love are often modest and unsure, while the models of the opposite forces are verbal and certain, and I wondered if I ought to have shared more of my attitudes. On the other hand, I also recalled the words, attributed to the Chinese Hsin Hsin Ming, who said "the great way is not difficult for he who has no preferences; but make the slightest distinction and Heaven and Hell are set infinitely apart." [58]

As we put the food away, Baba provided background about the three students. Before I'd arrived, Mr. 90% Sure had entered a café across the road from the campus, where Baba and Paul were lunching. The student greeted them and sat at a table of his own. He subsequently left before them, saying, "see you Saturday" on the way out. Within minutes, their lunch concluded, Baba approached the cashier to pay the bill and was told that, as was the custom, it had been taken care of by the fellow who had just left!

"You're such a kind man, Dr. Dhuru," Mr. 90% Sure, once had said to Baba, when they were in class together. Then he appended, "You should be a Muslim."

This sort of statement can be, and apparently was, taken in different ways. One non-Muslim colleague suggested a kind Muslim should join his particular religion. Searching for the highest thought I could muster, I decided the message between the collective lines was that each religion strives for and believes in the superlative level of their own sense of kindness.

The Camel Souk

The next afternoon, Thursday, Baba called a North American acquaintance that had expressed an interest in going to the Camel Souk, on the outskirts of town. We both liked it there. So first, Daniel came over for tea and then we set off.

Arriving, we pulled the car on to what appeared to be an out of the way bit of sand, off a well-worn path. We wandered, memorizing the shapes of camels, sheep and goats. Acres of them spread before us, in dozens of roughly constructed pens, beasts in a variety of colors, coats, and ear-lengths. Adjacent to our car, a large brown dromedary, tethered to a stake by a single foot, wore a circular channel into the ground, as it munched hay, its lower lip flapping loosely. I made myself thoroughly at home. Ambling on, pens of colorful goats scurried about. When the small, white ones with long ears sat down, they looked like large white rabbits.

Eventually we got back to the car. Pick-up trucks had been coming and going from this same area, near black camel hair tents and a long red rug. We finally figured out this wasn't just a stray bit of sand. We must actually have parked in somebody's private driveway. Maybe that's why a man in *thob* and *shmal* kept greeting us. Just before driving away, he came right over to our car and waved at Baba.

"Hello brother," he shouted.

Then he leaned into the car and spoke to the rest of us.

"Hello sister" and again "Hello brother" to Daniel.

He was a farmer and butcher and this was his place of business. Muhammed welcomed us profusely and invited us to walk across the gray crushed stone yard, along the red carpet and past predominantly red prayer rugs, into his tent, where seven assorted Sudanese, Saudi and Indian customers, friends and the help, all men and one boy sat, in an oval, on predominantly red carpets, around a campfire. As we

Ala Tool

compared notes later, Daniel confided he never would have gone to the souk alone, leave aside into the tent, and I certainly wouldn't have. But Baba created this kind of adventure for himself all his life, so once again I had him to thank for the opportunity. I approached the tent with an attitude of one part nervousness, two parts excitement and three parts believing that whatever transpired there would be good.

The tent was really more of a lean-to, about 4 x 7 meters (12 x 20 feet), open on the long side nearest us, with a wooden roof covered with heavy plastic tarp for rainy weather, black camel hair walls lined on the inside with gray blankets. The fire was in the center on gray crushed stone and surrounding it, within the walls, were luxurious carpets and carpet covered, elongated cubes and cushions for resting backs and elbows.

The sun was setting. The men had just completed their *Maghreb* prayer and were about to break their fast. A metal tray of dates was passed around, along with porcelain demitasses of Saudi coffee. The hourglass shaped coffee pot with a toucan bill spout was kept warm by the embers. The coffee consumed, the little cups were put into a small pail of water. Then we were offered the smallest root beer mugs I've ever seen of tea, warming by the fire in its own, squatter, metal pot. Empty mugs went into a second bucket. Against my better judgment, but unwilling to risk offending our hosts, I consumed most of both, with enough caffeine and tannin to keep me wired most of the night. No matter. It was, perhaps, once in a lifetime.

While all this coffee and tea drinking was going on, a most fascinating moment was unfolding. Conversations were going in all directions. Once we'd been introduced as "brothers" and "sister," that designated our position in the group, Baba explained later, conversant with the related Indian culture as he was. We were no longer outsiders, so business and social interactions could go on in our presence.

Muhammed, Baba and then I sat in a line, Daniel sitting askew nearest me. Muhammed and Baba talked while I listened. When Baba occasionally turned to look at me, what I read in his eyes was a pure form of fun.

Muhammed was 36 years of age and happily unmarried. He was shorter than us and had a large tummy. His business card, printed in Arabic and English, showed a color graphic of the heads of a goat and a camel facing in opposite directions with a long carving knife slicing vertically between them. He had just sold a camel to a customer for 2000 SR, about $600.00 U.S. Others talked to each other while a cell phone was whipped out to seal the deal.

When I'd lowered myself to the ground, my touchy muscles concerned me. I summoned all my powers of adaptation to help make this experience a positive one. Those acquainted with bioenergetics and aruvedic principles will be aware of the eight *chakras* on the body, like energy centers, the first being located at the base of the spine and the 8th being above the head, each relating to a specific endocrine gland, color and type of power. The 8th *chakra*, located about 30 cm. (12") above the head, and also called the Soul Star, enables us to take an objective squint at ourselves, to see ourselves doing and being synchronously. As the proceedings became more animated, part of my consciousness ascended to this perch, so I could enjoy the double benefit of being part of the group and observing the group at the same time.

Comments and questions flew back and forth. The most pleasingly choreographed set of synapses spanned perhaps only six minutes when signals were sent and received sometimes in sequence and sometimes simultaneously.

"Are you Muslim? Why didn't you come for *salah*?" a customer asked Baba.

"No, no, he's Hindi," meaning Hindu, the butcher said, answering for him.

A Saudi asked in Arabic if we had children. Fast on the heels of my answer, "*Wahid walad wi wahda bint*," came the inevitable question about our daughter's age and after my answer, a comment from him that brought laughter from the whole group. His words had come too quickly for my comprehension, but I was certain a marriage proposal hid in there somewhere. It happened all the time. In the meantime, a Sudanese fellow, recognizable from his bulbous white head wrap, directed a question to Daniel.

"Can you get me a job in America?" he queried.

The two Indians, it turned out, spoke Baba's mother tongue, one of 16 Indian languages. The house of one of their Grandfather's was situated in Baba's Mumbai neighborhood. So their conversation, across the bonfire, added a third language to the mix. When Baba told them I spoke a little *Marathi* too, of course, I had to confirm with,

"*Ho, mala pun yete*," and they nodded shyly in appreciation. Meanwhile the cell phone was being passed about so constant comment was coming from our camp.

Baba and I muttered to each other that it might be an idea to fetch the camera from the car, but even as we said it, my Soul Star told me that would have desecrated the precious memory already being recorded, and he seemed to know it, too, so the camera stayed put. The sun had set while we were in the tent. From my vantage point at the carpet's outer edge, I saw kittens come in and out of the attached tent, perhaps sleeping quarters. The fire and half moon were the only sources of light after the orange tones in the sky behind the camels had ceased to outline their curvy silhouettes. But intermittent gruff grunts continued.

After what we deemed a decent interval, we took our leave. To my amazed relief, sitting there had not aggravated my back and hip. It had actually been quite comfortable. We bid adieu to the assembled guests, the shyer ones looking away as I smiled, but more than half nodding and smiling back at me. Muhammed walked us to our car, parked beside his dusty pick-up truck. He asked us to wait and dug around in his back seat, eventually emerging with a bag full of fresh, small, white eggs from his own hens. He shook all three of our hands warmly and invited us to his farm sometime. The excitement of that brief half hour stayed with me for weeks and even now is a memory that conjures up the feeling that all is right with the world.

On the drive home, tents were strung with bright colored lights. These hubble bubble or Sheesha tents, Daniel pointed out, were shelters where men and boys smoked fruit flavored hookak pipes, drank tea and coffee, ate *schwarma* and played cards.

Lunch at a Cottage Compound

The next day, *Jumma*, Joseph invited us for lunch. He lived in a compound of quaint cottages. Within the ubiquitous barricades, narrow, rural roadways meandered through thick trees, abodes with both front and back yards and see-through fencing for semi-privacy. Beautiful plants grew in his yard: bougainvillea, roses, olive, rosemary, hibiscus and even an orange tree surrounded a small lawn and the inside was just as cheerfully decorated as the outside. Hazards abounded, of course: a leaky roof, limited water supply during dry months and a phone service that was erratic and wearisome, at best. But the atmosphere was peaceful and down the road were a swimming pool and clubhouse. He prepared a gourmet three-course lunch, which we ate on his patio, overlooked by compound cats.

By late afternoon, we prepared to go home. To reciprocate in kind to this gentle gourmet would have been like trying to sculpt a piece for Michelangelo as a gift, assuming he'd given us the Pieta in the first place. Some other way to help him would present itself in time.

We said our so-longs and I felt wonderfully relaxed as we drove away from the cottage. As we swung around the last corner, though, the walls reemerged and I realized, anew, where I really was. That might have alerted me, but it didn't. It wasn't until we got to our own parking lot that it suddenly dawned on me. As I exited the car wearing a red patterned outfit, I noticed I'd forgotten my black draperies on the cottage coat rack. My head told me to stand up straight, breathe deeply and walk slowly, but as I self-consciously walked to our building, my body wanted to hold its breath and move quickly. Still no key for the flat and now, not even an *abaya*.

The Art Gallery Lady

The last week before we left for *Ramadan* vacation, I looked into the possibilities of tutoring English and getting artwork into a show. In response to ads Baba had put up offering tutoring, I met educated families whose children did well in school, except for English grammar. I thought, not for the first time, that English is not the easiest language to learn, with its idiosyncratic spelling, numerous irregularities and loads of exceptions to rules and I thanked my lucky stars for the umpteenth time that it was one of my first languages.

I hoped to share my skill with Breathwork when the opportunity arose. Nothing to do with religion, but everything to do with spirituality, increasing one's awareness of the power of the breath to energize, to relax, to get in touch with what's inside and to release it. The subject would have to be broached carefully. My source of counseling clients from the first trip was gone and I felt sufficient turmoil in my own life that I didn't want to actively invite clients into it at that time. If a coincidental exchange of life's experiences occurred, that was another matter. I'd no doubt, when the time was right, things would take shape. This was too important to rush.

Ala Tool

Craft bazaars, usually held on private grounds, were now prohibited. *Mutawas* had discovered belly dances at one and bachelors at another. So now bazaars were fewer and even more undercover. This was not where I wanted to exhibit, anyway.

Instead, through an embassy, I'd heard of a Saudi woman who owned an art gallery in a large center, attached to a big hotel. On the phone, she sounded pleasant, articulate and competent, both times we spoke. We arranged for both Baba and I to come to the gallery at 9:30, two evenings hence, to meet her and show her my work.

"The last *salah* is at 8:00 PM," she explained "and with the traffic, the earliest I can get there is 9:00 o'clock."

This sounded too good to be true, I thought. Was it really going to be this easy?

We arrived at 9:25 P.M., using the side entrance, which she had informed me, had no stairs. On to the gallery on the second level. Her shop was surrounded by other small shops and restaurants, but hers was locked and unoccupied. Maybe the traffic was heavy. Maybe a child was sick. We asked the neighboring shopkeepers. No, they hadn't seen her.

Conveniently, uninhabited café tables were right outside the gallery, with views of both main entrances. We could have juice and watch for her at the same time. Baba waved to the waiter in the restaurant just off the hall. Both he and his manager came over together. Since they were nearer me, I could hear them better as they spoke than Baba could.

"Sorry sir, but we cannot serve you here ... *mutawas* ...a Family Section is inside ... for the ladies."

As I understood the predicament, I said it was all right. We didn't need any juice. But until Baba had heard what they'd said, they looked at and explained only to him. Once he'd answered the same way I'd already done, they left. They'd been versed in the art of treating a woman as invisible unless she was in her allotted spot. As I pondered what that was all about, I decided my human voice had inherent value, and the day I became so used to this Saudi style that I didn't bother even to try and speak for myself, that was the day I'd be in trouble.

We went downstairs to wait on black padded seats. In that short time, two Filipinas, one after the other, came and sat opposite me while Baba wandered the lobby. The first wore a black hat with a curled brim, had a 'what am I going to do now?' air about her and said she didn't know she wouldn't be allowed to hear the seminar about investments in the hotel's conference room, with her husband. In the Kingdom, neither tax nor interest was allowed, so savings commonly go out of the country. She left to walk around a nearby shopping center.

When the second woman came, her hair uncovered, she sat opposite me and looked in every direction but mine. I decided to invade her privacy and asked if she was attending the seminar.

"My husband," she answered, and added that she regretted forgetting to bring along a book. I wished I'd had one to lend her. We talked for a bit. After a 40-minute wait for the gallery owner, I left a note for her with the concierge and we went for ice cream.

Two days later, not having heard from the gallery owner, I called her residence several times. The only response I got occurred when a frail voice uttered *"mafee mawjood"*-"she's not present," and hung up. Was I the object of the 'tell them what they want to hear syndrome' again? I'd wanted an appointment. She gave me one.

Chapter 26: Christmas In India

"Infinite gratitude to all things past, infinite service to all things present and infinite responsibility to all things future" [59]
—Huston Smith, about Buddhism, *The Wisdom of Faith*

I love the Christmas season: music, candles, poinsettias, visiting, pumpkin pie and eggnog, and when I don't have to be in it for long, even snow. When I filled out the visa application for *that place*, several lines pertained to Religion. Without declaring yours, you didn't get into the country. Although raised Christian, more or less, I found myself unable to write that down. As a result of life's events, travel, education, friendships and a lot of thought, my personal beliefs became reformulated to a philosophy which I later discovered already had a name—Taoism. Symbolized by flowing water, it's characterized by effortless action, simplicity, spontaneity and compassion. Daily, I worked on lessening the turbulence in my waters.

So I took the plunge and wrote Taoist on the application—declared publicly. Before the processed visa arrived, though, a woman from the embassy phoned asking what Taoist was. Not understanding my explanation, she asked, "Is it Buddhi?" Technically, it bears more similarity to Buddhism than any other major religion, but Taoism is gentler in nature. For the sake of official expediency, I agreed to be categorized as Buddhist, on their form, and so it was written.

Still, I love Christmas: carols, colored lights, and good cheer. That year, a new South African acquaintance described her yuletide south of the equator. There, the school year ran from January until December and then let out for summer vacation. Their Christmas was full of end-of-school-year as well as end-of-calendar-year parties and crowds heading for the beach!

Two years earlier, Christmas had been in Riyadh because *Ramadan* vacation didn't begin until January 11. Since then, the juxtapositions of the Islamic and Gregorian calendars had shifted 11 days, twice, so that current year, *Ramadan* vacation got underway on December 21. One member of our expat group took pity on the 'poor *mutawas*', because they wouldn't know who to harass, Christians celebrating openly or Muslims not doing their duty.

Jewel Dhuru

Our Christmas that year was to be in India. That meant no snowy evening drives looking at twinkling lights, no stuffing or eggnog, but there would be homemade date and walnut cake, huge bamboo-plastic-tissue paper stars on the sides of buildings and a large measure of goodwill.

Before the gaiety, however, my usual bath, as I knew it in Riyadh in a long, deep tub would become a casualty of travel. Silt, the persistent powder in Riyadh, was replaced, in Mumbai, with a steady stream of dust coming in from the dry street. Windows were kept open and ceiling fans running to keep the temperature comfortable, between 24-32 C. (75-90 F.). It usually did not rain in Mumbai in the winter, only during monsoon season, June to September.

The family's 68-year old bungalow, a veritable villa, had been a model in both design and materials in its heyday. Three balconies and a terrace provided comfort but the bathrooms were still old-fashioned. Once Baba laboriously dragged me up the long, circular staircase, we exchanged greetings with family, and I recovered a bit. Relief for my sore muscles came in the form of sitting on a large, flat stone on the floor in a ceramic tiled bath room and using a tumbler to splash warm water over myself, scooped from a bucket after it had tricked in from a heating geyser on the wall. As I sat on my stone, visions of a luxurious bathhouse swam before my eyes with a sunken tub, lots of bubbles and window casements looking out over a forest. Outside the window of this bathroom, a neem tree and songbirds provided their own touch of the exotic.

Alternatively, a week later, when we traveled to a summerhouse in a city 56 km. (90 miles) away, in a more modern almost Western style bathroom, I faced an actual showerhead but perhaps I hadn't really gotten the hang of it. The diminutive size of the geyser, appropriate for trickling water into a bucket, necessitated keeping the volume low for the shower head as well, so most of my warm water got lost in the translation as it dribbled close to the wall. Still, compensation was in the form of smiles and good conversations from the family, privileges I wouldn't have when I returned to my tub in Riyadh.

Because of that long staircase, just like two years earlier, there would be no outings to my favorite spots in Mumbai: no ride on Marine Drive called the Queen's Necklace along the Indian Ocean, no visiting friends in Bandra and Dadar or movies or shopping with the

Ala Tool

kids, no drinking sugar cane juice, freshly squeezed by a sidewalk vendor, no lunch by Jahangir Art Museum, no sightseeing around the grand old train station Victoria Terminus or the Oberoi Hilton or the Taj Mahal Hotel or eating freshly roasted nuts at Malabar Hill park. Baba went out quite a lot, though and came home with stories of long chats with childhood friends.

Despite it all, I didn't feel isolated because there were balconies and lots of visitors. Indeed the bell rang easily forty times a day, including during the supposed naptime after lunch. Coincidentally, two friends from Wisconsin were in Mumbai at the time and arranged to come over. And I was delighted when the plan to go to the summerhouse materialized.

Christmas Day found us and various family members hurtling down the warm, dusty, bumpy road between Mumbai and a neighboring smaller city in a chauffer driven 11-seater SUV Tata Sumo, alongside all manner of Marutis, Hyundais, Fiats, Bajaj Tempos and Ambassadors, all Indian made, not to mention lorries of all sizes with musical horns, scooters and bicycles.

We passed villages and towns, prolifically flowering trees, rectangular green fields surrounded by lighter green and yellow fields, wayside temples, fruit stands, donkeys and monkeys and stopped at tollbooths and roadside spreads of local pottery. Heading up a steep grade into a suddenly cooler 700 meter (2000') mountain called a *ghat*, we overlooked a hydroelectric project, and looked up to the sight of the landmark rock-formation resembling a Duke's Nose, then passed low stone walls which prevented us from tumbling into yawning, terraced gorges and towns in valleys. We passed by rustic bungalows on hill station roads with hairpin turns, under bunches of dangling roots of banyan trees with green parrots in their top branches and arrived at a house where a 50 cm. (20") Poinsettia plant grew in the back yard and a cake that said Merry Christmas sat on the table.

Now here was hospitality from the heart. Yes, sometimes born of duty, but combined with courtesy. Of course, I was biased. Elsewhere in the yard grew a thorny lemon tree, papaya, hibiscus, aloe, a coconut palm, purple morning glories spilling over the fence and bushes with Indian names that I'm still learning to pronounce, all bordering a small lawn of short Korean grass that grew horizontally and didn't need mowing.

Jewel Dhuru

For Eid, beginning December 31, 2000, a nearby cyclone sent a drenching rain to wash the streets of Mumbai in preparation for the New Year, the only time in six trips I'd ever experienced rain during the Mumbai winter. It sat in puddles in the front garden and soaked everyone in sight. In Riyadh, we would have had silt. In Mumbai, the downpour had temporarily grounded soil and dust, which we had to thank for the lush vegetation: coconut palms, periwinkle, dieffenbachia, all varieties of croton, a neem tree and the ubiquitous bougainvillea. Unlike these, which were being rained upon, our houseplants would be prostrate when we got back to Riyadh, but we were warned to resist the temptation to water them too often. They would tolerate drought better than excessive water.

Between Christmas and New Years, I continued to bounce between *Marathi*, the language of Maharashtra, and Arabic. In Mumbai, sitting around the dining table, the family spoke fluent English some of the time and the rest, they naturally reverted to *Marathi*, their mother tongue. But due to the lag time in my brain, half of what I attempted in *Marathi* came out Arabic and I would have the reverse problem when I got back to Riyadh.

On New Year's Eve 2000, at the turn of a new century, we had a festive meal, and watched *Crorepati*, India's answer to Who Wants To Be A Millionaire? Literally meaning the owner of a crore, or 10,000,000 rupees which translates into $250,000.00 US, I kept in mind that the cost of comfortable living in India is significantly less than in the United States. We were to find on our return to Riyadh that an Arab version of the program had sprung up, too.

A month later, after we'd left Mumbai, the lights in that same family dining room were to sway and the cutlery in the kitchen was to rattle in answer to the 7.9 earthquake in Gujarat, 600 km. (375 miles) north. Tenants of the nearby apartments in Mumbai were to go down into the street, but there was no damage to the buildings.

While our January 2nd flight to Riyadh was boarding, Christmas carols were piped over the public address system. In that part of the globe, Orthodox Christmas is celebrated between January 7 and 15, depending on whether one is Armenian or Coptic.

Back in Riyadh a couple of days later, I took stock. A scant two months earlier, I'd been in the Midwest, then two weeks in New York, four in Riyadh, then two in Mumbai Now, back in Riyadh again, it would be only two more months before Baba's Hajj vacation.

I was becoming so adaptable, I felt like a veritable gypsy, alternating between searching for someplace to belong long-term and acknowledging that there will never be a better place than to be fully here with myself, at this moment.

Sometimes in the midst of meditation, in Riyadh, I perceived myself as a falling leaf, purple, red and green, detaching and fluttering away from the parent plant, circling a weathervane, being blown up, down, edgeways and in swirls, milling about with other leaves falling around me, being trodden on underfoot, muddied and forgotten, being rained upon by dust and silt and even washed off by rain, finding my way to the side of a path until I'm whipped up by a car racing by, perhaps lifting other fallen leaves on my way up, landing on a cat's sticky nose, getting singed on the edge of an open fire, recoiling and rising again on the blaze's warm current, shining in the sunlight, displaying the beauty still in my worn colors, and finally fluttering out of sight on to my next adventure.

Chapter 27: Adjustments, Re-Adjustments and More Adjustments

"Opportunities are things we haven't noticed the first time around" [60]
—Catherine Deneuve

"Oh, botheration!
I thought my 'sentence' was up on May 20 (6 months from Nov. 20), but I just found out time spent on trips out of the country don't count, so I have an additional 26 days to 'serve', time added on for two 'escape attempts' (one to India & a proposed trip to Damascus). So that takes me to June 16, which is Dad's last day of work anyway."

Sitting at Baba's computer in the dining room, I sent an email to my kids on January 20, 2001 when I thought 1/3 of my time was up.

Getting in touch with my own anger about being there at all without blaming Baba was a big job, which ultimately just began at two months after I arrived. Two months before I could even start to stop feeling like a captive, see the humor in my self-imposed predicament and go through the process with a happier heart. The loving intention behind my anger was to remove barriers that kept people from connecting. Who was I really mad at anyway? What about all those lessons I came to learn? What was happening to my connection with my best friend, my self?

There was much to be thankful for: my health—more or less, despite my recent complaints, a stable family life—more or less, travel and the opportunity to work—more or less. And I could write. I asked Baba to look at my chapters, so he could keep in touch with the rapid changes inside me, and so we could hash the issues out together and come to terms with them. But unless the passage I offered was short and I really insisted, he usually had something more pressing to do: editing for a professional journal with a deadline looming, a pal with an arm in a cast to drive to a soccer game or a space station to find in the heavens. I mused that those astronauts came closer to our house and kids, daily, than we were.

Eventually, I learned not to share a-l-l my feelings with Baba and he really listened the third time if I didn't mind repeating what I said

Ala Tool

more than twice. I would help him maintain a semi-museum like state in the sitting room if he didn't complain when I claimed workspace here and there. Obviously, we were both works in progress.

While sitting on the couch, I recalled the comment of several friends back home when they heard I was returning to *that place*.

"Well, at least you know what to expect," they assumed.

From the culture, that was true. But if someone had told me the few people with whom I felt a heart connection at first would vanish in some way, I might have been better prepared.

A number of supports I thought I had put in place for myself stayed out of reach. Linda, who'd left the Kingdom, kept in only sporadic touch. Three other more tentative acquaintances were still in the city and had heard I was back, but the social rules being what they were, channels for getting in closer touch were blocked. The culture had a large repertoire of social sidesteps, unstated, unexplained but subliminally understood, like making oneself perpetually unavailable or sending an emissary with a message of 'another time, *inshallah*'. There was no response, either, to Baba's overture to Miss Modern's father. Did I regret exchanging a morsel of my heart with disappearing people? Was it really an exchange? Self-doubt is a terrible thing.

Mr. Wrong Number was gone. He might have been still in the city, and he might be married, but now, we had a different phone number. Mr. Saudia Bent didn't work on the campus anymore and couldn't just appear at the guard kiosk asking admittance so he could keep in touch with someone else's wife. And Rana, my little English student. I had received a post card from her months before, and I had replied, but her family now remained incommunicado as well.

It was as though all those shared experiences were relegated to that time in the past. Even Munawer, our old flat cleaner, who had bought our refrigerator to send it to his family, had disappeared. Baba heard of his whereabouts through his buddies and sent messages, but no show. We learned later that campus cleaners weren't allowed to take private jobs any more, not even in their spare time. Even Baba's mirth-filled lunches with his cohorts had stopped in favor of the prevailing serious atmosphere. Even wrong numbers were rare.

Three months later, I was to get a call from a woman who spoke Arabic-only. She asked a couple of short questions, which I didn't understand. Finally after saying "wrong number" a couple of times, I had little choice but to hang up. Ten minutes later, the same voice was on the line again—a rather uncultured voice. She gave her name as Suja... S-Something. She seemed to know me and wouldn't accept that it was the wrong number. But, No, she didn't know any *Ingelese* and No, she didn't have a friend who did either.

I recognized by the cadence that she asked the same few short questions over and over, but I couldn't understand them. Then she uttered a word I did know. In the same breath as *Ingelese*, came *mudaresa*—a female teacher. Ahhh. Could she be asking for English lessons? She seemed encouraged by my recognition, so again with the repeated questions, and when I didn't answer that time, she hung up. I could have used the distraction in the early months. But this one was not to come until three months later and it didn't lead anywhere anyway.

In those early days, transportation was different, too. Gone were the days when Baba brought a taxi around from the corner stand. We had our own car now, more comfortable for me physically, but more isolating from the locals. Now that I was prepared for the taxi drivers, I wouldn't have to deal with any. We would not run into the kind Samaritans we did last time, either, when we were new and needed them. Now, we were in a position to extend helping hands. Being in the front seats, though, did provide a closer view of idiosyncratic Saudi driving.

Our furnishings were different, too. We had sold all our furniture the first time. The second time, Baba wasn't told until he got there that only one furniture allowance per family was allotted and that was used up the first time. It sounded reasonable; I only wish we'd been told sooner. As a result, Baba had bought just the minimum for his needs. He filled the dining room with music equipment on a small table, so we were not set up for entertaining. I felt like I was starting all over again, but with more self-assuredness and self-reliance than before.

My priorities took a different trajectory this time, too. I didn't study Arabic too much. With reduced exposure to Arabic-only speakers, there didn't seem much point. The enunciation on TV was so poor, I couldn't make out enough to look up in a dictionary. Indeed some fine-tuning came from Baba this time. In my absence, he'd been practicing. I already knew words varied from country to country. There was Egyptian Arabic, Syrian Arabic and every other variation from 20 other countries. I studied from mainly Egyptian cassettes, never Saudi. Baba had been learning Saudi Arabic. He was better at numbers better than I, now comprehending prices, when rattled off rapid fire at shops and gas stations. "To buy lentils at the farmer's market," he instructed, "ask for *adis*, not *ads*."

I was not to know, the second trip I would be almost cut off from children. I usually got along well with kids, reading stories and answering 'why' questions. But there, most kids showed a degree of what I interpreted as distrust, even kids Baba knew. Saudi kids avoided us entirely.

I had hardly done any needlework that second time. Again, my sore shoulder told me to experience this slice of life more joyfully, not as a burden. Last time, I had made an effort to not completely lose touch with the three types of work I did. The second time, perhaps I was meant to engage in other work, broadening my spectrum of knowledge. I would continue to use my talents and skills as opportunities and I merged, but I looked for something else worth trading seven months of my life for. Getting to know Baba's pals and especially their wives, when they came, was more fruitful than having bunches of students or clients. It would help me keep in touch with his new world once I went back home. But I didn't show my kids' photos to people anymore. That was a separate part of life. Neither did I identify myself by my work.

It took two months before I could semi-consistently strive for the highest thought, before I didn't feel tears pricking the backs of my eyes, or worse, daily. Tears were a welcome release but were not in keeping with a 'making the most of the present moment' philosophy. It was two months before I finished swinging from one emotional posture of getting into a lather about everything but saying little about it—at least not verbally, to another strategy of trying to accept everything as normal and not letting anything upset me—at least not too often. Finally, I was able to try to maintain a more balanced course of being com-passionate with myself and selective with my comments, using them where they might do some good—at least most of the time.

In other words, two months before I stopped feeling sorry for myself and adopted a 'get on with it' attitude, accepting that nothing and no one really interferes with my path or purpose, not if I recognize myself in everyone and everyone in myself.

Jewel Dhuru

Perhaps it was no surprise that about this time I had a dream about a horse in distress in my front yard. When first aid was administered, it shape-shifted into a man, reminding me to look past outer appearances. Disdain of anyone else was only a reflection of what I don't like about myself. Criticizing another was a sign of my own feelings of weakness. It was within my power to create, to change and to find alternatives to an impasse. Whatever I imagined had been taken away from me, no one could take my self-respect unless I agreed to relinquish it. It became part of me when I behaved respectably, striving for my highest and treating others as equal human beings I often felt my Dad's indefatigable sense of humor near me, even though he'd passed on years before. Many a time, he helped to keep me from analyzing too much and to laugh it off.

I finally finished a painting of a Saudi coffee pot and demitasse in front of a tapestry. I started to understand how Saudi women could get wrapped up in goings on inside the home, although our choice of activities might have varied quite a bit. They had children to occupy their time; I didn't. I even took advantage of a perk of being female in those segregated circumstances. I didn't have to entertain friends of Baba's who dropped in unexpectedly, when inconvenient for me. After a greeting, I could just excuse myself, go to my bedroom, close the door, leave Baba to make tea and nobody thought anything of it. I did it once. It was the first time I recall doing such a thing and it felt odd, but at the same time, a relief.

Things were changing. Some days, I was so pre-occupied, I forgot to look out the window. I routinely kept two books in each the sitting room and bedroom, books in the slow process of being read. That way, when I went from room to room, I'd have a choice between submerging myself in Tolkien or a murder mystery, between Wodehouse or a novel. Choices. Variety. I had to create them myself, no matter how temporary, artificial or vicarious. I welcomed the mental wrangling of keeping characters straight and not letting the subtle details from one plot cross over into another. For an unexpected dividend, Paul offered to give my Tolkien trilogy back. I accepted with delight, having unspoken pangs of regret for ever having left them behind at all. When I emerged from listening to 'Klik and Klak', the two hilariously helpful Car Talk brothers on NPR or a humorous novel set in a British library or a dusty Eastwood western on TV, I passed a window and noticed, with a shock, that the view

Ala Tool

outside had a Middle Eastern look to it and the sun was shining brightly.

'Where was I?' I wondered. It looked quite cheery. Warm bodies were out there, too. 'Oh yes', now I remembered. How insolated I had become, as though our flat was enfolded in a layer of gelatin.

The phone so seldom rang, when it did, I didn't rush to answer it. When part of me realized that another part didn't care much if I missed a call, I knew then, too, that I had changed. I was slipping—slipping inside. Every few weeks, when I retrieved the electric bill slid under our door, the empty hallway looked like the border of foreign territory. I was more content within. The influence from without was larger than life but it was up to me whether or not the quality of my life got smaller. Still, it was startling to see how comfortable Baba had become with the customs, while I was becoming less so.

Difficulty Following Directions

One Friday morning, as the stentorian recitation at *salah* filled the air, Baba discovered an article in the Arab News (2001) about the side effects of cardiac bypass surgery, the kind he'd had. My ears pricked up from my comfy position on the couch where I was wrapped in the purple-blue sarong and two sweaters I wore most Friday mornings. It took me a while to realize why I was always drawn to that sarong on *Jumma*. Blue for the 5th *chakra* at the throat is for hearing, assimilating and speaking, and purple for the 6th one at the forehead is for visualizing and applying ideas practically. Both were conducive to good talks with Baba on Fridays. Our talks were valued exercises because Baba had learned well the lesson to avoid stress. Before the bypasses, occasional arguments cleared the air, but now tension could only be discharged when opportunities for fruitful dialogue appeared. Baba began reading from the article.

"The New England Journal of Medicine reports that some coronary bypass patients had more difficulty following directions, doing mental math and planning complex actions ahead of time." [61]

Maybe that's how he managed to forget his laptop at home when he left for Riyadh the second time. Mental math? I still relied on him to help me change currency at borders and to change from metric to non-metric. But maybe that's why Mr. Last Minute didn't have things ready for me when I arrived. Oh well, as long as he was still a whiz at the really essential stuff: his work, what time the space station came around, computers, cars and cameras.

As he read, I got up off the couch and went over to kneel beside his chair. We'd had a lot to work out lately. My mind drifted to times when our attitudes threatened to polarize us and we struggled to achieve a meeting of minds.

"Why did you insist on coming here when you knew I didn't want to?" I'd once asked him in an agitated moment.

"Why do you think?" he'd countered.

"To get your way?" I'd ventured.

Then quietly, he'd sighed and uttered, "That's the tragedy."

Deep in my heart, I knew this was his way of providing for his family and he'd hoped for my appreciation. I valued his motivation, but what exactly was he providing? That's what I wondered about. The tragedy for me was that I didn't think he recognized that the experience for me was very different than it was for him, but just as valid.

He continued reading the technical parts of the article. We laughed as we each silently contemplated the impact on our lives of his surgery and convalescence, travel strains and every other inconvenience. We'd been through a lot together. Our 28th anniversary was later that month. It was difficult to separate which changes were because of his heart and his age, or my age and biological fluctuations, which because of the stage of our relationship and which because of the Saudi experience. Then I thought of something. Did the article say following directions, mental math and planning ahead? I leaned closer and whispered into his ear.

"But you never were very good at following my directions," I whispered."

And a fresh spasm of laughter gripped us. After the mirth subsided, he went on with his paper and I retreated to the couch to think. I recalled the words of a counselor colleague of mine. She had elaborated on a technique used to get at hard to swallow personal truths.

"When you're tempted to tell your partner something about himself, starting with 'you'," she explained, "turn the statement around, put an 'I' in front of it, say it to yourself instead and keep re-working its form until you can believe it."

Using this method, "You never listen" begins as "I never listen" but might change form until it gets to "I never listen to the loving intention behind your fear" or "If I really listened to what you were trying to tell me, you might be more interested in listening to my heart."

She gave another example. "You don't appreciate anything I do" might really mean "I don't appreciate myself and so demand it from others."

I recalled two occasions when Baba was telling me about a problem plaguing one of his pals' wives. Some of the women, having been harassed by feelings of menace or *mutawas*, didn't answer the door or phone the whole time they were in the Kingdom. Twice, I watched a thoughtful look overcast Baba's face for a scant few minutes and I thought privately that now he was getting the feel of what we women lived with every minute, day and night. But then the phone would ring or another distraction would occur and he was back into his own reality again.

City Map

After two months, I got the hang of the street directions in Riyadh. Before then, I never knew where we were or how to get home. Streets that I thought were perpendicular to each other were really parallel. I'd never had so much trouble adjusting to a city, in more ways than one.

When out for a ride with another couple one day, the four of us had the brief conversation probably every expat couple has had at some point.

"If we were out," Baba asked, "and I became incapacitated and couldn't drive, would you drive me to a hospital? he asked me." I had already given that consideration.

"In this standard transmission car, with my back?" I answered, "Yes, I'd drive, but then we'd have two emergencies."

It would have helped though, if I could figure out the lay of the streets. To alleviate my bewilderment, Baba finally explained it in a way I could grasp. City maps did not have North neatly lined up at the top. The top slanted to the Northeast. A Ring Road encircles the city, each of the four sides aligning with compass directions and most streets followed suit. But the main street, King Abdul Aziz Street, and three or four other old ones nearby run diagonally through the middle of town. So maps were slanted so those historical, core streets could be straight. With this understanding, the abstruse, lost feeling started to abate.

Back to Batha

Once when we went back to Batha to search for a particular tailor, we were, again, in an area where very few women roamed and those in the vicinity had their heads covered. As Baba combed the area for the shop, to save me unnecessary steps, he asked me to stay put for a few minutes while he milled about. With a grimace, I agreed and he was off.

As the powers that be would have it, I stood just outside a small mall, my head unsuitably uncovered. Nearby, a salesman stood alone outside his lingerie shop. All manner of colorful and skimpy unmentionables hung in the display window while three comfortable, empty seats beckoned inside. Dozens of such shops decorated the city, all serviced by men. How women could shop under those circumstances, I couldn't grasp.

So there I was in the middle of the arena again. But the stares of passersby and of the guard, who pretended to be reading a magazine in his chair just inside the mall doorway, didn't pester me this time, and the vague sense of menace from that first episode had faded.

Indeed, in time, when other expat women told me it was not safe to go out by myself, I was the one who played devil's advocate, told them to choose their spots carefully, plan their trips with successful outcomes in mind and urged them to create safety within. While I waited on the corner for Baba, alas, I realized that had perfected my version of the big city technique of putting on a counterfeit countenance and looking right through people, the system of semi-seeing from the sidelines. My attitude had become one of 'this is the allotted spot on this planet to which I had been called, for this moment, and I'm going to make myself comfortable here'.

On the way home, we bought a bag of cat food. Often, we meandered through residential streets, and invariably cats, all colors—tabbies, calicos, and gold or gray tigers—prowled near, on, around and inside dumpsters. I would stop and sprinkle a handful of food near them and watch after we'd moved off a bit. The cats in the

DQ, we found, appeared less scrawny and more readily identified the substance I dropped as food. The most responsive cat was on a dark DQ back road. We'd been watching the sun set over palms in parks when the light ran out. As we putted along the dark road, a cat came out of the brush and then ran halfway back in again.

"Cat, cat," I exclaimed to Baba, who stopped the car and backed up.

I opened the door, dropped a handful of food at the side of the road and we backed further away. In our headlights, the cat scarfed down the kibble and I wished I had sprinkled more. Watching it eat was nourishing for me, too. It was too dark to even see its color and I wondered where it lived, how old it was, and whether male or female—all questions to remain forever unanswered. Satisfied, we drove off.

Although plenty of 16^0 C. (61^0 F.) days still chilled us, it started warming up, sometimes reaching 22^0 C. (72^0 F.) and no more rain for a while. The dates seemed to change more quickly on my laptop. It was almost the end of January.

One Marathon Week and the New Abaya

One unusual week, we attended three dinners at the homes of acquaintances. I had become so accustomed to being alone with my thoughts, the idea of repeatedly getting on and off a social merry-go-round was dizzying. I was glad to be with people but it was physically taxing with the added walking, two steps up here, three down there, not to mention coping with artfully shaped chairs that were beautiful to look at but that bore no similarity to the human shape.

Just before this week, we'd agreed my original black *abaya* had become travel worn enough that it was still serviceable for drives or the supermarket but not for visiting. It saddened me. I asked myself, yet again, why I wore one at all. My answer was—for my convenience. Being exploited by a dozen eyes and fear of more serious punishment was inconvenient. Besides, I didn't want Baba arrested by some overzealous *mutawa*. But I usually fastened only the top snap and left the rest flapping in the wind because my respect for this particular cultural rule was marginal. I believed in a higher law than the one espoused by this scant 8,000,000.

Jewel Dhuru

Still, I didn't want to turn into a person who thinks being well dressed means owning a collection of black encasings with imported lace trims and hand embroidery, so I struggled against the idea of investing in a second one at all. I felt sorry for my black burden, though. It had been the object of my disdain practically from the moment I'd bought it, reluctantly, as a necessary evil. It was actually quite pretty. It was plain black with snaps down the front and on the cuffs, with a stand up collar, and machine embroidery surrounding black stones on the front and back upper bodice. But the time had come to give it a rest.

So we ordered a new one before the first of the three dinners but it wouldn't be ready until just before the third. I could have just walked into a shop and bought a black one off the rack, but that second time, I was determined to purchase a garment I could wear elsewhere on the globe, so that meant color. I had seen a few cover-ups being worn on the streets in olive green and deep red. We went to an *abaya* shop and listened while a non-Saudi, Muslim male spoke articulately about straight and bias cuts, sleeves made in one or two pieces, front and side closures, how he could give me a better discount if I bought a matching scarf, to which I shook my head, and how the pockets I wanted him to add would ruin the fall of the material.

When the time came to select the color, a clandestine operation, I was aware that while preparing to return to the Kingdom, I had found myself attracted to oranges, yellows and greens. In the study of kundalini and color, it's understood that when I stand in the closet irresolute about what to wear, I'm really just seeking the color that supports me in my need at that moment. Orange, yellow and green were connected to the 2nd 3rd and 4th *chakras* on the body, located just below the navel, at the diaphragm and at the heart respectively, and also corresponding to partnership power and experiencing pleasure (2nd), personal power, wisdom and intuition (3rd) and the central powerhouse of a loving heart and an openness to life (4th). Those pretty much summed up my challenges in Riyadh. I ended up ordering an olive green, bias-cut, flared-skirted, with tassels on the flared sleeves *abaya*, with the addition of side-seam pockets on which I had insisted. *Thobs* had pockets. I didn't see why *abayas* couldn't have pockets

The tailor asked me to put an *abaya* off the rack on over my own so he could check the size and length. Since I'm tall, I prefer longer to

Ala Tool

shorter and told him so. The tag in the neck of my current black millstone signified 58 but I had forgotten it at the time.

He murmured as he began his meticulous work. The *Dhur salah* was about to start, at about noon and he would have to shoo us out and lock up the shop. "Just put this on ... 56 ... and an inch longer" and then he made notes. He seemed quick and competent. "length 59 ... it will be ready on Tuesday," he concluded. Four ears pricked up—59?

"No, that should be 57," Baba corrected. I had also noticed the cognitive dissonance, but had the feeling the tailor knew what he was doing, so I planned to trust his judgment. Still, Baba being better in math than I, I scanned the tailor's face for explanation, which in turn looked at Baba's face and then without a word, the tailor crossed out the 59 and wrote 57. My inner voice niggled, but maybe Baba was right. *Salah* began and we filed out, the tailor heading for the mall men's mosque and we to get a Mama Noura juice when the shops reopened.

The first two feasts filled Thursday and Friday evenings: imaginative food, interesting conversation and company and the chairs weren't too bad, either.

On the following Tuesday, normally I would have gone along to pick up the *abaya*, in case of a glitch, but the pick up date being the day before the third dinner, I asked Baba if he could just bring it. I would lay low that day. "*Mafee mishkole*," he agreed. Two hours later, he finished his errands and walked in with the cloak for making me invisible.

It looked good: well pressed, expertly sown, bias cut, and tassels. I checked the unadvocated pockets. They were deep and finely serged to keep from unraveling. Yes, I could see a slight wrinkle where they affected the fall of the fabric, but well worth it to have pockets. Then I swung it around to try it on. And when I looked down—oh my! It was short. I didn't mind if slacks were so long they bunched up at the ankles but too short brought dismay.

An image of the crossed out 59 on the paper flickered before my eyes and in a flash it all became clear. I knew how this happened. When the tailor said "56," he must have been referring to the *abaya* from the rack. When I hung my duo on hangers side by side, the 58 on the black one confirmed that if we'd said nothing, it would have been all right.

Jewel Dhuru

I knew how it happened, but it took two weeks before I understood why and even longer before I could begin to keep something similar from happening again. At the moment the two men had made eye contact, if I had given voice to any lack of understanding, a group problem-solving mechanism might have been triggered, airing the tailor's concern and leading to resolution. But to the tailor, the husband's word was law; there was no negotiation. Only I had the power to activate it.

The length of this garment was not very high up on a list of life-altering issues. It was really quite trivial, even reparable, but I had a feeling the same dynamic and all its mutations was being played out in a myriad of ways, over petty and large issues—like when and where to go out, how to dress the kids, how to talk to girls differently than boys, whether the wife should go to school or not, what to read, what people to talk to—issues played out in families all over the country, and it had been happening for some time.

Baba's feelings, whenever he saw my splash of green, moved over time from *chagrin*, because his mathematical comment had been made so offhand he didn't even recall it, to guilt, to eventually forgetting the whole thing. My initial bewilderment gave way to annoyance. Then, as I released the sting from the memory, that *abaya* became a symbol of my vow to myself to use personal power combined with heart, when needed. I had the power to attend to my inner voice along with the power of my outer one to draw out the truth. Perhaps if Baba and I eventually learned to work together better, with our hearts open, indeed, it had turned out all right.

The last of the three dinners combined couples, whole families and a handful of temporary bachelors. Besides experiencing the environs of yet another manicured, but walled compound, the accommodations were more than comfortable. We took part in stimulating conversation, alternating among pairs and trios talking, then women and men conversing in separate groups and then combined topics of interest to all. Ironically, the usually taboo subjects of politics and religion surrounded us so they were discussed in spurts with large modicums of tolerance. As a group, we sorted out whether or not there was a phobia for the desert, how to find the best satellite dish and the perils for kids of too much TV.

During one interval, the men, in their nook, tackled cars, cigarettes, computers and shoptalk. Meanwhile, the women

Ala Tool

embellished each other's horror stories about coming to Riyadh through Jiddah. Unless their husbands drove for a day and a half from Riyadh to pick them up, expat women faced having their passports confiscated and having to sit in a waiting area in full view of the officials for 24 hours until the next flight to Riyadh, for the ostensible purpose of keeping out of trouble. Passports were given back just before the women embarked.

For one 20-minute period, we women shared coping strategies. Each of us that evening, men and women, were members of relatively stable marital relationships, who liked our spouse's jokes, for the most part. We were all in the Kingdom for a purpose, primarily educational. Most of the families maintained two households, in as many countries. In many cases, where one member of each duo perceived crisis, the other saw opportunity, so balance came from between the two. Most of the women agreed to be caretakers of the joint property, and to be both Mom and Dad to the kids when Dad was away. Some referred to their phone bills as astronomical.

A unique by-product of our circumstances was that we did not define ourselves by our occupations. One educated woman traveled between Riyadh and home a great deal, and transported her kids when at home. About a job, she said, with a wry smile, "no one will have me." So without gainful employment, we had to figure out what our presence there was really worth, identifying ourselves by what we liked. We threw ourselves into soul nurturing hobbies, like pot making, writing, sewing and tutoring, hobbies that could be turned into employment, or better still, could be done just for fun. My personal questions were about how that part of the world was better off for having me there and how my life was enriched by this episode.

Our little group was in the unique position of creating a sisterhood of people from widely varying backgrounds for support and inspiration. How could we bring the best out of ourselves and others in an emotionally charged atmosphere?

The female conversation went on. One woman started a familiar narrative, leading down the road of perfectionism to overload, being taken for granted and ending with learning the hard way to put herself first on her care-taking list, for the sake of all. One reiterated of our joint thoughts of helping our husbands domestically while there, especially with entertaining, but basically, we felt like visitors, not wanting to disturb his status quo. We were all aware of the delicate balance between wife and husband. No place for one-upmanship or inflated egos.

This conversation was different from those with Baba's female colleagues. They talked about always getting their messages at work last, sometimes being left out of meetings because as a result. The written notice of one end-of-year send-off party, in which both male and female colleagues were going to be leaving, was clearly marked 'for males only'. When the females' objections were finally noted, a female-only party was arranged.

But at this dinner, it was all wives of employees. The mention of each new minor atrocity that hit home brought inner ripples of sighs, nods, smiles, empathy and acknowledgment of how we felt that only another who'd been through it could know. Increasingly, those back home with whom I could have meaningful conversations without skirting around my situation as if it was an embarrassing skin condition, decreased to a core few. I could choose between either becoming more sequestered, wherever in the world I was, or learning a new way of talking to people, understanding myself instead of expecting them to understand. I had to find other common ground between us on which to dwell.

I, having the eldest children of the group of wives, and the only one with a married child, shared my thoughts about holding kids with open hands, recognizing that what we want for them might not be what they want for themselves, trusting in the good job we did raising them and reducing our input to playing a supportive role while they learned from their own mistakes.

We even touched on our biological changes because of environmental stressors, travel and cultural adjustments and on dietary supplements to keep ourselves on an even keel.

My battery charged up, I warmed to these new sisters. It didn't matter that we may never sit together in our real houses. Our liaisons were made of mist and moonlight. Home was in our hearts. This lifestyle seemed more palatable now, respecting Baba's inner voice. He wanted to have more international impact before he retired for good and all. When we stood up, I noticed my hip wasn't so tender anymore. What was the significance of hip pain in bioenergetics? Fear of going forward in major decisions? Nothing to go forward to? There were solutions here.

Still, I guarded against getting attached to the women so as not to succumb to the lure of an artificial existence. Even as I was making a potential new friend, I knew the one I enjoyed most would be leaving in four days, not to be back soon. These global friendships were as potent as childhood friendships. They were just different. We didn't have a long history together, but what we shared was personal, exposing feelings we don't usually wear on our public faces. Our support could be felt across continents. Physical absence did not sunder the fellowship.

The evening drew on and it was time to go. I had almost made it through the marathon week and I felt pretty well. As all bid good night, one of the guys spoke to me, tongue in cheek.

"You looked more comfortable today than earlier in the week. Maybe you're getting used to this sitting around!"

Chapter 28: Soaking Up Local Color

"Be courageous. It's one of the only places left uncrowded" [62]
—Anita Roddick

The end of January brought the 16th annual two-week Celebration of Saudi Culture and Heritage at Janadriah Village. We'd missed it the first year, so we were trying again. On the way there, Joseph, Baba and I saw picnickers with blankets and baskets, sometimes even with TVs, spread out on any shady spot on freeway embankments.

Like everything else, at this Village, men's, ladies' and family days were separate. Getting lost resulted in our just missing the last family day for the year. The last days, naturally, would be ladies' days. Resigned, we headed for home, stopping at the Camel Souk and Batha as compensation.

But twice a day, Janadriah Report came on TV, so I learned about it that way, as well as from friends who'd gone. The gate and surrounding walls were modeled after the ramparts of old forts and inside were artisans, all men of course, grisly bearded, corrugated complexioned curmudgeons, demonstrating 5000 year old arts from what some considered the glory days:

- how to fashion clay pots from sandy soil,
- to construct a bee hive from a hollowed out palm log,
- to set up an animal powered irrigation system,
- to weave cloth for tents and garments from sheep and camel wool thread,
- to make palm-leaf rope, and
- to use natural dyes to color fabric.

Camel races and horse shows were held not far from handicraft tents full of prayer beads of all colors and types of stone, and near the ubiquitous lines of dancing men, tongues loosed in song, waving swords and flags, springing up from left and right like popping corn.

February was to be rich in varied experiences, too, one piled on top of another. We ran into Tanya and husband a few times, in the hall or outside the building. They were atypical in that they stopped and spoke when they saw us. The conversation was always the same, though. He, looking relaxed, was just on his way out of town but they'd have us over next week, *Inshallah*. She, looking anxious, was sorry she had not called yet.

"My husband's cousin is in the hospital ... it's so busy with children ..." And so it went.

Economic reform

Economic reform had been going on in the country since 1999. A new influx of domestics was due from Nepal, to add to the mainly Filipina force. They would work in Saudi households for 500 SR per month, about $125.00 U.S. Their days were filled with hard work and when not needed, they stayed in their rooms.

Synchronously, the Arab News (2001) extolled how the Internet, the virtual oasis, had gotten out of control. Some authorities advocated allotting attention to educating kids that not all that was accessible worldwide was good for those special 8,000,000, instead of pumping money into filtering out objectionable material.[63] Hot on the heels of this came a Los Angeles Times article, written by a female. She claimed Saudi boys and girls, 43% being 14 or under, were fed up and were turning to chat rooms to grumble about no dating, no driving and the standard of living falling with the price of a barrel of oil. Incidentally, they were discovering the rewards of double income families, worldwide news, foreign investment and wanted to let the world in on the world's terms instead of just the forefathers' terms.[64] But ideas have to incubate before they can hatch, so change would take time.

Camel Meat

Muhammed, the farmer from the Camel Souk phoned a couple of times, always at 2:00 AM when we were asleep, asking Baba when he and the other brother were going to come and visit his farm. Since we were planning our Hajj getaway at the time and I was not invited, anyway, Baba took his time making plans. But we did taste camel meat.

Baba brought some from the supermarket. As it sizzled in the pan, dark brown and greasy, I recalled the voice of my college Biology professor in Canada.

"Botulism is odorless and tasteless," he had lectured. "We don't see it much in this part of the world. They mainly see it where people eat their camels after they've died of old age!"

I eyed it with trepidation. Camel meat not exactly being a low fat item, we only had a small bite each. It was just like hamburger, but had a wild taste to it, like venison or pemmican. But it was a scary prospect and a single mouthful sufficed.

Farmer's Market

Out for a ride one afternoon, to mail letters to people whose Christmas cards had reached us on February 1, 2001, we found ourselves driving by a 0.4 hectare (acre) patch of farmer's market, not too far from our corner of Riyadh. We circled the long concrete arches, shading parallel rows. Before deciding where to stop first, we perused the sections for fruit, vegetables, hanging sheep carcasses, a fishery, a pottery shop and one for bags, bins and jars of herbs and spices, nuts and honey.

Then we stopped at fruits and vegetables. What a delightful change from the usual urban atmosphere. The Saudi guys in their late teens manning the stands actually nodded and smiled, wrestling with their limited English.

"Welcome to Saudi Arabia," they greeted as we approached, succeeded by "how are you?" and the usual "what is your country?"

Their produce was a horticultural treat for the senses. The colors of apricots, corn, peppers, kiwis, eggplants, bananas, radishes, pineapples and plums, mangos and melons, lettuce, lemons and local crops—some vivid, some muted—blended into a dripping watercolor when I squinted at them, looking so rich in this sandy beige country. The heavy scents of fresh, ripening tomatoes and earthy mushrooms combined with the sight of a crate of oranges with leaves still attached, transported our spirits onto some stranger's farm.

One guy was generous with his labor, putting a couple of extra zucchinis into the bag while charging us only the measly 2SR, about $.55, for the ½ kilo (1 lb.) we asked for. Another pressed an extra couple of zipper skin oranges into my hand after the ones we selected had been paid for. An older man, an Indian from Kashmir asked Baba about his origin. His young assistant and I exchanged smiles when the two Indians started chatting away in their common lingo. The elder

Ala Tool

plunked half a dozen earthy scented tomatoes into a bag and wanted to give them to us free. This was not uncommon, but knowing how hard laborers work in any country, we tucked a few Riyals under a pen on his scale.

The herb and spice shop was an old world treat: bins of green shelled pistachios, beige cashews and brown hazelnuts, reddish cinnamon bark peeled right off the tree, whole nutmegs, black peppercorns, red saffron, fennel and dried garlic, vats of pickled olives and olive oil, bulky burlap bags of sage leaves, figs, dates, dried apricots, currants, boxes of herb teas, along with sesame and cumin seeds and everything else one could ever need to make a savory dinner.

To be sure, the same attitudes we'd encountered among city folk still flourished, but with less intensity. Or maybe I was just getting past them faster. When we answered the question about our nationalities, one of the bunch still said, "India? ... Canada?" with that 'it'll never work' look in his eyes. All in all, it was a delightful half hour escapade. Maybe the urban-rural disparity is the same the world over.

We went home in good spirits with so much produce, we would never finish it all before Hajj. We would share it with neighbors. Istanbul, Turkiye had been our first choice for vacation but the direct flights had just stopped for the season. So we opted for Damascus, Syria and began studying the tour books.

The Slippery Gootra

The next week, while pouring over a map, I had the TV on. The scheduled Feature Film wasn't shown, English instruction taking its place, given by an Instructor with a slippery *gootra*. With one of his hands, he applied a squeaky blue marker to a white board while the other hand kept the *gootra*'s central crease aligned with his forehead. On this call-in program, he answered grammar questions. He did a superb job of giving examples for how to change from active to passive voice and how to pluralize countable and non-countable nouns, all while adjusting his headdress every time he turned to the board and back to the camera. First example—slip, slide, readjust; second example—flip, flop, pinch pleat. But there was a glitch when he gave examples on how to combine two short questions into one.

Jewel Dhuru

The first example looked great. But the second!
"What's the time? Do you think?" he wrote on the board.

Then with a straight face, and another adjustment of the errant folds, he proceeded to demonstrate the proper way to combine them. "What's do you think the time?"

Oops! I suppose five out of six wouldn't have been bad, had he been a student. Overall, I couldn't have done as well in Arabic as he was doing in English, with or without a *gootra*.

The News and Other Local Color

Next came the news. BBC and CNN reported differently there than they did in North America: more regional issues, a distinct view of the bigger picture and more news anchors, with accents, who weren't intimidated by foreign names. The Middle East being separated from the continent of Africa only by the Red Sea, and connected to Asia through Turkiye, we heard Asian news and of tragedies in progress that kept the Red Crescent Society busy:

- Kim Dae Jung of South Korea was aglow when honored with the Nobel Peace Prize,
- The Alahabad—70,000,000 people wrapped in white gathered at the Ganges River in India,
- Nkosia Johnson, the 11-year old South African boy, became a spokesperson for AIDS,
- Nawad Sharif, exiled Prime Minister of Pakistan, arrived for asylum in Jiddah,
- The UN left Afghanistan because of Taleban restrictions,
- The Serb leader, Radaman Karadzic, turned himself in to the War Crimes Tribunal,
- The Lockerbie verdict in the Netherlands was announced to tense spectators,
- The Turkish economy went into shock,
- The War Crimes Tribunal judged rape and sexual slavery were crimes against humanity,
- Kuwait recognized 10 years since its most recent fiasco with Saddam,
- Sudan was short of food and water and a border war was stopped by a UN enforced deadline,

- Angola exported 100s of 1000s of barrels of oil a day but had none for hospital generators,
- Nigeria emerged from 30 years of military rule and a dozen coups to a civilian government not able to provide access to health services or safe drinking water for half its people,
- Sierra Leone's war between regime and rebel groups left civilians without humanitarian aid,
- Congolese outbreaks of polio, plague, AIDS, sleeping sickness, meningitis, measles and cholera caused the life expectancy to drop to 45, and
- 40,000 Ethiopians had to leave Eritrea.

My heart was heavy when I listened to the News. Not much was new. Ironically, a new, sprawling, pale pink Ethiopian embassy in the DQ was nearing completion, with lush gardens and lawns watered by sprinklers day and night.

But that wasn't all. Refugees of all types were in distress.
- Thousands of Iraqis were landing in rusty, beached tankers on the French Riviera,
- Britain was inundated with refugees from a number of countries,
- 330,000 refugees from Liberia and Sierra Leone piled into Guinea, West Africa,
- Rohingya refugees from Myanmar were abused and malnourished in Bangladeshi camps,
- Boatloads of refugees from northern and sub-Saharan Africa were landing in Spain,
- Indonesians were leaving Borneo for Java where indigenous people clashed with migrants,
- and Shiploads of children from Benin were being carted about.

The strongest global warming warning yet came from environmental agencies, predicting climate changes and an increase in freakish weather conditions. On its heels came reports of continuing devastating flooding of the Zambezi River in Mozambique, the worst drought and famine in Kenya in 60 years, and the earthquake in Gujarat, India.

Jewel Dhuru

For some reason, we didn't get much news in the United States of the African countries, the cradle of our common civilization. As usual, to find news that was uplifting, rather than dispiriting, was an individual quest.

About this time I noticed the words Saudi and Arabia didn't carry a high emotional charge anymore. I didn't have to call it *that place* anymore. It was becoming more of an inert substance, a neutral location, like any other, only able to have the effect on me that I allowed. I took a deep, clearing breath and reclaimed power I had previously given away.

Jerusalem

I didn't even try to keep up with all the politics in the area, although the history of how four cultures managed to inextricably intertwine their lives in a single square kilometer in the center of Jerusalem continued to fascinate me. Two BBC journalists surveyed the Armenian, Christian, Jewish and Muslim Quarters and commented that the streets between them were almost equivalent to international borders.

The ancestors of all four had swept through the city and settled it for a time, one after the other. So each of their holy places are underneath or beside or obscured by or on the other side of the wall of or on the very same spot as the holy places of the other three. What continued to surprise the journalists was how some residents blindly passed each other on those bordering streets without even seeing each other or developing any communal understanding or coming to terms with the joint history. This sounded familiar. In Riyadh, on a different scale, this technique was also achieving perfection. There were lessons here, too.

On February 7, 2001, Ariel Sharon became Prime Minister. A new Palestinians-Israeli chapter was about to begin. So with all the other unrest in the area, within a week, that patch of Earth reverted to chaos. As one report put it, referring to the former Yugoslavia, but applicable to other regions: "Peacekeepers wondered what peace there was left to keep."

During my years of teaching academic writing to foreign college students, I'd had two Palestinian students, *Philistine* in Arabic. Coincidentally, my worst and one of my best. Both were in

Ala Tool

Engineering. The worst student's father had chosen his subject for him. Jabbar spelled phonetically, was absent frequently, and participated in class only sporadically. In his Journal writings and essays, he pontificated about the Intifada and molotov cocktails. I phoned the Engineering Department office to glean insight into his intentions. The mention of his name brought exasperated chuckles from the department secretary. They'd tried to drop him because of the lack of quality in his work but his father kept getting him reinstated. It took him three semesters to finally complete all the requirements of my one semester course and barely secure a passing grade.

Yousef, one of my best, had gentle, intelligent eyes and asked appropriate questions in class, taking a heavier than average course load, so he could graduate sooner. One winter day he came in with a bad cold and hungry, wearing a black and white *shmal* wrapped around his throat, like Yassar Arafat wears on his head. It was *Ramadan*, he explained. He couldn't eat until after dark, but by the time his last class finished, the cafeterias were closed. It was rough. Other Muslim communities on campus, like Malaysians and Indian Muslims, were larger and helped each other cope, but too few Palestinians studied on campus to form a cooperative network.

A couple of months later, he informed me he was transferring to a smaller university. His parents couldn't afford to keep him in this private school. Sometimes I wonder how the two students and their families are doing, if they're still alive, if I'll see either of them on the news, and what at least one of them has done with his engineering degree.

From my limited perspective, in chronic disputes, as long as each member

- resists developing the understanding of how their own input into joint history has created and perpetuates the present friction—not their neighbor's input—but their own,
- and resists learning to replace mere impulsive reaction with thoughtful action,
- and resists developing the mentality of win-win negotiations—nothing will change.

Jewel Dhuru

Without a change of approach, new generations will grow up stuck in loss.

More News

Watching such news had a physical effect. My muscles stiffened and ached. They felt the strife of ancient personal skirmishes and got right into the flight or fight. Not for the first time, I thought about my own chronic conditions, how my history created them. Besides what was already in my repertoire of mental-emotional-spiritual exercises, what vision would it take to release tension? The loving intention behind fear was to learn not to make the same mistakes over and over again. I could change, even if my circumstances didn't. That would free up energy for joy. Bits of wisdom kept running through my mind like a fever. Confucius is purported to have expressed the thought— Don't concern yourself with being known by the right people; concern yourself more with being someone who is worth knowing.

If I wanted peace in my life, I had to make it myself. My present situation was uppermost in my mind. My strained friendship with Baba, tenuous contact with neighbors and international tempers flaring. It took the attitudes and actions of all the participants to create the current states of affairs. One couldn't do it alone. I closed my eyes, took a deep breath, blew out a long, tired sigh and offered a silent prayer to remove all prejudice from my heart. Help me to see through the illusion of my separation from the rest of humanity.

Coincidentally, that same week, two days before Valentine's Day, the genetic code, common to all humankind, was cracked. Most of the billions of bits of genetic information we all share is ancient history. We have only about 30,000 genes that can reflect change from generation to generation so the actual difference between any one of us and a neighbor, regardless of origin, is very small, perhaps only a comparatively miniscule 10,000 genes. It was encouraging, thinking we could concentrate on the similarities, if we had a mind to, rather than clouding issues with ancient history, genetic baggage.

We took more notice of Valentines Day, February 14, that year, than usual. In India, shops were raided. The cards were called vulgar and burned. It was not part of their culture to be demonstrative in the street, they asserted. Actually, in both cultures, Indian and Saudi, men did hold hands and walk arm in arm, and Saudi men hugged and kissed cheeks in the street. In Riyadh, the inventory of ordinary card shops, under critical scrutiny most months was suddenly put under a magnifying glass. Email cards sent using the university account were intercepted. Year round flower shops were compelled to remove all roses, even the Jury variety, the only one that had any scent. Conventional wisdom had it that roses could still be procured for black market prices, if anyone found them that indispensable.

Friends encountered other sudden changes of policy, too. Allegedly 24-hour grocery stores used to allow shoppers to mill around during *salah* once they were already inside, as long as they stayed in the back and didn't come near the register, where a *mutawa* might see them. Likewise restaurants used to just put decorative screens around occupied tables and allow customers to sup quietly in the semi-darkness.

But this had recently changed. Grocery stores and restaurants, even McDonalds, locked their doors after enforcing a mass exodus.

"But we haven't finished our food yet," lamented our friend, to the establishment.

"Leave it on the table," she was told. "You can finish it in a half hour!"

We guffawed as we conjured up mental images of customers with appetites only half satiated looking longingly through darkened windows at congealing food.

When *mutawa*s were especially vigilant, it was not uncommon to hear about women, particularly blonds, who were harassed for not having their heads covered in public. The wife of a friend would have been compelled to enter the nearest shop and buy a scarf, had her husband not absent-mindedly shoved a dishtowel from their kitchen into his pocket!

The decibel level in the hall changed, too. We were used to kids noisily playing in the elevators and under our windows but one day, there was so much screaming in the hall, I was sure someone had broken a bone. I opened the door just in time to see a young boy rounding the corner, on roller blades, followed by several gleeful, marauding compatriots, female and male, on all manner of wheels. Annoyance rising in my throat, I adopted my most neutral expression before looking toward Tanya's door. A specter stood there, only eyes showing, maybe a relative of Tanya's husband, adding her brood to the bunch. When she became aware of me, she began chasing the kids and herding them together with orders of "come on" and "don't shout."

Remembering Tanya's girls when I previously tried to give them flowers, I was reluctant to get involved with this bunch again. On that occasion, I had smiled and said hello as I passed them, engaged in raucous play in their doorway. From our flat, I plucked the two finest freesias out of a vase on the coffee table, and went back to their door. Before I reached them, the 3-year old scampered inside but the 7-year old wordlessly accepted both blossoms and shut the door.

I would have liked to offer these kids a book or puzzle from my pantry, but didn't think they'd be allowed to accept them. The invisible barrier was almost palpable. Was it there's, or mine, I wondered. Instead of speaking, I raised my eyebrows at whoever was rolling by at the moment and closed my door. Even after the roundup, I didn't notice any drop in the decibel level. I submerged myself in a paperback comedy about forged books in a British library.

Two days after Valentine's Day, the United States and Britain bombed Baghdad. From local news, I picked up two tidbits: Iraqi civilians were dejected, because they'd thought in the previous two years, they'd come some distance toward ridding themselves of sanctions, but now, with a shock, they found they were back at Square One and secondly, other Arab countries agreed Palestine was the issue of the day, not Baghdad. In Riyadh, helicopters hovered overhead.

More news kept the emotional roller coaster rising and falling:
- NASA's NEAR spacecraft landed on the asteroid, Eros, to collect astronomical data and to spread our harmony or disharmony to yet another astral body,
- An American nuclear submarine hit a Japanese fishing trawler at Pearl Harbor,
- a 24-year old Brit sailed around the world alone,
- recovering Sarajevo was preparing to host the 2010 Olympic games,
- an old copy of *The Seven Pillars of Wisdom*, by T. E. Lawrence, Lawrence of Arabia, was auctioned off, found in the cellar of a Scottish female writer,
- a British rock group played to appreciative audiences in Cuba,

- Mad Cow Disease took on larger proportions, Brazil and Canada getting into the fray with a game of tit-for-tat, Canada refusing Brazilian beef and Brazil pouring out Canadian wine,
- and the 11-month long foot and mouth disease crisis began in Britain.

Disquiet became so commonplace, I became more hardened to it and kept my spirits up easier. This callousness was a sad side effect, but keeping my own spirit strong was the best thing I could do for everyone else around me, too.

I wiped the cobwebs from my brain and reflected on the pleasant in my life. Beige and gray sparrows and dark blue pigeons with iridescent necks and pink feet and eyes came to eat the food I sprinkled on the two-foot wide bedroom windowsill. They were a delight, strutting about, pecking at cookie crumbs, remnants of hot cross buns, scones and rice grains. When out of food, they tapped at the window at 5:30 AM, endearing themselves to me with their pointed plea.

By the time I had completed three months, I was even able to appreciate the humor when Baba announced, "I'm not taking the car today so you can go where ever you want."

"I don't have keys," I countered.

He considered his pocket for a moment, then suggested, "Just hotwire it!"

About mid-February, the temperatures became ideal again, in the upper 20s C. (70s F.), although still in the low 20s C. (60s F.) mornings and evenings. We needed neither heat nor AC. It would percolate again soon enough. For a few days, a blizzard of sand exploded on the *shemal* winds and rained hazy silt down on us all day. The air had a smoky, bleary quality and the sunset was obscured. On the streets, out came blue tinged halogen vapor headlights.

Saudization

Then, true to form, just as I began to get the hang of this stage, it shifted abruptly and I was on to the next one. Baba came home one day and announced we would not be coming back for another year after all. Saudization. Laws passed a few years earlier began the process of eliminating expats in every business and replacing them with indigenous people, to the tune of an additional 5% per year. So this was the way our odyssey was to end? With a bang, just the way it started? The news was bittersweet. I didn't know whether I felt reprieved or let down.

Finally, an end to this insufferable seclusion. I could be nearer the kids, be outside more and drive. On the other hand, I had been looking forward to going to India next *Ramadan*, only a 3 1/2-hour flight. We were planning next Hajj vacation, maybe a Mediterranean cruise. I was just beginning to make friends.

In particular, I had two preferences: to avoid being around for the chaotic selling of the furniture and car, and to have time alone back home to restore my version of order between the advents of my son and my husband. Perhaps I was to have neither. If Baba had been going back to Riyadh for a third year, he would have had a scant few weeks in the Midwest before doing an about face. Now, it would all be different.

As the others in Baba's department came to know about our not staying, the women I knew best and I commiserated with each other. One spoke of how I hadn't yet seen the real bubbly, social her. She hadn't met the real friendly, helpful, willing to listen me yet either. Another, with depression flickering just under the surface, confided she was watching her personality change before her eyes. I felt like I was escaping and leaving them behind. Exit wounds. With my time now limited, I felt freer to show my inspirational literature to selected others and to speak more freely about my own coping strategies. When I dipped into my lending library, seeking just the right pieces for a particular individual, I rejoiced inwardly that my skills had found some application. Vital signs. I wished I had shared my strategies sooner.

I had resolved not to thrust my precious artwork, done with care, imagination and heart, into this erratic environment, even if they were born there. I would concentrate on other pursuits. At Hajj, I had finished the needlepoint of a wooden Saudi door. With that completed, too, everything could go to the framers.

Thumamah and the New Moon

Life went on. The weekend of our 28th wedding anniversary, we were out driving and stumbled upon a park of sorts with a sign over

Ala Tool

the main gate reading *Thumamah* Village. We'd heard of *Thumamah* preserve for gazelles. Prince Charles of England had just visited it the previous week. At first we thought they must be one and the same, but when we saw a fort gate, two giant incense burners, a Ferris wheel and strings of colored lights, we decided the preserve must be a place apart. So this was where kids went on the weekends?

Across the street stood a row of ten white, teepee shaped umbrellas, covering booths with local wares for sale: spices, sweets, nuts, bakery, candles, carpets and rummage sale items. It looked like a fair. We walked up the row just to look and on the way back, bargained for a few incidentals. Our big find was a camel bag, a sturdy beige weaving with red and brown designs, and lots of red tassels. It was 100 x 60 cm. (40 x 24") and had deep pockets. Such bags usually hung by loops from a wooden and leather camel seat, one bag on each side.

Back in our sitting room, I threw the loops of the bag over the corners of the door and sat down to read a notice in the Arab News (2001), entitled Call to Look for New Moon.

"The Supreme Judicial Council has called upon all Muslims ... to look for the new moon ...urging those who sight ...(the crescent) to testify before the nearest Shariah (Islamic) court."[65]

This new moon would herald the arrival of *Dulhijj*, the month of Hajj vacation. TV Programs on How To Perform Hajj and Safety at Hajj came in all languages: Turkish, Indonesian, Malay, French, the Persian Farsee and Urdu, as well as Arabic and English. Commercials between programs instructed pilgrims not to let others use their blankets for picnics, not to share towels, razors and toothbrushes and to be as careful of potable water as washing water. And an advertisement came in the newspaper offering meningitis vaccines.

An adolescent-looking Sheikh TV gave instruction about what is forbidden during Hajj, like hair and fingernail cutting, although he admitted nobody could remember why. They just do it. He continued that the first ten days of the month of *Dul Qadah* were similar to the last ten of *Ramadan*, in that no good deeds will be as rewarded by Allah as much as those performed during those intervals, not even engaging in *Jihad*, actions taken to spread Islam. That is, except for one. If a man uses up all his wealth in the service of Allah, that is more rewarded at any time.

Chapter 29: Driving: Hazards And Hilarity

"Man's character is the product of his premises" [66]
—Ayn Rand, *The Fountainhead*

On the streets of Riyadh, daily, we witnessed maneuvers guaranteed to evoke that *now I really have seen everything* feeling. In 1999, before Baba could drive a rented car, he was required to get a Saudi driver's license. That meant a road test after merely identifying a half dozen road signs on a chart—no rulebook. Two years later, when we bought a car, a 2000 Nissan Sunny, white, like 90% of the country's cars, the dealer looked at him with amused shock when Baba asked for the likes of a user's manual. Other cues told us that the system of automobile locomotion was still in its infancy. Safety regulations do exist, but not everyone knows about them or understands their importance.

Most Saudis on the road learned to drive in rural areas, around the age of 10, maybe with a camel in the back of their pickup truck, and they brought their driving etiquette to the big city.

Roadways

I've seen something of the driving habits in 17 countries but have only seen the more risky of the following antics, occasionally, in large, nonstop cities. But in Riyadh, they were everyday occurrences. Every day, we avoided cars on freeways or 6-lane divided roadways, squeaking between two others at twice the velocity everyone else was going, zigging and zagging from shoulder to shoulder, crissing and crossing like a renegade horse in the Royal Canadian Mounted Police Musical Ride, that intricate, precisely timed, wagon wheel shaped performance with horses and riders. Sometimes, 2/3 of windshields were obscured by cardboard or cloth, presumably to keep the sun out. Using the *shmal* as a curtain on each side of the eyes cut down on glare, too, and on having to be overloaded with peripheral information. Many cars had smoked windows in the back seats for the ladies, or curtains across the back window, but a new trend was to have white frosted glass everywhere, even across the windshield. We couldn't even see the eye color of the people who almost ploughed into us.

On non-divided highways, a car coming from the other direction seemed to be a cue to pass. Lane markers didn't mean much. Cars careened with two wheels on one side of them and the other pair on the other side. Cars jutted out from side streets or lanes without regard for who was already there before them. We didn't see too many accidents, but an oral surgeon friend told us plenty of mangled faces needed repair.

Red Lights

Three Saudi cars in each lane routinely went through red lights, police standing placidly unperturbed at the corner by their motorcycles. And the only reason the rest of the cars didn't follow suit was that the cars from the other side had started coming. The authorities, we found, were looking for unfastened seat belts or for expats to harass who put one tire tread into the marked pedestrian crossing. So when Baba stopped at the red, the cars behind honked. At times, honking from six or seven rows back was aimed at the front row of roadblocks. They didn't see much traffic going across, so honked a 'why are you stopping?' query.

Honking

Honking was reserved for these special circumstances. A single car could be laboriously weaving its way against traffic on a narrow one-way street and nobody honked. Bicycle or motorbike riders, though usually not Saudis, could take seemingly carefree meanders, in the wrong direction on the side of a freeway or major street and nobody honked. But two seconds before every red light turned green, a whole chorus started up. Of course, it didn't help that signal lights and crosswalks were in the same plane, so with the fenders of the front cars crowding the crosswalk, the light was practically right over the drivers' heads.

Nobody honked either at double parkers. Strings of shops bordered frontage roads on both sides of 6-lane roads with boulevards of palms down the middle. Angle parked cars were tightly packed in front of popular shops, and behind them sat a row or two of straight,

Jewel Dhuru

double parkers. If you came out and didn't see the driver who was blocking you, you could look around, or just wait. We'd been on both ends of this situation. When we were blocked, we didn't have to wait more than a few minutes and once, while I waited for Baba, the uniformed driver of a Mercedes with tinted back windows walked pointedly by my window, then quietly went back to his car to wait. Private space is a luxury in most of the world. No need to honk.

U-turns

U-turns at intersections were routine at the proper light, a small one, located lower on the pole than the main traffic light. They were essential because long stretches of two-way roads with central boulevards were uninterrupted by cross streets, so we could either turn right and go around the whole square block or make a U-turn at the next corner, often a mile down the road.

So at intersections where four cars squeezed into three lanes, the left two or three lanes either turned left, made a U-turn or went straight. You never knew in advance what anyone else was going to do. Turn signals gave little indication of drivers' actual intentions. You just proceeded cautiously and found out at the same time as everyone else.

This was not the only way to make a U-turn. Frequently, U-turns to the left were made from the extreme right lane, across the front of three other lanes of cars, all sitting at a red light. The first couple of times, the spectacle was a shock; later it became predictable. It was better entertainment than Ad Vision, the huge public commercial screens on the tops of high buildings at every major intersection. At the 2-minute red lights, each of the four directions of traffic went one at a time. A big screen was just what was needed, another distraction, given that easily 1/5 of the drivers were driving as a secondary activity, the primary one being talking on a cell phone.

Yet another style of U-turn involved drivers just passing the turning point they wanted, being reluctant to go ahead another mile to the next intersection, so backing up a block on the right side of the road, against the flow of traffic, and then crossing over three or more lanes of traffic to turn left and ultimately back.

More Red Lights

Several times, we witnessed the phenomenon of four cars abreast stopped at a red light, when a driver from the second layer back, perceiving two front runners having a space almost big enough for a car between them, started to slowly, persistently wriggle up to the space. Both the intruding driver and male passenger extended their hands from open windows in that palms upturned wheedling, appealing position, until the cars on each side creped over a few inches to make room. When the intruding vehicle achieved an equal place at the front, right under the red light, a quick look to left and right told the driver it was safe to go straight across, so he did. Now I think I really have seen everything.

We had the distinct impression that if drivers could, they would treat red lights like they do stop signs—ignore them. One STOP in a residential back lane was so bleached, we recognized it only by its shape and location. A NO ENTRY showed similar signs of wear. Baba proposed they both were faded because of lack of use. This was the same logic that conjectured that the Canadian province of Quebec wanted to separate because it didn't like the winter.

Headlights? After it got good and dark, most people used them, but on every street, several navigators used only parking lights, dim lights, one light or no lights. Once a car went merrily along for miles with only its flashers on, perhaps because they were the only lights working or perhaps because it was an emergency waiting to happen.

Pedestrians? Mostly men on the sidewalks. You usually parked near where you wanted to go, but a few people did brave crossing wide streets at crosswalks. Jay-walking? People crossed wherever they could get a foothold without getting their foot run over. Even on freeways, there was often a *thob* climbing over a concrete barrier. If he got across without getting killed, he was in the right.

Some Saudis courteously waved us around them when they stopped right in the middle of a lane, or let us ahead of them onto a crowded street, remarkable occurrences because of their rarity. The unexpected made a lasting impression.

I could tell about the almost every day spectacle of two teen boys, each in a Mercedes, circling a boulevard in a populated shopping area, screeching tires in a 15-minute duel. Or about the time four Saudi boys in a car with special plates slid in front of us, one standing up out of the sun roof and two in the back, each hanging out of side windows from the knees up. But these instances would not be unique. This would probably be true of select other cities as well, the common denominator being kids who are too affluent and have too much free time.

Coincidentally, an Arab News (2001) article appeared, entitled Accident Rate Still High in Kingdom, declaring that in 2000, in this country of only 15,000,000 people (6,000,000 of whom are expats), despite newly enforced seat belt laws, there were in excess of ¼ million accidents, with 4200+ deaths and 3000+ injuries, that this number was up from 1999, and that 40% of those killed were under the age of 25. [67]

It was a source of poignant mirth that, synchronously, although I was not to see it for two more months, an article was being prepared for the Winnipeg Free Press (2001), my hometown newspaper, about their driving habits. It seemed, although the residents of the province of Manitoba were not aggressive drivers, they were quite well known for talking too much on cell phones, putting on make-up, shaving and combing their hair during rush hour. [68]

On one occasion in Riyadh, Baba found himself in a middle lane of three, just pulling up to a red light.

"Oh I wanted to turn left there," he exclaimed.

Mafee mishkole, I thought. He gave me a wry smile when I responded, "So what's stopping you?"

Chapter 30: Damascus And Environs

"The world is most wonderful when explored with a youthful heart" [69]
—K. DeElle

Damascene Students

At Hajj, on the flight to Damascus, Syria, I recalled faces from the college academic writing class I taught. In the back row of a class of 15 students from ten different countries, sat Shamcy, a pleasant young man from Damascus. One assignment was to Freewrite in a Journal on topics of their choice, to aid in becoming fluent thinking and composing in English. Munjed wrote a hilarious story about how he and three buddies went, in one of their father's cars, for a picnic to the grounds of a monastery halfway up a mountain overlooking Damascus. It seems they locked themselves out of the car, then were motivated to find a way back in by the sudden arrival of half a dozen small wild dogs, who jumped all over it. The dogs only retreated when two giant dogs on leashes with a monk in tow emerged from the monastery. The enormity of those dogs was such that the guys wished earnestly for their half dozen small ones back. Then, the ignition became disabled, so one of them went down the mountain to bring back a latently incompetent locksmith. The story rambled through the piece-by-piece destruction of the dashboard, their eventual homecoming and tall tales to parents to cover their tracks. In more than seven years of teaching, it was the Journal entry that gave me the most entertaining glimpse into a student's life. In time, Munjed finished the course and moved on.

A year later, imagine my surprise when Rami, another Syrian student, wrote the same story in his Journal. This must be one of the buddies, I surmised and wondered if eventually I'd meet the whole bunch.

Damascus

I awoke from my reverie as our mechanical flying carpet landed where dreams and legends spring to life from the soil. To get a flavor of Damascus, it would be best to take a moment to imagine the most charismatically antiquated city you ever saw. Add 2000 years to that, more charisma, ignore the dust, broken bricks, uneven lanes and missing stones. Then, imagine the drivers and pedestrians are good judges of distance, are generally courteous and it's safe to walk alone in the evening. And you have Damascus, or more accurately, Dimashq.

Dimashq, on the old Silk Road, is one of the few cities on our globe claiming, with 5000 plus years of civilization, to be the most ancient populated city in history. Every cultural group in the region settled some part of it at one time: Egyptians, Israelis, Assyrians, Alexander the Great's Greeks, Nebuchadnezzar of Babylon, Persians, Nabataeans, Romans, Christians, Muslims, Abbasids of Baghdad, Crusaders, Nur ad-Din and the Turks and his successor Salah ad-Din a Kurd, Mongols, Mamluks of Egypt, Ottoman Turks, Germans, French and the British, until finally Dimashq became the capital of an independent Syria.

We checked into a hotel and while I settled in, Baba wandered. Dimashq is nestled in the Barada River valley and stretches up the sides of the surrounding mountains. In the central area, city squares, roundabouts with fountains, souks, residential areas, embassies and museums all vie for space. But what is historically interesting lies in the compact Old City, surrounded by ruined fortress fortifications, and accessible through the remnants of nine enormous arched stone gates. The Ummayed Mosque was of central importance and is where Baba set his sights. My biases show when I avoid opulent buildings, be they mosque, cathedral, temple or palace, especially when they are described thusly by the tour book: the "caliph Khaled ibn al-Walid considered it necessary to empower the image of his city with 'a mosque the equal of which was never designed by anyone before me or anyone after me'." [70]

It's not that I don't appreciate the feats of the artisans or the beauty, but I'm more impressed by a high percentage of literacy or the absence of poverty, or harmonious relations between neighbors. As long as there are children without enough to eat, perhaps it's unfair, but such opulence becomes a monument in my eyes to indifference. But I suppose, when this mosque was built in 636 AD, they weren't too concerned with literacy or immunizations.

Beginning in the 9th century BC, the site the mosque now occupies originally held the Armenian temple of Hadad, expanded into the Roman temple of Jupiter, and then a Christian basilica dedicated to St. John the Baptist. Perhaps there was a story of harmonious relations among diverse neighboring cultures here after all, spread out over 1100 years. In any case, I spared myself from being swaddled in a brown *abaya*, provided for women at the site and trudging up and down stairs with no shoes. But I did eventually peek through the entranceway and what I saw myself and through Baba's two rolls of film of mosaics, precious stones imbedded into prayer niches, inlaid wood and gold ceilings were beautiful.

When page two of the information booklet began with the prophetic salutation, "Dear Quest," I knew we were in for a fun ride. Not only were Qs and Gs taxing for Arabic writers; Bs and Ps posed a problem as well. The menu from the Al Basha Restaurant, referring to Light and Useful Meals, listed a Cheese Blatter.

We smiled and laughed a lot in Dimashq. We laughed when Baba walked in after his solo exploratory excursion to the mosque and announced, "I bought new shoes." When he pulled up his pant legs to reveal a pair of broken down black loafers with gold buckles, his heels hanging out past the ends, I knew something was up. I had forgotten to convey to him the tour book's warning to carry your shoes with you when you remove them at the mosque. Without this tidbit, to get back to the hotel, Baba had to rely on the little old codger who passed for a caretaker to provide him with an abandoned pair that he guarded in a back room. Haves and Have Nots. In this city, where crime was infrequent, for some it was worth the risk to pinch shoes from comparatively affluent tourists, even if breaking the laws of the Syrian version of Islam. Our American dollars equaling 45 SL, (Syrian Lira) each, Baba replaced his size 11 Clarks for a fraction of the original cost and returned the borrowed pair to the so-called caretaker.

Similarly, I smiled with appreciation when Alim, our first taxi driver-tour guide, explained it was out of consideration for my back that he slowed down and rumbled gently over railroad tracks, enduring the perturbed honks of the driver behind him. I smiled when I sat on steps near the remnants of the 3000 year old Roman Temple of Jupiter waiting for Baba and a young Syrian passerby asked me where I was from before suggesting that it being winter, I might like to sit in the sun around the corner rather than there in the shade. We had hoped to take in as much of Syria, Lebanon, and Jordan as time allowed, but I had laughed when Baba talked about not only going to Beirut, but also to Jerusalem. Getting back into an Arab country with an Israeli visa stamped into a passport was tricky at best, assuming we could manage to get the visa at all. Getting back into Saudi Arabia with it would be next to impossible.

The garb in Dimashq was eclectic. For men, it ranged from traditional long striped *galibiyyas* to predominantly Western clothes. And for women, from a few covered in black except for the face to long gowns of all colors to tight slacks and tops. Headscarves matching outfits were common along with capricious make up. Heads of hair in all shades of russets and auburn were left uncovered, but the roots, like that of the children's following behind were brown or black.

The best part was the smiles and being regarded by kind eyes again. People asked where we were from and said 'welcome'. They seemed less tense or starved for conversation. Kids in passing cars waved. Baba and I could have our photo taken together in public again, without fear of being overlooked, overheard, or over-inspected. I didn't see that uncomfortable condition of not knowing if it's all right to look at another human being or not, or wrestling with where on the anatomy to look. Business did not grind to a halt for *salah* and going to pray was not even compulsory. This was hospitality creating an at-home feeling, genuine, unencumbered by unreasonable restrictions, not just used as a temporary distraction to help forget your plight.

Alim didn't speak too much English but knew the city well, listened with his heart and intuited what we wanted. We used his services for four days and it was wonderful to feel a meeting of minds with a stranger again, even if fleeting and about elementary subjects. At times I waited in the taxi while Baba got just a few more pictures. Alim helped me pronounce Arabic names in our tour book. His brown toothy smile didn't bother me since we found out minerals in the water can cause such speckling. We asked about each other's families and he did not suggest that I have another child.

Driving was like locomoting in any city of 5,000,000 people with narrow one-way streets and few parking spots. Traffic police with shrill whistles, manned roundabouts and intersections. In this compact space, it was not unusual to have your clothes brushed harmlessly by a slow moving vehicle. Yes, drivers were a little casual with lane changes and more than one scooter curb crawled in the opposite direction as the flow of traffic, but people were basically courteous, flashing lights as a request to pass on the left. And women drove, too.

Alim took us from site to site. Once we entered a gate to The Old City, about a mile square, invariably we found our way past the Citadel and to the central Ummayed Mosque courtyard. The Pope was to follow the same path in Syria two months later. From the mosque continued narrow winding lanes full of timeless oriental bazaars and vendors' carts. One other way in to the Old City was to walk in through the 6 meter (15') wide Souk Al Hamadiyah. This 650 meter (1/3 mile) long, cobbled stoned two-storied, roofed, tunnel with khans, cubbyholes, emporiums, nooks and crannies, with merchants and wares all along the sides was the oldest shopping area in the city. In shadowed corners, black market members offered to exchange our money. From across the street, the entrance was a gaping black hole, right off the sidewalk between buildings, promising riches like Ali Baba's cave. Upon entering, it resembled the innards of an undulating caterpillar. The blackened and vaulted corrugated iron roof was full of rusted holes, giving the impression of a starry night, as daylight pinpricked its way through the orifices. Besides pseudo starlight, elegant 2 meter (6') light fixtures, made from stained glass or wood with inlaid glass, dangled from the cavernous ceiling.

Even the Nur ad-Din *hammam* bubbled inside, a public bath, although open at different times for men and women. It contained a hot room for sweating, a warm room for washing and rinsing, a massage area and a cold room for refreshments and conversation. And it was named after the Turkish uncle of Salah ad-Din (1138-93), the local Kurdish hero whose statue on horseback sat right outside the souk. He is credited with driving the crusaders out of the area, portrayed in history as a true knight in the romanticized European tradition.

Kaiser Wilhelm II of Germany had visited the Old City and restored Salah ad-Din's mausoleum in the 1800s, presenting the site with a white marble tomb with inlaid stones. I'm not sure who's in there, but Salah ad-Din's cenotaph, just beside it in the same room, was austere by their standards, of walnut and painted with Ayyubid motifs.

Jewel Dhuru

Taxiing through the Souk Al Hamadiyah one day, a group of teen boys walked past us chanting, *"soora, soora"*, meaning photo, when they saw my camera. Baba jumped out, echoing *soora* to them. They smilingly lined up and after the flash, thanked us politely and went off. Baba had pictures of people of all ages, and most of them didn't even want a copy. They just wanted to be photographed. On the other hand, Baba had made friends with the proprietor of the photo shop he frequented. When Baba offered him a copy of the photo the two of them had taken together, the proprietor confessed he'd already made one for himself!

When we exited the souk, through the spacious Ummayed courtyard and past the remains of the temple of Jupiter, the lanes became narrower. Cars going in one direction could barely pull over letting opposing cars pass, but not without coming nose-to-nose with a vendor's cart or storefront. Meandering on inside, more mosques appeared, along with chapels of St. Paul fame and more souks and khans. Buildings and barricades used *ablaq* architectural techniques, alternating black basalt limestone and sandstone, resulted in a banding effect. Old houses and restaurants were undistinguished from the outside but once you cross the threshold—wow!—marble, wood, stained glass, mosaic and inlaid tiles. More old residences now used for schools, palaces with courtyards, more *hammams,* Roman arches and blind alleys where people still lived.

On one street, passing a bakery, I commented on the overwhelming aroma of fresh bread pouring out of the shop. Alim wedged the taxi over in a corner and went into the shop, followed by Baba. They came out with still warm bread, but Baba complained Alim wouldn't let him pay for it. That was because whatever Alim told the baker, the latter wouldn't accept any payment. As our trio walked, taking in the details of overhanging balconies with latticed shutters, we broke bread together and munched. Once we headed down the narrowest lane, only wide enough for a single small car to inch through, passing perilously close to front doors. Flowerpots, lanterns and coach lights wisely hung above car and head level. Pedestrians flattened themselves against walls as we passed. When we encountered another vehicle going the other way, we backed up and enjoyed the view a second time. Finally, out through a gate and back into the big city.

Alim showed us the mosque of Sayyida (Lady) Zeinab, the granddaughter of Muhammed (pbuh), and the daughter of his daughter, Fatima. It was strikingly colorful, Persian by design, with shades of blue tilework and a gold onion-shaped dome.

My special request was to see the mosque and tomb of Ibn Arabi, the Spanish Sufi mystic who died in 1240 and whose big-hearted beliefs impacted Islam for centuries. On a crowded shopping route, it was very much a community mosque, drawing in throngs, even for picnics.

Alim repeatedly suggested a place out of town, so eventually we arrived at Maloola, meaning entrance, a village with houses pressed up against the cliff face, one above the other. At the top of the cliff sat the Greek Catholic Monastery of St. Sergius. I wondered if this was the same monastery as Munjed and Rami wrote of, but the only little shaggy dog around was guarding a donkey, tethered to a fence.

A door, half our height, led into the monastery. A serene roofless courtyard went on to an allegedly pre-Christian alter, for pagan sacrifices. Another half door off the courtyard opened into a museum with jars, jugs and implements once used throughout the monastery and a gift shop where religious items and homemade wine and honey were sold. I came away with a segmented fish carved from olive wood and the memory of the priest's reciting the Lord's Prayer in Aramaic for us. The atmosphere was so peaceful and calm, it was difficult to leave and I'm thankful if I can evoke a fraction of the contentment and tranquility when I think of it.

On Tour in Syria

Later that day, we made plans to visit neighboring countries. At the Syrian Embassy in Riyadh, Baba had applied for multiple entry visas, allowing several border crossings, but they gave us only a single entry visa. Once in and once out. So Jordan and Israel were still just a dream, but Syria didn't recognize Lebanon as a separate territory. So, we embarked on a 2000 km. (1200 mile), 5-day journey in a Hyundai van with a round green Persian carpet in the mid-section, complete with Rasheed, our mild mannered, English speaking, Syrian driver. It was a comfort that neither of our drivers asked about our religions, nor tried to push theirs on us.

Jewel Dhuru

We explored cities and towns along the way. The tour book referred to the people of Hims, the third largest Syrian city, as rather backward. We might have guessed without being told, from the black *abayas* aplenty again. It was like entering a time warp.

From there, a short side trip revealed 800-year old Krak des Chevaliers. Some 22 crusader castles adorn Syria, Lebanon and Israel and Krak is the best preserved. With its gothic arches, vaulted halls and towers, it is the epitome of the castle of childhood fantasies, even impressing Lawrence of Arabia. The story goes that the fortress wasn't actually recaptured from the crusaders. With the surrounding territory already taken back, the crusaders just gave up and left. At lunchtime, from the window of the restaurant across the gorge from it, the fairy tale qualities were even more apparent than when we had stood beside the massive walls looking up.

On to Hamah with its lovely *norias*, 21-meter (60') creaking, wooden water wheels, built in Mamluk and Ottoman times. They dished up river water and fed it to what still stood of high stone Roman aqueducts. Again, the same spectrum of dress modes, but leaning towards the conservative. Many women wore lovely long coats in muted colors with matching scarves. Young men were the clichéd tall, dark and handsome, all with moustaches, and many with two bushy eyebrows knit into one.

Aleppo, really Halab, the second largest city in Syria, vies with Dimashq for the title of the world's oldest. Eid, the 4-day holiday at Hajj's end, was in full swing most of that night: noisy music, singing and fireworks. Halab has a citadel with moat, fortified keep for raining down arrows and boiling oil, bastion, armory, throne room and mosque. Its sprawling Old City had souks, a Great Mosque and Hammams. Its Baron Hotel, since 1911, has such names in its guest book as Charles Lindbergh, Theodore Roosevelt, T. E. Lawrence and Agatha Christie.

Our last two stops before leaving Halab were old hotels and restaurants. The first was the 400-year old Martini Hotel, adapted from two Arab-Italian looking houses with a courtyard between. Walking down a narrow cobbled lane, we ducked under an arch and entered a new world. It was charm personified. History lingered in every enchanted corner. Carved stone arches, gingerbread beige stone walls, black scrolled iron balustrades, inlaid marble floors and inlaid wooden chairs, courtyard window-boxes with Poinsettia and English ivy cascading passed round-topped, stained glass windows, wood-framed etched glass skylights, an ancient looking stone well with bucket and rope tucked into one corner of the dining room, intricate wood carvings and carpets in the Arab dining room and stone relief work in the wine cellar, all accessorized by metal plates, swords, clocks, latticed lanterns, flower pots and candlesticks.

By the time I had packed as much as I could into my memory, my back needed a rest, so I recouped in the van while Baba popped a new roll of film into my camera and went with Rasheed to see the other hotel. Baba had not wanted to limit himself to just one digital flashcard on this trip. But without his laptop, the card couldn't be unloaded and reused, and he only had the one card, so he left his digital camera in Riyadh and sustained himself by taking over mine. When he got back with stories of a similarly enchanting hotel, we headed for the open road.

As we got into more rural areas, not only the odd scooter putted along the curb in the opposite direction, but bicycles, townspeople walking, little boys on a donkey, its two saddle bags full of green leaves and the odd father and son shepherding their flock of a dozen sheep across the road after a nibble where the grass is greener. Hitchhikers from all over the world thumbed their way. If we'd been traveling alone, we would have picked up a few and exchanged stories, but Rasheed's employer wouldn't allow it.

Diminishing Returns

The road wound through one hilly, picturesque farming community after another. Everything yellow had come into bloom at one time, flooding the fields with quavering sunlight. Seemingly miniature olive groves and terraced rows of crops appeared on each side, interspersed with petite stone quarries. A donkey brayed in a field of scrub vegetation, grasses, scarlet poppies and yellow and purple wildflowers. Hedges of 3-meter (10') high beavertail cactus bordered the road. On hills, whole rows of fir trees leaned at a $40°$ angle because of the whipping wind from the west.

It was down just such a road, not far from the Turkish border, that we jaunted through low, undulating hills, on the way to Byzantine ruins. The terrain looked like either a terminal moraine had retreated stutteringly and melted on that spot, or an invisible hand had just plain

Jewel Dhuru

planted a crop of rocks. Around each curve the view was more stunning than the last. This can't get much better, we thought. Before we reached a point of diminishing returns, Baba just had to take photos, so he asked Rasheed to pull over.

When he faded from view, I took in the scene. The left side had fir and eucalyptus trees, lines of olive groves in the distance in rich, reddish brown soil, wildflowers and outcrops of white, gray, yellow and red textured rocks. Sheep, penned in by a wooden fence running parallel to the road, came in the same assortment of colors as the rocks and were hard to pick out at first glance. Would the day ever come that all such hills looked this way, I wondered: the hills of Sarajevo, the ones between Macedonia and Albania, Russia and Chechnya, around the Golan Heights and Kashmir. Those hills were never created for shooting and strife. They were meant to bear fruit, to provide sustenance for stomachs and souls.

To the right were more sprinkled rocks and a low rock wall, edging obliquely from the road to the top of the hill, where there was a line of—barbed wire? It seemed out of place. Oh, oh. Too late. Baba was already too far out. I wasn't to know then, but out of my sight, a man in fatigues at the top of that hill began waving his arms at Baba as soon as he saw the camera. Within seconds, Baba jumped back into the van and ordered, "Let's go." But before the engine could be started, raucous honking and a screeching of brakes brought a large SUV, springing from nowhere, to a stop across our bow, eliminating any possibility of escape. Two officers were in the front seat, women in black and half grown children in the back.

"Problem?" Baba asked the driver. Rasheed just sat with his eyes lowered. Before the officer even reached our van, the talk in Arabic had started, to the tune of, we were told later, "You're Syrian; why don't you tell your passengers it's not allowed to take pictures here?" ... talk ...talk... The officer asked for Baba's passport and Rasheed's ID and car information. It seemed, beyond the barbed wire was a military installation. So these lovely hills were not immune either. In the meantime, the women sat and stared and the older boys came out to listen.

At one point, Rasheed asked Baba," Can you give him the film?" to which Baba answered, "I'd rather not." Baba half stood wanting to join the two men outside, but strained to sit tight since he wouldn't know what they were saying anyway and Rasheed didn't appear at all

Ala Tool

rattled. Rapid talk ... more talk... After all the papers were handed back, Rasheed leaned in and pleaded, "Please, if you don't mind, give him the film." I suppose we were lucky Baba was using my camera at the time, not his fancy digital one. This guy didn't look like he would have understood flashcards. I registered the number 10 in the little window before I started rewinding ... rewinding. The shots of the second hotel were in there, the hotel I hadn't seen. I handed the film to Rasheed who surrendered it and the officer immediately headed for his vehicle.

Not wanting to give up that easily, Baba asked Rasheed if the officer spoke English. It seems he did, so he came back to hear Baba out. The officer leaned into the car and with a kindly face said, "welcome." Baba explained we were tourists and he had not taken a single photo yet, to which the officer repeated, "welcome."

"So may I have my film back?" Baba inquired.

The officer squeezed Baba's right hand with both of his and said, "Excuse me."

"What?" asked Baba.

"Excuse me," repeated the officer.

He looked at my hand but I didn't move. He raised both hands, touching ten fingers to his temples and left. Not violent, but warlike. Baba resigned himself. It had been worth a try. As we drove away, minus one roll of film, a lookout tower reared up from beyond the barbed wire.

Then, on to Ladhiquiyah, the hometown of Haffiz El Assad, the previous Syrian President, who had just passed on in June. His likeness was everywhere in cities and towns: on billboards, posters and pavilions, but never more than there. A few showed his son, the current President, Bashar, as well. They were almost as ubiquitous at the photos of King Fahd in Saudi Arabia, whose framed portrait hung in every restaurant, shop, grocery store and even post office.

Ladhiquiyah, a port on the Mediterranean was an atypical Syrian town. Russian and Greek influence was evident, on signs and in the dress. Fewer headscarves, but more redheads, make up and tight pants. In the evening, the locals were celebrating Eid with a carnival of sorts around the ruins of a towering Roman gate with four arches. As I craned my neck to take in the detail at the top, two young Syrian boys came on bicycles, one about 7 years old, asking me in Arabic if I

Jewel Dhuru

liked it and the other, age 10, saying "happy to meet you." It was heart warming.

Our hotel balcony looked out over a lovely park with a colorfully lit up fountain, but Baba said when he walked by himself in the evening, it was the first time in Syria he didn't feel safe on the streets. The next morning, the usual local fare of flat, round Syrian bread with butter, apricot jam, feta cheese and olives made up breakfast.

Phoenician ruins dated back to 1000 B.C., not far from where Alexander the Great, in 333 B.C., passed through this fishing village. While I played at amateur archeology, 10 cm. (4") lizards hid in patches of wild cyclamen and I stumbled upon a field of red poppies in bloom. The words of the poem *In Flanders Fields*, memorized in school as a child, raced through my mind. "Take up our quarrel with the foe, to you from failing hands we throw the torch, be yours to hold it high," it rambled. Who was the foe now, I wondered. Did we have to have one?

By this time, the topography had changed—not so rocky and lusher green. After all, this was the Syrian Riviera: orange, grapefruit and lemon groves, patches of glossy leafed avocado trees and rows of grape vines, curving up and down hills. Orange trees were heavy with fruit.

Further south, Tartus is Syria's only other seaport. It was quiet but had a diminutive Old City that grew up originally in and of the Crusader fortress of Tortosa. Artfully restructured and adapted as a residential quarter, traces of the fortress were easy to discern, including a surrounding depression in the ground, which was once a moat.

The remnants of another crusader castle, renamed Qala'at Salah ad-Din, apparently, had impressed T.E. Lawrence even more than Krak des Chevaliers. It perched dramatically on top of a wooded ridge with precipitous sides, dropping away to ravines. The site was incomparable, but few ruins remained, just jagged ramparts. A siege of two days was reportedly all it had taken Salah ad-Din to drive out the crusaders in the late 1100s.

As we drove along on a Monday near sunset, Rasheed announced he was watching for a gas station. Our tank was on the edge of empty. Tuesdays, almost everything was closed in that part of the Arab world, but with Eid and the towns being small, who knew how many days off they would have. Rasheed stopped to ask locals, who directed us back a couple of kilometers. The people there said, no, it was closed, that we'd have to keep going forward. We asked again; no go. So we kept driving. Each of the three of us silently took stock of our situation. As I saw it, we were traversing a balmy mountain, at the beginning of March, and the scenery above and below was gorgeous. We had a bag of oranges, a few bananas and two liters of water. In a pinch, with reclining front seats and a Persian carpet in the spacious mid-section, there was room to sleep comfortably in the van, even more if we removed the luggage from the back. Of course, the custodian of the van was a Muslim male. That might cause a wrinkle. There was nothing to fear in terms of theft, not there. In any case, a Samaritan would come by and help in the morning or earlier. I didn't see a problem. I enjoyed the view and prepared to accept whatever came. Then an open gas station appeared.

At lunch the next day, for the first time, Baba asked Rasheed about his family. His joint family home contained his parents and the wives and children of several brothers. Sisters lived with their husbands' families. Affection filled his eyes when he spoke of his kids. His wife and kids must have missed him when he traveled with tourists, I speculated. I privately recalled my days of confinement with our young children when Baba was away for conferences and dinners. My job done, it was my turn to go joy riding with Baba and this Muslim male. His wife had the rest for company and support in his absence. I wondered if this episode with us influenced his life, as hearing about his provided understanding for me.

Lebanon

We passed within minutes of the Turkish border but had no visas to cross it, so on to Beirut, or more accurately, Beyrouth. The crossing process looked haphazard, but no doubt there was method to it. First, Syrian passport control to get out of the country, then the Lebanese one to get in, then we pulled the van up to a kiosk for a cursory check. For some reason, passport control wanted to know my father's first name. That sounded familiar. My hospital card in Riyadh said Jewel Martin. It took only a ½ hour but it gave me time to take in the fashions.

A most memorable pair was two young women, one in a skin-tight magenta sweater festooned with a fleecy boa collar and hair of exactly the same color. The other wore a glitzy steel gray top. Both looked as though they'd been poured into black slacks. They wore earrings dangling to the shoulder and eye make up and lip liner that captured my gaze. The impression was incongruence. First I noticed the make up, and only when I could look past it, could I see the face. No slaves to the school of perfect blending, these. The pair was only memorable because it was my first time in person to see such a showcase. On Lebanese TV in Riyadh, I had seen the like but was to discover that Lebanon was saturated with such styles.

Is this what Saudi women looked like under their veils, I wondered? Is this why they fingered the extreme fashions in shops? Come to think of it, when I was at the campus hairdresser-dressmaker getting an easy care cut for the trip, a number of outrageous gowns hung on a rack. She'd asked about my salt and pepper hair, mentioning the buckets of dye she used on the locals.

In the town of Byblios, more Roman ruins, attached to commercial, overpriced shops. The hubbub encircled an outdoor café, where we lunched. I asked Baba to order something light for me while I rested in the van. When I returned, the Arab at the next table had ordered a fruitwood hookah pipe for his wife, the only time we saw such a public display. Baba and Rasheed were munching on yummy chicken *schwarma* but a mutton burger awaited me. I would have been happy with *schwarma*, too. Still, I ate half the burger and greasy fries, leaving the rest. The next morning, my stomach was distinctly rumbly.

Then came Beyrouth, the Lebanese Riviera. The traffic had picked up considerably, to the tune of bumper to bumper. Gone were the citrus groves and grape vines. Since Lebanon was once a French colony, many traffic signs were in French. Stimulating the senses was loud music and billboards advertising all and sundry, including women in provocative poses presenting perfume and lingerie. Although Muslim, Lebanon thinks of itself as more European than Arab.

Terracotta pots of poinsettias and English ivy lined the Napoleon Hotel entrance, on a lovely, quiet street downtown. The neighborhood had so much to offer: a magazine shop, tavern, fresh produce and flowers, clothing shops and cart vendors all on our block. Our inexpensive seventh floor room included a balcony large enough for a dining set for six and two window boxes. Each bunch of 1500 LL,

Ala Tool

(Lebanese Lira), in my black travel bag was worth only $1.00 U.S, but the cost of living comfortably was higher than in Syria.

The first day in that room, only soda and bread passed my lips. Then came the chills, body aches and weakness, as if needed any more. Baba wanted to go for an evening show but the festivities started late, so he went exploring on his own or with Rasheed and let me rest. From that day, my bread and sugar water diet was to carry on into Riyadh and I was to lose 10 cm. (4") around my waist. It would be 2 1/2 weeks before I could eat normally again.

We didn't use the balcony much. It was still winter. Another reason was the mother mourning dove nesting on an egg laid in the bare shrubbery of the window box. I could watch her and her mate's comings and goings through the sliding glass door, and throw cookie crumbs out for them. This was the only hotel I had ever stayed in that included a pet—of sorts.

Was that an explosion? No, just fireworks for Eid. Just the name Beirut conjured up images in my brain of war, but in two days of exploring, only once did we see a now empty apartment building with bomb and shrapnel holes puncturing the walls. It looked quite out of place. Stereotypic representations from the news gradually gave way to those fitting many Mediterranean resorts: rows of off white, buttercup and beige houses, apartment buildings, shops and restaurants, ornate balconies and terracotta roof tiles. Mounting the slope to the summit, *telefrik* cable cars were ascending to churches on the tops of low mountains and descending to waterside grottos. Dazzling blue water all along the shores—sailboats and cruisers. Mountains were snow capped. In Beyrouth, one can ski in the morning and swim away the afternoon.

Plenty of checkpoints, to be sure. Soldiers in army green fatigues and red berets manning check posts on major roads mostly waved cars through. We slowed down long enough for them to see we weren't dangerous and for us to see long-barreled weapons slung over their shoulders.

Dead dogs and a few cats lay off highway. Stray dogs, surprisingly, were not the mid-sized, mixed breeds, found worldwide. A rotweiler, a sheepdog, a German shepherd and a retriever lived wandering, solitary lives. They had none of the usual affectionate, selfless, tail-wagging dog demeanor. I do understand a culture's not putting a high priority on pets, when resources are all wrapped up in

Jewel Dhuru

providing for the immediate needs of people. It's like not having a contingency plan and returning instead to the same house even when one's ancestral land is flooded out every year. But not being allowed by religion to touch dogs? Maybe it was because of parasites, but I was saddened they missed the opportunity to let such enrichment into their lives. The same old Western perspective? Perhaps. Still, animals inhabited this earth before we did, and abused it less. We owe them. I carried the ashes with me of our beloved pet, the same ones I had sprinkled in the DQ wadi in Riyadh. His spirit roams at some spectacular sites.

On to Baalbek, arguably the best Roman ruins in the Middle East. A square mile of temples and pillars of size and power stood serenely next to bustling present day Baalbek, also named after the Roman god, Bal.

Then a final stop at Aanjar. This time, instead of ambling through Byzantine ruins, we sat outside the gate and had refreshments under a cedar tree with Rasheed and the Armenian Catholic gentleman who ran the coffee and spirits shop. This grandfatherly figure and I walked the few steps to the roadside and he pointed out rows of peach trees in bloom, just across a field.

"The next comes plum, then apple and grape, and then all will turn green when the leaves sprout," he explained.

"At the foot of the hills in the distance," he pointed out, "are the famous wine caves. From the anise grown here, we make *arak*."

I'd wanted to sample *arak* ever since I'd read about its being a specialty of the area.

While pouring and stirring the milky potion, he elaborated on the process.

"It is distilled three times from the same grapes as wine," he instructed, juggling glasses, "then add the anise and dilute with half water, or more or less water, according to your liking."

I had a sip. The atmosphere, the view and the company, I relished; the *arak*, with its strong licorice taste, not so much, but I valued the chance to sample it. As we four sat under the cedar, I was aware of the grandfather's attentiveness whenever Baba and I spoke to each other. I felt as though all our secrets were visible under the scrutiny of his benevolent gaze. It was, otherwise, so peaceful, it was difficult to get up and get into the van. Or maybe it was the *arak*.

Ala Tool

Crossing the border back into Syria took longer than on the way out. European tour buses, luxurious with heavy maroon drapes, cluttered the parking lot. Completing the formalities, we started toward the 3 km. (mile long) buffer zone through the Anti-Lebanon mountain range. Only army trucks, wayward sheep, a donkey, poppies and other flowers peeped out in the wooded hills. We were near the Golan Heights, a beautiful name, but largely abandoned because of the shooting back and forth. It was hard to believe we were so close to the West Bank and Gaza Strip. They were near the glorious Mediterranean, too.

While we traveled, the international news was mostly the same.

- The foot and mouth plague was a virulent strain, perhaps unresponsive to vaccines, perhaps yet turning us all into vegetarians,
- A Taleban edict ordered the destruction of the Bamyan Buddhas in Afghanistan. A Muslim gentleman insisted Islam was a religion of peace, tolerance, and respect for the diversity of faiths and values.

Perhaps back in Sufi times, that was true, but this was not the impression I had gotten from Saudi Arabia. But there, in Syria and Lebanon, with vestiges of the Phoenician, Mamluk and Ottoman springing up everywhere, where the worlds of ancient cathedrals intersected with that of old mosques, both of them coexisting on top of the roots of the Roman Temple of Jupiter, maybe it was. In Beyrouth, near minarets and steeples, a billboard had advertised a restaurant, with a picture of the ten commandment tablets and a handful of loaves and fishes.

- International Women's Day was celebrated in the first week of March. Lebanese TV reported a rural Empowerment Program.

On offer were literacy classes and lectures about marital abuse, probably common problems throughout rural regions of much of Asia and the Middle East. By the second week of March, however, I would be back in our Riyadh sitting room reading an article in the Arab News (2001) entitled Women Enjoy Important Status in Saudi Society.

"Ustazah Zakiah Al-Awidi, the well known writer said that it is a very nice thing that the world celebrates the women's day ... She said

Jewel Dhuru

that women in many parts of the world suffer injustices. Islam was the first religion that granted woman her full rights..." Elsewhere in the same article, Fawzia Al-Tassan, manager of Al-Faisaliya Women Charitable Society in Jeddah, said, "... status of the women in Islam became an example for the others to follow." [71]

Back in Damascus

We headed back to Dimashq for three last days. In the evening, we tried again to go for a show, but I still didn't feel up to it. So we drove through more of the Old City and up to *Jabal* Qassioun again. On that Thursday evening, about 10 PM, the streets were full of young people all dressed up, some crouching in the beds of open-back trucks, going to Ali Baba's Cave or a disco at the Hotel Omar Al Khayam. We did end up finding a bright spot for dinner, a restaurant near our hotel. When the maitre D' understood why I was not eating much, he had *shay binanaya,* mint tea, brought to me, with real mint leaves dipped into boiling water.

On this 10-day foray, I was restored with some milk of human kindness. I recalled other times I was the recipient of unsolicited consideration. In 1976, Baba and I were touring Italy when our son was one year old. We were the last three to board a tour bus in Rome. I mounted the stairs first, our little one in my arms. As the bus started to move, I was catapulted down the aisle, with 9 extra kilos (20 pounds) in my arms, but my center of gravity having shifted, I wasn't totally aware of my movement. From a side seat, an unknown arm shot out across my abdomen, to stabilize me and keep us from taking a nosedive. The arm achieved its purpose and within seconds, was withdrawn. I never knew who it was, not even if a man or a woman, but I'm grateful to this day that my benefactor was not inhibited by my gender or marital status.

The Flight to Riyadh

The day after the mint tea dinner, Rasheed took us to the airport and it was Baba who got a hug from him while I got a quick nod and 'good-bye'. With my back in its usual state and my intestines churning, I couldn't wait to get buckled into my seat, recline it and close my eyes. But as soon as I began to edge my seat back, a small uproar started behind me. Pummeling the back of my chair, three Saudi males in *shmals* were animatedly discussing, in Arabic, which one would get stuck sitting behind me. They summoned a male attendant to whom I explained before he too joined in the fracas and got everyone relocated. A thin man, whose face I never saw, got the short straw and sat behind me cross-legged, so I was told later by a man across the aisle from me. As soon as I began to recline my seat, the pushing and shoving began anew, in earnest.

After lift-off, the seats being tight, I didn't get up but half turned in my seat and ventured a "Sir, do you speak English? I have problems with my back and need to recline my seat." No response came from the rear, but I subliminally registered a male face from across the aisle taking an inordinate interest in my words. I decided saying any more to my neighbor to the rear wouldn't have helped, because I didn't know what had already been ventured by the male flight attendant on my behalf and the anger that usually bubbled just under the surface in such situations, like lava, was rising up to my throat, so I didn't trust myself to speak.

To calm myself, I drew on all the theory and past experience that would come to a clouded mind. Anger is for removing barriers, and some headaches come from anger with no place to go, I reminded myself. When one has lost one's voice, anger turned inward becomes depression, I warned myself. My milk of human kindness was getting rapidly diluted. The prodding and kneeing of my seat didn't stop through the entire 2-hour flight. I never did recline more than 5 cm. (2"). Silently I prayed 'Remove all prejudice from my heart'.

Baba was zoned out through most of the goings on, exhausted from his foray, the night before, into the world of belly dance. I had said I wouldn't mind if he and Rasheed went to his long awaited show, starting at the usual 11:30 PM, and he didn't get in until 3:30 AM the morning of our flight. He described the show as tastefully done: a female singer, a female belly dancer and then a male singer, all with orchestral accompaniment.

Later in the flight, I asked a female attendant a question but she couldn't understand me. The young man from across the aisle, the eavesdropper from earlier on, volunteered to help communicate my needs to her. Afterwards, we started talking. He was Lebanese American and taught at a Saudi high school. He gave me an earful about the school: about the students, no self-discipline, low motivation and no curriculum and about the teachers, having to be physically in the building 10 hours a day although classes were only scheduled for 15 hours a week. A Western perspective? I suppose so.

For a whole week afterwards, I didn't want to see a *shmal* or *gootra* or hear a voice come out from under one. Naturally, I didn't get my wish. But, we'd gotten a rare Saudi taxi driver on the way home. He was a gentle driver and soft spoken. He had started by opening both passenger side doors for us, the front one for Baba. I suppose he was preparing for a guy chat in the front. The day would come again when it would feel natural for Baba to do just that, but at that moment, freshly arriving from a land of more equitable reciprocity, without hesitation Baba came around the other side of the car and sat in the back with me.

Chapter 31: Lull and Storm

"Advice is what we ask for when we already know the answer but wish we didn't" [72]
—Erica Jong

If I was leaving on June 17, March 4 was exactly half time, so after our return from Hajj, the clock seemed to tick faster. In our absence, March had heralded spring's arrival with mostly dry and 30^0 C. (85^0 F.) days. Roadwork was being attempted outside our sitting room. A particularly bumpy speed breaker had been leveled, but the rest of the surface was now bumpier than before. Then, selected sections of the new surface were marked off and dug up again. Then came two days of heavy rains, so the whole thing just sat. Eventually, it was finished and we rumbled over a smoother speed breaker. It was a reminder for my mental, physical and emotional speed breakers to mellow out, too. Ebb and flow. Lull and storm.

The campus cloverleaves were getting facelifts, too. Instead of replenishing the existing monochromatic pale yellow exterior, though, the vertical rows of protruding balconies were being splashed over with refreshingly contrasting beige or russet. Our building got beige. Inside halls were reborn to sea foam and a darker green. Chemicals from the painting and roadwork hung in the air for two weeks. Workers in orange coveralls scraped and painted the halls all morning, sat on the floor where they stopped work, lunched in the cloud of vapors and then started up again an hour later, breathing fumes all day.

Only on drizzly afternoons was it safe to open the windows. The dust and fumes were temporarily grounded. But the car! It looked like a bucket of watery mud had been tossed over it. They all looked that way. Car washers at shopping centers had lots to do.

Two weeks after our return, we had two rainy evenings and nights. At least this was a self-cleaning rain, leaving little residue on the car. One evening, we were out when the rains started, so we pulled over and watched the lightning display its powerful, long jagged, yellow streaks over rooftops. It felt like a real prairie rainstorm. We could close our eyes and visualize wheat fields undulating in gusts of wet wind. The power of imagery never failed to transport us.

In cadence with the rain, on the edges of unlandscaped streets, low growing plants with red flowers had sprung from the sand. Wherever sand was undisturbed, bordering freeways, in empty lots and on city outskirts, dormant, deep roots burgeoned into crimson patches.

Flower gardens all over the city were reaching their peaks: snapdragons, petunias, marigolds, nasturtiums, cana lilies and every other annual. Before it got too hot, the semi-annual bougainvillea blaze erupted in profusion, too. Like poinsettia, these tropical plants have colored leaves, commonly mistaken for the flower, with actual miniscule flowers tucked inconspicuously inside. What were a month earlier long sprays of green branches, nondescript except for their poetic arches, now burst into strands tinged with color, transforming in tone and hue.

Bushes, hedges and trees came in all sizes, shapes and colors. As we drove around the corner of one compound, a most spectacular display emerged. Solid, thick, bright masses branched at the ends and curved unpredictably, artistically, over 3 meter (10') beige walls. A riot of color cascaded in shades of deep, bright pinks, reds, and dark and light oranges, down the length of the whole street for a distance of 100 meters (290'), interrupted only by the changing of the colors. It commanded our attention, like a beacon, like a scream, like the high note in an opera, and stopped us cold. Approaching that corner, drips and drabs of vivid oranges and pinks had built to a crescendo and suddenly, without warning, the whole streetful appeared in its glory. We just sat for a minute and drank it in, the awe of nature's bounty. In a couple of weeks, they would begin to fade and then rest until the next time.

While the bougainvillea raged, an Arab summit, involving 22 national leaders did, too. It convened in Amman, Jordan, just 200 miles south of Dimashq. Ostensibly, Arabs were meeting to find more ways to support Palestinians in their crisis, besides just sending money and bringing the injured to their hospitals. But the proceedings were eclipsed by Iraq trying to get UN sanctions lifted. Journalists at the summit reported that all of the Arabs, including Kuwaitis, wanted to see the sanctions lifted, but that would mean Iraq's complying with UN requirements including weapons inspectors, which Iraq opposed, and so the go-round continued.

On the way out one evening, we noticed a woman standing in front of Tanya's door. I had seen this specter standing in the same spot before. It was the woman who'd chased after roller bladeing marauders. I said "Hello" as I passed and she froze into a wax museum exhibit, so I went on to the elevator. I could hear Baba behind me saying, "Hi" and then after a pause, "Are you all right?" to which her murmured response was, "Yes." We both went on.

In the car, Baba mentioned he'd been wanting to do some entertaining at home, to have a catered dinner for colleagues who'd invited him in my absence and to introduce me to pals I hadn't met yet. It would be a good chance to include temporary bachelors, too.

My first reaction to his suggestion was mixed. I visualized a room full of people, music and laughter and I felt an internal smile forming, right next to a cringe. I could get all my artwork framed and put it out on display. Our camel bag, Damascene fabrics, inlaid wooden chess set and silk saris could be conversation pieces and my puzzle clocks could serve as comic relief, if it was needed. But at the same time, a feeling of foreboding followed me. I hoped this wouldn't be the straw that broke the camel's back.

Chapter 32: Treks: Lush Rivers, Coral Reefs And Dune Buggies

"Should you shield the canyons from the windstorms, you would never see the beauty of their carvings" [73]
—Elizabeth Kubler-Ross

During the last half of March, between making plans to have the dinner and getting the spare sitting room presentable to take the overflow from the main sitting room, we indulged another dream. A book, *Desert Treks from Riyadh,* was a fountain of information and on free weekends, we explored. It described short and long, 2 and 4-wheel drive treks, jaunts to human-made rivers, natural waterfalls, ancient camel trails, dams, forts, coral reefs, natural arches, standing stones, graffiti rock and weekend excursions to Madain Saleh—a Nabatean town, and the Wahba Crater, 4 km. (about 2 miles) wide and thought to be volcanic in origin.

Riyadh River

Our first trek was to a river, near Al Hayr, flowing for 48 km. (30 miles) down the Wadi Hanifa, to a spot where sedimentary rocks edged down from the roadside to a riverside thicket. Tall reeds and casuarinas bushes played hosts to goldfish, moorhens, snipes, stilts and other water birds. Its origin was our own city wastewater, but with treatment and purification, it gave birth to vegetation so lush that would do any river proud. There was no odor at all and in the desert to have such luxury, one can't be too choosy anyway.

On that 30^0 C. (85^0 F.), sunny day, Baba trooped up and down the bank with his camera, stopping to soak his bare feet in the clear water and I spread my old black *abaya* out on a sandy patch to lie down and soak up Vitamin D. The average temperature had jumped up $5°$ that week and the next week it would do the same.

Though fewer flies than at the Camel Souk, vitality encircled me. The wind quivered in the tops of 3 meter (10') pampus-grassy looking stalks, gentle chirps and chortles escaped the shrubbery, wings fluttered and bees hovered. When I sat up, a black beetle had zig-

Ala Tool

zagged its way carefully around me and a butterfly had landed on a bush just an arm's length away.

More exploring, more pictures and we started heading back. By this time, it had become second nature to scan others standing by the roadside in uninhabited regions. Whether with or without a vehicle, we looked to see they were all right, to stop and ask if they needed a ride or help, as others had done for us.

So on the way back to town, after Baba finished investigating a big dune and we were rolling again, we couldn't fail to notice a lone male Saudi, in *thob* and *shmal*, standing at the roadside, waving a round, red, greasy engine part at us with his equally greasy hand.

When Baba opened the window, "*sayara*"-car, and "*Al Hayr*" were all the hitchhiker needed to say, while gesturing towards town, for us to figure out he needed a ride to *Al Hayr*. Of course we would give him a ride, but those hands. This was going to be tricky. Baba opened the back door for him, moved over our emergency bag of food and water and our trek book left on the seat, so he wouldn't have to touch anything, except the paper towels I handed him.

We were on the only road to town, so off we went. For some reason, from the moment he got in, he spoke mostly English to us and we spoke mostly Arabic to him. Not that there was that much conversation but the smiles and expressions in the eyes were warm. On his part, it consisted of, "thank you, thank you, thank you, *Ana Saudi. Intumma min fein?*" (I'm Saudi. Where are you from?) "*Araby quayes* (your Arabic is good), straight, right, left," and gesturing towards his house with a broad smile, he asked "tea? coffee?"

And on our parts, it was "*mafee mishkole, T'oreed moya?* (No problem, Do you want water?), *yimeen?* (right?), *yasar?* (left?), *a la tool?*(go straight on?), *shukran* (thank you)," and "*le, shukran* (no thanks)" to the tea or coffee.

Between his not needing any water and giving us turning directions, we drove in silence until we heard the sound of pages turning. Then I remembered the trek book in the back. Having blackened the paper towel, he searched for a diversion and started paging through our book. Oh no! I wanted to snatch it out of his hands, but the damage would already have been done anyway, and I couldn't think of how to do it without being rude.

Once we dropped him off, Baba hazarded a reluctant glance back and his face told the story even before I saw the book myself. After

Jewel Dhuru

that, whenever we used our trek book, this first outing would leave an indelible mark on us. If ever our hitchhiker became a wanted man, we had several sets of fingerprints.

Coral Reefs

For our second trek, I hunted for fossils and Baba sought dunes. On the way to a coral reef, the same shimmery vapors-sitting-on-the-desert-floor phenomenon reappeared on the highway, evaporating on approach, with the backdrop looking closer than it actually was.

A few large trucks and the odd car were the only traffic. Parallel power lines and sparse, grass verges in barren soil were the only sights as featureless miles ran under us. Then, a phone booth would appear. Or a water pumping station would go by, resembling a Japanese restaurant, low and green, with sleek straight lines and a flat roof. Or a solitary group would be picnicking on a blanket, their vehicle equipped with ropes, sand ladders, and other self-rescue paraphernalia.

After 96 km. (60 miles) of unremarkable driving, we passed through the band of dozing Dahna Dunes again, where we'd gotten stuck two years earlier. In the distance were the cliffs of the Tuwaiq Escarpment, looking pinkish purple. As we drove, I realized this was a sandy beige country to me no longer. There was more here than met the eye at first glance.

When we stopped for a stretch and to rest our eyes, I could distinguish as many shades and textures of sand as shades and shapes of leaves in a forest. They weren't all blurred together like ink on a wet newspaper anymore. Rich reddish brown sands stood distinct from pinks and beiges, yellows and oranges. Some coarse grains lay heavily on the ground and some were so powdery light, a wind could whip them into a granulated froth.

And our excursion followed two days of heavy rain, so olive and gray green leaves were appearing, too. We had it all! Tiny blossoms everywhere—purple, yellow, red. Not ostentatious like bougainvillea in the irrigated city. In the dry soil, flamboyance was a luxury that couldn't be afforded. But peering closely, I discerned quiet, dry bursts of jubilant color atop almost every plant. When no one witnessed it, what was the sound of such silent splendor, I wondered.

Ala Tool

The low ridge of hills near Khurais contained the fossilized remains of marine life, deposited in a shallow Eocene seabed 40-55 million years ago. We parked off the road. Between two hills, just 0.8 km. (½ mile) from the highway, a 0.2 hectare (½ acre) area of white coral with lots of bits of black, orange and grayish stone and bone sat in more mute magnificence.

I sat at the epicenter of the reef and visualized it in its heyday, teeming with sea life: urchins, rays, sharks, gastropods and bivalves. Fossils were sold in shops, but I preferred to find my own. If books told how to find the reef, I guess the locals didn't mind my collecting the bones. Baba wandered and took pictures while I amassed a small bagful, kneeling beside sharp burrs and avoiding camel doo. I was surprised by several freshly disturbed patches of soil, 10 cm. (4") in diameter, exposing still wet sand, surrounded by otherwise parched sand. They looked freshly dug up, but during the half-hour we were there, we had not seen another living thing. Could it have been snakes or scorpions, as our trek book warned? I was glad I wore my high top boots.

On the way back to Riyadh, we stopped to play in the 20-meter (60') dunes. Baba traversed the narrow ridge on top, and when he turned to come back, his footprints were already silted over, just as the ledge I had dug out to sit on nearer the bottom had filled itself in before I even got back to the car. Perhaps this is a third place on the globe where we ~~get~~ can get a sense of our actual relationship with the universe, our position and duration, besides looking up at a starry night sky and floating over a great coral reef. Looking at the photos later, showing human specks at the bottom of peaks way up above our heads, we looked much more insignificant than I had felt at the time.

Wildlife Research Center and Dune Buggies

On a *Jumma* afternoon, at 3:30, as we'd agreed, Baba came out of his computer cave. He said he wanted to show me where a Saudi superior had treated him and his colleagues to dinner. We grabbed our trek book, almost as an afterthought, just before going out the door.

We looked through the grandiose gates at white chairs and tables in a walled-in garden, lawn and trees. It was 20 minutes drive from our flat, just past *Thumamah* Village. This Sheesha Club was for fine dining and smoking hookah pipes and it had a Family Section. For 50

SR admission, about $13.00, the whole family, defined as a collection of acquaintances, could dine. Across the adjoining wall, another gated enclave was a kids' park with pony and mechanical rides. Baba recounted his memories of the dinner evening as we turned onto the highway.

More signs for *Thumamah* indicated it was 25 miles distant. Then came a sign for *Janadriah*. This must be the elusive King Khaled Wildlife Research Center, the wild park Prince Charles of Britain had toured. And *Janadriah*, or alternately *Jinadriyah*, or *Janaderiyah* as other signs said, the Saudi culture and heritage fair that we couldn't find in February. So this was where they were? We decided to go for it. I got out the tour book and read about them.

Not for the first time, Baba mentioned a place his pals went to see dune buggies. For him, that would be as much fun as his observing MIR passing overhead, or sighting the space station crossing the sky at the precise times listed on the Internet. As we drove, the rounded, harder, undulating dunes were different from the soft pointier Dahna Dunes. Spattering the hillsides were Bedouin tents, pens of sheep and camels, trucks, and even colored lights on gates. Regular homesteads. Short grass even covered large areas, with truck tracks dividing it up into sections, giving the illusion of cultivated fields. We passed an Equestrian Club with a slanted red roof, stands, paddock motif and quarantene area. And after that came *Janadriyah*, 4 hectares (10 acres) of walled in exhibition grounds with the fortress gate I had seen on TV.

Then on to the wildlife preserve. On the left side of the highway, at first, were large fields of crops, irrigated by slow moving metal contraptions and later on, hard dunes sprung up at an unusually busy intersection. On the right, a sign stood pointing to *Thumamah*. The land opened into a sunken dry wadi, extending up to the sharply ridged Buwayb Escarpment. The preserve, our book said, was originally the private collection of the late King Khaled, and had all Arabian species: ibex, oryx with long, straight horns, idmi and rheem, mountain and sand gazelles.

We pulled up to a checkpoint complete with guard. Our trek book, written in 1994, didn't mention a checkpoint. It only said if we made a day visit, a stop at the ranger's camp down the road was unnecessary, but if we wanted to camp there, we needed a permission letter from the Secretary General in Riyadh and that would take three

Ala Tool

weeks to get. We had just planned the trip that very afternoon. We had nothing to lose.

The checkpoint, a gray kiosk, was just big enough for a chair and a shelf for papers. The Saudi guard in fatigues came out and smiled. He spoke little English but was quick at non-verbal communication. After exchanging greetings, we indicated the oryx picture in our trek book and pointed to the wadi. He asked for our permission letter.

"*Mafee*," Baba said, "only *Iqama*," our infamous passport substitute.

"Sorry," said the guard.

We took in the acres before us of wind-scorched green scrub brush for animals to hide behind, leading up to steep escarpment in shades of rock and sand, and wondered if this was as close as we would get to the animals.

Still smiling, the guard asked where Baba worked and where we lived and he reached in to the car for Baba's *Iqama*. That handed over, he asked if it was our first time there, to which we assented. He had a polished way of communicating with non-Arabic speakers, using gestures and repeating, more slowly, trying alternate words, never raising his voice, as though we were deaf. His smile remained relaxed throughout, giving that all-in-a-day's-work impression. Still, the words he strung together sounded dismissive, like it was too bad we didn't have papers or that he didn't recognize us from a precious visit. My authoritarian roots had found fertile soil in the Kingdom and it had become harder to keep them from taking a firm hold. So, my tendency to give up was usually triggered at such a point. The authority figure had spoken. But Baba was hampered by no such malady. His limitation was the language. I didn't see any signs of resignation on his part, like putting the car into reverse.

"It's our first time," he declared. The guard shrugged his shoulders and shook his head. He didn't understand. It was up to me.

"*Mumkin nuss saya bess ege?*"—May I go in for only half an hour? I requested, along with an accompanying going ahead and coming back motion with my index finger. I opted for 'I' instead of 'we' because, under pressure, I forgot the verb form for we.

"*Tayib*"—Ok, he relented, nodding and backing up but still holding on to Baba's *Iqama*. We hesitated to leave the precious document in the hands of any stranger, but it became clear that if we wanted to go in, the *Iqama* would be collateral. He gave us directions, but there appeared to be only one road in and out. I felt rather pleased with our three-way effort. *Ala tool.*

When we passed the ranger's camp, signs directed us to breeding pens and a closed visitor's center. With the sun threatening to set, there was no time to lose. In a scant half hour, there wasn't the luxury of a thorough search, even with binoculars, for one of a thousand shy, sandy colored animals resting under shady bushes or standing on rocky slopes, visible only if they moved. Only flocks of sheep walked with shepherds. At a high fence and an inner kiosk, another guard said *"mafee mishkole"* to Baba's getting pictures of the colorful escarpment, sharp cliffs and the dry plants blooming away in their quiet quest for self-actualization.

"Only ten minutes left," Baba alerted me. Time to head back. I had never seen him so conscious of the time, but then again, the guy had our *Iqama*. As we approached the exit, he stood there waiting for us. He handed the *Iqama* back, shook Baba's hand and then mine. No matter that we had not seen an oryx or rheems. A sense of satisfaction went with this cooperative, impromptu undertaking. And we still had ten more weekends. We might be back.

Dusk approached. This was my favorite time of day, for reflection, relaxing, home and sleep. We backtracked to the busy intersection. Cars and trucks were going to the right, the dune side of the highway, up a hill. We would go to the top and see what the attraction was.

Just over the ridge, suddenly appeared lines of 2-wheel drive cars and trucks, parked up and down the sides of the road. On the left was a high chain-link fence, but on the right a scene unfolded. From the shoulder, the ground dipped into a sandy furrow about 100 meters (290') wide and rose again on the far side to join undulating orange-tan hard packed dunes with a 5 cm. (2") softer top layer, all set off against a bluish white darkening sky. Scattered over the dunes were mostly white 4-wheel SUVs, pickups and jeeps, little groups of young men and boys sitting on the sand, talking and watching. No blankets, not even any food. Just tea thermoses and the guys, chatting and relaxing. A couple of tracks threading up one dune entertained three or four dune buggies, to 100 assorted spectators.

Baba parked the car and jumped out. I could just see him figuratively rubbing his hands together and chuckling, his spirit soaking up nourishment. So this was where the dune buggies were!

Out came the digital camera and the binoculars. Low, wide-wheeled dune buggies with just bare skeletons for chassis, engine and gas tank meandered sedately around the beds, revved their engines, struggled to the top, then coasted down and around again. No roll bars over the top to provide protection as a couple of them raced up and down. The scene was quiet for the first five minutes; not even any sibilant strains of *salah*, not way out there.

Evening crept up, tinting the sky in stages. A ceiling of shade descended. A spellbinding melee started. Boys jumped into cars and half of them cleared out within minutes, but not before first tearing around in circles in the flats. Several kids splayed themselves out over trunks and roofs of cars with wild-eyed inhabitants before streaking onto the road to vacate the area.

We headed for the white teepees at *Thumamah* Village. More camel bags hung on lines but we didn't buy. We came away with two packages of fresh date and fig mini mammouls. Another weekend complete, we headed for home.

Chapter 33: Reluctant Students and Welcome Guests

"Where the telescope ends, the microscope begins. Which of the two has the grander view?" [74]
—Victor Hugo, 1862

It was the beginning of April 2001, that quiet period when neither the heater nor the AC was needed. But, 'solar max' was on the way. It was time to realign all the wall switches and the compressor down the hall from HEAT to COOL. Then, the blowers in each room could provide cool air within minutes of pressing the same button as for heat. There was no advantage to leaving blowers running in unoccupied rooms for hours. Both heat and cool dissipated within minutes of being turned off.

Our voices sounded scratchy, the linings of our noses were swollen and sometimes I swore I sensed my skin sizzling. The annuals had all fizzled and even bougainvillea, so vibrant a couple of weeks before, had shivered and shed their blossoms, their short season ending as the heat of spring rose.

A period of sun activity, 'solar max', occurring about every 11 years, characterized by the ejection of radiation and particles into space, was happening right then, at the beginning of April. While these disturbances created beautiful auroras in the skies over the Poles, the colorful shifting needles I recalled as a child, these same solar flares wrecked havoc with radio and TV transmissions for three days. Some radio stations sputtered and became speechless and the TV picture went blank just when it got to the interesting part of the movie. Then our email became sporadic, and then it got worse. My personal account shut down completely and only Baba's censored work email account was available to me, involving several time-consuming steps. Either it was the sun or one of the times the local authorities allegedly unlinked everybody's Internet for a while. That explosive region of the sun would rotate away from us, but would return in a couple of weeks.

The international news was hotting up, too. South Korea recalled its Ambassador to Japan because Japan's new history book, allegedly, glossed over its own wrongdoing. Slobodan Milosevic, sought for war crimes, was arrested and I wondered how the Bosnian contingent of our family was doing. Without United States participation, the rest of the world prepared to implement a plan for limiting greenhouse gases. An Iraqi tanker trying to avoid UN sanctions, sank off the United Arab Emirates coast, three hours drive from us. After three days, a UAE desalination plant was shut down to prevent contamination, causing residential water shortages. China and the United States were into a game of Tit for Tat over the spy plane debacle and within a week, the U.S. would sell modern arms to Taiwan. It was business as usual.

Prospective Students

Yet another Saudi woman called asking for an English tutor, for her sister. They both studied grammar from a book but needed conversation. I had received several such calls, referred through acquaintances of acquaintances.

Br-i-i-n-g-g. Br-i-i-n-g-g. Another young woman identified herself as a banker.

"I and my friend, want to practice the American accent," she explained.

I invited them to come to our flat.

"I will try to get the special permission from my family," she explained. "I will call you tomorrow."

She called back the next day. No, her family insisted they would stick to the usual rules. Her driver was only allowed to take her to work, to friends' houses, or to the well known all women's club in town.

Would I like to meet at the women's club, she asked? All right, I said. She would call back in the morning. "I and my driver will pass you," she offered, meaning they'd pick me up.

When noon came and went with no phone call, I called her.

"Oh, umm, I was going to call you," she stammered. "My friend cannot come today … I'll call you next week … *Inshallah*."

Inshallah was the last word I ever heard from her.

I was surprised to learn one day from Daniel that a male student he'd referred to me claimed he'd called us. The student reported that he'd spoken to Baba, who told him we were not taking any new students!

Then a call came on behalf of a Saudi woman from a well-to-do local family. She'd called her own English tutor, a female expat acquaintance of ours, asking for a yoga teacher to do stretching and somehow, my name came up. I briefly explained breathwork to the English tutor, who suggested I call Miss Well-to-do anyway. She told me a code name I'd have to give to the male, Arabic-only telephone receptionist, because this prospective client could not accept calls from unknown westerners.

I dialed ...code name ... got through ... again explained it's not yoga ... it was more like psychological stretching.

"I am tired and don't feel well," Miss Well-to-do explained. "Could you come to work with me, my mother and my sister after two days?" she asked. "My driver will call you on the afternoon of that day and pick you up, *Inshallah.*" Another last word. Unfortunately, her mother became ill and was hospitalized the next morning.

When going out that evening, Tanya and her husband stood in the hall with some of his relatives. Baba said hello and I gave as much of a cheery wave as I could muster in the face of what I perceived as their stoicism when extended family was present. Only the daughter who'd previously accepted a flower from me and I exchanged smiles and waves and I passed on.

One day, I welcomed into the sitting room the new student whose sister had called about conversation. Noor was the most memorable student this trip: a buxom, dark-eyed, longhaired, 18-year old Saudi female. Each time she came, only her eyes showed. While she left her *abaya* and *burka*, veil, on one chair, I placed refreshments on a side table. Then Noor and I sat near the balcony door and potted croton.

Her sister came, too, the first day, introduced us and then retreated into the background so we could get acquainted. Noor wanted to be an English teacher but when I asked if she could visualize herself as one, she couldn't. Shy and quiet at first, she had limited English vocabulary and a narrow range of interests to match. I suggested she read a newspaper article of her choice for the next day and we would talk about that. The next time, she brought an article about the movie industry but had understood little of it. I asked if any other section captured her interest.

"I don't like scientific things," announced Noor, "only romance, comedy and fashion."

That second time, she came alone, but the same elder sister, also studying English, had her driver bring her at the end of our session.

"I want to be a translator," the sister said, "but there are only jobs for teachers," so she settled for that. The next week, in her own class, the sister said she was to have a test on a Dickens book she hadn't read yet.

"How much would you charge," she queried, "if you would read the book and tell me about it?"

I suggested we get two copies, both read it at once and she ask for clarification whenever she got stuck.

"I have two copies," she assured me. Her words indicated she would bring the second copy the next day, but her face told me something different. The next day, Noor came alone.

As we talked, I got to know her better. Her birthday was a couple of days hence and mine was later that same month. But that was this year; hers moved 11 days each of 18 years. I helped her with a writing assignment for her English class in which she was to describe her bedroom in detail. As she spoke, she embellished the image of a spacious room with lots of furnishings and frills and I learned about her taste in colors and music.

We had some similar preferences: flat shoes, not too much jewelry and oranges. When her cell phone rang, I had no difficulty distinguishing the respectful tone to her sister from the brusque one to her Indian driver. Over the weeks she was with me, her range of interests increased. Useful resources were a child's magazine I had picked up in India, with articles about friendship and sharing and a child's science and history question and answer book I had bought in Beirut. Noor took a liking to the subjects, especially how Elizabeth Barrett met Robert Browning. So we read through and discussed the topics.

Looking into the dark placid eyes of this pudgy 18 year old, with too soft a voice, apathetic, unobservant, naïve, seemingly wholly unprepared for life, I saw myself at that age. Counselor, understand thyself. I came all these thousands of miles to sit in a global schoolroom, to get a glimpse of myself, to see how much I had learned or hadn't. At that moment, my life in the Midwest seemed very remote, a lifetime or two away.

Jewel Dhuru

Guests For Dinner

In early April, it was a couple of weeks before 18 guests were to come for a quiet dinner. Baba had been talking about it for months, having his pals and their wives over. Still, when he walked into the sitting room one day a few weeks before, his very pores exuding energy, saying "Hey, help me set a definite date for this dinner," things started to take on a more ominous shape.

I continued to cringe inwardly whenever he mentioned it. In my recent socially-deprived state, part of me welcomed the congenial company but another part had become so used to solitude, I regarded any formal production as an invasion of my personal space. I hated feeling that way. I wanted to feel that anyone who crossed my threshold was a welcome guest.

I knew he didn't expect me to cook, but plenty still needed doing. As slowly as I did physical tasks, it was taking me weeks to prepare for the mere three hours of festivities. There was something irksome, too, about his making all the arrangements, he who worked all day, while I who had loads of spare time, trailed along for the ride. I satisfied myself by getting artwork framed, other decorative touches in place and conversation pieces out of storage.

Baba had everything under control, he said. He insisted on Indian food for his pals. He knew a restaurant that would let him use their serving dishes and spoons but they didn't deliver. We just had to get their menu, make our choices and he would pick up the food that day.

He wanted to invite everyone for after the last salah, 8:30 PM or so, but I insisted we plan for a little earlier, 7:30, with food arriving between the last two *salahs*. Even if I was hostess in name only, I didn't want to be yawning before dessert. He knew where we could borrow ten more chairs. He would get help to rearrange the sitting room couch, armchairs, coffee and end tables. Since we didn't have a regular cleaner, we would have to get one in, a stranger to me, working against local prohibitions. He knew where he could find one. We'd have to decide whether to use plastic plates and cups or to buy whole sets of china, glassware and cutlery and large snack bowls, just for that one evening. He knew about that, too. He knew a fellow who did catering. Shiraz was known and liked by his pals but was unknown to me. He would come early and stay with us half the evening to help serve, presiding over Baba's kitchen.

Baba would take care of everything. I would just have to remove my stuff from the coffee table and couch! I started to feel not only superfluous, but downright in the way. The more enthusiastic he became, the more I wanted to withdraw. There were moments I could see in a flash, how couples married 35 years could grow so far apart, they want to separate.

My head started to ache. Control seemed to be the issue, each of us wanting to have things our own way. Those who would have given up on the relationship over less than this were ones who couldn't remember the foundation of friendship they shared 34 years before, or maybe they just couldn't see how they could get back to the tender feelings of that happier time.

At least there, in Riyadh, I contemplated, if I needed to lie down in the middle of the evening, the bedroom was right down the hall. At home in the Midwest, those who came over understood when I retired to the family room or when I stretched out on the couch for 15 minutes while we talked, but in Riyadh, I didn't know the people well enough for that. I tried to think how I could be more efficient. With the added challenge to my endurance, every step counted.

At 8 days before our dinner, it started getting hotter, 30^0 C. (85^0 F.) and we needed to start the compressor, so our six ACs could cool. We'd hoped it would be cool enough that day so we could turn off the noisy sitting room AC just before people came. But first, Baba said he'd call a campus repair fellow in to service them so they didn't blow dust all over the rooms.

About 7 days before the dinner, I began trying to bake a dessert myself. At least this was something I could do to feel part of a plan that was taking up weeks of my life. Normally, I loved to bake breads and desserts. So I experimented with the gas oven, yet again. This oven had two pilot lights, one at the top and one just above the floor, both having to be relit every time the oven was used. So Baba lay down on the kitchen floor with a flashlight and match after match. I spent an entire Thursday morning turning out very little that wasn't burnt on the outside and raw on the inside. I decided my time and energy were better used elsewhere. I gave up.

At 6 days, temperatures soared into the mid 30s C. (90s F). Baba still had not done the paperwork to get the ACs checked. I turned them on anyway, dust or no dust.

Jewel Dhuru

At 5 days before, wrinkles appeared in the plan for whether to stay another year or not. Baba was asked for a copy of his curriculum vitae, to be sent to Kuwait. They were looking for new faculty there. It was disconcerting, not to know what we were going to do. Baba brought home a Bangladeshi fellow, Rafiq, who would come and clean for three hours the next day.

At 4 days, there was talk of not being enough faculty for the next year in Baba's department and expat colleagues urged him and the department to reconsider his leaving. Rafiq came, all smiles and did an admirable job on the kitchen and bathroom. Then, he tackled dusting and vacuuming. I thought I could write in my makeshift bedroom office while he worked, but he called me so often with questions that I just stayed and talked to him, probably what he really wanted anyway. His narrative about his needy family told me he wanted me to convince Baba to up his wages. Between the AC repair people coming in and out, Rafiq's going room to room, and Baba's taking a nap just when I was finally able to start writing, words from the 1964 movie, *The Chalk Garden*, flavored my mood: "Life without a room to oneself is a barbarity." [75]

At 3 days before, when it reached 35^0 C. (97^0 F.), the ACs ceased to cool. They blew only heat and it took two days of servicemen coming to and fro to get them working properly.

At 2 days before, the difference in our styles became super-amplified. My style leads me to make major decisions and prepare all the physical trappings ahead of time, with a high resistance to change after this point, and leave the last couple of hours for myself, to restore inner calm, so I can reach maximum enjoyment when the company comes. Baba's style, building momentum as the pressure of the last minute approaches, leads him to prolonged thinking about how to do things, saving major adjustments spontaneously for the end, when his fastidious fidgeting and cleaning up after the cleaner, reaches its peak. In days past, the combination of the best parts of our two styles had worked wonders—when we could work together.

So at 2 days, when the menu had already been chosen, but the plates, glasses and cutlery hadn't, Baba remembered another good restaurant that would provide china and cutlery, and would deliver. So, he decided, we'd have to go to that restaurant, sample their food and select from their menu on the spot. When we went, increased security added to the intrigue, since the day before, a bomb had exploded outside a bookshop, near the restaurant.

By the day before, I had already prepared the second, ladies' sitting room, across from the bedroom, as an overflow room. A blue Indonesian sarong curtained the window, a couple of paintings hung from the light fixtures so as not to make holes in the wall and a blue Damascene cloth covered a box that would serve as a side table. The dining room was prepared in comparable fashion. Baba would move the L-shaped table he used as his desk to the dining room, to use as a buffet table just for that day. Then he got the idea of setting up that same buffet table in the ladies' sitting room instead of the dining room and using the real dining room as an extension of the main sitting room, so we could stay together as one big group.

The feeling of going in several directions at once tore at me. During this last couple of weeks, a lifelong habit, at times of stress, became accentuated—nibbling at my fingernails. At such times, some people curse, some drink and some get ulcers. I nibble at my nails. On the mental level, I knew this particular trait symbolized wanting to take a bite out of something or someone but not being able to, for whatever reason. So we take bites out of ourselves instead, until we can figure out how to express our wants and needs less self-destructively. On emotional and physical levels, however, it couldn't be resolved that quickly. I had to go through the stages.

That day, I recall reaching a stunned immobility, a state of rigid apprehension while Baba dragged furniture from room to room. The TV was on right in front of me, but I didn't hear a word. How can I function under such pressure, I asked myself, the pain in my neck and thorn in my side aching, my head throbbing. Everything was out of control. It seemed nothing in my life was the way I wanted it.

Ac-Cept, I reminded myself. Don't sweat the small stuff. Infinite organizing power, nature's balancing act, everything guided by a finer, wiser, more harmonious hand than my own, would rule. Trying to maintain control over every detail of my life, I had gotten off course.

Suddenly I remembered Mr. Jokey Jeweler. In that episode of our lives, exactly two years before, that very month, our actions had been at polar opposites, too. Back then, I'd insisted that when Baba went back to the jewelry shop, he mention to the fellow that I had felt offended. As I uttered my request, I had watched Baba's eyes cloud over, fogged with a private preoccupation. The day he went and returned, it was the same old impasse. The jeweler hadn't meant anything by it. It was just his way. A simple 'Never mind the jeweler or anybody else. I'm sorry you felt hurt' would have gone farther to sooth ruffled feathers and strengthen our relationship than more explanations about the culture. But it was not to be.

I learned two lessons that day. I promised myself I would never deliberately put Baba into a position of having to go against his own grain again. It was like insisting he swallow a bitter pill without water. Nothing was gained by it—not for us. Instead, it had taken something out of him—away from us. That's not what I meant to accomplish. And I was reminded that some problems, I would just have to resolve within myself.

Now, two years later, here was the same position again, with me in the middle this time. Back then, he was caught between trying to please me and showing understanding of the jeweler's culture. Now I was stuck between espousing his pet project and upholding my personal values, caring for my emotional and physical needs. As usual, we were co-creators of our own circumstances.

I'd stayed stunned on the couch, in its new location against the wall across the room from the balcony door, for a good half hour. From the garble of thoughts running through my mind, I breathed the positive ones in deeply and resolved to do better. I left it to the management of the fine hand of the universe and stopped worrying, more or less. I roused myself, snatched my finger from my mouth and clenched my fist. That's one thing I can control, I determined. I don't have to chew myself up over this—or anything! The onslaught was from within. That's where the solutions were, too. Whatever came, my nails were not going to be nubby.

That Thursday evening in April, everything was ready as the first guests pressed the buzzer. Extra white plastic chairs completed an oblong oval interspersed with our own blue ones. Three chairs that were comfortable for me were evenly spaced around the room, so I could eventually sit with everyone. Baba had picked up the glassware the day before. Shiraz was preparing snacks and ready to pass out fruit juice and soda.

Buzzzzz! Clad in a short-sleeved green patterned gown, I stayed in the sitting room while Baba, in blue, went into the hall to open the door. Then, couple after couple and groups of temporary bachelors came on each other's heels. The evening was not set up for kids but when three came through the doorway with a neighbor lady, I got out 3-D puzzles, collapsible tissue paper snowflakes and our karaoke microphone.

"Now isn't this the way you like to see women dressed?" Baba beamed, appreciating our collectively colorful garb. The enthusiastic assents from both sexes were ice breaking.

A group of women sat in one corner and chatted contentedly. Others sat in between the men and talked shop. All twenty of us fit cozily in the sitting room-dining room. The food was delivered right on time, at 8 PM. Shiraz was a valuable asset, companionable competent and comfortable with the crowd. A van pulled up in front and he helped a troop of men carry foil-covered containers and boxes of plates and cutlery to their allotted spots. I used a cream Syrian tablecloth on one wing of the L-shaped table and blue-green sari material for the other. I only saw the food I was serving two minutes before I called the women to come and try some.

"Oh, you mean we get to go first?" Elizabeth asked.

The dinner itself was delicious: curried chicken, lentils, *raitha* with cucumber and yogurt, *birjani* with mainly rice, a mixed vegetable *bhaje*, bready round flat *nans*, and a creamy *khir,* sweet vermicelli for dessert. Everyone seemed to enjoy it, and went back for seconds.

At 9:00 PM, Elizabeth and Paul announced they had to make an important phone call from home and left. Soon after, the mother and kids, the father being at a conference, took their leave, too. A few of the guys took an interest in my artwork and had suggestions as to how to get the alleged fossils identified. The women who didn't talk shop reverted to personal stories about local social conditions. By 11:30PM, en masse, as they had come, they all filed out.

I didn't find out until after everyone was gone that several had brought brightly wrapped packages. To my chagrin, as guests entered the hall, but before they reached the sitting room, packages were spirited into a back room. I would have liked to thank bestowers for their generosity, to connect gifts to givers as parcels were presented, even if not actually opened right away. Instead, it became a game of match-up, Baba's trying to remember what size or shape or color who was carrying. One box of marbled onyx goblets sat on the coffee table for two days before Baba's casual inquiries helped ascertain to whom to address the thank you note.

Cleanup the next day was fairly quick. Even though I'd savored the efforts of the chefs, such times always highlighted my uncommon attitude to food. Food tastes best to me when I'm hungry and I eat to take the edge off hunger, not to get so stuffed, I can hardly move. I feel most nourished if I eat consciously, rather than mindlessly. I prefer six snacks a day to three large meals. Snacks keep fatigue and jitteriness from low blood sugar away better and the lower extremities of my digestive system don't get stretched out of shape, either. The most nourishing contact I had with that food occurred the next day when I prepared care packages from the mountain of leftovers, for Baba to give away to the skinny workers outside.

For most of that day and the next, Baba and I barely spoke. There was a lull in our inadvertent antagonism, but the quiet catastrophe that surrounded us was ongoing, precluding an immediate resolution. We had not hosted the dinner as friends; we were merely husband and wife. My head throbbed again and, he, by himself, went in search of the space station. While I slipped inside myself for solace and strength, he slipped away.

Over the next week, our current version of normality began to return, slowly, with another twist. I felt stronger and more in charge of my own destiny. Baba never talked about how he felt about that day, but afterwards, he tuned out even more easily when disagreement reared its head. Still, life would go on. The sun would rise again. Other challenges to our powers of cooperation would come and go. In time, I would learn to handle such stressors with more equanimity, if not humor, but it didn't happen overnight. I had to grow through the stages.

If I understood correctly the theory, of how we choose life partners, the two levels of attraction are the ego level and the spiritual one. On the ego level, we chose to merge paths 28 years earlier because our strengths and weaknesses complemented each other's. Where I sought solace from within, he found it in activity. On the spiritual level, each of us was the perfect mirror, reflecting deeper parts of each other and reaffirming each of our wholeness, as well as our connections to the other. If the theory was true, we each were due for a look in the mirror.

Chapter 34: Happy Fiftieth

"The thoughts we have held and the words we have repeatedly used have created our life and experiences up to this point. ... What we are choosing to think and say today, this moment, will create tomorrow and the next day ... The point of power is always in the present moment"
—Louise Hay, *Heal Your Body* [76]

The day was approaching that I'd gone through 50 years of life to reach. Just before that, my two closest female companions had left within a couple of days of each other, in mid-April, one unexpectedly because of a death in the family and the other for the summer. More wrinkles appeared in the grand scheme of whether we were leaving the Kingdom or not. A new professor was interviewed for the department, but he was almost unanimously deemed unsuitable.

On my 50th birthday, I treated myself to phone calls, wrote letters and a few cards had come. There's something about getting a birthday wish from the heart that says 'I'm glad you were born'. To my delight, Michael Palin's wonderful wit in Pole to Pole, promised but not delivered by Saudi TV two years earlier, was shown on BBC, this episode being about Istanbul, to which we hoped to go one day. The pleasure was to be more rare than I had imagined. By the next week, BBC broadcasts were reduced to a blank blue screen and remained so for our last seven weeks. It couldn't have been solar flares. One Indian and two Arabsat channels were gone as well, as if unplugged. Maybe someone had tripped over the tangle of cords on the roof, lines running between 16 balconies and several dishes up top. No more of my favorite BBC diversions: World Trek Series, QED, Correspondents, Mastermind-India and Simpson's World.

Just that week, we'd finally gotten our new video recorder working. So we rented videos, all with Arabic subtitles and all in a semi-bleeped state, non rewound, removing all female-male affection, but not the bad language. Over five weeks, I watched Rob Roy, Bossa Nova, Instinct, As Good as it Gets, Dead of Winter, Grumpy Old Men, Double Jeopardy and Gladiator.

The last week of April, a most unusual weekend was about to begin. One Thursday morning, I woke up from a dream about a panting, brown, immature eagle, 1/3 meter (a foot) high, with a broken wing, glazed over eyes, and a general demeanor of distress. I recognized it as the same eaglet that had appeared in the same condition, in my dream the previous week. It was a figure of pathos then, too, but I had forgotten about it until its reappearance. My heart went out to the poor thing. Hadn't it gotten any relief since last week? Once fully awake, I turned to my animal medicine book, knowing without looking that eagle symbolized Spirit.

The eagle's tale spoke of the power to connect to both Divine and Earthly realms. Eagle medicine invited me to broaden my sense of self beyond the presently visible, to gather courage and soar above the mundane. Wisdom comes in strange and curious forms and illumination will come on the air to my higher mind. Go past clipped wings and seek higher ground, it said.

That weekend, it was hot even at night, the heat of the day holding at a shade over 35^0 C. (95^0 F.). The bedroom AC had stopped sloshing, but even without sound effects, it still ran loudly. I would have awakened feeling like a wet noodle anyway, but with the added noise, I felt as though I had been transported to Niagara Falls in my sleep. Either that or my flight was already taxiing out and I wasn't even packed.

Thursday morning, after Baba did some laundry and hung the clothes out on the kitchen balcony, he went to one pal's to get pointers on choosing a Persian carpet, then to another pal's to drop off borrowed CDs. I planned to lie low that day, moving slowly and limiting in-house excursions to short distances because later that evening, several of us were going for my birthday dinner. Since no close friends or family were nearby, except for Baba, I invited new acquaintances to share the event. I usually only tackled the three stairs in and out of our building once a day.

Baba came home after noon and went to take a nap and I started to bring the laundry in. While I unpinned socks from one end of the line, at the other end, the wind snatched up one of Baba's dress shirts, buttoned onto a hanger with the hook bent down enough, so Baba thought, to prevent just such an unplanned flight. I looked down and there it was lying in the sand, still buttoned, but 1½-meters (4 feet) away from the hanger. I remembered Baba's saying another of his shirts was missing and his pajama top, too. I could have wakened him but resolved to brave the stairs twice that day. If I didn't go down now, somebody might make off with the shirt.

After the rescue, I started getting dressed for the evening, because at 5:00 PM, Baba's Saudi student was coming to talk shop with him. I had not met Faisal yet but he'd helped deliver our sitting room set before I had arrived. Faisal turned out to be a very pleasant, mild-mannered young man. I made tea, and leaving them to their labors, went to the bedroom to work on my last clock puzzle, which was approaching completion. Just as I was hoping Faisal wouldn't leave without saying goodbye, Baba popped his head in saying Faisal was looking at my artwork on his way out and did I want to come and talk to him, and then his head disappeared.

For five months, a rather thickish cord lay on the floor on my side of the bed, running along the side and the foot of the bed for the purpose of hooking up my laptop. Every morning, my shoes knocked against it, but even during the first disoriented weeks, in a jet lagged state, in the dark, I was always aware of its position and I didn't mind. It was one of my lifelines. But somehow at that moment, when I got up from my puzzle, I didn't sense where it was. So instead of rounding the corner of the bed, I found myself on the floor with two skinned knees, one matching elbow and a left ankle, which I heard, rather than felt, c-r-a-c-k-l-e as I went down.

Baba reappeared immediately, kneeling beside me, his foot perilously close to my glasses, which had flown off my face in mid-fracas. He wanted to examine the ankle, but having had experience with sprained ankles, I felt sure nothing was broken, and didn't really want him wrenching at it. So he went to get an ice pack and I could hear him telling Faisal what happened.

When I sat up, still on the floor, I told him to ask Faisal into the bedroom because I didn't want to rush. Soon, the ice pack was in place, and the two guys were sitting on the end of our low bed beside me, Faisal liked this better than being in the sitting room—more like Bedouins. His great grandfather had been a farmer. We chatted for a few minutes. I soaked up the healing potential of this homey moment, all the barriers down and our essences intermingling.

My ankle didn't hurt all that much. My concern was for the imbalance this injury would bring. I had planned to start organizing six months of accumulated stuff, on Saturday, two days hence, since we only had 6 ½ weeks to go. Perhaps this ankle would be the impetus to become even more efficient in my movements or to just let go more. In the true Arab style, Faisal said he would come and pack for me. On that fanciful note, my ankle having achieved a sufficiently numbed up state, I got up, my left arm around Baba's shoulder and my right around Faisal's. It seemed the most natural thing in the world.

On the way back to the main sitting room, I insisted we stop off at the second sitting room, right across the hall so Faisal could see the paintings hanging from the light fixtures in there. He went in by himself while I leaned on Baba and made explanations from the hall.

My ankle stayed chilled until four more friends and acquaintances gathered in the sitting room. They were to be our guests at a restaurant. Earlier, by phone, I had ascertained that if we were seated and ordered dinner before 7:30 PM, we could be served before the last *salah* began at 7:55. Otherwise, we would have to sit and wait until 8:15 for service. I bandaged my joint and put on my olive green *abaya*. "Right or left?" Baba asked as he prepared to help me down the stairs. My two halves were so dis-integrated, I didn't even know on which side to lean. Someone was alighting from a taxi just as we came down. Good, because we wouldn't all fit into our car. My ankle and I got the front seat and we set off in convoy.

My cane was in the back seat, I remembered with relief, the bamboo shaped one with the black handle. I had not used it much yet but it was for just such an unexpected eventuality that I had bought it. Baba had taken it to the car one day with the intention of getting a rubber tip for it. When we got out at the restaurant, Baba handed me the cane. But as I grasped it, it sagged in the middle! It was broken! It must have been the car cleaner for whom Baba had left the door unlocked the day before. Maybe he'd sat or knelt on it. It was a nasty shock.

I hobbled into the Italian restaurant with a lot of help, only enjoying the stained glass windows, murals and other Italian décor half as much as I would have liked. We got our order in on time and collectively feasted on Saudi champagne, lasagna, pizza, grilled chicken, fish, dumplings in mushroom gravy, olives, tirimisu, cream caramel and apple pie and ice cream. If it hadn't been for the Filipino waiters and lack of Italian street sounds, we might have thought we were in Italy. Being otherwise fulfilled, we hardly perceived the lights dimming during *salah*. A screen painted with an olive grove was

Ala Tool

pulled around our neighbor's table, but not ours. Communal good humor and sparkling conversation helped the candle and pink orchid on our table keep the ambiance bright. On the way home, well, maybe all six of us would fit into our car after all. With four in the back, it was snug, but with all the laughing, who noticed.

On Friday, I grappled with tedium I hadn't felt for a while. Swelling and bruising began to show. Most of the next few days were spent re-learning how to get the right leverage to stand up from low furniture and to walk. When I leaned on my weaker right side, it spoke back sharply, resenting the demand. This was all I needed to become even more sedentary.

Naturally, my posture and gait would change. Perhaps my outlook could, too. Drawing again on the philosophy espoused by Louise Hay, that every physical sensation of dis-ease has an emotional root [77], I began to assess. Left ankle problems referred to inflexibility or the inability to receive pleasure from relationships! I had already decided it was enough left side activity for a while—the receptive, mothering side. It was time to engage my right side more—the taking action, letting go side. Is this what the eagle from my dream meant by wisdom coming in curious forms, going past clipped wings, soaring above the mundane, illumination coming on the air, or perhaps while I was flying through the air, to my higher mind?

The discomfort on my right shot up threefold. Baths to soak my left ankle, along with my now bitterly complaining right ankle, hip, side, back, arm and wrist took three times as long. On Friday morning, the pigeons on the bedroom windowsill tapped on the glass for food, which was in the kitchen, at the other end of the now, seemingly, even longer hallway.

Baba did more laundry that day and stepped onto the balcony just in time to see another shirt taking a flying leap from the clothesline. When he went down to rescue it, he found it, his other shirt and his pajama top, still on their hangers, hooked to the side of a nearby dumpster.

Meanwhile, even with my sense of balance in tatters, I was determined to shuffle over to the campus hairdresser that very day and get an easy care cut, one less thing to look after. The Filipina hairdresser I'd had the last time had just left the Kingdom the day before. That was always the way. No sense in getting used to anything or anybody. The new Filipina already had a Saudi woman in the chair with black dye seeping into her hair, so she asked me to sit down for a minute, using typical Filipina phrasing.

"For a while, Mumm," she had said, and then offered to take me in a second chair.

"What would you like, Mumm?"

As I explained, the repetitive clicks of the dressmaker's sewing machine came through a screen, on which hung the spaghetti strap styles she was stitching. As the hairdresser snipped, she talked. She had been cutting hair for years, she assured me.

"But I have only been in the Kingdom four days, Mumm." Still, it was long enough to decide to get her husband's resume in shape and to secure him a position there, too.

"For two years, I cannot survive if he is not here, Mumm." It was an often-told story.

And so ended the birthday weekend. Life took on a surreal quality as I looked down at my burgeoning bruises. One primary thought remained in my mind as I surveyed my left ankle, 1 ½ times its usual circumference. This was my driving foot!

The Art Gallery Lady

Br-i-i-n-g. Br-i-i-n-g. A most unexpected call came the next week, the 30th of April. It was the Saudi art gallery owner with whom I'd had an ill-fated appointment in December.

"I have just seen the message you left with the concierge," she apologized.

She and her driver had been in a car accident that evening.

"The front of the car had been destroyed … nobody was hurt … but the other driver wouldn't let us leave until the police arrived … I didn't have your number with me …your note got shuffled into a folder with unimportant things … I'll be happy to see your work."

She was anxious to correct the impression I must have gotten from her not calling.

"I learned a lesson that day," she continued, "to always carry the number with me when I have an appointment with someone new."

My right side was telling me to be decisive. I greatly appreciated the call. It had made a difference and I told her so, but there wasn't much time left. I would think about it and let her know. Privately, I was glad I had already focused my energies on writing and teaching English.

Chapter 35: Hitchhikers, Dunes and Souks

"There is no logical way to the discovery of these elemental laws. There is only the way of intuition, which is helped by a feeling for the order lying behind appearance" [78]
—Albert Einstein

Crossroads

May began with three days in a row of sudden, short, downpours, unusual for dry Gulf summers, but global weather reported heavy cloud activity on the ocean in preparation for the Asian monsoon season, so maybe that explained it. Bursts of liquid assets left streets swamped for a few hours and then soaked into the sand. Spectacular sunsets shone, with ultra bright spots seeping through the edges of bleached, billowy clouds. Alternately, reddish glows superimposed by blue and white striped rays emanating from the sinking sun were followed the next day by clearing and a temperature of 38^0 C. (100^0 F.).

One week after spraining my ankle, it was already going through the second of six color changes. It looked green and misshapen. Still grappling with reestablishing better balance when I walked, if I looked as unsteady as I felt, I didn't want to see my reflection in a mirror. Swaying broadly from side to side, it took all that was left of my agility to walk a straight line. I could see the parallels between my physical condition and emotional state. I guess there were still more lessons to learn. It did my heart good, though, to realize I didn't feel disconnected from my source. When my feet touched sand and stone, I felt more grounded than I had for weeks. Life was getting better with each step and breath.

I was down to my last six weeks in the Kingdom, packing for the last time. I had reached a crossroads. Many of Baba's friends and acquaintances assured us they'd see us before we left and I had no doubt they meant to try, impromptu dinner invitations and dropping in. I looked forward to seeing those with whom I had a heart connection even if they dropped in without calling, but casual acquaintances coming before I was dressed in the morning or at 9:30 at night was another matter.

And now it was going to be even more difficult to pack than usual because my left ankle made it harder than ever to work at floor level, where the suitcases were. Either I had to learn a new brand of gracious assertiveness and consider my needs first or sacrifice them to maintain the appearance of competence, without letting visitors in to my inner world. How to best align my energies with the flow? And whose flow? Mine? Or everybody else's? Or a collaboration? Or one that was universal, bigger than all of us? That was the challenge.

Given that half my mind and ¾ of my heart were already back home near the kids, I had to make choices as to whom I was willing to spend time and energy on. I could feel my personality changing. If that wasn't enough, the time was impending to advertise and have strangers parade through our flat again, window-shopping. As it was to turn out, though, friends abroad of our friends in Riyadh were coming to the Kingdom shortly after we were to leave. They considered taking our flat furnished. If the deal worked out, it would save us trouble and save the other couple from having to shop for the basics while in the thick of jetlag, as we had had to. So we got involved in negotiations over the email with them.

The Hitchhiker Talks Nonstop

On our Saturday after-work outing that week, we dropped off a roll of film, picked up the dry cleaning, and then we went riding. We found ourselves on unfamiliar turf near closed shops and open mosques, so Baba drove slower and we took in the details. Rounding a corner, a lone Arab male in *thob* and cutwork cap stood by the side of the road and put his arm out as we approached. There wasn't anyone else around and it was hot. Why not, we thought. I rode with my seat reclined, as usual, but as Baba's dry cleaning was on the seat behind him and hitchhikers never stayed with us very long, I righted my seat and unlocked the back door behind me.

"*Salam wa laqum*" our passenger began. I gave my usual disclaimer about knowing only a little of the language. Unperturbed, he sat in the middle of the seat, leaned forward and started a constant low monologue in Arabic. Not a word of English was to escape his lips.

"*A la Tool?*" we asked, to which he responded with his hand held vertically between us, motioning ahead, his monologue unabated.

Ala Tool

Baba wondered aloud to me if he was going to ask for money. It had happened before. One man in a Saudi *thob,* near the DQ, with a needy story, admitted he wasn't Saudi, though, and the fellow who'd approached Baba's car window in Taif was probably masquerading, too. Back then, neither one even got into the car. This fellow wore neither *shmal* nor *gootra,* only an Arab cap, so his origins remained unclear.

Eventually directions were given, though too late to bear left on a small turnpike, so around we went again. The only words I could pick out from his soliloquy were *"kul mara"*- every time, and *"mafee akl"*- nothing to eat. We didn't have any food in the car to offer him either, not even water. We decided he probably wasn't Saudi. Saudis usually had full bellies. His lament suddenly ceased and Baba looked back sharply. Noticing the fellow's head bowed and his fingers pressing against the inside corners of his eyes, Baba whispered, "he's crying." Two weeks ago, my ankle had broken down barriers and now this.

Our hearts opened to him at the same time as we wondered if he was just jerking us around. Where were his friends and family? Then I remembered Mr. Wrong Number, the bachelor. This was probably the same sort of mourning.

As we came around the same turn again, we bore left and he resumed his verbal grieving. Then suddenly, as a short strip of shops came into view, within five minutes of getting into the car, he pulled himself together and shuddered *"halas"*-finished. We'd already agreed I would give him a bill from my bag before he left. Just before he got out, for the first time since we'd passed him on the road, I saw the side of his face as he leaned forward to touch and then kiss my left shoulder, through my clothes, and then he performed the same benediction on Baba's right shoulder. Heaping blessings on us, he opened the door. Lastly, he took the bill, without appearing overeager.

He stopped at my window, tarrying a moment to look into our faces, raising his hand again in a gesture of gratitude, answered by our raised hands. It was only then, before he moved off, that I took a good look at his face. He was young, in his 20s, short and thin. I contemplated those who'd helped us unhesitatingly when we were in need or lost. He didn't look like a person who contrived to make this same trip half a dozen times a day with different carloads of expats to fleece, and it saddened me that I was so suspicious. The few shops in that section were quiet and looked slightly derelict. Perhaps business had taken a turn for the inconvenient.

As we pulled away, we rehashed the episode. When Baba had looked back sharply, he was giving in to a reflex to watch his back with strangers. When I first saw the extended arm, I had appreciated the luxury of helping in this way, too. In many countries, picking up hitchhikers was outside the realm of possibility. Riyadh was quite safe in that respect, but we hadn't brought anyone to tears before.

The other comparison that ran through my mind was between the behavior of this fellow and numerous others who'd been afraid to look in my direction or to talk to me, especially if Baba was there, perhaps not even because of what was in their minds but because of what they thought might be in Baba's. Could those perennially repeated scenarios just be endless versions of a cat and mouse game, where the two change identities depending on the circumstances, to the point of having compound cats or multiple mice, and one rarely seriously pounces on the other, only torments them at length?

Along came this fellow. Yes, perhaps in the grip of a personal crisis, perhaps feeling he had nothing left but his humanity. He'd shared his emotions with us, treating our shoulders equally and openly and that meant a lot.

The Dent

A dent of unknown origin appeared on the corner of our car one day, so before Baba started offering the car for sale, he took it in to a shop. He made the arrangements and the Asian mechanic drove home with us so he could take the car back. As we rode, the mechanic talked.

He'd been in Saudi Arabia for seven years. He wasn't an ordinary worker; his rank was a little higher up, he said. But regardless of what alleged higher or lower rank one held, all non-Saudis worked the same, he disclosed. All companies were Saudi owned. The only real ranks were Saudi and non-Saudi. In his line of work, he continued, the longer he stayed there, the more it hurt him professionally. Even though he got experience with a greater variety of cars in the Kingdom than he would in his homeland, there was no potential for advancement. Everything stayed the same, even the low salary.

Ala Tool

In his job, he was not allowed to have family with him. No life—only work. Every time he'd had enough and planned to go home, a political situation arose at home making it impossible to find a job there. But, then again, he said, although he missed his family, he wouldn't have been able to build his house back home or educate his kids, had he not worked abroad. We were lucky, he conjectured, that we could have our family there. Yeah, lucky. Double binds come tied in all varieties of knots.

The Dreams

That whole past week, I had been blessed and plagued with dreams, most not remembered consciously but probably reflecting the turmoil in my conscious state of mind. Heritage and history huddled together to hash out the meaning of my life.

One dream I recalled when triggered by an Ad Vision days later was of being in my hometown, lost and alone, no transportation, not recognizing any landmarks, asking strangers for directions but not remembering any street names. Another time, images were before me of getting off a bus on a familiar street, which suddenly shimmered and turned into a wavy, sandy shoreline and a stretch of shingled seaside with shells and waves. Another was about living in a trailer park with scarcely room to turn around. And one about giving a friend a ride and the car seat falling into pieces at our feet, all the hinges and bolts failing at once. Two nightmares recurred, the first about getting kids out the door too late to catch the school bus and forgetting their lunch money and the second about being very lost in my old high school, without a class schedule. Graphic symbols permeated the dreams, presumably representing parts of myself.

Kuwait had received Baba's application and he heard the Emirates were looking for people, too, so he sent another one there. I didn't want to ask him not to send the letters. If his heart were really elsewhere, insisting that he stay home would just bring disharmony.

Back to the Dunes

Five weekends before I was to leave, we went back to *Thumamah*, the dune buggy dunes, Lookout Point—Saudi style. Only one buggy this time, to 100 cars and trucks. The trucks in the bed were more widely spaced, uncovering the snaky tire track pattern crisscrossing the expanse, like a quilt with no color variation but lots of texture. Trucks crazily traversed the dunes, spattering sand as they revved along, like snow blowers spitting snow. On well-established vertical paths, trucks tried to thread their way up to the crest, failed and slid down backwards while others, alongside, backed up the hill, the two face-to-face going in opposite directions.

This time, we followed the main road farther as it curved to the right, behind the upper dunes. Two roadside refreshment trucks sold swirled ice cream cones and drinks. It was quieter on this back road. Here were the blankets, women, children and picnics. Ah! The obscure Family Section of the dunes! As I read in the car, Baba wandered with his camera, met people, drank their tea, and helped five youngsters push their truck off a sandbank. He followed their directions; they knew when and how to rock the truck better than he.

Our car had been running continuously for hours, Baba always leaving the AC on for me. The temperature had reached 41^0 C. (106^0 F.) that day, not unusual for the time of year. It was to reach 42^0 C. (108^0 F.) two days later and stay there the rest of May and half of June, but only the usual 15% humidity. Previously, the engine's overheating concerned me, but now I knew even with continuous use, the temperature indicator barely moved off C-cold. We left before the sundown free-for-all started, stopping at the white teepees to get a second camel bag.

On our last trip to the dunes, two weeks later, few cars of any type buzzed by. Not even the ice cream truck. Mostly, Baba wandered and I read. At one point, he and a borrowed video recorder came back after a 45-minute absence, as passengers in a 4-wheel drive SUV that pulled up alongside. He introduced me to a Saudi Major of Special Forces who shook my hand and then, as was customary, didn't look at me again. On the dunes, the Major had shown Baba the best angle from which to film and the Major's driver had given him an invigorating ride up and down the slope, him videoing all the way. He animatedly described his experience, until he saw my face and my dropped jaw. Then he asked, "Oh, would you have liked a ride on the dunes?"

Old Habits Die Hard

The same feeling had surrounded me a week earlier, when we'd gone to the Camel Souk again. That time, leaving my apparition apparel in the car, I approached one group of white dromedaries, sitting, chewing their cuds, while Baba wandered with his digital camera and borrowed video recorder. I had no doubt the livestock owners had seen me from their tent. They didn't seem to object when I picked up stray wisps of grass blown out of the feed box, onto my side if the fence and offered it to the dromedary nearest me. The beast was already stretching its neck over to me. It sniffed the tufts with collapsible nostrils and plucked them from my hand with yellowed teeth. Meanwhile, I took a look at the brand on its neck, its almond shaped eyes, long curly lashes, split articulate upper lip and small ears and it let me rub its elongated, velvety muzzle. Another reclining dromedary nearby started rocking forth and back to build up the momentum to get to standing. Yet another turned on its side to scratch on the ground, wide hoofs flailing in the air. It was molting, thick, itchy bits of fur remaining only on the hump.

While I fed the docile beast, Baba called to me that he'd been invited for tea at the same tent and by the time I had figured out what he'd said, he'd moved off to sit down on plush carpet with three Arabs in flowing robes. With a pang, I went back to the car to read. A half hour later, he returned with stories and a photo on his flashcard screen of a brown lamb that had been trotted out for his benefit. "Oh," he said, "Would you have liked to see the lamb?" Old habits die hard.

Three days after the Major of Special Forces incident, we returned to the Camel Souk. By that time, Baba had printed out the photos he'd taken of the farmer with the brown lamb and he wanted to deliver them. This time, instead of parking at the side of the thoroughfare as we'd done last time, Baba pulled the car right into the tent's sandy driveway and announced to the farmer that his wife was with him. Without hesitation, I was welcomed in with a smile and a handshake. I sat on his red carpet, ate his dates and sipped his cardamom coffee and sweet tea.

All the while, customers, all men, came in and out of his enclosure. He was delighted with the printouts and hesitantly permitted the video camera in. But as Baba filmed, I detected a flutter of uneasiness among the other men when they glanced at my ankles, 5 cm. (2") of which were uncovered between socks and pant legs when I sat on the carpet. It didn't bother Baba, but I rearranged my *abaya* for their comfort and my own.

Afterwards, the Bedouin farmer walked us to adjoining pens of white sheep and brown goats where I inhaled deeply, soaking up the atmosphere with all my senses, felt the hot, inquisitive breath of lambs and kids on my fingers and Baba videoed to his heart's content. Twice, the Bedouin offered to put a lamb into the car for us. We laughed and explained our situation. He shook our hands again and we headed back to the main track. We didn't get far.

We got out again. Swaying over my head were the necks of dromedaries, especially one with a gray grizzled muzzle, and my Biology professor's voice echoed once more: "Botulism … mainly seen in countries where people eat their camels after they've died of old age!"

Baba and his equipment wandered. At another tent, he'd been asked for tea again. He declined but just chatted for a minute, while I returned to the air conditioned, comfortable car and finished the last chapter of yet another book. Lots of Sudanese fellows passed, smiling, one stopping at my window. I opened the door. After "*Salam wa laqum*," he asked "*Biritani?*"

I answered, "No, Canada."

"Ah-h, Can-a-da," he said smilingly, as he lingered over the words. Then he closed the door and caught up to his friends.

On this last time we would ever go to the Camel Souk, the sun was setting, just like the first time we watched it from a campfire in a tent. As we left, the dromedaries were vociferous, men were kneeling to pray and the full moon was brightening by the moment. We drove away slowly. We wanted the molecules and memories to cling to us for a long, long time.

Chapter 36: The Elusive Saudi Woman

"Only your illusions prevent you from seeing that you are—and always have been—free" [79]
— Antony de Mello, *The Heart of the Enlightened*

My days in the Kingdom were numbered and I was determined to get a handle on this phenomenon of the Saudi woman before I left. From what I had heard, read and saw for myself, I felt like I had a lap full of confetti to piece together to get the big picture.

Shreds of the story were everywhere. Husbands were held responsible for the alleged misconduct of their wives. But, if a female uncovered her face and a strange male nearby lost his head, and subsequent control over his hands, she was considered culpable.

Expat friends told of Saudi female neighbors, who were cordial and even raised their veils to talk in hallways, until kids or husbands appeared, and then a dark veil dropped over the whole proceedings. But, one of Baba's Saudi male colleagues spoke for more than just himself when he complained his wife was too dependent on him, her errands and chauffeured shopping trips requiring too much of his time.

A Saudi TV program, 'Not For Women Only' featured a Muslim female Ophthalmologist who predicted future research on genetic disorders of the eye would come from Saudi Arabia because of the abundance of cases for study. I recalled the sad common knowledge of the high incidence of birth defects due to advanced maternal age and infectious diseases of a personal nature and plentiful institutional homes for disabled children. But, the International Women's Day Saudi newspaper article insisted Islam was the first religion to grant women full rights.

The playground women, Tanya, the disappearing hostess and the mother who believed forgiveness of past sins was a perk of being female all were permitted only a narrow range of behavior but were dedicated to family in their own ways. Baba's impressions of his female students were that their motivation and diligence outshined the young men. They contrasted with my own English student, good hearted but underexposed to most of life, except shopping. The pervading impression was Saudi women stuck together, to commiserate and keep each other in line, but not to further personal growth. If, by chance, the real purpose of their silent gatherings at bus stops and waiting rooms was the illicit planning of a communal *abaya* burning, they'd hidden their plans well.

To add to the puzzlement, the topic of harassment came to light with a male journalist's article, entitled Harassment of Job Seeking Women. It shared a letter from a young lady, who described herself as university educated, fluent in English, wearing a face cover and with a serious speaking style. She wrote that five years earlier when going through a "critical financial moment," she was looking for any job anywhere, even a low salary at a hospital.

At that time, she wrote, Saudization was vigorous. Even so, she and other covered women were put in back rooms to answer phones and were treated more strictly than others in full make up, who handled reception. She told of a covered co-worker who was fired for being absent for only one day and of another who was docked three days salary for wearing a black veil instead of a blue one. When given notice of her own forthcoming termination, the official reason was she was unqualified to answer phones but the unofficial one was her veil. She related other stories of alleged harassment and claimed that unreasonably, even government hospitals requested meeting women in person and seeing their faces. [80]

How did this fit with the fashions at weddings, where every muscle shows through material as flimsy as apple peels, lower than low necklines and strident color schemes in leather, on chatelaines with faces made up like caricatures, with shiny stars stuck to plucked and rerouted eye brows, neon hair extensions and glittery green and purple nail polish on hands that bore half a kilogram (a pound) of gold jewelry?

Behaviors spanned a wide range, only heavier at the extremes, depending on whether a person was urban or rural, homebound or in the public eye and on how straight-laced or experimental her family was. Were those women now seeking education the mid-range, interested in pushing the limits? To integrate all the features and factors comprising Saudi womanhood would take the creation of a unique mental framework on my part, a new plan with a distinct pile of pieces. Their system wouldn't fit into my existing picture of womanhood.

How had this all started, I wondered. Remembering the goddesses and the Sufi roots, historically, which had come first, the restrictions or the behavior being restricted? Presumably, a society doesn't make laws against something nobody does. But then again, didn't only men decide which behavior was problematic and make the rules accordingly?

To this collection of chippets, another article by a male was added. Entitled Weekend Marriages, it enlightened about the mentality behind marriage in general. There was a new type of marriage, valid from a religious point of view and spreading in the Kingdom. Wives were interviewed in the Qassim area in the northeast. They were willing to speak in detail about their lives, while no husband agreed to comment. This area was the country's breadbasket. A non-Saudi, female, Muslim neighbor, that had lived there, told me how strict it had been. All women were veiled and gloved. When she raised her veil to make out a blurry shop window sign, she felt a *mutawa*'s tap with a stick on her shoulder. Her reaction was to stay home a lot and resent Saudi Arabia's considering itself representative of Islam in general.

Weekend marriages were popular because they circumvented the responsibilities and commitments of the traditional wife, like social calls and civilities. The contract is officially recorded and specifies spouses may see each other on Thursdays and Fridays only, and must not meet on weekdays. The "contract should also specify that the husband should provide a normal wife's entitlements if a 'weekend wife' demands them." [81]

The relationship is characterized by generally being secret, not openly admitted, known only in the circle of the couple's relatives and friends. Many husbands conceal second marriages from first families and explain their absences as business trips, especially if first wives are incapacitated, because according to the contract, the first wife's knowledge is not a condition.

Reasons abound for such marriages. Some husbands are unhappy in the first and seek a second without upsetting first wives. One wife didn't want to leave her job when her husband's position required relocation and another didn't want to move when he was transferred, so both unions were altered to weekends only. Some widows had busy weekdays living with married daughters but wanted to fill weekend voids. It is claimed that a marriage a woman is forced to accept is illegal, so this type satisfies, where a traditional one couldn't.

Still, divorces occur. One woman, whose aim in marrying was to have more children, since her first brood was grown, found her new husband uninterested in children, but he wouldn't grant a divorce unless she returned the dowry. Another's husband wouldn't allow her to go out on weekdays while he was gone. A third divorced and repaid the dowry after getting pregnant because she only really wanted a child anyway, but she found that since her contract was for specific days only, she could not claim the full rights of the 'normal' wife. [82]

Children, apparently, feel like victims when they sense something is different in their parents' relationship. Sadly, this would be true anywhere.

Trying to fit all the facets and facades together, I needed all the hands of a Hindu god. What thickets of human emotion did Saudi women go through? What compartments of Saudi womanhood was I not yet privy to? Are women ensnared in a state of national asceticism, concealing a hunger for living or do they live in veiled majesty? Do some really feel safer behind veils, because they believe uncultured men outside their homes don't deserve to be able to look at women?

When we were out exploring, I often mentally poured over the pieces. Near the end of our stay, one Thursday afternoon, we turned onto a quiet street with a line of huge Eiffel tower shaped structures, with high-tension lines strung between them. The whining buzz of go-carts at the side of the road caught Baba's ear. The little boy in him edged the steering wheel to the curb and stopped. On a low sandy hill, a few carts circled inside their ring of rubber tires. Only a few adults and children moved to and fro. Just ahead of us on the sidewalk stood an elderly man in a green and brown long, striped *galibiyya*, a buxom woman with only eyes showing and an energetic teen girl, in colorful skirt and top.

I stayed in the car, my *abaya* resting casually on my shoulders over short sleeves, while Baba mounted the hill to satisfy his curiosity. When he returned, his battery charged, he began pulling away from the curb, and then, suddenly he stopped.

"Oh, that guy is waving at us," he exclaimed, referring to the *galibiyya*. He backed up to the curb on my side, and it being easier for

Ala Tool

me to push open the door than to roll down the window, I opened it, exposing 45 cm. (18") of my bare arm. We thought the trio needed a ride and I began mentally sizing up the stretching potential of the back seat.

The girl bounced forward from behind her mother, bringing her face close to mine and asking "*Naam?*"–Yes? As I struggled for words, the striped *galibiyya* grabbed the girl's forearm, thrust her behind her mother and waved us on. While we both just looked at him, mystified, he took hold of my door and closed it.

My jaw dropped, until I saw the mother's face. Her eyes were creased at the corners and she was nodding. Keeping the elbow farthest away from her husband close to her body, she was waving at me. The dropped jaw changed to the lower half of a grin and I waved back.

'I know. I know. Just go on and be happy. It'll be all right,' her eyes seemed to say. As Baba tentatively moved the car away, Father looked relieved, daughter looked perplexed, but Mom and I maintained eye contact, waving for half a block. I wondered if she would have to pay the piper for her actions and how much, but I had a feeling, she could handle it. The image of her indomitable spirit has stayed with me to this day.

It tided me through the turmoil that came to the fore as I gathered the issues. How to apply the lessons of the Riyadh microcosm to my own world of mothers, daughters, sisters and mothers in law? Perhaps the aloofness I sensed was actually my own self-protection that got in the way of keeping my eyes, ears and heart open to other women.

I was about to conclude that the elusive Saudi female was either multi-faceted or searching for direction, or both, when a most remarkable article appeared in the green, Leisure section of the Arab News (2001). Alongside entertainment columns like Sidelights and Newsmakers was one called Close Encounters. The date was May 12, Mother's Day. Written by a man, it was entitled *On being a Woman*.

The author asserted that some decades back, he was born male for which he's grateful, considering today's times. He went on to explain that he does not look down on women or rate them less as human beings, but that in this culture, men have come out of it better off.

If he were a female, he wrote, he couldn't imagine getting dressed to go out and having his hairstyle flattened by a head scarf. Or getting into the back seat of a car, and enduring bouts of carsickness, his only recourse being hand signals to the driver or groans. They wouldn't help anyway because of the driver's speed and lack of safety, his being originally a villager and unused to automobiles.

If he wanted to pursue a profession, he would have to limit himself to accepted female professions, like teaching, banking or medicine. Or there would always be homemaking or being a kitchen slave, as some call it. Or else, he could kill time sleeping in, chattering idly, or refurbishing his house for the seventh time that year!

And if he wanted to sell some jewelry, he would need his male guardian's permission. But if the jewelry were a tasteless gift from the guardian, wouldn't the request hurt his feelings? And if he wanted to travel, would the guardian not have to sign him out? But what if he wanted to escape the guardian for a while? Who wins? If he became ill, he would have to ask the guardian to take him to see a doctor. But if the guardian were napping, his maladies would have to wait. And if the guardian was the cause of his maladies, he might never get to a doctor.

And if he wanted to start a business, who would push through the paperwork? His male guardian, naturally! That is, if he condones the idea at all. And what about the way he's treated in public places? Intimidating gazes and gawks make him want to rush back to the purity of home. In his hot and heavy robe, he would be a non-person. And if he had a son, wouldn't he miss out on his picnics, presentations and school contests? While his sisters stay home playing with dolls, the son would excel at school. He would not have a single photo document for identification and would have no say on his fate.

He ended with "Yes indeed. I thank God that I was born a male! And a Happy Mother's Day to all you mothers out there."[83]

Chapter 37: Taking Stock And Counting Down

"Some luck lies in not getting what you thought you wanted but getting what you have, which once you have got it you may be smart enough to see is what you would have wanted had you known" [84]
—Garrison Keiller, *Lake Wobegone Days*, 1985

While still trying to untangle the perpetual puzzle of womanhood—Saudi style, the countdown for my departure began. At 4 weeks before leaving, I sensed the uneasiness that comes with saying so-long to the measure of stability I had, regardless of quality. In transition again. After our life-altering experiences, there would be no going back to the way things were in the old neighborhood, in the old days.

I was glad I had started filling my suitcases with gifts, artwork and the warm clothes I wouldn't need anymore and bagging up the extras for cargo boxes, as time and ankle permitted, because at about 3 ½ weeks before departure, things started popping.

The long awaited university tickets arrived, two weeks after the airlines threatened to cancel my reservation. The university said the airlines were just playing games. I had a government ticket; the airlines would wait. I had gotten so accustomed to being caught in the middle it almost didn't matter anymore. The grip was loosening. I was allowed a New York stopover but not a direct flight to Milwaukee. So I made more phone calls and Baba made another trip to the airline office. Finally, the ticket was sorted out, *Inshallah*, but I was cautioned to carry receipts and if any hiccough occurred in New York, I might still have to purchase a ticket on the spot.

Baba had not decided on his plans yet. He would be abroad another few weeks after I left, but when to leave or where exactly to go or even before that, whether to sell the car in Riyadh or to drive to a car fair in Jordan to sell it, wasn't determined yet.

The last weekend in May was another exceptional one with dinners two evenings in a row, Wednesday and Thursday, the first with the family of a non-Saudi, Muslim colleague of Baba's and the second with basically the same bunch that met at our place in April. The dinners were of the starting at 9:00 P.M. variety, dinner being served at 10:30, with a lot of laughter, sharing quiet talks in small groups, louder discussions as a large group, taking lots of pictures, getting home at 12:30 AM and waking up too early in the morning with still too full a stomach.

There was talk of a trip to a golf course on Friday and of the same bunch meeting at a fish restaurant the next week. The so-long social circuit had begun. It was ironic that this close circle had developed in this simulated society, or perhaps it made perfect sense. I had warmed to this group despite myself. I was leaving with more budding affiliations than when I had arrived.

With each farewell, I watched the barriers to our being our real selves slip away a little more. I let some members of the group share in the ups and downs of my journey and I in theirs.

Starting with Wednesday morning, I intended to reactivate my semi-nocturnal side and be careful not to overdo it during the daytime. Unfortunately I woke up exhausted, probably from anxiety, at 5:00 AM, two hours earlier than usual. I attempted an afternoon nap but without success. I ultimately found myself doing something I rarely ever did, drinking coffee, and at 7:00 PM at that. Artificially wide awake when I normally would be winding down, my life shifted abruptly between neutral and overdrive and back again, ignoring sunup or sundown.

On *Jumma*, at 10:00 AM, I was sore and sluggish. It felt well over 38^0 C. (100^0 F.) when we set out for a literal oasis in the midst of flat, dry, treeless sand. Joseph had invited us to see his new compound and its nearby country club, both surrounded by palms and eucalyptus trees. When we opened the car door, we flinched as a wave of scorching heat hit us. The steering wheel and seat belt buckles were too hot to touch at first and I sensed that same sound of skin sizzling. Approaching the compound, a valley of rock appeared suddenly along one side of the road and disappeared just as swiftly when we changed direction. When the shallow gorge first opened up beside us, we both uttered the same phrase at once—"Qu'appelle Valley!"

Years earlier, we two were driving across Western Canada at dusk searching for a campsite. Unexpectedly, a valley appeared ahead of us in the waning light, the road dipping down into an enormous field of prairie, light bush and farmland. We descended and set up camp, practically in the dark, and after a night's rest, dawn brought the revelation that we'd rolled out our modest hermitage right beside bushes bearing wild blueberries, which I picked to supplement our

Ala Tool

breakfast. After decamping, we drove back up the slope, glancing back to take a last look at the vale before we reached level ground. Once we joined the main road at the top, just as abruptly as it had laid itself bare the night before, the valley had vanished. We later learned the name of the basin—the Qu'appelle Valley. To us, the name will always carry the essence of the mythical.

The valley beside Joseph's compound was a mere rocky ravine in comparison but just as ethereal. Driving to the club, a modern day fortress bordered the road. The low ornamental walls surrounded a palm and eucalyptus nursery. An extension of the same ravine served as a dry moat around the walls, with an occasional short bridge branching away from the road, crossing the dry water and leading to the gate. Meanwhile, the rural *Jumma* processions to nearby mosques were beginning. In the bed of the pick up truck ahead of us, eight farm workers in Punjabi outfits doubled as acrobats as they held each other in over the bumps.

Incredibly, Joseph and his neighbor endured the stupefying, sun-baked driving range for a ½ hour, and then came into the clubhouse to rest, eat and drink. Baba took his photos and I stretched out with Tolkien on the comfortable, long, curved couch in the clubhouse, ceiling fans chortling over my head. Back at the compound, we met two sets of his neighbors, congenial, down to earth people, who suggested yet another get-together before we left.

For six months, I had looked forward to cleanly clipping strings and ties and making my getaway. Now life was threatening to get messy. The strings proved resiliently strong. We had seen each other under pressure, subjected to injustices, and in adversity. We'd seen frailties and helped how and when we could. I would have liked to spend more time with some of them, but elsewhere. It was easier to make quality contact at this eleventh hour, with most barriers down.

One colleague and his wife, who had kept up the appearance of a unity of minds for five years, with her going back and forth all year, suddenly heard his contract was not renewed after all, even though the week before, his continuing service had been all settled. Suddenly they were at a loose end, with no commitment to or from an educational institution for the coming year. When we saw the couple, the chronic, simmering exasperation was spilling over the top. We all understood. The dream I'd had ten months earlier, about the turkey wing in the dishwasher with broken bone china, flashed before my

Jewel Dhuru

mind. Perhaps this explained the message from the turkey wing not to mix the organic with the inorganic. Some things are just too different to blend well.

This was May, but a few other couples were to have similar turnabout announcements sprung on them in June, just before the summer exodus, with not enough time to even sell their furnishings. Saudization. A nurse I had just met talked about strains on herself and her husband. She'd been called anti-social because she found it difficult to eat a heavy meal at 10:00 PM!

Faisal, my right hand crutch, suggested to Baba, a desert picnic with other students, but that never materialized. The group dinner at the fish restaurant turned out to be up a flight of stairs, so we gave that one a miss. One neighbor invited us for dinner in the middle of a week that I was already teetering on overload, so Baba went alone.

I suspected people I had only met over the phone, connections of Baba's, might just call and turn up at the last minute and I hoped I could muster up time and energy when they did. One Asian lady's mother was undergoing serious medical treatment back home, with unsatisfactory results, but her Saudi employers wouldn't release her early. She called me just to talk. She needed an ear, a sounding board, so I walked her through problem solving steps to explore alternatives, over the phone. Another caller needed moral support so we talked about her background and current concerns. We all needed moral support. I shared my experiences, too and we gleaned lessons from each other. I felt closer to these telephone acquaintances, sight unseen, than I did to some who had the leisure to observe the proprieties of visiting.

I would have liked to phone certain people before I left, but for the same intangible cultural, political, social reasons some didn't call me when I first returned, my felt sense told me it would be best to let it go. My elastic banded, burgundy colored, leather bound address book did not increase in girth in Riyadh, except for a few email addresses. I would wait for another significant change in my life to get the next in my series of little books.

June took on a blurry quality, but at least it was June. Way back in November, I had squinted through the lens of a figurative seven-month spyglass, drawing in the distant view of my departure day. Since April, it had zoomed up. I had catapulted to the same corner of the calendar as my coveted cruising time. My vigil was over.

Ala Tool

The spyglass had collapsed along with a few illusions. No going back. With a mixture of trepidation and an I-don't-care attitude, I thought of the people who had not responded to my emails or letters over the preceding seven months. More than a few relationships would likely go through a transitional stage, the one of lost-and-found that is a side effect of changing circumstances. But genuine ties of friendship would stretch and hold. It was in June, 30 years earlier, that Baba and I had met. Another milestone was passing.

The light of my little candle had not been snuffed out but the composition of the wax had been altered, changing my reality system. I hesitate to use 'never' in reference to the future, but at that time, it seemed I would never think of Tolkien again without seeing myself stretched out on my Saudi couch engrossed in his trilogy, 1420 popping off the page at me. I would never look out my living room window again without appreciating the freedoms I enjoyed, privileges of birth. I would never meet another person without assessing their intentions. I would never see male-female relationships in the same light, evaluating my own uses of agreement and acquiescence. Whether the nevers were irrevocable or not, time would tell. I hoped my experience would ultimately translate into taking each circumstance, personal encounter and relationship individually, focusing on merits, and planning for mutually beneficial outcomes.

Back in North America, it would be some time before a full moon didn't mean two weeks to Baba's payday, months before a curved water tower peeking above treetops didn't remind me of the dome of a mosque, and a year before I would be comfortable in dresses shorter than ankle length. The words *mafee mishkole, inshallah, mumtez!* (wonderful!) and *a la tool*, would become part of my vocabulary. Whenever we saw an Arab family whose female covered her head in black on a sweltering day, Baba was to say *Salam wa laqum* to them and smile at their startled reaction while I was to wonder if they felt their lives were better here or there.

After months of mood fluctuations in Riyadh, I had begun to mellow out and align my energies with the divine flow, not letting the lows get so low, nor the highs so high. I had become both tougher and softer, and I hoped more able to blend the two harmoniously. I became more confident that things would work out as long as I took them in stride and listened to my inner voices of guidance and

Jewel Dhuru

warning. At age 50, on good days, I felt freer of the needless need to impress anyone and went more for a sharing from the heart.

A couple of months down the road, Baba was to find it irksome that I was not as excited as he was about shopping for a second car. I had changed. Perhaps too detached? Time would tell.

Countdown

At 2 ½ weeks before my voyage began, two very windy days culminated in the blowing over and hauling off of a bougainvillea tree across the street. But it was cooler, only 39^0 C. (102^0 F.). I could tell that first thing in the morning because during the night, I had covered up with our fleecy, plaid blanket. The non-air conditioned bathroom was not the usual fiery furnace either. And the air in the usually stifling sitting room didn't make my breathing as raggedy.

Gas prices had reached their highest ever in the Midwest, more than $2.00 a gallon, but still only 6 SR ($1.50 U.S.) per liter ($0.40 a gallon) in Riyadh.

Through the email, we'd completed the transfer of our furnished flat to the friends of friends who would occupy it in August. Ultimately all we would have left to sell was our car, sitting room furniture and vacuum, that is, if the repercussions of our unorthodox sale could be smoothed over with certain contrary campus authorities.

The same week, Elizabeth and Paul's building had no tap water for 8 hours one hot day, so we sent over a load of 2-liter bottles and filled up a couple for ourselves while we were at it. Since the previous week, a not-so-small hiccough had plagued the citywide water system, except on campus. But the water tankers that provided sustenance for trees and bushes sat for days in the parking lot down the road, men stringing hoses between the tanks and large blue vats, so we thought something was up. If each consecutive building was to have a dry spell and my pessimistic prediction was correct, our turn would come on the last day, the most hectic time. Until then, rolling blackouts and water rationing had only touched us marginally.

At 2 weeks before, tension mounted in my back and between my temples. My left ankle was yellow, the five-week old sprain's last color change, but the outer shape and inner feel weren't quite right yet. Still, I felt so acutely that relief was in sight that keeping aligned with my natural rhythms, and concentrating on breathing and

Ala Tool

meditation became difficult once more. I was distracted, unable to focus too long and sometimes searched for solace in nervous nibbling when I wasn't even hungry. Other expat females told the same story, finding false comfort in food, but I was determined not to give in to it, at least not more than just now and then. I had to work at countering the untrue thought that I didn't need to actively keep in touch with my regenerative source anymore, that it didn't matter so much now because I would be geographically nearer to it soon. Our common source can be as close or far away as we choose at any given moment.

Late one morning, Baba called to say the Saudi superior who'd treated the fellows in his department to dinner, several times, wanted to go out again that same evening. This would be the fellows' second attempt to treat their superior to something other than the standard Saudi food he preferred. This time they met with some success. They did return to the same non-negotiable restaurant but took the waiter aside and privately ordered something else. Before Baba left at 9:00 PM, we finished our errands. The next morning, I saw the parting gift the group gave Baba and a card with genuine expressions of sadness at his leaving. I was happy for him. I just wished our stint wasn't so hard on me. He was, too.

While Baba was at dinner, I continued packing. Wanting to show our daughter and son-in-law in New York the Dimashq specialties and my Indian roadside acquisitions, I gave priority in my suitcase to those items. The rest would be shipped. A hefty fine was assessed for every kilo over two 32-kilo (70 lb.) cases. I began carefully packaging up a cache of precious personal possessions I wouldn't need for a while and putting them on a separate shelf in the kitchen pantry for Baba to ship: my paintbrushes, Arabic notes, my Tolkien trilogy, an English grammar book I used for teaching, a few paperbacks and two unique Arab designed candles.

By that time, we were on the last of Baba's seven original plants. I did the best I could for them, providing what I thought was the right lighting and not over-watering, but one by one, all the others had quietly faded away; leaving only the meter (3') tall croton. When dried out and freshly watered, it alternately drooped and was refreshed. But it also dropped leaves. Half the leaves had browned, crinkled up and fallen off. I could hear them crackling from across the room, trying to tell me something, crying for help, but whatever I had

Jewel Dhuru

tried, it hadn't helped. Ultimately, Baba would leave it with Joseph, who had a greener thumb.

Even with numerous phone calls for the car, serious customers were at a premium. Most callers haggled over price, and some didn't even show up while Baba waited for them half comatose in the scorching parking lot. Time was short. With most expats leaving simultaneously, if it didn't get sold that week, it wouldn't get sold at all and then we'd have a problem. So while I finished up the last paperbacks, Baba went to the car souk, with lots of wheels and megaphones announcing great deals, where young men jumped into our car to inspect it almost before it had rolled to a stop. With practiced eyes, they picked out the dent that had been painted. Knowing little English, they punched in numbers on their cell phones to signify their offers. Before long, Baba got a good price and rented a car on the way home, a turquoise Lancer.

The next week, we were entering our cloverleaf while two women with only eyes showing were approaching the same wide doorway, going out. We skirted around them, one on either side. I was just passing them when the taller one spoke to me.

"Hi—How are you?" she chirped in a cheery voice.

I was so taken aback by this discordant note, a cheery voice directed at me from a veiled face, that it took me a moment to recognize the fact and turn back. Seeing no one else in the hall, I answered an uncertain "Hello—OK" and passed on. When we rounded the corner near the elevator, I whispered to Baba.

"Who was that?"

It was Tanya! The other figure must have been the teen daughter who had swished passed me near the elevator months earlier. My gosh! I passed their door whenever I went in and out but had forgotten all about them. It was sad, the engrained pattern into which I, too, had fallen. At that moment, the memory came to me of the Saudi woman at JFK airport, who'd sat in Baba's seat with her back to me. What would a look into those mirrors reveal, I wondered, as the image of four jars of marbles rattled past my eyes.

A phone call came. Elizabeth, Paul and we two were invited for another long, late, heavy dinner to the home of an African Muslim couple, both students of Baba's several years earlier. Even though they'd known our kids through formative years, I hadn't seen them for years or met their youngest children. It would be the last days in the country for all four guests, and busy, so I felt freer to try to tailor the evening to our collective needs, after I reached a meeting of minds with Elizabeth. To the former student-hostess, I suggested just soft drinks and snacks right after the last *salah*, since my first hint at an afternoon visit met with a stunned silence. She was willing to collaborate, and her husband even allowed us to come at 8:00 o'clock, instead of waiting until *salah* finished at 8:40 PM.

Fortunately, Elizabeth applauded my cheekiness. She had more packing to do than I, dispersing ten years of stuff in preparation for their move, so they didn't have a whole evening to spare and preferred to eat earlier and lighter, too. So it was settled, in principle.

In the meantime, Baba decided to move his desk from his backroom office to the dining room. On his short wave, for months he'd been hearing Arab music he wanted to tape, but the stereo was in the dining room. So he moved, hooking up wires. The problem was this competed with the TV, so out came Baba's earphones and the spirit of compromise on both our parts.

On the news, a guilty verdict was handed down to Arabs accused of bombing of American embassies in Nairobi, Kenya and Dar Es Salam, Tanzania three years earlier. Since Osamah bin Laden was alleged to be the mastermind, the high level of alert in Riyadh continued.

At the 1½-week mark, two Indian fellows bought our sitting room set, agreeing to pick it up after I left. With videos and movies on other channels, Saudi feature films weren't as pleasurable anymore. My mood alternated between periodic elation at being able to see my kids soon and a numbing detachment from the present circumstances. I hardly looked out the window. My present moment was tying up loose ends, notifying friends that I'd soon be sprung and writing, so the view outside would soon be a thing of the past. I would, however, miss twice-weekly talks with Elizabeth. We'd only gotten to this point of familiarity in the last month and now it would end. By this time, my left ankle was functioning at 90%, with the help of cold packs, warm water, intensive massage and stretching. My spirits were rising as well and I had the feeling nothing could happen to me in the last measly 12 days that I couldn't handle. But the unexpected was about to reawaken.

One evening, driving on a busy street that we'd frequented too many times to count, five lanes of cars were moving along abreast of

Jewel Dhuru

each other, when a Saudi college student rear-ended us in the center lane. After the initial shock, we moved one lane nearer the curb while he streaked to the side of the road beside me, stopping just centimeters from a parked car right outside my window. He didn't understand why Baba was annoyed since there was no damage to either car. My back and leg muscles were the only casualties. At the moment of impact, a shockwave radiated across my lower back and down my right leg and my muscles were to remain more tender than usual for a week. There it was again. A reminder to move forward with support and joy. If it was true that the physical really mirrored the emotional state—oh dear! Perhaps just the boost I needed to get me ready for the long journey home.

Baba took the student's name and license number, but the country's fledgling insurance business had not yet touched his life. We started off again and not 30 seconds later, a car s-c-r-a-p-e-d along our left side. From the interior, it sounded like a meter-long (3-foot) crease but this time nobody stopped, not even us. Six and a half months and no collisions and now twice in five minutes! Suddenly I felt unsafe. Home stretch or not, the unpleasant could still happen to me, even on that taken for granted street. Later, viewed from the exterior, the surmised meter-long crease turned out to be a 10-cm. (4") scrape the rental agent said he would touch up himself.

The next day, in my state of super-sensitivity, I scanned the landscape as I rounded the corner of our building, heading for the parking lot. Perhaps what I thought of as the local mentality had finally affected my vision. Things looked fuzzy, distorted, like a giant board game, the white pieces being incommunicado, the black being non-entities and all other colors being expendable in this ebbing zone. But what was the object of the game, I wondered.

The evening with the former students arrived. Soft drinks and snacks were served at 8:00 PM, as promised. I was glad I had insisted on a short visit, because that morning, Baba's pal's computer program had become corrupted and he came over to print out an important file. Our printer cartridge chose that moment to run dry, as he sat there in mid-print, so he and Baba hiked over to another neighbor-colleague's to finish printing. And a female student of Baba's phoned to say she wanted to visit me. Fine. I completed preparations for her visit just in time to answer the phone and hear her say her uncle was ill and she couldn't make it after all. Shifting sands.

The following evening was the last and best gathering, in the loveliest of compounds. We sat around the table like a family, catching up on news, thrashing out issues, commiserating over situations, empathizing with problems, giving congratulations and wishing each other well.

We heard the latest stories about those who'd just been notified they would be leaving, and about the progress of those trying to secure visas for their children for the summer. Stories followed convoluted trails, relating the hoops parents had to jump through over six weeks, tackling one obstacle after another until in the end, applications for their sons were not approved anyway. Each time, the Kingdom succeeded in keeping out yet another dreaded bachelor. We parted that day exchanging contact information and conveying messages to absent wives.

Although I didn't know it at the time, the same week as our gathering, another celebration was in progress. An article from my hometown's Winnipeg Free Press (2001), entitled Unveiling of Pooh Art at Legislative Building Draws Young and Old, announced the unveiling of the only known oil painting of the little bear, Winnie the Pooh, painted by E.H. Shepard, immortalized in stories by A.A. Milne. A flyer was reproduced in the article. What caught my eye was that along the bottom of the flyer, Everyone is welcome! was printed in big letters. Unlike the notice in Riyadh from two years earlier of a one day Sportsfest where the everybodies in question turned out to be adults with only Y chromosomes and their children, at this gathering at the Manitoba Legislative Building, Winnipegers, other Manitobans, visitors and pets manageable in a crowd were indeed welcome to the celebration of the historical connection of the bear to the city that had given him his name. [85] It was heart warming.

At 1 week before I left the Kingdom, Baba made his reservation for India, leaving a week after me. At the Dean's End of Year Meeting, those leaving the university and the Kingdom were honored. Baba enjoyed accolades and congratulations. The Baba I knew was usually guarded when discussing feelings. But, in an interesting turnabout, at various dinners and meetings that week, Baba made speeches expressing his deeper feelings to Saudi and non-Saudi colleagues alike. In one, he claimed he was about to begin work for a new boss—his wife. Meanwhile I had become more reticent.

At ½ a week, my suitcases were ¾ full, with lots left over to ship. Baba entertained invitations to get involved in reviewing journal articles and consulting—after this, his second retirement. Baba called from work one day to say that his friend from work with whom I had shared moral support over the phone, would like him to bring her over on her lunch break. We had a quick 15-minute visit, I passed on paperbacks to her and then, she was gone.

Another colleague gave us a CD of Arabic Christmas carols. I played it in June and enjoyed every note, particularly a French song, *Il est Ne, le Divine Enfant*. A special French Canadian couple had introduced me to in decades earlier. The last public place I heard it memorably was a hotel in Bangalore, India while Baba was conferencing one Christmas and now the same song had followed me to Riyadh. At that moment, the globe seemed very small indeed.

We got our last take-out hamour and chips and finally purchased a Tabrizi Persian carpet for our family room back home. The Kingdom Center, the unfinished downtown skyscraper, whose glass face had been inching skywards for months, had hit a snag and stopped. It would not be completed before we left.

The last 3 days before I left, I became unusually wakeful at night, alert at 2:00 AM for a few hours or at 4:40 AM for the whole day. Jet lag started even before the jet. I suppose it was the anticipated excitement and upheaval. At 2:00 AM, my right nostril was completely plugged, burgeoning from merely being swollen for weeks. In fact, my eyes were itchy and white matter filled the inner corners that morning. And I had sneezed six times the day before. Annoying symptoms for one who'd experienced few allergies. Mercifully, my back had settled down the last couple of days before I took on the added burden of travel again

That week, everyone started leaving the country. While the call was still local, I enjoyed an extended conversation with the wife of one fellow who'd gone home alone. Fortunately, she had a job, so got out on weekdays. We reviewed some of our extraordinary experiences. In passing, she mentioned the blooming fantail palms, dangling white fluffy stuff. In her neighborhood, cars were covered with fuzz. Ah! The itchy eyes, the nostril, the sneezing. Was all that I was allergic to in the Middle East?

The next day another two fellows would go, the day after even more and so on in geometric proportions. We made a last pilgrimage to the site of our dog's ashes and I brushed residual crumbs off the bedroom windowsill. The birds knew the system's rhythms better than I. We stopped at the neighborhood bread maker to buy bread and say so long. Normally Baba went into the shop to chat with him and I waited in the car, but this time, the baker came out and treated us to cartons of orange juice from the shop next door. We stood on the sidewalk sipping, but the proceedings were awkward. Baba translated questions from Urdu but the baker diverted his gaze to Baba or to the ground while he listened to my answers in Arabic. Still, not only was the juice a treat, but this time, he wouldn't even take our money for the bread. More exit wounds and vital signs. With contacts back home reestablished, the healing had already begun. I heard the scintillating strains of my last Saudi *salah* at 8:15 PM on Saturday, June 16, 2001.

Chapter 38: The Blink Of A Cosmic Eye

"Love people even in their sin, for that is the semblance of divine love and is the highest love on earth. ...Love every leaf ... every grain of sand ... If you love everything, you will perceive the divine mystery in things" [86]
—Fyodor Dostoyevsky

On the flight to New York, the word that kept running through my mind as I sat wedged in the tight, uncomfortable seat that reclined very little was grueling. I got little sleep, perhaps 4 hours of 13 in the air, during a confinement that had begun at 1:30 AM.

If I thought the dreams rattling my consciousness a few weeks before were disconcerting, the images that punctuated in-flight short snooze spurts, contorted catnaps, wakeful winks and disrupted, drifting dozes bordered on strange, choppy, weird and disjointed. My body screamed to me to lay it down but I placated it by throwing a shawl around my loose slacks and long blouse, walking to the restroom and stretching and then stuffing pillows in different positions when I sat down again. It was like living in a pressure cooker. In what passed for morning, the Pakistani woman two seats away, who'd answered my previous attempts at communication with monosyllables, surprised me by asking me to fill out her Customs forms, handed out by attendants during what passed for the evening before. She said her eyesight was poor even with specs. With my own puckered eyes, I asked her the questions necessary to do a half decent, if exploratory, job to complete the forms. Her hearing didn't seem too good either, because my questions reached a sufficient volume for the American male in the seat ahead to get up, come back and ask me a question about his form, as though I knew what I was doing. Baba would have smiled.

A couple of hours later, as we prepared to disembark, the same man leaned down over me and muttered "worst flight of my life" under his breath. With the light in the kitchen, just beside him, going on and off all night, people like me going for a stretch to the restroom just in front of him and an upset infant in the second seat away from him, he'd spent most of what passed for the night with a blanket thrown right over his head.

Ala Tool

With other presumably indispensable information, the TV screen in front showed which direction East was at each moment so those who wished to pray on the carpeted area in a back corner could orient themselves to the *Kabah* in Makkah, spelling it *Al Qibhah*. Prayer rules provided for skipping or combining two prayers when on a voyage, uncomplicating the process.

After 13 hours aloft, we landed in New York. I went from a nation of 6,000,000 expats and 9,000,000 Saudis to 8,000,000 in The City alone. Since Baba had checked my bags 12 hours before the flight, mine were probably the first two loaded into the hold. First in—last out. I waited 50 minutes for the belly of the plane to disgorge them, then 30 seconds to get through Customs and into the waiting hands of our son-in-law.

And suddenly my half-life was all over in the blink of a cosmic eye. No more black sackcloth on my person and hot ashes in the air. More greenery, music, neighbors, birds, dogs, and color enriched the ever-changing street scenes. The movies I had craved in order to pass the time, no longer held my interest and neither did jigsaw and crosswords puzzles. I couldn't stay in one spot for hours anymore. For a while, every time I heard a whirring kitchen appliance or a car alarm, I misconstrued it as *salah* and every loud buzz was a limo driver on reconnaissance. The lives of this young couple, my kids, seemed so cheerful in comparison, with a kaleidoscope of activity within easy reach. Our daughter had left up Christmas garlands and colored yuletide lights, just so I could see them—a rare treat.

After letting Baba know I'd arrived, I wanted to do everything from my old life at once, like a child with a gift certificate to a new toy store: to go out on the balcony with my Grand cat who eyed me patiently from the door, to phone our son and good friends, to show the kids what I'd stowed in my suitcases, to hear their news and to see favorite TV programs. But I also found it easier to pace myself than before, confident that everything would occur in its own time.

The contrast between New York and Riyadh was sharp. New York had green parks, people playing ball, talking or just stretching out on green grass. I came to life, too. But what life? What was I going to do now? It would take time to pick up old threads again.

Back in Riyadh, surrounded by suitcases and five cargo boxes, Baba called to say he'd have the phone disconnected the next day, allowing three days to tabulate the final bill. The expat sport of

Jewel Dhuru

signature gathering had begun weeks before, Baba eliciting the help of secretaries. With no phone, emails would come only through his office account, so he would be semi incommunicado until he changed cities again.

Three days later, our sitting room furniture would be picked up, *Inshallah. A*nd the Housing Office would inspect the flat for that final clearance signature. Baba would give the vacuum to a friendly Sudanese fellow. That's the way it was, cycling through many hands and hearts. I recalled with a smile that when we left the first time, Baba gave, to a friend, the 20-liter plastic water can we'd kept in our trunk when we explored Abha and Najran. The friend had a jeep and traveled, so he could use it. But the second time, when we bought a car of our own, the same friend gave the same can back, a red ribbon stuck to the top. Now Baba would pass the can on again. Then, two days after I arrived home, Baba would leave for two weeks in Mumbai.

In New York, entertainment meant healthful influences along with commercials, nudity, bad language, crime and violence. But at least I had a choice and I now knew well violence came in more varieties than just physical. On the other hand, most countries I've visited have a comprehensive range of world news, including Canadian and American. But what was labeled World News for that week was often condensed into The Global Minute, the other 59 elbowing out much of global concern and focusing instead on the antics of local politicians and celebrities.

On the Wednesday in my kids' suburb, just after they left for work, the scene across the street was transformed. Seven long fire trucks pulled up on the river side of the street, in front of an apartment building, sirens whining, hoses extending, smoke fuming, fire fighters' juice drinking and when it was all over, neighbors' sidewalk gawking. One apartment was ablaze but no one hurt. After 1½ hours, apart from roof doors being left open for aeration, I couldn't have told anything had happened, at least not from the outside. *Ala Tool.*

In Riyadh, Baba attended a thesis defense, a dinner and a breakfast that Saudi weekend, but I would have to wait two more days for mine to start. Meanwhile, I enjoyed the balcony with my Grand cat. I must have kept, at the bottom of my lungs, molecules of inhaled desert wind because when I exhaled deeply over the river, the surface ripples were the same shape as the rivulet pattern the wind had carved

Ala Tool

into the dunes. As I watched, a solitary V of Canada Geese wove its way northward up the very center of the river, honking as its shape undulated from a V to a U to a W. I would be leaving this serene spot in a few days, too. Over the phone, our son in Wisconsin described the deep pink peonies in our front yard, nearing their peak. I might just get home to catch the end of their eruption.

On the weekend, my kids acted as guides. We three saw deer spring from between trees at a national park and a couple of 200-year-old battlefields. We rumbled drove past lakes with swans floating freely, around Sleepy Hollow and through the grounds of West Point. My perception was influenced by recent history, piled on top of the less recent and filtered through vestiges of jetlag. At one point, my garbled gaze seemed to see the filigree of ornate Arab doors, but that was another world.

Jet lag didn't take as long to get over when I returned as when I went. Within two days, I was sleeping 9:00 PM to 5:00 AM, with an afternoon nap, and by five days the headaches and back strain were almost gone, too. Of course, in New York, boredom and depression had abated.

My maverick airline ticket went off without a hitch. As I was settling in at home, I realized I had been away long enough to forget things I thought I never would. I forgot the first half of my social security number, my car license plate number, the names of wildflowers in my own back yard, the phone number for the neighborhood library, which button started the car radio, that I had to slow down to 20 mph in a school zone, the names of the neighbors' kids, how to reengage the TV dish, what utensils I had in this kitchen as opposed to the Saudi one, that the end of the movie doesn't have to be chopped off, how refreshing newly mowed grass smelled and how delightful it was to be buoyant in a pool of water.

I had forgotten, too, the system behind the overstuffed shelves near my desk so when I started to make places to keep papers from the suitcase, I didn't remember they already had places. I just didn't know where they were right then. I wanted to make space too, for the cache of books in the Saudi pantry that would arrive as cargo.

A couple of days after my arrival, the steering wheel, indeed, the whole car felt stiff as I maneuvered our Volvo for a first time in eight months, this trip being to the chiropractor. I needed that treatment after our two bang ups in Riyadh two weeks earlier.

Jewel Dhuru

Back in the pool for exercise, I had lost some of the strength I had gained before I left home but perhaps I had developed other strengths. The stairs presented the same old problem. Not only no going back, no going upstairs either, not more than every third day or so. The old formula for healing, two steps forward and one back seemed apt, but the global strides I stumbled along with moved in unexpected directions and challenging distances.

I hadn't forgotten the scent of my pink peonies, though. Their fragrance took me back to a childhood farm, where, incidentally, we were going in five weeks. Although the timing was taxing, I looked forward to it. The back patio of my modest hermitage was heavy with the scent of moisture and the sounds of songbirds and wind rustling through leaves. Squirrels had planted corn and sunflower seeds in the flower garden and I left them where they'd sprouted. But I wasn't used to bugs whizzing past my eyes and ears anymore, except for nocturnal mosquitoes. In my absence, the grape vine had officially rounded the corner and brought a bird's nest and strikingly yellow June Beetles with in, both near the same spot where seven months earlier, our son and I had looked at Orion's belt. I hung up my black travel bag, communed with the spirit of my dog running free in the yard, sat in my lounge chaise and sipped a glass of wine.

As I unpacked, I had that transitory feeling again, of straddling two worlds. A Damascene tablecloth and Saudi incense burner would adorn a teak table. The Saudi coffee pot painting would complement crockery. Frankincense, myrrh and ood would reside with beeswax candles. Baba's "body by chocolate chip" magnet would cling to the fridge near a native Canadian dream catcher. Arriving in cargo, the plaid indigo and black blanket would lay by a hand knit one and a camel bag would hang on the door near my needlepoint of an English countryside.

In the evening, the chirping and rasping of crickets and frogs was so loud, I felt like I was camping out. In the morning, a squirrel's signal was suspiciously like a 'baa-a-a'. For a moment, I thought I had fallen asleep in *Diraaya* and a flock of bleaters was going by.

While sorting months of mail, I picked up the Journal of Counseling and Development to soak up restoration for the soul. An article spoke of specific people who were reassessing their priorities, reaching sagacious insights. They developed a new appreciation for family, good friends and humanity in general and treated each new day as a gift. This sounded familiar. Their attraction to the trappings of success was extinguished. I thought of travel and contact with cultures, but at what cost to cooperation and closeness. I thought of shadowed women with glamorous gowns, gold galore and cell phones but undetermined maladies and drivers who couldn't drive. As I read of savoring joyful moments, transcending the mundane and letting go of toxic relationships, I thought of those I had missed, whether or not they'd kept in touch and where the quality of life lay. One voice decried the injustices humans inflict on each other and I thought of Israel and Palestine, Muslims and Hindus, women and men and even Baba and I.

My reassessment had been along these lines, I reflected, and my voyage of discovery was not over. Surprisingly, the article was entitled *More Wisdom From People Who Have Faced Death*. Their life-threatening experiences had inspirational and revitalizing effects. Perhaps a bit dramatic, comparing my feelings to theirs, yet I knew better than to deny what I sensed. Then, universal timing being what it is, our son, who'd delayed having his own place due to us, decided since I was back and house and yard were in order, the time for him to go was now.

I read on. When asked if they cared what others thought of them, voices in the article answered that they did, but not to the point of people pleasing or worrying about image. Rather, they appreciated close friendships more and focused on being true to themselves. Their view of the future of humankind, in general, was that we're in trouble but that there was hope. Human frailties, they believed, came from being immature developmentally; humanity would eventually outgrow it. The World News came to mind and I was not so sure. If we don't learn from our mistakes, we repeat them. When asked about the most gratifying experiences in their lives, topping the list were enjoying small pleasures and handling ordeals gracefully. [87]

There's more than one kind of death. My life wasn't snuffed out. Nor were my circumstances changed as completely as victims of natural disasters or witness protection program participants. For me, it was the demise of attending to the superficial, of holding on to old attitudes or unhealthy relationships, of looking at life through a mundane monocle or of thinking that appreciation is owed me but I don't have to reciprocate, the death of illusions.

During my second week, an unexpectedly pleasant episode unfolded. With our son now reappearing only on weekends and Baba not back yet, I solicited help for mid-week tasks. One friend brought groceries, one helped unpack and a third trimmed the grape vine and elderberry bush. One day I asked a female friend to help me shop for more than I could carry myself.

"Did you get everything you needed, too?" I asked my friend as she shifted my selections from cart to counter. She answered in the affirmative, but a pleasant looking, curly black-haired cashier, whose nametag read 'JJ', interjected in a sweet voice: "I didn't."

"You didn't?" I repeated, looking at her interrogatively.

" I could use a hug," JJ said, mixing forlorn and impish in her look.

"Oh, I have one to spare," I offered, thinking of recent times female support would have made a difference.

The cashier went through the motions of checking us out, packing up our purchases and wishing us a good day, but I did not forget her offhand remark. While my friend took the bag, I took my change with my left hand and extended my right hand to her, wishing JJ the best. For a moment she stood mystified and then looked down at my hand. Then grasping it warmly with both of hers, she leaned her head and shoulders forward across the counter and I followed suit, creating a momentary tactile connection. My friend appreciated JJs openheartedness as well and we all three parted richer than when we'd arrived.

Chapter 39: Home At Last

"Our deepest fear is not that we are inadequate. Our deepest fear is that we are powerful beyond measure. It is our Light, not our Darkness that most frightens us. ... And as we let our own Light shine, we unconsciously give other people permission to do the same"[88]

—Marianne Williamson, *A Return to Love*

The last week before Baba's return home, when I planned to get so much done, a burning scent emanated from my laptop again, and back to the shop it went for two weeks. I could have completed the sewing project I had started in November, but the bobbin chose that time to knot itself into a tangle. So there I was. No writing or sewing that week. But what to do? Back to books and music. But here, I had variety, along with the car, friends and neighbors to phone and exercise in the nearby pool. There wasn't much point in starting any other kind of work besides writing, because we would be traveling again in five weeks.

Baba's Back

By the time Baba got home on July 20, 2001, a still higher level of alert erupted over Saudi Arabia and the UN deployed outside monitors to observe Palestine and Israel. Baba had had a fruitful trip and we could finally share semi-unhurried stories about all that had happened since I had left Riyadh. I told him about the Broadway actor I'd met on the flight from New York, and he recounted his visit to the Oxford University Press-India, in New Delhi, in connection with a book he was editing. And lots of family news.

Once Baba had unwound a bit, we began to get in touch with the changes in each other. It had been four years since our first dose of empty nest syndrome, but here was another. No time to dwell on it, though. With Baba and his luggage came the cargo boxes. Inside would be the plaid indigo and black blanket I wrapped around myself in the winter, camel bags from the *Thumamah* teepees and my cache of books, brushes and binoculars.

Jewel Dhuru

Complicating our settling in was the fact that while still in Riyadh, we'd planned to attend a family reunion in Canada. We were to leave in 11days. Gifts for relatives went right out of a shipping crate and into the just vacated suitcase. My travel bag couldn't rest, either.

After four weeks of pseudo independence, having no one to please but myself about meals and schedules, once again, we had to come to joint terms about whether the house would be kept warmer or cooler, who would use the car when, and whether things in general would be done this way or that. With Baba now used to cooking for himself, a new collaborative order would have to be established in the kitchen, too. The first time Baba went to get groceries, he moaned the unavailability of fresher than fresh, hot out of the oven, yeasty Arab bread from his pal, the baker across the street and the fact that now we would have to cook every day. No more inexpensive gourmet meals to pick up from our choice of a dozen ethnic kitchens.

Because of the responsibilities of living, raising a family, jobs, other travels and a number of other excuses, we had not set foot in the western half of Canada for 19 years. The day after my laptop arrived from repair, it was almost time to go. With piles of pages of notes to construct into the shape and sounds of a manuscript, I had a scant half-day to check the laptop out. I would subsist a little longer on notes shoved into a folder for potential pages.

Just before leaving, we made time to sit down and show our son some photos we'd taken. He fit stories of his own doings in between ours about Baba's colleagues, the Mumbai relatives, Phoenician ruins, Crusader castles and where in the world we'd sprinkled our dog's ashes.

The Arab-North American Northwest

On August 1, 2001, my binoculars still in the depths of an unpacked cargo box and everything left in the competent hands of our son, we were off again. Cruising 5 km. (39,000') above the planet's surface, we watched the land form patchwork Iowa farm fields, then roughen into Mt. Rushmore's Black Hills, then thrust higher into Yellowstone's Grand Tetons divided by wiggly rivers, suddenly rise even further into the snow-caps of Montana and eventually subside into the potato plots of Idaho. As our plane dragged its shadow across the Rockies, I thought I saw a brick fortress wall lining up neatly along the uppermost rocky ridge. Roman ruins or Crusader castle? Perhaps we were too far West for that, far too far—the wrong continent. And then, in my imagination, a snow-crested peak became a sandy dune and snowy patches with dark flecks on flat terrain became Bedouin camps in the sand. The flight ended in Seattle, with a view of Mt. Rainier's sun-drenched crater, a single peak on the global Ring of Fire. At that very moment, Sicily's Mt. Etna's spectacular natural fireworks display was wrecking havoc on refuges, ski resorts and towns, but Mt. Rainier, disposed to spew mudslides at times, was serene.

Inexplicably, on the flights coming and going, even though we'd requested two low fat meals, Baba got his, but plunked down before me were kosher meals. I ate both with relish after perusing a note in each package, in English and possibly Yiddish, assuring me the utensils used to prepare each meal had been bought new and had never been used before.

Meeting our daughter and son-in-law in Seattle, we rented a car together for as long as they had leave, and then we two would continue on our own. Our daughter took us back to the dormitory that was her temporary home when she studied at the university and to a new chapel remarkable for its gathering of lights playing on the walls. We set more of our dog's ashes free, inviting his spirit to romp, rest in the shade and sniff in campus botanical gardens. A few days hence, we would park outside the old farmhouse of my childhood and I would recount stories about my grandparents' farm: the strawberry patch, the cream separator, the milk cans, the weeping willow tree, Grandma's cookie jar, the electrified fence, the chicken coop, hummingbirds in the hollyhocks, the hay loft, the pile of firewood, the pig sty, and Shaggy, the German Shepherd.

But first we had to get there. We set off in the car, taking in Seattle's Pike Place Market, and colorful statues of painted, tinted, clothed, tiled, rosemaled and otherwise gimmicked pigs that stood and sat their way to fame. Heading north through the Cascade Mountains, the Blue Angels aerobatic team saw us off by rehearsing noisily overhead for an air show that weekend.

Still accustomed to desert travel, green freeway road signs near Seattle took on unexpected connotations. My fuzzy brain misread Tukwila as the Tuwaiq Escarpment with its fossils and dry coral reef, and the exit to the Kingdome sports stadium seemed to pave my way back to the Kingdom of Saudi Arabia, no longer, *that place*. As we crossed the border into Canada, the disorientation increased when along the freeway, not only did a minaret topped by a crescent moon appear above the treetops but also a whole attached mosque with dome, ornate windows and arches, then another mosque and within a minute, a third one, all in a cluster.

A road sign pointing to West Bank, a suburban area, had me wondering whether we were in Palestinian or Israeli territory. Houses glued to mountainsides took me back to the slopes of Dimashq's *Jabal* Qassioun and Maloola. Trees set flat into alcoves along freeway sound barriers resembled those sprawling laterally against walls off Prince Abdullah Street in Riyadh.

Gasoline was now $0.66-Canadian per liter (about $1.77-US per gallon) whereas it had been $1.25 US per gallon down south, both a far cry from the 4 SRs per liter ($0.25-US per gallon) in Riyadh. Approaching Vancouver, the difference in the fine for littering did not escape our notice. South of the 49th parallel, $100.00 per infraction changed to $2000.00 up north!

In downtown Vancouver, the feeling of being on the honor system was heart warming, being trusted by strangers. The Royal Canadian Mounted Police presence, in their white cars, was minimal, but try anything shady and they'd appear. British and Scottish named streets, like Cavendish, Hawthorne, Argyle and MacKenzie, had a familiar feel. At red lights, Baba murmured that he kept expecting other drivers to honk just before they turned green. Threading our way through the city, he liberally used his now polished skill at not-quite legal U-turns.

Seeing and hearing the French language again, on merchandise labels and on TV, was music to my ears. News of the provinces and territories on CBC, took me back to my single days. Canadian bacon was conspicuous by its absence. What we Canadians call Back bacon doesn't bare much resemblance, in shape or flavor, to the tubes of ham labeled Canadian bacon elsewhere. In one hotel room, I temporarily abandoned my boycott of caffeine and munched the unique chocolates of my childhood, Cherry Blossoms and bubbly Aeros.

In Vancouver, we just had enough time for a quick jaunt through the white globe lit streets of historic Gastown, the classical Chinese gardens of Chinatown, where Kung Fu the series was filmed and then into the peninsula of Stanley Park where The X Files was filmed. In the park, the totem pole display, cricket oval, lighthouse and horse drawn tour carriages all added charm. From a cool, shady, spot on the coast, under 200-year-old evergreens, we overlooked the not-too-high rises of the teeming downtown of this city of 800,000 and the bustling harbor with private yachts, pontooned seaplanes and a grand sea bus terminus. Time too, for a quick rattle over the grand Lion's Gate Bridge and on to the Capilano Suspension Bridge, the latter for pedestrian traffic only, looking down onto tumultuous torrents in a deep gorge of a Pacific inlet. The rockeries at Capilano were so brilliant with color and texture that more of our dog's ashes were set free to roam and rest.

Reunioning meant more than words can describe. A cavity behind my breastbone, rubbed raw at times and coated in doubt, was now filled with soothing warmth, caring and confidence. Certain personal pockets of recollections were unique to each of us, not corresponding to any one else's, and isolated in time, while other vivid memories were shared by all.

When not meeting with relatives, the four of us explored the mountainsides. For a time, I wanted, habitually, to continue carrying lots of bottled water on treks. As vestiges of disorientation faded, I smiled at myself for doubting the safety of drinking the water straight out of the tap. Our ears popping, we drove through transparent clouds suspended in the roadway. Signs reminded us to Be Bear Aware. We followed the contours through thick stands of undisturbed pines, Douglas firs and other conifers. Infrequent clearings made room for ski lifts that stretched up to touch ever-changing clouds. Trees were quenched by sparkling bubbling brooks or rivers tinged green from glacial silt—Sasquatch country. A bonus was that the terrain reminded our Bosnian son-in-law of the land of his birth and he felt at home there, too.

When the kids left us to return to their jobs, we would resist the temptation to indulge a new habit, offering rides to hitchhikers. Alas, the crime rate wasn't negligible there. For now, as we rode, my thoughts went to those natives and workers, 100 or more years earlier, who had blazed and blasted that very forest trail, and those who later paved the same road, erecting telephone poles and fences along cliff edges. When they removed felled trees in logger trucks, I suppose they'd had the same view as we did then. The sun filtered through thick-trunked greenery on bright days, and on rainy ones, the runoff from the top created waterfalls, splashing down, polishing shiny streaks onto rocks or eroding jagged vertical cracks into rocky mountainsides. Day after day, as the builders had edged forward into moose, deer, cougar and bear country, they must have replaced the sounds of wildlife with that of picks, shovels, chain saws and cement mixers. As we drove, I hummed a tune from my childhood about silver birches, beavers, blue lakes and rocky shores and returning once more.

For days, we mingled with more than 90 relatives. My burgundy address book, quite dormant of late, fell on fertile ground once more. Its girth increased as the snail and email addresses and business cards of grown up cousins tugged at its encircling elastic band. I endeavored to capture the essence of this enchanted pocket of time and was reluctant to leave.

Flashing Forward

Our kids were to be off for home. Before Baba and I were to leave the city, though, we would follow the Wine Route to vineyards called Quail's Gate, Gray Monk and Mission Hill. Pasquale, a guide, directed us to a wine tasting cellar where Brahms Lullaby tinkled inside and a mission bell tolled outside, providing mood music while we sipped Pinot Noir and Riesling.

After two days, we two would head back to Seattle for our flight home, but by the scenic route. Alluring names on the map—Revelstoke, Burnaby, Chilliwack, Salmon Arm, Penticton, Abbotsford and Esterhazy—looked even better in 3-D. We were to stop at Osoyoos, home to Canada's only desert, a scant 26.8 hectares (66 acres) but with more than 100 species of rare plants and 300 of vertebrates. Claiming globally unique species of invertebrates, many were either Red-listed (endangered) or Blue-listed (vulnerable). And this desert was just a few miles from the Okanagan waterfall—more extremes.

Then across the border again into Washington State, leaving behind one of the lands of metric measurement, of hectares, liters, meters, grams and the Celsius scale. On the Colville Reservation of Twelve Confederated Tribes, unassuming abodes were to blend into the landscape. We headed for the brimming reservoir on the Columbia

River that is dubbed the Grand Coulee Dam. Then, on to Leavenworth, a once dying town, now turned into an attractive Bavarian village, with gingerbread looking roof shingles on hotels, houses and shops, with bright buds spilling out of window boxes, scrollwork and goats. While we breakfasted, a character in lederhosen, a brown Tyrolean cap, red vest and high socks, walked through the dining room of our hotel out onto the balcony and stepped up onto a second floor ledge to blow a curved wooden 6 meter (19') long Alpenhorn. A crowd gathered below and applauded his country concerto, a sound oddly reminiscent of the strains of *salah*.

Right after breakfast, Baba recalled aloud that just about then, most of his expat pals would be arriving in Riyadh for a new semester, while he was in the North American Northwest, retired. And not one minute later, on the car radio, a DJ was to announce that his daughter was in Kuwait, just north of Saudi Arabia and that the temperature there was 34^0 C. (130^0 F.).

The highway to Seattle wound through tunnels chiseled into mountainsides and into the national park that was home to the volcanic and glacial majesty of Mt. Rainier. Sub alpine hillsides burst with blossoms, carpeting it in white, yellows and purples and some short red stalks that couldn't have been the same but from a distance, looked just like the red flowers that sprung up, after the winter rains, in sandy patches all around Riyadh. Exiting the park, an Ad Vision screen near Tacoma took us right back to the busy intersection of Riyadh's Olaya and Akariya Streets, with its two-minute red lights and advertising entertainment.

We weren't to hear the news until we returned home, four days after the kids left us, that four Brits were allegedly to confess to some of the bombs that had flared in Riyadh in November and December when we were there. Soon after, Al Khubar, right across the causeway from Bahrain, was to be bombed. Leavenworth was to be thrust into a smoky limelight because Washington winds were to fan the flames of seven forest fires in the state, one of them causing evacuations in that same alpine resort town, the wonderland we'd just discovered. But the worst fire was already blackening 15,500 hectares (50,000 acres) of the Colville Reservation.

Faisal, the Saudi student who acted as my right crutch was to phone from across the continents to keep Baba abreast of his activities. About that time, the expat couple that was to take our old furnished flat in Riyadh arrived to objections from the Housing Office. Fortunately, a college Dean intervened, pouring porcelain on the rough spots.

A week after getting home from this vacation-come-retreat, we were to begin a joint, comprehensive mental-emotional housecleaning. With Baba retired and the stairs in our house a thorn in my back, changes were needed.

By mid-September, we were finally to unpack the last cargo box. To my dismay, my cache from the pantry had been overlooked in Baba's last minute scramble to depart: my brushes, Tolkiens, Arabic notes and Arab candles, all left behind. Fortunately, I had carried the last of the trilogy with me, but it missed its mates.

We were to find out later that after Baba vacated the old digs, campus workers remodeled the kitchen, so the new occupants found the flat more disheveled and less complete than Baba had left it. But some of my precious package was located, although it was to be eight months before the Arabic notes reappeared and the two Tolkiens rejoined their mates.

Ultimately it was to take many months to work the Saudi strains and accompanying personal politics out of our systems, while retaining the good memories. The culture and circumstances had cultivated traits in each of us that we had not needed before, but that we now valued, perhaps to the chagrin of the other. Baba enjoyed the superlative camaraderie at work and spontaneous travel without the responsibilities of home and hearth. I valued my increased decisiveness when having only my own needs to consider and the added measure of inner calm I had gotten from my glimpse of a bigger picture. But our pictures, when superimposed, didn't always match. It became harder work to benefit from the ways the other one had grown. We each enjoyed more autonomy but with a lasting connectedness, holding each other with open hands and keeping a benevolent eye out from a distance.

Oftentimes, Baba was to wake early and go out to revel in the sight of the space station that he'd sought incessantly in Saudi skies. For evening appearances, I sometimes accompanied him to dark hilltops and joined in his reverie for the few minutes it took the orbiting craft to cross the heavens. It struck me, again, how much more pleasure he seemed to get from such celestial searches than from being at home.

We were to buy a second car, having left only an aging Volvo behind while we traveled. And my desired hot tub was to finally arrive. Once it was all set up, friends were eventually included in the soothing spa atmosphere. Talks with friends turned therapeutic as tensions melted away. The 3-D Bavarian clock puzzle that was born in Riyadh ticked off the seconds of steamy satisfaction. There was a price to pay, though. Negotiating the two steps between family room and hot tub twice daily and exercising in a swimming pool again, to regain the stretching and stamina I had sacrificed for travel meant giving up struggling with the longer flight of stairs and access to clothes and other of my possessions that couldn't be stored downstairs practically. At night, I slept on the main level, creating more changes in our household and relationship.

We were to continue searching our hearts for what we really wanted to do with the rest of our lives, whether to move and where. Wherever we went, it would have to have lots of windows and privacy. Shelves and closets were gradually to be turned out to see what to give away and what to keep. Baba maintained involvement in several projects at once and I signed up for a yearlong personal enrichment course with plenty of soul-searching homework to do between monthly classes. I began studying Feng Shui, to understand energy balance in the home, and finally grasped why I so enjoyed my chaise in the central position on the patio, the energies there symbolizing Unity—Oneness.

At East Indian gatherings, we were to get reacquainted with those who'd missed us, whether or not they'd kept in touch. It was at those times that I began reemerging from under the shadow, the path to normalcy appearing clearer. Other Indians had been to the Arabian Gulf and had surmounted the adjustments.

We were to host our long time neighbors at a Round Robin at Christmas 2001, one last get-together with the small group who were beginning to drift apart. For conversation, they preferred the local political buzz to our Arab tales, but liked our Aladdin's lamp. Family Christmas was to be very low key. Since we'd first left for Riyadh in October 1998, all our kids had moved away.

Through emails with Riyadh pals, Baba was to keep attuned to Saudi school semesters, while I felt more disconnected. Perhaps the lowest point, for me occurred when I realized that not only did I feel as though he'd moved very far away, but that he showed signs of feeling that I had. It was to be some time before he would realize that, as close as they were to him, his expat pals would not be the ones that backed him up when he was forgetful or that stayed up at night with him when his stomach was upset. With his wanting to take on more temporary teaching in Trinidad, Tobago and Timbuktu, I was reluctant to fall into a state of total dependence on him again. A new state of independent interdependence was a must. I thought of the self-supporting spirit showing through the eyes of the woman at the go-cart rides under the Saudi Eiffel tower, and knew that whatever the challenges, if she could do it, I could, too.

Eventually, smiles between Baba and I were to come more spontaneously, developing a new kind of considerate caring, a sort of symbiosis. We more actively negotiated our needs and were to formulate a new kind of appreciation. Regrets began gradually to fade into the past.

Then on September 11, 2001, while Canada Geese honked over my head, something else was to happen overhead. A finely tuned fiasco was to unfold, causing frenzied fortnights, having far flung effects, requiring from a traumatized world, fortitude on all fronts. It would be impossible to exaggerate the collective shock and pandemonium that was to engulf the American nation, similar in caliber and scope to events and wars in other parts of the globe. Deep disquiet was to descend on a world on edge, civilizations awakening to danger. Disturbed slumber and disjointed dreams once more were to dull my mind. Higher levels of alert and more wounds.

Our kids in New York were to sleep uncharacteristically late that same morning. Our son-in-law, whose job routinely would have placed him right in harm's way, ultimately arrived only in time to feel rubble flowing under his feet. I heard my daughter say that this was another time in her life that she found herself in an atmosphere smacking of *persona non grata* because of the shade of her skin and I felt it more than if it had happened to me. Baba felt the strain, too, as he curbed his usual habit of confidently initiating conversations with strangers.

Humankind was not merely starting a new chapter. By September, we were well into a new volume, an unfortunately violent volume of American-Arab-Israeli relations. Our lives were never to be the same. How we handled it would ultimately determine whether what remained of our lives would be better than before or not. Recalling

Superman and green kryptonite, his own home planet, perhaps we would find that life was too short to carelessly neglect misunderstandings and stubbornly insist on our own way rather than taking steps towards collaborative interdependence. An enlightened and ennobling approach to all relationships, not merely repeating new versions of old ineffective policies, was needed more than ever before.

Eventually, a new kind of cooperation would grow up between Baba and I, even while working in the kitchen. There would be no point in combining our two heads if we couldn't work together. If we worked against each other, we'd cancel each other out. And then where would we be? But bumps still littered the road. We had both contemplated moving away from the Midwest, so I had detached from people and routines, and then he became ambivalent about leaving. Ironically, the objectivity I had achieved from fending for myself freed me to share my personal brand of humanity with more people.

Baba began to share more broadly, too. On New Year's Eve 2001, he was to stop a complete stranger walking passed our house to explain the rare phenomenon of Jupiter shining brightly near the full moon and the pair stood in the frosty air enjoying the spectacle. I was to keep in closer touch with newfound relatives from the reunion, sharing from our hearts by long distance. I finished reading *The Return of the King*, the sojourners still stuck in the year 1420, while Riyadh had moved on to 1423 and I became more firmly grounded in my own present moment. Approaching our 29th wedding anniversary in February 2002, Baba and I each had seen how far we could push developing 'me' without losing 'us'.

The Lord of the Rings movie was to create a sensation amongst Tolkien fans, it basking in its status as a modern-day myth. We were to begin informal instruction in the Bosnian language in preparation for Baba's travel there the next fall. For our 29th anniversary, we reserved a quiet table for two by a restaurant window, surveying a winter rock garden and patio. When we first sat down, the dining room was practically empty. In our private nook, we talked and ate and talked some more, even indirectly broaching previously untouchable subjects. When we finally rose to leave, the place was full and I wondered when all these people had come in. I was to re-celebrate my 50th birthday that April by lunching with handpicked female friends.

Jewel Dhuru

By spring 2002, my attitude, on my best days, became less covertly complaining and more conducive to sustaining stability. I was to allow myself no more excuses for not being upbeat—none. If life was not what I wanted it to be, the quality of my day was still up to me. A long, long, time before, Baba and I had chosen each other as partners. Our growth was individually timed, sometimes in direct relation with each other and sometimes singly distinct, but growth all the same. It was never too late to renovate the room for improvement.

By a year after our return, summer 2002, with shifting responsiveness on both our parts, we were advancing in spurts towards a more effortless harmony that was quietly immense. We derived perennial pleasure from sharing in the growth of our adult children. Baba began reading my chapters and became more attentive to the ongoing consequences for me of our choices over the last three years, and I went to the IMAX Theatre with him to see a film about the space station. The show was not bad but the chairs were the most uncomfortable, straight-backed, short-seated, low-based specimens it had ever been my misfortune to adorn. Baba noticed them too, and appreciated my effort in coming. The increased strength of my muscles must have reached a critical mass because strengthening began occurring at the rate of bunches of inches. The World Cup Soccer final was especially unifying that year. Selected family and friends in India, the United States, Canada and Europe were all involved in the same thing at once. Even Baba's Riyadh pals, on summer vacation in their home countries, were enjoying the vicarious company of good sports with interesting names, physical features, languages and heritages.

By a year, I was to feel again that the my life was just right exactly as it was, that actions taken so long ago on both our parts in the heat of a Saudi experience were done for the best reasons and part of a larger plan. It would be up to us to draw conclusions and lessons from them that were life affirming.

A transformation had been taking place. We were not merely husband and wife any longer. Inadvertent wounding had been an opportunity for either ultimate separation and loss or for rising above the hurt. It also provided the chance to adjust erroneous, sometimes subconscious, decisions made as a youngster about who is essentially responsible for my self-care. In time, Baba was to realize that some, though not all, of my more inexplicable actions over the last few years had been done out of friendship, though it might not have seemed so at the time. And in time, I was to realize that some of his actions were motivated by friendship, too. I was to temporarily loosen the threads of tutoring, painting and working with clients. Writing had become a more pressing priority. Life's pieces were never to fall into the places they used to fit. Instead, by being, thinking and growing, we were to create a whole new picture.

Flashing Back

In August 2001, the old, new enchanted pocket seemed to stretch without limit. Right that moment, here—right here, sitting with my aunt on a hillside in beautiful British Columbia, between rows of blueberry bushes, overlooking kilometers of grape vines and apple, apricot, peach, plum, pear and cherry orchards, sustenance for stomach and soul, time stood still. With the multiple perspective of years of memories, my vision included wooden swings in gardens galore of stalky, swaying hollyhocks, Russian sage, tiger lilies, pale pink wild roses, gloriosa daisies, pale blue snow ball hydrangeas, buttercups, Quail Crossing signs down below and hummingbirds buzzing above, weeping willow, silver birch, poplar, mountain ash, maple, hazelnut and chestnut trees, and sheds and bushel baskets around hillside barns. In the kitchen, sauerkraut, cheese, homemade bread and sausage, bread 'n butter pickles, peas fresh out of the pod and currant scones were set out ready to nourish.

Hearing long remembered voices of relatives once more, catching ancient whiffs of Grandpa's cigar and Grandma's canning still lingering in the old kitchen and the musty fragrance of hay in the loft, the years dropped away and my roots surfaced, becoming visible, exposed. The more things appeared to have changed, the more we were connected, all from the same source, all children of the universe.

Ogopogo, Canada's answer to Loch Ness's Nessie, was safe in its niche in Okanagan Lake, paddling underneath jet skis that whizzed on the surface near poplar trees with 10-meter (30 foot) circumferences. Baskets repleat with dangling fuchsia, hung from white globes lighting the paths on the lake's edge to hotels, a convention center, an amphitheater and quaint shops while colorful parasailing chutes studded the azure sky.

Jewel Dhuru

This time when I got back home, I would retire my black bag once and for all, its pockets distended and its ribbing threatening to come unstitched. It could rest now that my spirit had become supremely mobilized. Here and now—right now, I would sprinkle more ashes of my precious pup. His spirit dwelled in some fabulous places, though none more satisfying than his own back yard and perhaps here, in the shadow of rose bushes of a treasured aunt and uncle. I think, later today, I'll go out and look for a new address book.

REFERENCES

Badawi, J. (1995). *Gender equity in Islam.* Plainfield IN: American Trust Publications.

Bakhtar, L. (1976). *Sufi: Expressions of a mystic quest.* NYC: Avon.

Caesar, J. (1997). *Crossing borders.* Syracuse, NY: Syracuse University Press.

Carson, D. & J. Sams. (1998). *Animal medicine.* NYC: St. Martin's Press.

Graham, D. (1991). *Saudi arabia unveiled.* Dubuque, Iowa: Kendall/Hunt.

Gray, J. (1992). *Men Are From Mars, Women Are From Venus.* NYC: HarperCollins.

Hay, L. (1984). *Heal your life.* Carlsbad, CA: Hay House.

Hitti. P.(1970). *History of the Arabs.* 10th ed., NYC: St. Martin's.

Humphries, A. & D. Simonis.(1999). *Syria.* London: Lonely Planet Publications.

Mackey, S. (1987). *The Saudis.* Boston: Houghton Mifflin.

McLean, A. (1989). *Triple goddesses: An exploration of the feminine.* Grand Rapids,

MI: Phanes Press.

Rodinson, M. (1971). *Mohammed.* NYC: Pantheon.

Thompson, I. (1994). *Desert treks from Riyadh.* London: Stacey International.

Wilson, P. & Graham, D. (1994). *Saudi Arabia: The coming storm.* NYC: M.E. Sharpe.

Jewel Dhuru

ENDNOTES

1. Attenborough, R. (Producer) (1982). *Gandhi* [Film].
2. Hay, L. (1984). *Heal your life.* Carlsbad, CA: Hay House (p. 52).
3. Cather, W. (1996). In R. Byrne (Ed.) *The 2548 best things anybody ever said.* NYC: Galahad (#63).
4. Neame, R. (Director) (1964). *The Chalk Garden* [Film].
5. Scott Peck, M. (1978). *The road less traveled.* NYC: Simon and Schuster. (p.268).
6. Freud, S. (1996). In R. Byrne (Ed.) *The 2548 best things anybody ever said.* NYC: Galahad (#633).
7. Dhuru, J. (2001, April). "Exploring the neighborhood in Saudi Arabia." In R. Laird (Ed.). *Sacred journey*, (pp. 22-25). New Jersey: Princeton.
8. Batarfi, K. (2001, May 28). *Oppressed* bachelors in society. *Arab News*, (p.3).
9. De Mello, A. (1982). *The song of the bird.* Garden City, NY: Image Books.
10. Saudi TV Channel 2 News, January 27, 1999.
11. Ohsawa, G. In W. Spear (1995). *Feng Shui made easy.* NYC: HarperCollins (p. 111).
12. Graham, D. (1991). *Saudi Arabia unveiled.* Dubuque, Iowa: Kendall/Hunt (p.75).
13. Seattle, Chief, *Chief Seattle's 1854 Oration.* www.halcyon.com.
14. Thoreau (1999). 2000 29th C. Chronicles—Pocket Pal. Maywood, NJ: Myron Manufacturing.
15. Rodinson, M. (1971). *Mohammed.* NYC: Pantheon Books (p.31).
16. Johnson, S. (1967). In B. Stevenson (Ed.) *Home book of quotations - Classical and modern.* NYC: Dodd, Mead and Company (p. 2195).
17. Personal Communication, March 22, 2001.
18. Allen, P. G. (1995). "Where I come from is like this." In N. Silverman (Ed.) *Making peace.* NYC: St. Martin's (p. 49).

19. McCourt, F. (1996). *Angela's ashes*. NYC: Scribner (p. 95).
20. Wilson, P. & D. Graham (1994). *Saudi Arabia: The coming storm*. NYC: M.E. Sharpe (p. 226).
21. Badawi, J. (1995). *Gender equity in Islam*. Plainfield IN: American Trust Publications. (p. 27).
22. Ibid, (p. 2).
23. Ibid, (p. 24).
24. Ibid, (p. 29).
25. LeShan, E. (1972, May). How do your children grow? *Woman's Day*.
26. Badawi, J. (1995). *Gender equity in Islam*. Plainfield IN: American Trust Publications. (p. 3).
27. Hitti. P. (1970). *History of the Arabs.*10th ed., NYC: St. Martin's (p.439).
28. Ibid, (p. 587).
29. Bakhtar, L. (1976). *Sufi - Expressions of a mystic quest*. NYC: Avon Books (p.3).
30. Ibid, (p. 110).
31. Ibid, (p. 108).
32. Salahi, A. (1999, April 9). Guidance from the Prophet. *Arab News,* (p. 11).
33. Draz, M. (1999, April 26). Decisive refutation of counter arguments. *Arab News* (p.9).
34. Draz, M. (1999, May 3). The broadest meaning in the minimum wording. *Arab News*, (p. 10).
35. Badawi J. (1995). *Gender equity in Islam*. Plainfield IN: American Trust Publications (p.3).
36. Salahi, A. (1999, May 7). Universal virtues. *Arab News,* (p. 11)
37. Hoff, B. (1992). *The Te of piglet*. NYC: Dutton (p.19).
38. Salahi, A. (1999, April 16). The sensitive character of the prophet. *Arab News,* (p.11).
39. Badawi J. (1995). *Gender equity in Islam*. Plainfield IN: American Trust Publications (p.31-32).
40. Stowe, H. B. (1998). *Brilliance*. Edmonds, WA: Compendium Inc.
41. Roosevelt, E. (1998). *Brilliance*. Edmonds, WA: Compendium Inc.

42. Ibn (Ata) Illah. (2002, Feb.). In R. Laird (Ed.). *Sacred journey*, (pp. 24). New Jersey: Princeton.
43. Nouy, L. In W. Spear (1995). *Feng Shui made easy*. NYC: HarperCollins (p. 31).
44. Tolken, J.R.R. (1995). *The return of the king.* NYC: Houghton Mifflin (p.276).
45. Ibid, (p. 275).
46. Ibid, (p. 309).
47. Aquinas, T. (2002, Feb.). In R. Laird (Ed.). *Sacred journey,* (pp. 24). New Jersey: Princeton.
48. Blake, W. In Dyer, W. (Speaker) (1992). *The Keys to Higher Awareness*. (cassette recording). Carlsbad, CA: Hay House.
49. Cosby, Wm. Jr. (1996). In R. Byrne (Ed.) *The 2548 best things anybody ever said*. NYC: Galahad (#322).
50. Curie, M. (1999). 2000 29th C. Chronicles—Pocket Pal. Maywood, NJ: Myron Manufacturing.
51. Rogers, W. In W. Spear (1995). *Feng Shui made easy*. NYC: HarperCollins (p.175).
52. Ten Boom, C. (1971). *The hiding place.* Uhrichsville, OH: Barbour and Co. (p. 202).
53. Saudi TV Channel 2 News, December, 2000.
54. Japanese Proverb. (1996). In R. Byrne (Ed.) *The 2548 best things anybody ever said*. NYC: Galahad (#583).
55. Ramkumar, K. (2000, November 28). Cruise ship brings 307 British tourists to Jeddah. *Arab News*, (p.1).
56. Dickensen, E. (1999). 2000 29th C. Chronicles—Pocket Pal. Maywood, NJ: Myron Manufacturing.
57. Carson, D. & J. Sams. (1998). *Animal medicine*. NYC: St. Martin's (p.113, 178).
58. Levine, P. (1997). *Waking the tiger.* Berkeley, CA.: North Atlantic Books (p. 196).
59. Huston Smith's videotaped interview with Bill Moyers on The Wisdom of Faith, 1996.
60. Deneuve, C. (1999). 2000 29th C. Chronicles—Pocket Pal. Maywood, NJ: Myron Manufacturing.
61. Bowman, L. (2001, Feb. 9). Brain decline due to bypass still a problem years later. *Arab News*, (p. 17).

62. Roddick, A. (1998). *Brilliance*. Edmonds, WA: Compendium Inc.
63. Abid, K. (2001, January 3). Futile attempts at blocking the Internet. *Arab News*, (p. 2).
64. Abu-Nasr, D. (2001, January 8). New generation tugs at Saudi Arabia's veil, but change is slow. *Los Angeles Times*.
65. Call to look for new moon. (2001, Feb. 21). *Arab News*, (p. 2).
66. Rand, A. In W. Spear (1995). *Feng Shui made easy*. NYC: HarperCollins (p. 91).
67. Abuljadaye, S. (2001, Feb. 21). Accident rate still high in kingdom. *Arab News*, (p. 3).
68. Rollason, K. (2001, May 17).Yes, we really are bad drivers. *Winnipeg Free Press*, (p. A1, A4).
69. DeElle, K. (1999). 2000 29th C. Chronicles—Pocket Pal. Maywood, NJ: Myron Manufacturing.
70. Humphries, A. & D. Simonis, (1999). *Syria*. London: *Lonely Planet Publications* (p. 126).
71. Dawood, W. (2001, March 10). Women enjoy important status in Saudi society. *Saudi Gazette*, (p. 3).
72. Jong, E. (1999). 2000 20th C. Chronicles—Pocket Pal. Maywood, NJ: Myron Manufacturing.
73. Kubler-Ross, E. In W. Spear (1995). *Feng Shui made easy*. NYC: HarperCollins (p. 97).
74. Hugo, V. In W. Spear (1995). *Feng Shui made easy*. NYC: HarperCollins (p. 69).
75. Neame, R. (Director) (1964). *The Chalk Garden*.
76. Hay, L. (1984). *Heal your life*. Carlsbad, CA: Hay House (p. 3).
77. Ibid (p. 52).
78. Einstein, A. In W. Spear (1995). *Feng Shui made easy*. NYC: HarperCollins (p. 116).
79. De Mello, A. (1989). *The heart of the enlightened*. NYC: Doubleday (p.185).
80. Al-Suwayad /Al-Eqtisadiah, A. (2001, January 10). Harassment of job seeking women. *ArabNews*, (p. 3).
81. 81 Al-Nasser, H. (2001, January 19). Weekend marriages. *Arab News*, (p. 3).

82. Ibid (p. 3).
83. Al-Maeena, T. (2001, May 12). On being a woman. *Arab News*, (p. 20).
84. Keiller, G. (1996). In R. Byrne (Ed.) *The 2548 best things anybody ever said.* NYC: Galahad (#533).
85. Fallding, H. (2001, June 3). Unveiling of Pooh art at legislative building draws young and old. *Winnipeg Free Press*, (p. A1, A4).
86. Dostoyevsky, F. (2002, Dec.). In R. Laird (Ed.). *Sacred journey,* (pp. 26). New Jersey: Princeton.
87. Kinnier, R., N. Tribbensee, C. Rose & S. Vaughan (Spr. 2001). In the final analysis: More wisdom from people who have faced death. *Journal of Counseling and Development,* 79 (p. 171-77).
88. Williamson, M. (1993). A return to love: Reflections on the principles of a course in *miracles*. Boston: G. K. Hall (chap. 7, sect. 3).

Jewel Dhuru

Map of the Region

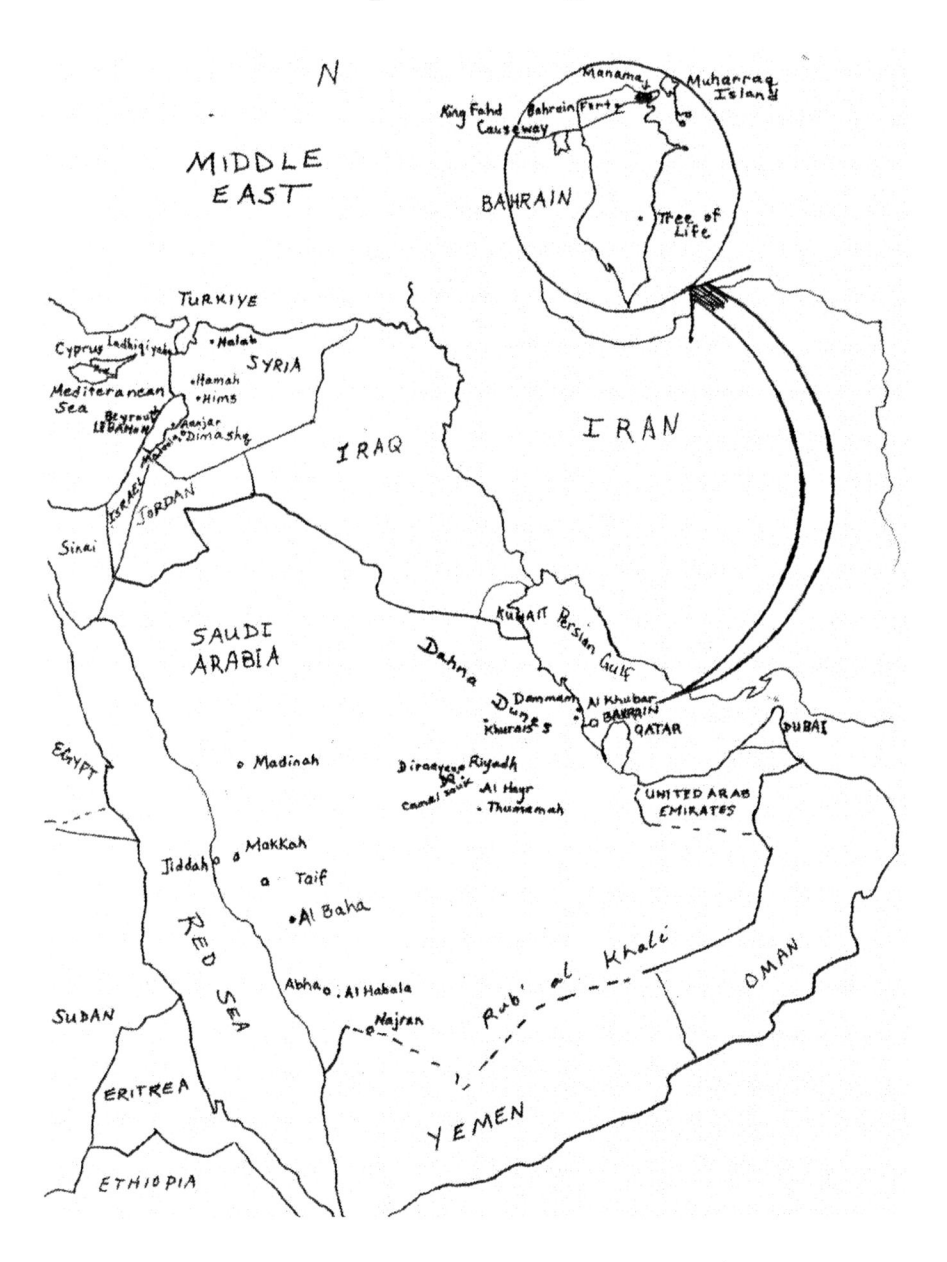

Jewel Dhuru

About the Book

Keep Going Forward! (English for *Ala Tool*). That's the option Canadian-born Jewel Dhuru, counselor, English teacher and artist chooses after two bittersweet sojourns in Saudi Arabia. As her Indian-born husband teaches at a Saudi college, she chronicles the daily delights and dreads of expatriates, women and bachelors, coping with polarities while holding on to common bonds of humanity. Not just another travelogue, this poignant, inspirational account describes sunset from a Bedouin tent at the camel souk and aromatic frankincense and ood perfuming Jewel's kitchen, and touches on the zealous morality police, lessons behind a clandestinely tailored green *abaya*, conflicting personal styles as guests gather for dinner, why a jeweler in bustling Riyadh won't shake Jewel's hand and visits to friendly smaller Saudi towns, four neighboring Arab countries, India and Canada. Underneath hilarious and harrowing anecdotes, this western woman grapples with questions of her identity and marriage, using this interval of 'about face' as a catalyst for her own continuing spiritual evolution. The story unfolds of a woman blooming in the desert not renown for female friendliness, feeling her life change substantially, discovering there is no going back to the way it was and choosing to *Ala Tool.*

About the Author

Jewel Dhuru was born and raised in Canada but has lived in the United States for thirty years. Besides being a wife and a mother of two, she taught English as a Second Language to college students at Marquette University for eight years and has been a counselor specializing in breathwork for seven. She has exhibited her paintings and ceramics at Milwaukee galleries and has contributed articles to *Sacred Journey*. She and her Asian Indian husband have traveled through seventeen countries and now live in the American Midwest.

Printed in the United States
1119800004B/43-168